THE HARVARD CLASSICS

The Five-Foot Shelf of Books

Vamana (Vishnu) Temple
Khajraho, Central India, 10th century

Vamana (Vishnu) Temple
Khajraho, Central India, 10th century

THE HARVARD CLASSICS
EDITED BY CHARLES W. ELIOT, LL.D.

Sacred Writings

IN TWO VOLUMES
VOLUME II

Christian, *Part II* · Buddhist
Hindu · Mohammedan

With *Introductions and Notes*

Volume 45

P. F. Collier & Son Company
NEW YORK

CONTENTS

CHRISTIAN

PAGE

THE FIRST EPISTLE OF PAUL TO THE CORINTHIANS 491
THE SECOND EPISTLE OF PAUL TO THE CORINTHIANS 516
HYMNS OF THE CHRISTIAN CHURCH 533
(See Special Table of Contents, page 534)

BUDDHIST

BUDDHIST WRITINGS, TRANSLATED AND ANNOTATED BY HENRY
CLARKE WARREN 573
(See Special Table of Contents, page 575)

HINDU

THE BHAGAVAD-GITA OR SONG CELESTIAL, TRANSLATED BY SIR
EDWIN ARNOLD 783

MOHAMMEDAN

CHAPTERS FROM THE KORAN, TRANSLATED AND ANNOTATED BY
E. H. PALMER 875
(See Special Table of Contents, page 877)

INTRODUCTORY NOTE

In the eighteenth chapter of "The Acts of the Apostles" an account is given of the founding by Paul of the Church of Corinth. At that time Corinth was a great seaport, with a cosmopolitan population and an apparently well-deserved reputation for immorality. Not long after Paul's departure, it appears that some members of the Church fell back into the evil ways of the place, and their brethren wrote to Paul for advice. Paul's reply, now lost, seems to have been misunderstood; and their answer, along with oral reports which had reached the apostle, called forth the first of the two extant epistles. This was written at Ephesus, probably in 54 A. D., though some scholars date it three or four years later.

Our second epistle was sent from Macedonia, after Paul had been forced to flee from Ephesus, a few months after the date of the first. Like the first, it deals with scandals and divisions in the Corinthian Church, but rejoices over some matters on which its founder could offer congratulations. The more painful part of the letter, chapters X to XIII, is supposed by some to be part of an epistle coming between the first and the second.

The two letters give a very vivid picture of the perils through which the infant church struggled in the midst of a vicious pagan society, before its fundamental principles were firmly grasped, and while opportunities abounded to be led astray by rival teachers. Paul addresses himself to the unpleasant task of discipline with straightforwardness and courage, yet with much tenderness; and in holding up to his converts the gospel as he conceived it, he rises to a pitch of sublime eloquence.

THE FIRST EPISTLE OF PAUL TO THE
CORINTHIANS

[1]

I

PAUL, called *to be* an apostle of Jesus Christ through the will of God, and Sosthenes our[1] brother, [2] unto the church of God which is at Corinth, *even* them that are sanctified in Christ Jesus, called *to be* saints, with all that call upon the name of our Lord Jesus Christ in every place, their *Lord* and ours: [3] Grace to you and peace from God our Father and the Lord Jesus Christ.

[4] I thank my[2] God always concerning you, for the grace of God which was given you in Christ Jesus; [5] that in everything ye were enriched in him, in all utterance[3] and all knowledge; [6] even as the testimony of Christ was confirmed in you: [7] so that ye come behind in no gift; waiting for the revelation of our Lord Jesus Christ; [8] who shall also confirm you unto the end, *that ye be* unreproveable in the day of our Lord Jesus Christ. [9] God is faithful, through whom ye were called into the fellowship of his Son Jesus Christ our Lord.

[10] Now I beseech you, brethren, through the name of our Lord Jesus Christ, that ye all speak the same thing, and *that* there be no divisions[4] among you; but *that* ye be perfected together in the same mind and in the same judgment. [11] For it hath been signified unto me concerning you, my brethren, by them *that are of the household* of Chloe, that there are contentions among you. [12] Now this I mean, that each one of you saith, I am of Paul; and I of Apollos; and I of Cephas; and I of Christ. [13] Is[5] Christ divided? was Paul crucified for you? or were ye baptized into the name of Paul? [14] I[6] thank God that I baptized none of you, save Crispus and Gaius; [15] lest any man should say that ye were baptized into my name.

[1] Gr. *the brother.*   [2] Some ancient authorities omit *my.*   [3] Gr. *word.*
[4] Gr. *schisms.*   [5] Or, *Christ is divided! Was Paul crucified for you?*
[6] Some ancient authorities read *I give thanks that.*

[16] And I baptized also the household of Stephanas: besides, I know not whether I baptized any other. [17] For Christ sent me not to baptize, but to preach[7] the gospel: not in wisdom of words, lest the cross of Christ should be made void.

[18] For the word of the cross is to them that perish[8] foolishness; but unto us who are[9] saved it is the power of God. [19] For it is written,

I will destroy the wisdom of the wise,
And the discernment of the discerning will I bring to naught.

[20] Where is the wise? where is the scribe? where is the disputer of this world?[10] hath not God made foolish the wisdom of the world? [21] For seeing that in the wisdom of God the world through its wisdom knew not God, it was God's good pleasure through the foolishness of the preaching[11] to save them that believe. [22] Seeing that Jews ask for signs, and Greeks seek after wisdom: [23] but we preach Christ[12] crucified, unto Jews a stumbling-block, and unto Gentiles foolishness; [24] but unto them[13] that are called, both Jews and Greeks, Christ the power of God, and the wisdom of God. [25] Because the foolishness of God is wiser than men; and the weakness of God is stronger than men.

[26] For behold[14] your calling, brethren, that not many wise after the flesh, not many mighty, not many noble, *are called:* [27] but God chose the foolish things of the world, that he might put to shame them that are wise; and God chose the weak things of the world, that he might put to shame the things that are strong; [28] and the base things of the world, and the things that are despised, did God choose, *yea* and[15] the things that are not, that he might bring to nought the things that are: [29] that no flesh should glory before God. [30] But of him are ye in Christ Jesus, who was made unto us wisdom from God, and[16] righteousness and sanctification, and redemption: [31] that, according as it is written, He that glorieth, let him glory in the Lord.

[7] Gr. *bring good tidings.* Comp. Mt. 11. 5.
[8] Or, *are perishing.*   [9] Or, *are being saved.*   [10] Or, *age.*
[11] Gr. *thing preached.*   [12] Or, *a Messiah.*   [13] Gr. *they called themselves.*
[14] Or, *ye behold.*   [15] Many ancient authorities omit *and.*
[16] Or, *both righteousness and sanctification and redemption.*

II

[1] AND I, brethren, when I came unto you, came not with excellency of speech[1] or of wisdom, proclaiming to you the testimony[2] of God. [2] For I determined not to know anything among you, save Jesus Christ, and him crucified. [3] And I was with you in weakness, and in fear, and in much trembling. [4] And my speech[1] and my preaching[3] were not in persuasive words of wisdom, but in demonstration of the Spirit and of power: [5] that your faith should not stand[4] in the wisdom of men, but in the power of God.

[6] We speak wisdom, however, among them that are fullgrown: yet a wisdom not of this world,[5] nor of the rulers of this world,[5] who are coming to nought: [7] but we speak God's wisdom in a mystery, *even* the *wisdom* that hath been hidden, which God foreordained before the worlds[5] unto our glory: [8] which none of the rulers of this world[5] hath known: for had they known it, they would not have crucified the Lord of glory: [9] but as it is written,

Things which eye saw not, and ear heard not,

And *which* entered not into the heart of man,

Whatsoever things God prepared for them that love him.

[10] But[6] unto us God revealed *them*[7] through the Spirit: for the Spirit searcheth all things, yea, the deep things of God. [11] For who among men knoweth the things of a man, save the spirit of the man, which is in him? even so the things of God none knoweth, save the Spirit of God. [12] But we received, not the spirit of the world,[8] but the spirit which is from God; that we might know the things that were freely given to us of God. [13] Which things also we speak, not in words which man's wisdom teacheth, but which the Spirit teacheth; combining[9] spiritual things with spiritual *words*. [14] Now the natural[10] man receiveth not the things of the Spirit of God: for they are foolishness unto him; and he cannot know them, because they are spiritually judged.[11] [15] But he that is spiritual judgeth[12] all things, and he himself is judged[11] of no man. [16] For

---

1 Or, *word*. 2 Many ancient authorities read *mystery*.
3 Gr. *thing preached*. 4 Gr. *be*.
5 Or, *age:* and so in ver. 7, 8; but not in ver. 12.
6 Some ancient authorities read *For*. 7 Or, *it*. 8 See ver. 6.
9 Or, *interpreting spiritual things to spiritual* men.
10 Or, *unspiritual*. Gr. *psychical*. 11 Or, *examined*. 12 Or, *examineth*.

who hath known the mind of the Lord, that he should instruct him? But we have the mind of Christ.

III

[1] AND I, brethren, could not speak unto you as unto spiritual, but as unto carnal, as unto babes in Christ. [2] I fed you with milk, not with meat; for ye were not yet able *to bear it:* nay, not even now are ye able; [3] for ye are yet carnal: for whereas there is among you jealousy and strife, are ye not carnal, and do ye not walk after the manner of men? [4] For when one saith, I am of Paul; and another, I am of Apollos; are ye not men? [5] What then is Apollos? and what is Paul? Ministers through whom ye believed; and each as the Lord gave to him. [6] I planted, Apollos watered; but God gave the increase. [7] So then neither is he that planteth anything, neither he that watereth; but God that giveth the increase. [8] Now he that planteth and he that watereth are one: but each shall receive his own reward according to his own labor. [9] For we are God's fellow-workers: ye are God's husbandry,[1] God's building.

[10] According to the grace of God which was given unto me, as a wise masterbuilder I laid a foundation; and another buildeth thereon. But let each man take heed how he buildeth thereon. [11] For other foundation can no man lay than that which is laid, which is Jesus Christ. [12] But if any man buildeth on the foundation gold, silver, costly stones, wood, hay, stubble; [13] each man's work shall be made manifest: for the day shall declare it, because it is revealed in fire; and[2] the fire itself shall prove each man's work of what sort it is. [14] If any man's work shall abide which he built thereon, he shall receive a reward. [15] If any man's work shall be burned, he shall suffer loss: but he himself shall be saved; yet so as through fire. [16] Know ye not that ye are a temple[3] of God, and *that* the Spirit of God dwelleth in you? [17] If any man destroyeth the temple[3] of God, him shall God destroy; for the temple[3] of God is holy, and[4] such are ye.

[18] Let no man deceive himself. If any man thinketh that he is wise among you in this world,[5] let him become a fool, that he

[1] Gr. *tilled land.*
[2] Or, *and each man's work, of what sort it is, the fire shall prove it.*
[3] Or, *sanctuary.*   [4] Or, *which* temple *ye are.*   [5] Or, *age.*

may become wise. [19] For the wisdom of this world is foolishness with God. For it is written, He that taketh the wise in their craftiness: [20] and again, The Lord knoweth the reasonings of the wise, that they are vain. [21] Wherefore let no one glory in men. For all things are yours; [22] whether Paul, or Apollos, or Cephas, or the world, or life or death, or things present, or things to come; all are yours; [23] and ye are Christ's; and Christ is God's.

IV

[1] LET a man so account of us, as of ministers of Christ, and stewards of the mysteries of God. [2] Here, moreover, it is required in stewards, that a man be found faithful. [3] But with me it is a very small thing that I should be judged[1] of you, or of man's judgment:[2] yea, I judge[3] not mine own self. [4] For I know nothing against myself; yet am I not hereby justified: but he that judgeth[4] me is the Lord. [5] Wherefore judge nothing before the time, until the Lord come, who will both bring to light the hidden things of darkness, and make manifest the counsels of the hearts; and then shall each man have his praise from God.

[6] Now these things, brethren, I have in a figure transferred to myself and Apollos for your sakes; that in us ye might learn not to go beyond the things which are written; that no one of you be puffed up for the one against the other. [7] For who maketh thee to differ? and what hast thou that thou didst not receive? but if thou didst receive it, why dost thou glory as if thou hadst not received it? [8] Already are ye filled, already ye are become rich, ye have come to reign without us: yea and I would that ye did reign, that we also might reign with you. [9] For, I think, God hath set forth us the apostles last of all, as men doomed to death: for we are made a spectacle unto the world, both[5] to angels and men. [10] We are fools for Christ's sake, but ye are wise in Christ; we are weak, but ye are strong; ye have glory, but we have dishonor. [11] Even unto this present hour we both hunger, and thirst, and are naked, and are buffeted, and have no certain dwelling-place; [12] and we toil, working with our own hands: being reviled, we bless; being perse-

---

[1] Or, examined.   [2] Gr. day. See ch. 3. 13.   [3] Or, examine.
[4] Or. examineth.   [5] Or, and to angels, and to men.

cuted, we endure; [13] being defamed, we entreat: we are made as the filth[6] of the world, the off-scouring of all things, even until now.

[14] I write not these things to shame you, but to admonish you as my beloved children. [15] For though ye have ten thousand tutors in Christ, yet *have ye* not many fathers; for in Christ Jesus I begat you through the gospel.[7] [16] I beseech you therefore, be ye imitators of me. [17] For this cause have I sent unto you Timothy, who is my beloved and faithful child in the Lord, who shall put you in remembrance of my ways which are in Christ, even as I teach everywhere in every church. [18] Now some are puffed up, as though I were not coming to you. [19] But I will come to you shortly, if the Lord will; and I will know, not the word of them that are puffed up, but the power. [20] For the kingdom of God is not in word, but in power. [21] What will ye? shall I come unto you with a rod, or in love and a spirit of gentleness?

V

[1] It is actually reported that there is fornication among you and such fornication as is not even among the Gentiles, that one *of you* hath his father's wife. [2] And ye[1] are puffed up, and did[2] not rather mourn, that he that had done this deed might be taken away from among you. [3] For I verily, being absent in body but present in spirit, have already as though I were present judged him that hath so wrought this thing, [4] in the name of our Lord Jesus, ye being gathered together, and my spirit, with the power of our Lord Jesus, [5] to deliver such a one unto Satan for the destruction of the flesh, that the spirit may be saved in the day of the Lord Jesus.[3] [6] Your glorying is not good. Know ye not that a little leaven leaveneth the whole lump? [7] Purge out the old leaven, that ye may be a new lump, even as ye are unleavened. For our passover also hath been sacrificed, *even* Christ: [8] wherefore let us keep[4] the feast, not with old leaven, neither with the leaven of malice and wickedness, but with the unleavened bread of sincerity and truth.

6 Or, *refuse.*   7 Gr. *good tidings.* See marginal note on Mt. 4. 23.
1 Or, *are ye puffed up?*   2 Or, *did ye not rather mourn, . . . you?*
3 Some ancient authorities omit *Jesus.*   4 Gr. *keep festival.*

[9] I wrote unto you in my epistle to have no company with fornicators; [10] not[5] at all *meaning* with the fornicators of this world, or
with the covetous and extortioners, or with idolaters; for then must
ye needs go out of the world: [11] but as[6] it is, I wrote unto you not
to keep company, if any man that is named a brother be a fornicator,
or covetous, or an idolater, or a reviler, or a drunkard, or an extor-
tioner; with such a one no, not to eat. [12] For what have I to do
with judging them that are without? Do not ye judge them that are
within? [13] But them that are without God judgeth. Put away the
wicked man from among yourselves.

VI

[1] DARE any of you, having a matter against his[7] neighbor, go to
law before the unrighteous, and not before the saints? [2] Or know
ye not that the saints shall judge the world? and if the world is
judged by you, are ye unworthy to[8] judge the smallest matters?
[3] Know ye not that we shall judge angels? how much more, things
that pertain to this life? [4] If then ye have to[9] judge things pertaining to this life, do[10] ye set them to judge who are of no account in
the church? [5] I say *this* to move you to shame. What,[11] cannot
there be *found* among you one wise man who shall be able to decide
between his brethren, [6] but brother goeth to law with brother, and
that before unbelievers? [7] Nay, already it is altogether a[12] defect in
you, that ye have lawsuits one with another. Why not rather take
wrong? why not rather be defrauded? [8] Nay, but ye yourselves do
wrong, and defraud, and that *your* brethren. [9] Or know ye not
that the unrighteous shall not inherit the kingdom of God? Be not
deceived: neither fornicators, nor idolaters, nor adulterers, nor ef-
feminate, nor abusers of themselves with men, [10] nor thieves, nor
covetous, nor drunkards, nor revilers, nor extortioners, shall inherit
the kingdom of God. [11] And such were some of you: but ye were[13]
washed, but ye were sanctified, but ye were justified in the name of
the Lord Jesus Christ, and in the Spirit of our God.

5 Or, *not altogether with the fornicators &c.*   6 Or, *now I write.*
7 Gr. *the other.* See Rom. 13. 8.   8 Gr. *of the smallest tribunals.*
9 Gr. *tribunals pertaining to.*   10 Or, *set them . . . church.*
11 Or, *Is it so, that there cannot &c.*   12 Or, *a loss to you.*
13 Gr. *washed yourselves.*

[12] All things are lawful for me; but not all things are expedient. All things are lawful for me; but I will not be brought under the power of any. [13] Meats for the belly, and the belly for meats: but God shall bring to nought both it and them. But the body is not for fornication, but for the Lord; and the Lord for the body: [14] and God both raised the Lord, and will raise up us through his power. [15] Know ye not that your bodies are members of Christ? shall I then take away the members of Christ, and make them members of a harlot? God forbid. [16] Or know ye not that he that is joined to a harlot is one body? for, The twain, saith he, shall become one flesh. [17] But he that is joined unto the Lord is one spirit. [18] Flee fornication. Every sin that a man doeth is without the body; but he that committeth fornication sinneth against his own body. [19] Or know ye not that your body is a temple[14] of the Holy Spirit which is in you, which ye have from God? and ye are not your own; [20] for ye were bought with a price: glorify God therefore in your body.

VII

[1] Now concerning the things whereof ye wrote: It is good for a man not to touch a woman. [2] But, because of fornications, let each man have his own wife, and let each woman have her own husband. [3] Let the husband render unto the wife her due: and likewise also the wife unto the husband. [4] The wife hath not power over her own body, but the husband: and likewise also the husband hath not power over his own body, but the wife. [5] Defraud ye not one the other, except it be by consent for a season, that ye may give yourselves unto prayer, and may be together again, that Satan tempt you not because of your incontinency. [6] But this I say by way of concession, not of commandment. [7] Yet[1] I would that all men were even as I myself. Howbeit each man hath his own gift from God, one after this manner, and another after that.

[8] But I say to the unmarried and to widows, It is good for them if they abide even as I. [9] But if they have not continency, let them marry: for it is better to marry than to burn. [10] But unto the mar-

---

[14] Or, sanctuary.
[1] Many ancient authorities read For.

ried I give charge, *yea* not I, but the Lord, That the wife depart not from her husband [11] (but should she depart, let her remain unmarried, or else be reconciled to her husband); and that the husband leave not his wife. [12] But to the rest say I, not the Lord: If any brother hath an unbelieving wife, and she is content to dwell with him, let him not leave her. [13] And the woman that hath an unbelieving husband, and he is content to dwell with her, let her not leave her husband. [14] For the unbelieving husband is sanctified in the wife, and the unbelieving wife is sanctified in the brother: else were your children unclean; but now are they holy. [15] Yet if the unbelieving departeth, let him depart: the brother or the sister is not under bondage in such *cases:* but God hath called us[2] in peace. [16] For how knowest thou, O wife, whether thou shalt save thy husband? or how knowest thou, O husband, whether thou shalt save thy wife? [17] Only, as the Lord hath distributed to each man, as God hath called each, so let him walk. And so ordain I in all the churches. [18] Was any man called being circumcised? let him not become uncircumcised. Hath any been called in uncircumcision? let him not be circumcised. [19] Circumcision is nothing, and uncircumcision is nothing; but the keeping of the commandments of God. [20] Let each man abide in that calling wherein he was called. [21] Wast thou called being a bondservant? care not for it: nay,[3] even if thou canst become free, use *it* rather. [22] For he that was called in the Lord being a bondservant, is the Lord's freedman: likewise he that was called being free, is Christ's bondservant. [23] Ye were bought with a price; become not bondservants of men. [24] Brethren, let each man, wherein he was called, therein abide with God.

[25] Now concerning virgins I have no commandment of the Lord: but I give my judgment, as one that hath obtained mercy of the Lord to be trustworthy. [26] I think therefore that this is good by reason of the distress that is upon us, *namely,* that it is good for a man to[4] be as he is. [27] Art thou bound unto a wife? seek not to be loosed. Art thou loosed from a wife? seek not a wife. [28] But shouldest thou marry, thou hast not sinned; and if a virgin marry, she hath not sinned. Yet such shall have tribulation in the flesh:

[2] Many ancient authorities read *you.*   [3] Or, *but if.*   [4] Gr. *so to be.*

and I would spare you. [29] But this I say, brethren, the time is[5] shortened, that henceforth both those that have wives may be as though they had none; [30] and those that weep, as though they wept not; and those that rejoice, as though they rejoiced not; and those that buy, as though they possessed not; [31] and those that use the world, as not using it to the full: for the fashion of this world passeth away. [32] But I would have you to be free from cares. He that is unmarried is careful for the things of the Lord, how he may please the Lord: [33] but he that is married is careful for the things of the world, how he may please his wife,[6] [34] and is divided. *So* also the woman that is unmarried and the virgin is careful for the things of the Lord, that she may be holy both in body and in spirit: but she that is married is careful for the things of the world, how she may please her husband. [35] And this I say for your own profit; not that I may cast a snare[7] upon you, but for that which is seemly, and that ye may attend upon the Lord without distraction. [36] But if any man thinketh that he behaveth himself unseemly toward his virgin[8] *daughter,* if she be past the flower of her age, and if need so requireth, let him do what he will; he sinneth not; let them marry. [37] But he that standeth stedfast in his heart, having no necessity, but hath power as touching his own will, and hath determined this in his own heart, to keep his own virgin[8] *daughter,* shall do well. [38] So then both he that giveth his own virgin[8] *daughter* in marriage doeth well; and he that giveth her not in marriage shall do better. [39] A wife is bound for so long time as her husband liveth; but if the husband be dead,[9] she is free to be married to whom she will; only in the Lord. [40] But she is happier if she abide as she is, after my judgment: and I think that I also have the Spirit of God.

VIII

[1] Now concerning things sacrificed to idols: We know that we all have knowledge. Knowledge puffeth up, but love edifieth.[1] [2] If any man thinketh that he knoweth anything, he knoweth not yet

---

[5] Or, *is shortened henceforth, that both those &c.*
[6] Some ancient authorities read *wife. And there is a difference also between the wife and the virgin. She that is unmarried is careful &c.*
[7] Or, *constraint.* Gr. *noose.*   [8] Or, *virgin* (omitting daughter).
[9] Gr. *fallen asleep.* See Acts 7. 60.   [1] Gr. *buildeth up.*

as he ought to know; [3] but if any man loveth God, the same is known by him. [4] Concerning therefore the eating of things sacrificed to idols, we know that no idol is *anything* in the world, and that there is no God but one. [5] For though there be that are called gods, whether in heaven or on earth; as there are gods many, and lords many; [6] yet to us there is one God, the Father, of whom are all things, and we unto him; and one Lord, Jesus Christ, through whom are all things, and we through him. [7] Howbeit there is not in all men that knowledge: but some, being used until now to the idol, eat as *of* a thing sacrificed to an idol; and their conscience being weak is defiled. [8] But food will not commend[2] us to God: neither, if we eat not, are[3] we the worse; nor, if we eat, are[4] we the better. [9] But take heed lest by any means this liberty[5] of yours become a stumblingblock to the weak. [10] For if a man see thee who hast knowledge sitting at meat in an idol's temple, will not his conscience, if he is weak, be[6] emboldened to eat things sacrificed to idols? [11] For through[7] thy knowledge he that is weak perisheth, the brother for whose sake Christ died. [12] And thus, sinning against the brethren, and wounding their conscience when it is weak, ye sin against Christ. [13] Wherefore, if meat causeth my brother to stumble, I will eat no flesh for evermore, that I cause not my brother to stumble.

IX

[1] AM I not free? am I not an apostle? have I not seen Jesus our Lord? are not ye my work in the Lord? [2] If to others I am not an apostle, yet at least I am to you; for the seal of mine apostleship are ye in the Lord. [3] My defence to them that examine me is this. [4] Have we no right to eat and to drink? [5] Have we no right to lead about a wife that is a believer,[1] even as the rest of the apostles, and the brethren of the Lord, and Cephas? [6] Or I only and Barnabas, have we not a right to forbear working? [7] What soldier ever serveth at his own charges? who planteth a vineyard, and eateth not the fruit thereof? or who feedeth a flock, and eateth not of the milk of the flock? [8] Do I speak these things after the manner of men?

---

[2] Gr. *present.*   [3] Gr. *do we lack.*   [4] Gr. *do we abound.*   [5] Or, *power.*
[6] Gr. *be builded up.*   [7] Gr. *in.*   [1] Gr. *sister.*

or saith not the law also the same? [9] For it is written in the law of Moses, Thou shalt not muzzle the ox when he treadeth out the corn. Is it for the oxen that God careth, [10] or saith he it assuredly[2] for our sake? Yea, for our sake it was written: because he that ploweth ought to plow in hope, and he that thresheth, *to thresh* in hope of partaking. [11] If we sowed unto you spiritual things, is it a great matter if we shall reap your carnal things? [12] If others partake of *this* right over you, do not we yet more? Nevertheless we did not use this right; but we bear all things, that we may cause no hindrance to the gospel[3] of Christ. [13] Know ye not that they that minister about sacred things eat *of* the things of the temple, *and* they that wait upon the altar have their portion with the altar? [14] Even so did the Lord ordain that they that proclaim the gospel[3] should live of the gospel.[3] [15] But I have used none of these things: and I write not these things that it may be so done in my case; for *it were* good for me rather to die, than that any man should make my glorying void. [16] For if I preach[4] the gospel, I have nothing to glory of; for necessity is laid upon me; for woe is unto me, if I preach[4] not the gospel. [17] For if I do this of mine own will, I have a reward: but if not of mine own will, I have a stewardship intrusted to me. [18] What then is my reward? That, when I preach[4] the gospel, I may make the gospel[3] without charge, so as not to use to the full my right in the gospel.[3] [19] For though I was free from all *men,* I brought myself under bondage to all, that I might gain the more. [20] And to the Jews I became as a Jew, that I might gain Jews; to them that are under the law, as under the law, not being myself under the law, that I might gain them that are under the law; [21] to them that are without law, as without law, not being without law to God, but under law to Christ, that I might gain them that are without law. [22] To the weak I became weak, that I might gain the weak: I am become all things to all men, that I may by all means save some. [23] And I do all things for the gospel's[3] sake, that I may be a joint partaker thereof. [24] Know ye not that they that run in a race[5] run all, but one receiveth the prize? Even so run; that ye may attain. [25] And every man that striveth in the games exerciseth self-control in all things. Now they *do it* to receive

<hr/>

[2] Or, *altogether.*   [3] See marginal note on ch. 4. 15.
[4] See marginal note on ch. 1. 17.   [5] Gr. *race course.*

a corruptible crown; but we an incorruptible. [26] I therefore so run, as not uncertainly; so fight[6] I, as not beating the air: [27] but I buffet[7] my body, and bring it into bondage: lest by any means, after that I have[8] preached to others, I myself should be rejected.

X

[1] For I would not, brethren, have you ignorant, that our fathers were all under the cloud, and all passed through the sea; [2] and were all baptized unto[9] Moses in the cloud and in the sea; [3] and did all eat the same spiritual food; [4] and did all drink the same spiritual drink: for they drank of a spiritual rock that followed them: and the rock was Christ.[10] [5] Howbeit with most of them God was not well pleased: for they were overthrown in the wilderness. [6] Now these[11] things were our examples, to the intent we should not lust after evil things, as they also lusted. [7] Neither be ye idolaters, as were some of them; as it is written, The people sat down to eat and drink, and rose up to play. [8] Neither let us commit fornication, as some of them committed, and fell in one day three and twenty thousand. [9] Neither let us make trial of the Lord,[12] as some of them made trial, and perished by the serpents. [10] Neither murmur ye, as some of them murmured, and perished by the destroyer. [11] Now these things happened unto them by[13] way of example; and they were written for our admonition, upon whom the ends of the ages are come. [12] Wherefore let him that thinketh he standeth take heed lest he fall. [13] There hath no temptation taken you but such as man can bear: but God is faithful, who will not suffer you to be tempted above that ye are able; but will with the temptation make also the way of escape, that ye may be able to endure it.

[14] Wherefore, my beloved, flee from idolatry. [15] I speak as to wise men; judge ye what I say. [16] The cup of blessing which we bless, is it not a communion[14] of the blood of Christ? The bread[15] which we break, is it not a communion[14] of the body of Christ? [17] seeing[16] that we, who are many, are one bread,[15] one body: for

---

[6] Gr. box.   [7] Gr. bruise. Lk. 18. 5.   [8] Or, have been a herald.   [9] Gr. into.
[10] Or, the Christ. Comp. Heb. 11. 26.   [11] Or, in these things they became figures of us.   [12] Some ancient authorities read Christ.   [13] Gr. by way of figure.
[14] Or, participation in.   [15] Or, loaf.   [16] Or, seeing that there is one bread, we, who are many, are one body.

we all partake of[17] the one bread.[15] [18] Behold Israel after the flesh: have not they that eat the sacrifices communion with the altar? [19] What say I then? that a thing sacrificed to idols is anything, or that an idol is anything? [20] But *I say,* that the things which the Gentiles sacrifice, they sacrifice to demons, and not to God: and I would not that ye should have communion with demons. [21] Ye cannot drink the cup of the Lord, and the cup of demons: ye cannot partake of the table of the Lord, and of the table of demons. [22] Or do we provoke the Lord to jealousy? are we stronger than he?

[23] All things are lawful; but not all things are expedient. All things are lawful; but not all things edify.[18] [24] Let no man seek his own, but *each* his[19] neighbor's *good.* [25] Whatsoever is sold in the shambles, eat, asking no question for conscience' sake; [26] for the earth is the Lord's, and the fulness thereof. [27] If one of them that believe not biddeth you *to a feast,* and ye are disposed to go; whatsoever is set before you, eat, asking no question for conscience' sake. [28] But if any man say unto you, This hath been offered in sacrifice, eat not, for his sake that showed it, and for conscience' sake: [29] conscience, I say, not thine own, but the other's; for why is my liberty judged by another conscience? [30] If[20] I partake with thankfulness, why am I evil spoken of for that for which I give thanks? [31] Whether therefore ye eat, or drink, or whatsoever ye do, do all to the glory of God. [32] Give no occasion of stumbling, either to Jews, or to Greeks, or to the church of God: [33] even as I also please all men in all things, not seeking mine own profit, but the *profit* of the many, that they may be saved.

XI

[1] BE ye imitators of me, even as I also am of Christ.

[2] Now I praise you that ye remember me in all things, and hold fast the traditions, even as I delivered them to you. [3] But I would have you know, that the head of every man is Christ; and the head of the woman is the man; and the head of Christ is God. [4] Every man praying or prophesying, having his head covered, dishonoreth his head. [5] But every woman praying or prophesying with her

[17] Gr. *from.*   [18] Gr. *build up.*   [19] Gr. *the other's.* See Rom. 13. 8.
[20] Or, *If I by grace partake.*

head unveiled dishonoreth her head; for it is one and the same thing as if she were shaven. [6] For if a woman is not veiled, let her also be shorn: but if it is a shame to a woman to be shorn or shaven, let her be veiled. [7] For a man indeed ought not to have his head veiled, forasmuch as he is the image and glory of God: but the woman is the glory of the man. [8] For the man is not of the woman; but the woman of the man: [9] for neither was the man created for the woman; but the woman for the man: [10] for this cause ought the woman to have *a sign of* authority on her head, because of the angels. [11] Nevertheless, neither is the woman without the man, nor the man without the woman, in the Lord. [12] For as the woman is of the man, so is the man also by the woman; but all things are of God. [13] Judge ye in[1] yourselves: is it seemly that a woman pray unto God unveiled? [14] Doth not even nature itself teach you, that, if a man have long hair, it is a dishonor to him? [15] But if a woman have long hair, it is a glory to her: for her hair is given her for a covering. [16] But if any man seemeth to be contentious, we have no such custom, neither the churches of God.

[17] But in giving you this charge, I praise you not, that ye come together not for the better but for the worse. [18] For first of all, when ye come together in[2] the church, I hear that divisions[3] exist among you; and I partly believe it. [19] For there must be also factions[4] among you, that they that are approved may be made manifest among you. [20] When therefore ye assemble yourselves together, it is not possible to eat the Lord's supper: [21] for in your eating each one taketh before *other* his own supper; and one is hungry, and another is drunken. [22] What, have ye not houses to eat and to drink in? or despise ye the church[5] of God, and put them to shame that have[6] not? What shall I say to you? shall[7] I praise you? In this I praise you not. [23] For I received of the Lord that which also I delivered unto you, that the Lord Jesus in the night in which he was betrayed[8] took bread; [24] and when he had given thanks, he brake it, and said, This is my body, which is[9] for you: this do in remembrance of me. [25] In like manner also the cup,

---

[1] Or, *among.* [2] Or, *in congregation.* [3] Gr. *schisms.*
[4] Gr. *heresies.* [5] Or, *congregation.* [6] Or, *have nothing.*
[7] Or, *shall I praise you in this? I praise you not.*
[8] Or, *delivered up.* [9] Many ancient authorities read *is broken for you.*

after supper, saying, This cup is the new covenant in my blood: this do, as often as ye drink *it*, in remembrance of me. [26] For as often as ye eat this bread, and drink the cup, ye proclaim the Lord's death till he come. [27] Wherefore whosoever shall eat the bread or drink the cup of the Lord in an unworthy manner, shall be guilty of the body and the blood of the Lord. [28] But let a man prove himself, and so let him eat of the bread, and drink of the cup. [29] For he that eateth and drinketh, eateth and drinketh judgment unto himself, if he discern[10] not the body. [30] For this cause many among you are weak and sickly, and not a few sleep. [31] But if we discerned[11] ourselves, we should not be judged. [32] But when[12] we are judged, we are chastened of the Lord, that we may not be condemned with the world. [33] Wherefore, my brethren, when ye come together to eat, wait one for another. [34] If any man is hungry, let him eat at home; that your coming together be not unto judgment. And the rest will I set in order whensoever I come.

<h1 style="text-align:center">XII</h1>

[1] Now concerning spiritual *gifts,* brethren, I would not have you ignorant. [2] Ye know that when ye were Gentiles *ye were* led away unto those dumb idols, howsoever ye might be led. [3] Wherefore I make known unto you, that no man speaking in the Spirit of God saith, Jesus is anathema; and no man can say, Jesus is Lord, but in the Holy Spirit.

[4] Now there are diversities of gifts, but the same Spirit. [5] And there are diversities of ministrations, and the same Lord. [6] And there are diversities of workings, but the same God, who worketh all things in all. [7] But to each one is given the manifestation of the Spirit to profit withal. [8] For to one is given through the Spirit the word of wisdom; and to another the word of knowledge, according to the same Spirit: [9] to another faith, in the same Spirit; and to another gifts of healings, in the one Spirit; [10] and to another workings of miracles;[1] and to another prophecy; and to another discernings of spirits: to another *divers* kinds of tongues; and to another the interpretation of tongues: [11] but all these worketh the

[10] Gr. *discriminate.*   [11] Gr. *discriminated.*
[12] Or, *when we are judged of the Lord, we are chastened.*   [1] Gr. *powers.*

one and the same Spirit, dividing to each one severally even as he will.

[12] For as the body is one, and hath many members, and all the members of the body, being many, are one body; so also is Christ. [13] For in one Spirit were we all baptized into one body, whether Jews or Greeks, whether bond or free; and were all made to drink of one Spirit. [14] For the body is not one member, but many. [15] If the foot shall say, Because I am not the hand, I am not of the body; it is not therefore not of the body. [16] And if the ear shall say, Because I am not the eye, I am not of the body; it is not therefore not of the body. [17] If the whole body were an eye, where were the hearing? If the whole were hearing, where were the smelling? [18] But now hath God set the members each one of them in the body, even as it pleased him. [19] And if they were all one member, where were the body? [20] But now they are many members, but one body. [21] And the eye cannot say to the hand, I have no need of thee: or again the head to the feet, I have no need of you. [22] Nay, much rather, those members of the body which seem to be more feeble are necessary: [23] and those *parts* of the body, which we think to be less honorable, upon these we bestow[2] more abundant honor; and our uncomely *parts* have more abundant comeliness; [24] whereas our comely *parts* have no need: but God tempered the body together, giving more abundant honor to that *part* which lacked; [25] that there should be no schism in the body; but *that* the members should have the same care one for another. [26] And whether one member suffereth, all the members suffer with it; or *one* member is honored,[3] all the members rejoice with it. [27] Now ye are the body of Christ, and severally[4] members thereof. [28] And God hath set some in the church, first apostles, secondly prophets, thirdly teachers, then miracles,[1] then gifts of healings, helps, governments,[5] *divers* kinds of tongues. [29] Are all apostles? are all prophets? are all teachers? are all *workers* of miracles?[1] [30] have all gifts of healings? do all speak with tongues? do all interpret? [31] But desire earnestly the greater gifts. And moreover a most excellent way show I unto you.

---

[2] Or, *put on*. [3] Or, *glorified*. [4] Or, *members each in his part*.
[5] Or, *wise counsels*.

XIII

[1] IF I speak with the tongues of men and of angels, but have not love, I am become sounding brass, or a clanging cymbal. [2] And if I have *the gift of* prophecy, and know all mysteries and all knowledge; and if I have all faith, so as to remove mountains, but have not love, I am nothing. [3] And if I bestow all my goods to feed *the poor,* and if I give my body to[1] be burned, but have not love, it profiteth me nothing. [4] Love suffereth long, *and* is kind; love envieth not; love vaunteth not itself, is not puffed up, [5] doth not behave itself unseemly, seeketh not its own, is not provoked, taketh not account of evil; [6] rejoiceth not in unrighteousness, but rejoiceth with the truth; [7] beareth[2] all things, believeth all things, hopeth all things, endureth all things. [8] Love never faileth: but whether *there be* prophecies, they shall be done away; whether *there be* tongues, they shall cease; whether *there be* knowledge, it shall be done away. [9] For we know in part, and we prophesy in part; [10] but when that which is perfect is come, that which is in part shall be done away. [11] When I was a child, I spake as a child, I felt as a child, I thought as a child: now that I am become a man, I have put away childish things. [12] For now we see in a mirror, darkly;[3] but then face to face: now I know in part; but then shall I know fully even as also I was fully known. [13] But now abideth faith, hope, love, these three; and the greatest[4] of these is love.

XIV

[1] FOLLOW after love; yet desire earnestly spiritual *gifts,* but rather that ye may prophesy. [2] For he that speaketh in a tongue speaketh not unto men, but unto God; for no man understandeth;[5] but in the spirit he speaketh mysteries. [3] But he that prophesieth speaketh unto men edification, and exhortation,[6] and consolation. [4] He that speaketh in a tongue edifieth[7] himself; but he that prophesieth edifieth[7] the church. [5] Now I would have you all speak with tongues, but rather that ye should prophesy: and greater

---

[1] Many ancient authorities read *that I may glory.*
[2] Or, *covereth.* Comp. 1 Pet. 4. 8.   [3] Gr. *in a riddle.*
[4] Gr. *greater.* Comp. Mt. 18. 1, 4; 23. 11.
[5] Gr. *heareth.*   [6] Or, *comfort.*   [7] Gr. *buildeth up.*

is he that prophesieth than he that speaketh with tongues, except he interpret, that the church may receive edifying. [6] But now, brethren, if I come unto you speaking with tongues, what shall I profit you, unless I speak to you either by way of revelation, or of knowledge, or of prophesying, or of teaching? [7] Even things without life, giving a voice, whether pipe or harp, if they give not a distinction in the sounds, how shall it be known what is piped or harped? [8] For if the trumpet give an uncertain voice, who shall prepare himself for war? [9] So also ye, unless ye utter by the tongue speech easy to be understood, how shall it be known what is spoken? for ye will be speaking into the air. [10] There are, it may be, so many kinds of voices in the world, and no[8] *kind* is without signification. [11] If then I know not the meaning of the voice, I shall be to him that speaketh a barbarian, and he that speaketh will be a barbarian unto[9] me. [12] So also ye, since ye are zealous of spiritual[10] *gifts,* seek that ye may abound unto the edifying of the church. [13] Wherefore let him that speaketh in a tongue pray that he may interpret. [14] For if I pray in a tongue, my spirit prayeth, but my understanding is unfruitful. [15] What is it then? I will pray with the spirit, and I will pray with the understanding also: I will sing with the spirit, and I will sing with the understanding also. [16] Else if thou bless with the spirit, how shall he that filleth the place of the[11] unlearned say the Amen at thy giving of thanks, seeing he knoweth not what thou sayest? [17] For thou verily givest thanks well, but the other is not edified.[12] [18] I thank God, I speak with tongues more than you all: [19] Howbeit in the church I had rather speak five words with my understanding, that I might instruct others also, than ten thousand words in a tongue.

[20] Brethren, be not children in mind: yet in malice be ye babes, but in mind be men.[13] [21] In the law it is written, By men of strange tongues and by the lips of strangers will I speak unto this people; and not even thus will they hear me, saith the Lord. [22] Wherefore tongues are for a sign, not to them that believe, but to the unbelieving: but prophesying *is for a sign,* not to the unbelieving, but to them that believe. [23] If therefore the whole church be assembled

[8] Or, *nothing is without voice.*   [9] Or, *in my case.*   [10] Gr. *spirits.*
[11] Or, *him that is without gifts:* and so in ver. 23, 24.
[12] Gr. *builded up.*   [13] Gr. *of full age.* Comp. ch. 2. 6.

together and all speak with tongues, and there come in men unlearned or unbelieving, will they not say that ye are mad? [24] But if all prophesy, and there come in one unbelieving or unlearned, he is reproved[14] by all, he is judged by all; [25] the secrets of his heart are made manifest; and so he will fall down on his face and worship God, declaring that God is among[15] you indeed.

[26] What is it then, brethren? When ye come together, each one hath a psalm, hath a teaching, hath a revelation, hath a tongue, hath an interpretation. Let all things be done unto edifying. [27] If any man speaketh in a tongue, *let it be* by two, or at the most three, and *that* in turn; and let one interpret: [28] but if there be no interpreter, let him keep silence in the church; and let him speak to himself, and to God. [29] And let the prophets speak *by* two or three, and let the others discern.[16] [30] But if a revelation be made to another sitting by, let the first keep silence. [31] For ye all can prophesy one by one, that all may learn, and all may be exhorted;[17] [32] and the spirits of the prophets are subject to the prophets; [33] for God is not *a God* of confusion, but of peace.

As in all the churches of the saints, [34] let the women keep silence in the churches: for it is not permitted unto them to speak; but let them be in subjection, as also saith the law. [35] And if they would learn anything, let them ask their own husbands at home: for it is shameful for a woman to speak in the church. [36] What? was it from you that the word of God went forth? or came it unto you alone?

[37] If any man thinketh himself to be a prophet, or spiritual, let him take knowledge of the things which I write unto you, that they are the commandment of the Lord. [38] But[18] if any man is ignorant, let him be ignorant.

[39] Wherefore, my brethren, desire earnestly to prophesy, and forbid not to speak with tongues. [40] But let all things be done decently and in order.

[14] Or, *convicted.*   [15] Or, *in.*   [16] Gr. *discriminate.*   [17] Or, *comforted.*
[18] Many ancient authorities read *But if any man knoweth not, he is not known.* Comp. ch. 8. 3.

XV

[1] Now I make known unto you, brethren, the gospel[1] which I preached[2] unto you, which also ye received, wherein also ye stand, [2] by which also ye are saved, if ye hold fast the[3] word which I preached[2] unto you, except ye believed in[4] vain. [3] For I delivered unto you first of all that which also I received: that Christ died for our sins according to the scriptures; [4] and that he was buried; and that he hath been raised on the third day according to the scriptures; [5] and that he appeared to Cephas; then to the twelve; [6] then he appeared to above five hundred brethren at once, of whom the greater part remain until now, but some are fallen asleep; [7] then he appeared to James;[5] then to all the apostles; [8] and last of all, as to the *child* untimely born, he appeared to me also. [9] For I am the least of the apostles, that am not meet to be called an apostle, because I persecuted the church of God. [10] But by the grace of God I am what I am: and his grace which was bestowed upon me was not found vain;[6] but I labored more abundantly than they all: yet not I, but the grace of God which was with me: [11] Whether then *it be* I or they, so we preach, and so ye believed.

[12] Now if Christ is preached that he hath been raised from the dead, how say some among you that there is no resurrection of the dead? [13] But if there is no resurrection of the dead, neither hath Christ been raised: [14] and if Christ hath not been raised, then is our preaching vain,[7] your[8] faith also is vain.[7] [15] Yea, and we are found false witnesses of God; because we witnessed of God that he raised up Christ:[9] whom he raised not up, if so be that the dead are not raised. [16] For if the dead are not raised, neither hath Christ been raised: [17] and if Christ hath not been raised, your faith is vain; ye are yet in your sins. [18] Then they also that are fallen asleep in Christ have perished. [19] If[10] we have only hoped in Christ in this life, we are of all men most pitiable.

[20] But now hath Christ been raised from the dead, the first-fruits of them that are asleep. [21] For since by man *came* death, by man

---

[1] See marginal note on ch. 4. 15.   [2] See marginal note on ch. 1. 17.
[3] Gr. *with what word*.   [4] Or, *without cause*.   [5] Or, *Jacob*.   [6] Or, *void*.
[7] Or, *void*.   [8] Some ancient authorities read *our*.   [9] Gr. *the Christ*.
[10] Or, *If in this life only we have hoped in Christ &c.*

came also the resurrection of the dead. [22] For as in Adam all die, so also in Christ[9] shall all be made alive. [23] But each in his own order: Christ the first-fruits; then they that are Christ's, at his coming.[11] [24] Then *cometh* the end, when he shall deliver up the kingdom to God,[12] even the Father; when he shall have abolished all rule and all authority and power. [25] For he must reign, till he hath put all his enemies under his feet. [26] The last enemy that shall be abolished is death. [27] For, He put all things in subjection under his feet. But[13] when he saith, All things are put in subjection, it is evident that he is excepted who did subject all things unto him. [28] And when all things have been subjected unto him, then shall the Son also himself be subjected to him that did subject all things unto him, that God may be all in all.

[29] Else what shall they do that are baptized for the dead? If the dead are not raised at all, why then are they baptized for them? [30] why do we also stand in jeopardy every hour? [31] I protest by that[14] glorying in you, brethren, which I have in Christ Jesus our Lord, I die daily. [32] If after the manner of men I fought with beasts at Ephesus, what[15] doth it profit me? If the dead are not raised, let us eat and drink, for to-morrow we die. [33] Be not deceived: Evil companionships corrupt good morals. [34] Awake to soberness righteously, and sin not; for some have no knowledge of God: I speak *this* to move you to shame.

[35] But some one will say, How are the dead raised? and with what manner of body do they come? [36] Thou foolish one, that which thou thyself sowest is not quickened except it die: [37] and that which thou sowest, thou sowest not the body that shall be, but a bare grain, it may chance of wheat, or of some other kind; [38] but God giveth it a body even as it pleased him, and to each seed a body of its own. [39] All flesh is not the same flesh: but there is one *flesh* of men, and another flesh of beasts, and another flesh of birds, and another of fishes. [40] There are also celestial bodies, and bodies terrestrial: but the glory of the celestial is one, and the *glory* of the

---

[9] Gr. *the Christ*.   [11] Gr. *presence*.   [12] Gr. *the God and Father*.

[13] Or, *But when he shall have said, All things are put in subjection (evidently excepting him that did subject all things unto him), when, I say, all things &c.*

[14] Or, *your glorying*.

[15] Or, *what doth it profit me, if the dead are not raised? Let us eat &c.*

terrestrial is another. [41] There is one glory of the sun, and another glory of the moon, and another glory of the stars; for one star differeth from another star in glory. [42] So also is the resurrection of the dead. It is sown in corruption; it is raised in incorruption: [43] it is sown in dishonor; it is raised in glory: it is sown in weakness; it is raised in power: [44] it is sown a natural[16] body; it is raised a spiritual body. If there is a natural[16] body, there is also a spiritual *body*. [45] So also it is written, The first man Adam became a living soul. The last Adam *became* a life-giving spirit. [46] Howbeit that is not first which is spiritual, but that which is natural;[16] then that which is spiritual. [47] The first man is of the earth, earthy: the second man is of heaven. [48] As is the earthy, such are they also that are earthy: and as is the heavenly, such are they also that are heavenly. [49] And as we have borne the image of the earthy, we[17] shall also bear the image of the heavenly.

[50] Now this I say, brethren, that flesh and blood cannot inherit the kingdom of God; neither doth corruption inherit incorruption. [51] Behold, I tell you a mystery: We[18] all shall not sleep, but we shall all be changed, [52] in a moment, in the twinkling of an eye, at the last trump: for the trumpet shall sound, and the dead shall be raised incorruptible, and we shall be changed. [53] For this corruptible must put on incorruption, and this mortal must put on immortality. [54] But when this[19] corruptible shall have put on incorruption, and this mortal shall have put on immortality, then shall come to pass the saying that is written, Death is swallowed up in[20] victory. [55] O death, where is thy victory? O death, where is thy sting? [56] The sting of death is sin; and the power of sin is the law: [57] but thanks be to God, who giveth us the victory through our Lord Jesus Christ. [58] Wherefore, my beloved brethren, be ye stedfast, unmoveable, always abounding in the work of the Lord, forasmuch as ye know that your labor is not vain[21] in the Lord.

[16] Gr. *psychical.*   [17] Many ancient authorities read *let us also bear.*
[18] Or, *We shall not all &c.*
[19] Many ancient authorities omit *this corruptible shall have put on incorruption, and.*   [20] Or, *victoriously.*   [21] Or, *void.*

XVI

[1] Now concerning the collection for the saints, as I gave order to the churches of Galatia, so also do ye. [2] Upon the first day of the week let each one of you lay by him in store, as he may prosper, that no collections be made when I come. [3] And when I arrive, whomsoever[1] ye shall approve, them will I send with letters to carry your bounty unto Jerusalem: [4] and if it be meet for me to go also, they shall go with me. [5] But I will come unto you, when I shall have passed through Macedonia; for I pass through Macedonia; [6] but with you it may be that I shall abide, or even winter, that ye may set me forward on my journey whithersoever I go. [7] For I do not wish to see you now by the way; for I hope to tarry a while with you, if the Lord permit. [8] But I will tarry at Ephesus until Pentecost; [9] for a great door and effectual is opened unto me, and there are many adversaries.

[10] Now if Timothy come, see that he be with you without fear; for he worketh the work of the Lord, as I also do: [11] let no man therefore despise him. But set him forward on his journey in peace, that he may come unto me: for I expect him with the brethren. [12] But as touching Apollos the brother, I besought him much to come unto you with the brethren: and it was not at all *his*[2] will to come now; but he will come when he shall have opportunity.

[13] Watch ye, stand fast in the faith, quit you like men, be strong. [14] Let all that ye do be done in love.

[15] Now I beseech you, brethren (ye know the house of Stephanas, that it is the first-fruits of Achaia, and that they have set themselves to minister unto the saints), [16] that ye also be in subjection unto such, and to every one that helpeth in the work and laboreth. [17] And I rejoice at the coming[3] of Stephanas and Fortunatus and Achaicus: for that which was lacking on your part they supplied. [18] For they refreshed my spirit and yours: acknowledge ye therefore them that are such.

---

[1] Or, *whomsoever ye shall approve by letters, them will I send &c.*
[2] Or, God's *will that he should come now.* Comp. Rom. 2. 18 marg.
[3] Gr. *presence.* 2 Cor. 10. 10.

[19] The churches of Asia salute you. Aquila and Prisca salute you much in the Lord, with the church that is in their house. [20] All the brethren salute you. Salute one another with a holy kiss.

[21] The salutation of me Paul with mine own hand. [22] If any man loveth not the Lord, let him be anathema. Maranatha.[4] [23] The grace of the Lord Jesus Christ be with you. [24] My love be with you all in Christ Jesus. Amen.

[4] That is O (or Our) Lord, come!

THE SECOND EPISTLE OF PAUL TO THE
CORINTHIANS

[1]   I

PAUL, an apostle of Christ Jesus through the will of God, and Timothy our[1] brother, unto the church of God which is at Corinth, with all the saints that are in the whole of Achaia: [2] Grace to you and peace from God our Father and the Lord Jesus Christ.

[3] Blessed *be* the[2] God and Father of our Lord Jesus Christ, the Father of mercies and God of all comfort; [4] who comforteth us in all our affliction, that we may be able to comfort them that are in any affliction, through the comfort wherewith we ourselves are comforted of God. [5] For as the sufferings of Christ abound unto us, even so our comfort also aboundeth through Christ. [6] But whether we are afflicted, it is for your comfort and salvation; or whether we are comforted, it is for your comfort, which worketh in the patient enduring of the same sufferings which we also suffer: [7] and our hope for you is stedfast; knowing that, as ye are partakers of the sufferings, so also are ye of the comfort. [8] For we would not have you ignorant, brethren, concerning our affliction which befell *us* in Asia, that we were weighed down exceedingly, beyond our power, insomuch that we despaired even of life: [9] yea,[3] we ourselves have had the sentence[4] of death within ourselves, that we should not trust in ourselves, but in God who raiseth the dead: [10] who delivered us out of so great a death, and will deliver: on whom we have set[5] our hope that he will also still deliver us; [11] ye also helping together on our behalf by your supplication; that, for the gift bestowed upon us by means of many, thanks may be given by many persons on our behalf.

[1] Gr. *the brother.*   [2] Or, *God and the Father.* See Rom. 15. 6 marg.
[3] Or, *but we ourselves.*   [4] Gr. *answer.*
[5] Some ancient authorities read *set our hope; and still will he deliver us.*

[12] For our glorying is this, the testimony of our conscience, that in holiness and sincerity of God, not in fleshly wisdom but in the grace of God, we behaved ourselves in the world, and more abundantly to you-ward. [13] For we write no other things unto you, than what ye read or even acknowledge, and I hope ye will acknowledge unto the end: [14] as also ye did acknowledge us in part, that we are your glorying, even as ye also are ours, in the day of our Lord Jesus.

[15] And in this confidence I was minded to come first unto you, that ye might have a second benefit;[6] [16] and by you to pass into Macedonia, and again from Macedonia to come unto you, and of you to be set forward on my journey unto Judæa. [17] When I therefore was thus minded, did I show fickleness? or the things that I purpose, do I purpose according to the flesh, that with me there should be the yea yea and the nay nay? [18] But as God is faithful, our word toward you is not yea and nay. [19] For the Son of God, Jesus Christ, who was preached among you by[7] us, *even* by[7] me and Silvanus and Timothy, was not yea and nay, but in him is yea. [20] For how many soever be the promises of God, in him is the yea: wherefore also through him is the Amen, unto the glory of God through us. [21] Now he that establisheth us with you in[8] Christ, and anointed us, is God; [22] who[9] also sealed us, and gave *us* the earnest of the Spirit in our hearts.

[23] But I call God for a witness upon my soul, that to spare you I forbare to come unto Corinth. [24] Not that we have lordship over your faith, but are helpers of your joy: for in faith[10] ye stand fast.

II

[1] But[1] I determined this for myself, that I would not come again to you with sorrow. [2] For if I make you sorry, who then is he that maketh me glad but he that is made sorry by me? [3] And I wrote this very thing, lest, when I came, I should have sorrow from them of whom I ought to rejoice; having confidence in you all, that my joy is *the joy* of you all. [4] For out of much affliction and anguish of heart I wrote unto you with many tears; not that ye should be made

---

[6] Or, *grace*. Some ancient authorities read *joy*.   [7] Gr. *through*.
[8] Gr. *into*.   [9] Or, *seeing that he both sealed us*.   [10] Or, *your faith*.
[1] Some ancient authorities read *For*.

sorry, but that ye might know the love which I have more abundantly unto you.

[5] But if any hath caused sorrow, he hath caused sorrow, not to me, but in part (that I press not too heavily) to you all. [6] Sufficient to such a one is this punishment which was *inflicted* by the[2] many; [7] so that contrariwise ye should rather[3] forgive him and comfort him, lest by any means such a one should be swallowed up with his overmuch sorrow. [8] Wherefore I beseech you to confirm *your* love toward him. [9] For to this end also did I write, that I might know the proof of you, whether[4] ye are obedient in all things. [10] But to whom ye forgive anything, I *forgive* also: for what I also have forgiven, if I have forgiven anything, for your sakes *have I forgiven it* in the presence[5] of Christ; [11] that no advantage may be gained over us by Satan: for we are not ignorant of his devices.

[12] Now when I came to Troas for the gospel[6] of Christ, and when a door was opened unto me in the Lord, [13] I had no relief for my spirit, because I found not Titus my brother: but taking my leave of them, I went forth into Macedonia.

[14] But thanks be unto God, who always leadeth us in triumph in Christ, and maketh manifest through us the savor of his knowledge in every place. [15] For we are a sweet savor of Christ unto God, in them that are[7] saved, and in them that perish;[8] [16] to the one a savor from death unto death; to the other a savor from life unto life. And who is sufficient for these things? [17] For we are not as the many, corrupting[9] the word of God: but as of sincerity, but as of God, in the sight of God, speak we in Christ.

III

[1] ARE we beginning again to commend ourselves? or need we, as do some, epistles of commendation to you or from you? [2] Ye are our epistle, written in our hearts, known and read of all men; [3] being made manifest that ye are an epistle of Christ, ministered by us, written not with ink, but with the Spirit of the living God; not in tables of stone, but in tables *that are* hearts of flesh. [4] And

---

[2] Gr. *the more.*   [3] Some ancient authorities omit *rather.*   [4] Some ancient authorities read *whereby.*   [5] Or, *person.*   [6] Gr. *good tidings:* see marginal note on Mt. 4. 23.   [7] Or, *are being saved.*   [8] Or, *are perishing.*
   [9] Or, *making merchandise of the word of God.* Comp. 2 Pet. 2. 3.

such confidence have we through Christ to God-ward: [5] not that we are sufficient of ourselves, to account anything as from ourselves; but our sufficiency is from God; [6] who also made us sufficient as ministers of a new covenant; not of the letter, but of the spirit: for the letter killeth, but the spirit giveth life. [7] But if the ministration of death, written,[1] *and* engraven on stones, came with[2] glory, so that the children of Israel could not look stedfastly upon the face of Moses for the glory of his face; which *glory* was[3] passing away: [8] how shall not rather the ministration of the spirit be with glory? [9] For[4] if the ministration of condemnation hath glory, much rather doth the ministration of righteousness exceed in glory. [10] For verily that which hath been made glorious hath not been made glorious in this respect, by reason of the glory that surpasseth. [11] For if that which passeth[5] away *was* with[6] glory, much more that which remaineth *is* in glory.

[12] Having therefore such a hope, we use great boldness of speech, [13] and *are* not as Moses, *who* put a veil upon his face, that the children of Israel should not look stedfastly on[7] the end of that which was[8] passing away: [14] but their minds[9] were hardened: for until this very day at the reading of the old covenant the same veil remaineth,[10] it not being revealed *to them* that it is done away in Christ. [15] But unto this day, whensoever Moses is read, a veil lieth upon their heart. [16] But whensoever it[11] shall turn to the Lord, the veil is taken away. [17] Now the Lord is the Spirit: and where the Spirit of the Lord is, *there* is liberty. [18] But we all, with unveiled face beholding[12] as in a mirror the glory of the Lord, are transformed into the same image from glory to glory, even as from the Lord the Spirit.

IV

[1] Therefore seeing we have this ministry, even as we obtained mercy, we faint not: [2] but we have renounced the hidden things of shame, not walking in craftiness, nor handling the word of God

---

[1] Gr. *in letters.*   [2] Gr. *in.*   [3] Or, *was being done away.* Comp. 1 Cor. 13. 8, 10.
[4] Many ancient authorities read, *For if the ministration of condemnation is glory.*
[5] Or, *is being done away.* See ver. 7 marg.   [6] Gr. *through.*
[7] Or, *unto.*   [8] Or, *was being done away.* See ver. 7 marg.   [9] Gr. *thoughts.*
Ch. 4. 4; 11. 3.   [10] Or, *remaineth unlifted; which* veil *is done away.*
[11] Or, *a man shall turn.*   [12] Or, *reflecting as a mirror.*

deceitfully; but by the manifestation of the truth commending ourselves to every man's conscience in the sight of God. [3] And even
if our gospel[1] is veiled, it is veiled in them that perish:[2] [4] in whom
the god of this world[3] hath blinded the minds[4] of the unbelieving,
that[5] the light[6] of the gospel[1] of the glory of Christ, who is the image
of God, should not dawn *upon them*. [5] For we preach not ourselves, but Christ Jesus as Lord, and ourselves as your servants[7] for[8]
Jesus' sake. [6] Seeing it is God, that said, Light shall shine out of
darkness, who shined in our hearts, to give the light[6] of the knowledge of the glory of God in the face of Jesus Christ.

[7] But we have this treasure in earthen vessels, that the exceeding
greatness of the power may be of God, and not from ourselves; [8]
we are pressed on every side, yet not straitened; perplexed, yet not
unto despair; [9] pursued, yet not forsaken;[9] smitten down, yet not
destroyed; [10] always bearing about in the body the dying[10] of
Jesus, that the life also of Jesus may be manifested in our body. [11]
For we who live are always delivered unto death for Jesus' sake, that
the life also of Jesus may be manifested in our mortal flesh. [12] So
then death worketh in us, but life in you. [13] But having the same
spirit of faith, according to that which is written, I believed, and
therefore did I speak; we also believe, and therefore also we speak;
[14] knowing that he that raised up the[11] Lord Jesus shall raise up
us also with Jesus, and shall present us with you. [15] For all things
are for your sakes, that the grace, being multiplied through the[12]
many, may cause the thanksgiving to abound unto the glory of God.

[16] Wherefore we faint not; but though our outward man is
decaying, yet our inward man is renewed day by day. [17] For our
light affliction, which is for the moment, worketh for us more and
more exceedingly an eternal weight of glory; [18] while we look
not at the things which are seen, but at the things which are not seen:
for the things which are seen are temporal; but the things which are
not seen are eternal.

[1] See marginal note on ch. 2. 12.   [2] Or, *are perishing*.   [3] Or, *age*.
[4] Gr. *thoughts*. Ch. 4. 4; 11. 3.
[5] Or, *that they should not see the light . . . image of God*.
[6] Gr. *illumination*.   [7] Gr. *bondservants*. Comp. 1. Cor. 9. 19.
[8] Some ancient authorities read *through Jesus*.   [9] Or, *left behind*.
[10] Gr. *putting to death*.
[11] Some ancient authorities omit *the Lord*.   [12] Gr. *the more*.

V

[1] For we know that if the earthly house of our tabernacle[1] be dissolved, we have a building from God, a house not made with hands, eternal, in the heavens. [2] For verily in this we groan, longing to be clothed upon with our habitation which is from heaven: [3] if so be that being clothed we shall not be found naked. [4] For indeed we that are in this tabernacle[2] do groan, being[3] burdened; not for that we would be unclothed, but that we would be clothed upon, that what is mortal may be swallowed up of life. [5] Now he that wrought us for this very thing is God, who gave unto us the earnest of the Spirit. [6] Being therefore always of good courage, and knowing that, whilst we are at home in the body, we are absent from the Lord [7] (for we walk by faith, not by sight[4]); [8] we are of good courage, I say, and are willing rather to be absent from the body, and to be at home with the Lord. [9] Wherefore also we make[5] it our aim, whether at home or absent, to be well-pleasing unto him. [10] For we must all be made manifest before the judgment-seat of Christ; that each one may receive the things *done* in[6] the body, according to what he hath done, whether *it be* good or bad.

[11] Knowing therefore the fear of the Lord, we persuade men, but we are made manifest unto God; and I hope that we are made manifest also in your consciences. [12] We are not again commending ourselves unto you, but *speak* as giving you occasion of glorying on our behalf, that ye may have wherewith to answer them that glory in appearance, and not in heart. [13] For whether we are[7] beside ourselves, it is unto God; or whether we are of sober mind, it is unto you. [14] For the love of Christ constraineth us; because we thus judge, that one died for all, therefore all died; [15] and he died for all, that they that live should no longer live unto themselves, but unto him who for their sakes died and rose again. [16] Wherefore we henceforth know no man after the flesh: even though we have known Christ after the flesh, yet now we know *him so* no more. [17] Wherefore if any man is in Christ, *he is*[8] a new creature: the

---

[1] Or, *bodily frame.* Comp. Wisd. 9. 15.   [2] Or, *bodily frame.*
[3] Or, *being burdened, in that we would not be unclothed, but would be clothed upon.*   [4] Gr. *appearance.*   [5] Gr. *are ambitious.* See Rom. 15. 20 marg.
[6] Gr. *through.*   [7] Or, *were.*   [8] Or, there is *a new creation.*

old things are passed away; behold, they are become new. [18] But all things are of God, who reconciled us to himself through Christ, and gave unto us the ministry of reconciliation; [19] to wit, that God was in Christ reconciling the world unto himself, not reckoning unto them their trespasses, and having committed[9] unto us the word of reconciliation.

[20] We are ambassadors therefore on behalf of Christ, as though God were entreating by us: we beseech *you* on behalf of Christ, be ye reconciled to God. [21] Him who knew no sin he made *to be* sin on our behalf; that we might become the righteousness of God in him.

VI

[1] AND working together *with him* we entreat also that ye receive not the grace of God in vain [2] (for he saith,

At an acceptable time I hearkened unto thee,

And in a day of salvation did I succor thee:

behold, now is the acceptable time; behold, now is the day of salvation): [3] giving no occasion of stumbling in anything, that our ministration be not blamed; [4] but in everything commending ourselves, as ministers of God, in much patience,[1] in afflictions, in necessities, in distresses, [5] in stripes, in imprisonments, in tumults, in labors, in watchings, in fastings; [6] in pureness, in knowledge, in long suffering, in kindness, in the Holy Spirit, in love unfeigned, [7] in the word of truth, in the power of God; by[2] the armor of righteousness on the right hand and on the left, [8] by glory and dishonor, by evil report and good report; as deceivers, and *yet* true; [9] as unknown, and *yet* well known; as dying, and behold, we live; as chastened, and not killed; [10] as sorrowful, yet always rejoicing; as poor, yet making many rich; as having nothing, and *yet* possessing all things.

[11] Our mouth is open unto you, O Corinthians, our heart is enlarged. [12] Ye are not straitened in us, but ye are straitened in your own affections. [13] Now for a recompense in like kind (I speak as unto *my* children), be ye also enlarged.

9 Or, *placed in us.*
1 Or, *stedfastness.*   2 Gr. *through.*

[14] Be not unequally yoked with unbelievers: for what fellowship have righteousness and iniquity? or what communion hath light with darkness? [15] And what concord hath Christ with Belial?[3] or what portion hath a believer with an unbeliever? [16] And what agreement hath a temple[4] of God with idols? for we are a temple[4] of the living God; even as God said, I will dwell in them, and walk in them; and I will be their God, and they shall be my people. [17] Wherefore

Come ye out from among them, and be ye separate, saith the Lord,

And touch no unclean thing;

And I will receive you,

[18] And will be to you a Father,

And ye shall be to me sons and daughters,

saith the Lord Almighty.

VII

[1] HAVING therefore these promises, beloved, let us cleanse ourselves from all defilement of flesh and spirit, perfecting holiness in the fear of God.

[2] Open[5] your hearts to us: we wronged no man, we corrupted no man, we took advantage of no man. [3] I say it not to condemn *you:* for I have said before, that ye are in our hearts to die together and live together. [4] Great is my boldness of speech toward you, great is my glorying on your behalf: I am filled with comfort, I overflow with joy in all our affliction.

[5] For even when we were come into Macedonia our flesh had no relief, but *we were* afflicted on every side; without *were* fightings, within *were* fears. [6] Nevertheless he that comforteth the lowly, *even* God, comforted us by the coming[6] of Titus; [7] and not by his coming[2] only, but also by the comfort wherewith he was comforted in you, while he told us your longing, your mourning, your zeal for me; so that I rejoiced yet more. [8] For though I made you sorry with my epistle, I do not regret it: though I did regret *it* (for[7] I see that that epistle made you sorry, though but for a season), [9] I now

---

[3] Gr. *Beliar.*   [4] Or, *sanctuary.*
[5] Gr. *Make room for us.*   [6] Gr. *presence.* Comp. 2. Thess. 2. 9.
[7] Some ancient authorities omit *for.*

rejoice, not that ye were made sorry, but that ye were made sorry unto repentance; for ye were made sorry after a godly sort, that ye might suffer loss by us in nothing. [10] For godly sorrow worketh repentance unto[8] salvation, *a repentance* which bringeth no regret: but the sorrow of the world worketh death. [11] For behold, this selfsame thing, that ye were made sorry after a godly sort, what earnest care it wrought in you, yea what clearing of yourselves, yea what indignation, yea what fear, yea what longing, yea what zeal, yea what avenging! In everything ye approved yourselves to be pure in the matter. [12] So although I wrote unto you, *I wrote* not for his cause that did the wrong, nor for his cause that suffered the wrong, but that your earnest care for us might be made manifest unto you in the sight of God. [13] Therefore we have been comforted: and in our comfort we joyed the more exceedingly for the joy of Titus, because his spirit hath been refreshed by you all. [14] For if in anything I have gloried to him on your behalf, I was not put to shame; but as we spake all things to you in truth, so our glorying also which I made before Titus was found to be truth. [15] And his affection is more abundantly toward you, while he remembereth the obedience of you all, how with fear and trembling ye received him. [16] I rejoice that in everything I am of good courage concerning you.

VIII

[1] MOREOVER, brethren, we make known to you the grace of God which hath been given in the churches of Macedonia; [2] how that in much proof of affliction the abundance of their joy and their deep poverty abounded unto the riches of their liberality.[1] [3] For according to their power, I bear witness, yea and beyond their power, *they gave* of their own accord, [4] beseeching us with much entreaty in regard of this grace and the fellowship in the ministering to the saints: [5] and *this,* not as we had hoped, but first they gave their own selves to the Lord, and to us through the will of God. [6] Insomuch that we exhorted Titus, that as he had made a beginning before, so he would also complete in you this grace also. [7] But

[8] Or, *unto a salvation which bringeth no regret.*
[1] Gr. *singleness.* See Rom. 12. 8.

as ye abound in everything, *in* faith, and utterance, and knowledge, and *in* all earnestness, and *in* your[2] love to us, *see* that ye abound in this grace also. [8] I speak not by way of commandment, but as proving through the earnestness of others the sincerity also of your love. [9] For ye know the grace of our Lord Jesus Christ, that, though he was rich, yet for your sakes he became poor, that ye through his poverty might become rich. [10] And herein I give *my* judgment: for this is expedient for you, who were the first to make a beginning a year ago, not only to do, but also to will. [11] But now complete the doing also; that as *there was* the readiness to will, so *there may be* the completion also out of your ability. [12] For if the readiness is there, *it is* acceptable according as *a man* hath, not according as *he* hath not. [13] For *I say* not *this* that others may be eased *and* ye distressed; [14] but by equality: your abundance *being a supply* at this present time for their want, that their abundance also may become *a supply* for your want; that there may be equality: [15] as it is written, He that *gathered* much had nothing over; and he that *gathered* little had no lack.

[16] But thanks be to God, who putteth the same earnest care for you into the heart of Titus. [17] For he accepted indeed our exhortation; but being himself very earnest, he went forth unto you of his own accord. [18] And we have sent together with him the brother whose praise in the gospel[3] *is spread* through all the churches; [19] and not only so, but who was also appointed by the churches to travel with us in *the matter of* this grace, which is ministered by us to the glory of the Lord, and *to show* our readiness: [20] avoiding this, that any man should blame us in *the matter of* this bounty which is ministered by us: [21] for we take thought for things honorable, not only in the sight of the Lord, but also in the sight of men. [22] And we have sent with them our brother, whom we have many times proved earnest in many things, but now much more earnest, by reason of the great confidence which *he hath* in you. [23] Whether *any inquire* about Titus, *he is* my partner and *my* fellow-worker to you-ward; or our brethren, *they are* the messengers[4] of the churches, *they are* the glory of Christ. [24] Show[5] ye therefore unto them in

[2] Some ancient authorities read *our love to you.*
[3] See marginal note on ch. 2. 12.   [4] Gr. *apostles.*
[5] Or, *Show ye therefore in the face . . . on your behalf unto them.*

the face of the churches the proof of your love, and of our glorying on your behalf.

IX

[1] FOR as touching the ministering to the saints, it is superfluous for me to write to you: [2] for I know your readiness, of which I glory on your behalf to them of Macedonia, that Achaia hath been prepared for a year past; and your¹ zeal hath stirred up very² many of them. [3] But I have sent the brethren, that our glorying on your behalf may not be made void in this respect; that, even as I said, ye may be prepared: [4] lest by any means, if there come with me any of Macedonia and find you unprepared, we (that we say not, ye) should be put to shame in this confidence. [5] I thought it necessary therefore to entreat the brethren, that they would go before unto you, and make up beforehand your aforepromised bounty,³ that the same might be ready as a matter of bounty, and not of extortion.⁴

[6] But this *I say,* He that soweth sparingly shall reap also sparingly; and he that soweth bountifully⁵ shall reap also bountifully.⁵ [7] *Let* each man *do* according as he hath purposed in his heart; not grudgingly,⁶ or of necessity: for God loveth a cheerful giver. [8] And God is able to make all grace abound unto you; that ye, having always all sufficiency in everything, may abound unto every good work: [9] as it is written,

He hath scattered abroad, he hath given to the poor;

His righteousness abideth for ever.

[10] And he that supplieth seed to the sower and bread for food, shall supply and multiply your seed for sowing, and increase the fruits of your righteousness: [11] ye being enriched in everything unto all liberality,⁷ which worketh through us thanksgiving to God. [12] For the ministration of this service not only filleth up the measure of the wants of the saints, but aboundeth also through many thanksgivings unto God; [13] seeing that through the proving *of you* by this ministration they glorify God for the obedience of your confession unto the gospel⁸ of Christ, and for the liberality⁷ of *your* contribution unto them and unto all; [14] while they themselves also,

---

¹ Or, *emulation of you.*   ² Gr. *the more part.*   ³ Gr. *blessing.*   ⁴ Or, *covetousness.*
⁵ Gr. *with blessings.* Comp. ver. 5.   ⁶ Gr. *of sorrow.*   ⁷ Gr. *singleness.* Comp.
ch. 8. 2.   ⁸ Gr. *good tidings.* See marginal note on ch. 2. 12.

with supplication on your behalf, long after you by reason of the exceeding grace of God in you. [15] Thanks be to God for his unspeakable gift.

X

[1] Now I Paul myself entreat you by the meekness and gentleness of Christ, I who in your presence am lowly among you, but being absent am of good courage toward you: [2] yea, I beseech you, that I may not when present show courage with the confidence wherewith I count to be bold against some, who count of us as if we walked according to the flesh. [3] For though we walk in the flesh, we do not war according to the flesh [4] (for the weapons of our warfare are not of the flesh, but mighty before God to the casting down of strongholds); [5] casting down imaginations,[1] and every high thing that is exalted against the knowledge of God, and bringing every thought into captivity to the obedience of Christ; [6] and being in readiness to avenge all disobedience, when your obedience shall be made full. [7] Ye[2] look at the things that are before your face. If any man trusteth in himself that he is Christ's, let him consider this again with himself, that, even as he is Christ's, so also are we. [8] For though I should glory somewhat abundantly concerning our authority (which the Lord gave for building you up, and not for casting you down), I shall not be put to shame: [9] that I may not seem as if I would terrify you by my letters. [10] For, His letters, they say, are weighty and strong; but his bodily presence is weak, and his speech of no account. [11] Let such a one reckon this, that, what we are in word by letters when we are absent, such *are we* also in deed when we are present. [12] For we are not bold to[3] number or compare ourselves with certain of them that commend themselves: but they themselves, measuring themselves by themselves, and comparing themselves with themselves, are without understanding. [13] But we will not glory beyond *our* measure, but according to the measure of the province[4] which God apportioned to us as a measure, to reach even unto you. [14] For we stretch not ourselves overmuch, as though we reached not unto you: for we

---

[1] Or, *reasonings.* Rom. 2. 15.   [2] Or, *Do ye look . . . face?*
[3] Gr. *to judge ourselves among, or to judge ourselves with.*
[4] Or, *limit.* Gr. *measuring-rod.*

came[5] even as far as unto you in the gospel[6] of Christ: [15] not glorying beyond *our* measure, *that is,* in other men's labors; but having
hope that, as your faith groweth, we shall be magnified in you according to our province[4] unto *further* abundance, [16] so as to preach[7]
the gospel even unto the parts beyond you, *and* not to glory in another's province[4] in regard of things ready to our hand. [17] But
he that glorieth, let him glory in the Lord. [18] For not he that
commendeth himself is approved, but whom the Lord commendeth.

XI

[1] WOULD that ye could bear with me in a little foolishness: but[8]
indeed ye do bear with me. [2] For I am jealous over you with a[9]
godly jealousy: for I espoused you to one husband, that I might
present you *as* a pure virgin to Christ. [3] But I fear, lest by any
means, as the serpent beguiled Eve in his craftiness, your minds[10]
should be corrupted from the simplicity and the purity that is toward
Christ. [4] For if he that cometh preacheth another Jesus, whom
we did not preach, or *if* ye receive a different spirit, which ye did not
receive, or a different gospel,[11] which ye did not accept, ye do well to
bear with *him*. [5] For I reckon that I am not a whit behind the[12]
very chiefest apostles. [6] But though *I be* rude in speech, yet *am I*
not in knowledge; nay,[13] in every way have we made *this* manifest
unto you in all things. [7] Or did I commit a sin in abasing myself
that ye might be exalted, because I preached[14] to you the gospel of
God for nought? [8] I robbed other churches, taking wages *of them*
that I might minister unto you; [9] and when I was present with
you and was in want, I was not a burden on any man; for the
brethren, when they came from Macedonia, supplied the measure
of my want; and in everything I kept myself from being burdensome
unto you, and *so* will I keep *myself*. [10] As the truth of Christ is in
me, no man shall stop me of this glorying in the regions of Achaia.

5 Or, *were the first to come.*   6 Gr. *good tidings.* See marginal note on ch. 2. 12.
7 Gr. *bring good tidings.* Comp. Mt. 11. 5.   8 Or, *May indeed bear with me.*
9 Gr. *a jealousy of God.*   10 Gr. *thoughts.* See ch. 3. 14.   11 Gr. *good tidings.*
Comp. ch. 2. 12.
    12 Or, *those pre-eminent apostles.*   13 Or, *nay, in everything we have made* it
manifest among all men to you-ward.   14 See marginal note on ch. 10. 16.

[11] Wherefore? because I love you not? God knoweth. [12] But what I do, that I will do, that I may cut off occasion[15] from them that desire an occasion; that wherein they glory, they may be found even as we. [13] For such men are false apostles, deceitful workers, fashioning themselves into apostles of Christ. [14] And no marvel; for even Satan fashioneth himself into an angel of light. [15] It is no great thing therefore if his ministers also fashion themselves as ministers of righteousness; whose end shall be according to their works.

[16] I say again, Let no man think me foolish; but if *ye do,* yet as foolish receive me, that I also may glory a little. [17] That which I speak, I speak not after the Lord, but as in foolishness, in this confidence of glorying. [18] Seeing that many glory after the flesh, I will glory also. [19] For ye bear with the foolish gladly, being wise *yourselves.* [20] For ye bear with a man, if he bringeth you into bondage, if he devoureth you, if he taketh you *captive,* if he exalteth himself, if he smiteth you on the face. [21] I speak by way of disparagement, as though we had been weak. Yet whereinsoever any is bold (I speak in foolishness), I am bold also. [22] Are they Hebrews? so am I. Are they Israelites? so am I. Are they the seed of Abraham? so am I. [23] Are they ministers of Christ? (I speak as one beside himself) I more; in labors more abundantly, in prisons more abundantly, in stripes above measure, in deaths oft. [24] Of the Jews five times received I forty *stripes* save one. [25] Thrice was I beaten with rods, once was I stoned, thrice I suffered shipwreck, a night and a day have I been in the deep; [26] *in* journeyings often, *in* perils of rivers, *in* perils of robbers, *in* perils from *my* countrymen,[16] *in* perils from the Gentiles, *in* perils in the city, *in* perils in the wilderness, *in* perils in the sea, *in* perils among false brethren; [27] *in* labor and travail, in watchings often, in hunger and thirst, in fastings often, in cold and nakedness. [28] Besides[17] those things that are without, there is that which presseth upon me daily, anxiety for all the churches. [29] Who is weak, and I am not weak? who is caused to stumble, and I burn not? [30] If I must needs glory, I will glory of the things that concern my weakness. [31] The[18] God and Father of

[15] Gr, *the occasion of them.* [16] Gr. *race.* Comp. Acts 7. 19.
[17] Or, *Besides the things which I omit.* Or, *Besides the things that come out of course.* [18] Or, *God and the Father.* See Rom. 15. 6.

the Lord Jesus, he who is blessed for[19] evermore knoweth that I lie not. [32] In Damascus the governor[20] under Aretas the king guarded the city of the Damascenes in order to take me: [33] and through a window was I let down in a basket by the wall, and escaped his hands.

XII

[1] I[1] MUST needs glory, though it is not expedient; but I will come to visions and revelations of the Lord. [2] I know a man in Christ, fourteen years ago, (whether in the body, I know not; or whether out of the body, I know not; God knoweth), such a one caught up even to the third heaven. [3] And I know such a man (whether in the body, or apart from the body, I know not; God knoweth), [4] how that he was caught up into Paradise, and heard unspeakable words, which it is not lawful for a man to utter. [5] On behalf of such a one will I glory: but on mine own behalf I will not glory, save in *my* weaknesses. [6] For if I should desire to glory, I shall not be foolish; for I shall speak the truth: but I forbear, lest any man should account of me above that which he seeth me *to be,* or heareth from me. [7] And by reason of the exceeding greatness of the revelations,[2] that I should not to be exalted overmuch, there was given to me a thorn[3] in the flesh, a messenger of Satan to buffet me, that I should not be exalted overmuch. [8] Concerning this thing I besought the Lord thrice, that it might depart from me. [9] And he hath said unto me, My grace is sufficient for thee: for *my* power is made perfect in weakness. Most gladly therefore will I rather glory in my weaknesses, that the power of Christ may rest[4] upon me. [10] Wherefore I take pleasure in weaknesses, in injuries, in necessities, in persecutions, in distresses, for Christ's sake: for when I am weak, then am I strong.

[11] I am become foolish: ye compelled me; for I ought to have been commended of you: for in nothing was I behind the[5] very chiefest apostles, though I am nothing. [12] Truly the signs of an apostle were wrought among you in all patience,[6] by signs and won-

---

[19] Gr. *unto the ages.*   [20] Gr. *ethnarch.*
[1] Some ancient authorities read *Now to glory is not expedient, but I will come &c.*
[2] Some ancient authorities read *revelations—wherefore, that &c.*   [3] Or, *stake.*
[4] Or, *cover me.*   Gr. *spread a tabernacle over me.*   See Rev. 7. 15.
[5] Or, *those pre-eminent apostles.*   [6] Or, *stedfastness.*

ders and mighty[7] works. [13] For what is there wherein ye were made inferior to the rest of the churches, except *it be* that I myself was not a burden to you? forgive me this wrong.

[14] Behold, this is the third time I am ready to come to you; and I will not be a burden to you: for I seek not yours, but you: for the children ought not to lay up for the parents, but the parents for the children. [15] And I will most gladly spend and be spent[8] for your souls. If I love you more abundantly, am I loved the less? [16] But be it so, I did not myself burden you; but, being crafty, I caught you with guile. [17] Did I take advantage of you by any one of them whom I have sent unto you? [18] I exhorted Titus, and I sent the brother with him. Did Titus take any advantage of you? walked we not in[9] the same spirit? *walked we* not in the same steps?

[19] Ye[10] think all this time that we are excusing ourselves unto you. In the sight of God speak we in Christ. But all things, beloved, *are* for your edifying. [20] For I fear, lest by any means, when I come, I should find you not such as I would, and should myself be found of you such as ye would not; lest by any means *there should be* strife, jealousy, wraths, factions, backbitings, whisperings, swellings, tumults;[11] [21] lest again when I come my God should humble me before you, and I should mourn for many of them that have sinned heretofore, and repented not of the uncleanness and fornication and lasciviousness which they committed.

XIII

[1] THIS is the third time I am coming to you. At the mouth of two witnesses or three shall every word be established. [2] I have said beforehand,[1] and I do say beforehand[1] as[2] when I was present the second time, so now, being absent, to them that have sinned heretofore, and to all the rest, that, if I come again, I will not spare; [3] seeing that ye seek a proof of Christ that speaketh in me; who to you-ward is not weak, but is powerful in you: [4] for he was crucified through weakness, yet he liveth through the power of God. For we also are weak in[3] him, but we shall live with him through the

---

[7] Gr. *powers.*   [8] Gr. *spent out.*   [9] Or, *by the same spirit.*   [10] Or, *Think ye . . . you?*   [11] Or, *disorders.*   [1] Or, *plainly.* Comp. 1 Thess. 3. 4.   [2] Or, *as if I were present the second time, even though I am now absent.*   [3] Many ancient authorities read *with.*

power of God toward you. [5] Try your own selves, whether ye are in the faith; prove your own selves. Or know ye not as to your own selves, that Jesus Christ is in you? unless indeed ye be reprobate. [6] But I hope that ye shall know that we are not reprobate. [7] Now we pray to God that ye do no evil; not that we may appear approved, but that ye may do that which is honorable, though[4] we be as reprobate. [8] For we can do nothing against the truth, but for the truth. [9] For we rejoice, when we are weak, and ye are strong: this we also pray for, even your perfecting. [10] For this cause I write these things while absent, that I may not when present deal sharply, according to the authority which the Lord gave me for building up, and not for casting down.

[11] Finally, brethren, farewell.[5] Be perfected; be comforted; be of the same mind; live in peace: and the God of love and peace shall be with you. [12] Salute one another with a holy kiss.

[13] All the saints salute you.

[14] The grace of the Lord Jesus Christ, and the love of God, and the communion of the Holy Spirit, be with you all.

<hr>

[4] Gr. and that.   [5] Or, rejoice: be perfected.

HYMNS
OF THE CHRISTIAN CHURCH

CONTENTS

HYMNS OF THE CHRISTIAN CHURCH

HYMNS BASED ON PSALMS   PAGE
    PSALMS XIX, XXIII, LXXII, XC, C, CIV 535

GREEK HYMNS
    GLORIA IN EXCELSIS—SHEPHERD OF TENDER YOUTH 541
    THE DAY IS PAST AND OVER 542
    THE DAY OF RESURRECTION 543
    ART THOU WEARY? 544

LATIN HYMNS
    TE DEUM LAUDAMUS 546
    VENI CREATOR SPIRITUS 547
    HIC BREVE VIVITUR 548
    URBS SION AUREA 549
    JESU, DULCIS MEMORIA—JESU, DULCEDO CORDIUM 550
    DIES IRÆ, DIES ILLA 551
    STABAT MATER 553
    ADESTE FIDELES 555
    O DEUS, EGO AMO TE 556

MODERN HYMNS
    A MIGHTY FORTRESS IS OUR GOD 557
    NOW THANK WE ALL OUR GOD 558
    BE NOT DISMAYED—IN TEMPTATION 559
    CHRISTMAS HYMN 561
    LIGHT SHINING OUT OF DARKNESS 562
    THE FUTURE PEACE AND GLORY OF THE CHURCH 563
    EARLY PIETY 563
    THE HOLY TRINITY 564
    EPIPHANY—SUN OF MY SOUL, THOU SAVIOUR DEAR 565
    ABIDE WITH ME 566
    THE PILLAR OF CLOUD 567
    NEARER, MY GOD, TO THEE 568
    MY FAITH LOOKS UP TO THEE 569
    A SUN-DAY HYMN 570
    THE PILGRIMS OF THE NIGHT 571
    LET THERE BE LIGHT 572

HYMNS BASED ON PSALMS

PSALM XIX

JOSEPH ADDISON

[*1672–1719*]

THE spacious firmament on high,
With all the blue ethereal sky,
And spangled heavens, a shining frame,
Their great Original proclaim.
The unwearied sun from day to day
Does his Creator's power display,
And publishes to every land
The work of an almighty hand.

Soon as the evening shades prevail
The moon takes up the wondrous tale,
And nightly to the listening earth
Repeats the story of her birth;
Whilst all the stars that round her burn,
And all the planets in their turn,
Confirm the tidings as they roll,
And spread the truth from pole to pole.

What though in solemn silence all
Move round the dark terrestrial ball?
What though no real voice nor sound
Amid their radiant orbs be found?
In reason's ear they all rejoice
And utter forth a glorious voice,
Forever singing as they shine,
"The hand that made us is divine."

PSALM XXIII

Henry Williams Baker
[*1821–1877*]

THE King of love my shepherd is,
  Whose goodness faileth never:
I nothing lack if I am his,
  And he is mine forever.

Where streams of living water flow
  My ransomed soul he leadeth,
And where the verdant pastures grow
  With food celestial feedeth.

Perverse and foolish oft I strayed,
  But yet in love he sought me
And on his shoulder gently laid
  And home rejoicing brought me.

In death's dark vale I fear no ill
  With thee, dear Lord, beside me,
Thy rod and staff my comfort still,
  Thy cross before to guide me.

Thou spread'st a table in my sight,
  Thy unction grace bestoweth,
And O! what transport of delight
  From thy pure chalice floweth!

And so through all the length of days
  Thy goodness faileth never;
Good Shepherd, may I sing thy praise
  Within thy house forever.

PSALM LXXII

Isaac Watts

[*1674–1748*]

Jesus shall reign where'er the sun
Does his successive journeys run,
His kingdom stretch from shore to shore
Till moons shall wax and wane no more.

Behold the islands with their kings,
And Europe her best tribute brings;
From north and south the princes meet
To pay their homage at his feet.

There Persia, glorious to behold,
There India shines in eastern gold,
And barb'rous nations at his word
Submit and bow, and own their Lord.

For him shall endless prayer be made,
And praises throng to crown his head;
His name, like sweet perfume, shall rise
With every morning sacrifice.

People and realms of every tongue
Dwell on his love with sweetest song,
And infant voices shall proclaim
Their early blessings on his name.

Blessings abound where'er he reigns;
The prisoner leaps to loose his chains,
The weary find eternal rest,
And all the sons of want are blest.

Where he displays his healing power,
Death and the curse are known no more.
In him the tribes of Adam boast
More blessings than their father lost.

Let every creature rise, and bring
Peculiar honors to our King,
Angels descend with songs again,
And earth repeat the loud Amen!

PSALM XC

Isaac Watts

[1674–1748]

Our God, our help in ages past,
    Our hope for years to come,
Our shelter from the stormy blast,
    And our eternal home,

Under the shadow of thy throne
    Thy saints have dwelt secure;
Sufficient is thine arm alone,
    And our defence is sure.

Before the hills in order stood,
    Or earth received her frame,
From everlasting thou art God,
    To endless years the same.

Thy word commands our flesh, "To dust
    Return ye sons of men:"
All nations rose from earth at first
    And turn to earth again.

A thousand ages in thy sight
    Are like an evening gone,
Short as the watch that ends the night
    Before the rising sun.

The busy tribes of flesh and blood,
    With all their lives and cares,
Are carried downward by thy flood,
    And lost in following years.

Time, like an ever-rolling stream,
    Bears all its sons away:
They fly forgotten, as a dream
    Dies at the opening day.

Like flowery fields the nations stand,
    Pleas'd with the morning light,
The flowers beneath the mower's hand
    Lie withering ere 'tis night.

Our God, our help in ages past,
    Our hope for years to come,
Be thou our guard while troubles last,
    And our eternal home.

PSALM C

WILLIAM KETHE

[(?) *circa 1562*]

ALL people that on earth do dwell,
    Sing to the Lord with cheerful voice,
Him serve with fear, his praise forth tell,
    Come ye before him and rejoice.

The Lord ye know is God indeed;
    Without our aid he did us make;
We are his folk, he doth us feed,
    And for his sheep he doth us take.

O enter then his gates with praise,
    Approach with joy his courts unto;
Praise, laud, and bless his name always,
    For it is seemly so to do.

For why, the Lord our God is good,
    His mercy is forever sure;
His truth at all times firmly stood,
    And shall from age to age endure.

PSALM CIV

Sir Robert Grant

[1785–1838]

O worship the King all glorious above!
O gratefully sing his power and his love,—
Our Shield and Defender, the Ancient of days,
Pavilioned in splendor, and girded with praise.

O tell of his might, O sing of his grace,
Whose robe is the light, whose canopy space;
His chariots of wrath the deep thunder-clouds form,
And dark is his path on the wings of the storm.

The earth with its store of wonders untold,
Almighty, thy power hath founded of old,
Hath 'stablish'd it fast by a changeless decree,
And round it hath cast, like a mantle, the sea.

Thy bountiful care what tongue can recite?
It breathes in the air, it shines in the light,
It streams from the hills, it descends to the plain,
And sweetly distils in the dew and the rain.

Frail children of dust, and feeble as frail,
In thee do we trust, nor find thee to fail.
Thy mercies how tender, how firm to the end!
Our Maker, Defender, Redeemer, and Friend.

O measureless Might! Ineffable Love!
While angels delight to hymn thee above,
The humbler creation, tho' feeble their lays,
With true adoration shall lisp to thy praise.

GREEK HYMNS

GLORIA IN EXCELSIS

ANONYMOUS

[4th Century or earlier]

GLORY be to God on high, and in earth, peace, good will towards men. We praise thee, we bless thee, we worship thee, we glorify thee, we give thanks to thee for thy great glory, O Lord God, heavenly King, God the Father Almighty.

O Lord, the only-begotten Son, Jesu Christ; O Lord God, Lamb of God, Son of the Father, that takest away the sins of the world, have mercy upon us. Thou that takest away the sins of the world, have mercy upon us. Thou that takest away the sins of the world, receive our prayer. Thou that sittest at the right hand of God the Father, have mercy upon us.

For thou only art holy; thou only art the Lord; thou only, O Christ, with the Holy Ghost, art most high in the glory of God the Father. Amen.

SHEPHERD OF TENDER YOUTH

ST. CLEMENT OF ALEXANDRIA. Tr. H. M. DEXTER

[(?) 170–220]

SHEPHERD of tender youth
Guiding in love and truth
  Through devious ways;
Christ our triumphant king,
We come Thy name to sing;
Hither our children bring
  Tributes of praise.

541

Thou art our holy Lord,
The all-subduing Word,
  Healer of strife:
Thou didst Thyself abase,
That from sin's deep disgrace
Thou mightest save our race,
  And give us life.

Thou art the great High-Priest;
Thou hast prepared the feast
  Of heavenly love;
While in our mortal pain
None calls on Thee in vain;
Help Thou dost not disdain,
  Help from above.

Ever be Thou our guide,
Our shepherd and our pride,
  Our staff and song:
Jesus, Thou Christ of God,
By Thy perennial word
Lead us where Thou hast trod,
  Make our faith strong.

So now, and till we die,
Sound we Thy praises high,
  And joyful sing.
Let all the holy throng
Who to Thy Church belong,
Unite and swell the song
  To Christ our King!

THE DAY IS PAST AND OVER

ATTRIBUTED TO ST. ANATOLIUS. Tr. J. M. NEALE

[*458* A. D.]

THE day is past and over;
  All thanks, O Lord, to Thee;
I pray Thee now that sinless
  The hours of dark may be:

O Jesu, keep me in Thy sight,
And guard me through the coming night.

The joys of day are over;
  I lift my heart to Thee,
And ask Thee that offenceless
  The hours of dark may be:
O Jesu, keep me in Thy sight,
And guard me through the coming night.

The toils of day are over:
  I raise the hymn to Thee
And ask that free from peril
  The hours of dark may be:
O Jesu, keep me in Thy sight,
And guard me through the coming night.

Be Thou my soul's preserver,
  For Thou alone dost know
How many are the perils
  Through which I have to go:
O loving Jesu, hear my call,
And guard and save me from them all.

THE DAY OF RESURRECTION

St. John of Damascus. Tr. John Mason Neale

[circa 780]

'Tis the day of resurrection,—
  Earth, tell it out abroad,—
The passover of gladness,
  The passover of God.
From death to life eternal,
  From this world to the sky,
Our Christ hath brought us over
  With hymns of victory.

Our hearts be pure from evil,
  That we may see aright
The Lord in rays eternal
  Of resurrection-light,

And, listening to his accents,
   May hear, so calm and plain,
His own "All hail!" and, hearing,
   May raise the victor-strain.

Now let the heavens be joyful,
   Let earth her song begin,
Let the round world keep triumph
   And all that is therein,
Invisible and visible,
   Their notes let all things blend;
For Christ the Lord hath risen,
   Our joy that hath no end.

ART THOU WEARY?

St. Stephen the Sabaite. Tr. J. M. Neale

[725–794]

Art thou weary, art thou languid,
   Art thou sore distrest?
"Come to Me," saith One, "and coming
   Be at rest!"

Hath He marks to lead me to Him,
   If He be my Guide?
"In His Feet and Hands are wound-prints,
   And His side."

Hath He diadem as Monarch
   That His Brow adorns?
"Yea a Crown, in very surety,
   But of thorns."

If I find Him, if I follow,
   What His guerdon here?
"Many a sorrow, many a labour,
   Many a tear."

If I still hold closely to Him,
   What hath He at last?
"Sorrow vanquished, labour ended,
   Jordan past."

If I ask Him to receive me,
  Will He say me nay?
"Not till earth, and not till Heav'n
  Pass away."

Finding, following, keeping, struggling,
  Is He sure to bless?
"Angels, Martyrs, Prophets, Virgins,
  Answer, Yes!"

LATIN HYMNS

TE DEUM LAUDAMUS

ATTRIBUTED TO NICETA OF REMISIANA

[*4th Century*]

WE praise thee, O God, we acknowledge thee to be the Lord.
All the earth doth worship thee, the Father everlasting.
To thee all Angels cry aloud: the Heavens, and all the Powers
therein.
To thee Churubin and Seraphin continually do cry,
Holy, Holy, Holy, Lord God of Sabaoth;
Heaven and earth are full of the Majesty of thy Glory.
The glorious company of the Apostles praise thee.
The goodly fellowship of the Prophets praise thee.
The noble army of Martyrs praise thee.
The holy Church throughout all the world doth acknowledge thee;
The Father, of an infinite Majesty;
Thine honourable, true, and only Son;
Also the Holy Ghost, the Comforter.
Thou art the King of Glory, O Christ!
Thou art the everlasting Son of the Father.
When thou tookest upon thee to deliver man, thou didst not abhor the
Virgin's womb.
When thou hadst overcome the sharpness of death, thou didst open the
Kingdom of Heaven to all believers.
Thou sittest at the right hand of God in the Glory of the Father.
We believe that thou shalt come to be our Judge.
We therefore pray thee, help thy servants whom thou hast redeemed with
thy precious blood.
Make them to be numbered with thy Saints in glory everlasting.
O Lord, save thy people and bless thine heritage.
Govern them, and lift them up for ever.
Day by day we magnify thee;
And we worship thy Name, ever world without end.

Vouchsafe, O Lord, to keep us this day without sin.
O Lord, have mercy upon us: have mercy upon us.
O Lord, let thy mercy lighten upon us: as our trust is in thee.
O Lord, in thee have I trusted: let me never be confounded.

VENI CREATOR SPIRITUS

ATTRIBUTED TO CHARLEMAGNE. Tr. JOHN DRYDEN

[742–814]

CREATOR SPIRIT, by whose aid
The world's foundations first were laid,
Come, visit every pious mind;
Come, pour thy joys on human kind;
From sin and sorrow set us free,
And make thy temples worthy thee.

O source of uncreated light,
The Father's promised Paraclete,
Thrice holy fount, thrice holy fire,
Our hearts with heavenly love inspire;
Come, and thy sacred unction bring
To sanctify us while we sing.

Plenteous of grace, descend from high,
Rich in thy sevenfold energy;
Thou strength of his almighty hand,
Whose power does heaven and earth command,
Proceeding Spirit, our defence,
Who dost the gift of tongues dispense,
And crown'st thy gift with eloquence.

Refine and purge our earthy parts,
But O, inflame and fire our hearts,
Our frailties help, our vice control;
Submit the senses to the soul,
And, when rebellious they are grown,
Then lay thy hand, and hold them down.

Chase from our minds the infernal foe,
And peace, the fruit of love, bestow;
And, lest our feet should step astray,
Protect and guide us in the way;

Make us eternal truths receive
And practise all that we believe.
Give us thyself, that we may see
The Father and the Son by thee.

Immortal honour, endless fame,
Attend the Almighty Father's name:
The Saviour Son be glorified,
Who for lost man's redemption died;
And equal adoration be,
Eternal Paraclete, to thee.

HIC BREVE VIVITUR

FROM "DE CONTEMPTU MUNDI" BY BERNARD OF MORLAIX
Tr. J. M. NEALE

[*cir. 1125*]

BRIEF life is here our portion,
    Brief sorrow, short-lived care;
The life that knows no ending,
    The tearless life, is there.

And after fleshly scandal,
    And after this world's night,
And after storm and whirlwind,
    Is calm and joy and light.

There grief is turned to pleasure,
    Such pleasure as, below,
No human voice can utter,
    No human heart can know:

The peace of all the faithful,
    The calm of all the blest,
Inviolate, unvaried,
    Divinest, sweetest, best.

That peace,—but who may claim it?
    The guileless in their way,
Who keep the ranks of battle,
    Who mean the thing they say.

Strive, man, to win that glory,
    Toil, man, to gain that light,
Send hope before to grasp it,
    Till hope be lost in sight!

URBS SION AUREA

From the Same

Jerusalem the golden,
    With milk and honey blest,
Beneath thy contemplation
    Sink heart and voice oppressed
I know not, O, I know not,
    What social joys are there,
What radiancy of glory,
    What light beyond compare!

They stand, those halls of Zion,
    Conjubilant with song,
And bright with many an angel
    And all the martyr throng.
And they who, with their Leader,
    Have conquered in the fight,
Forever and forever
    Are clad in robes of white.

Jerusalem the glorious,
    The glory of the elect,
O dear and future vision
    That eager hearts expect,
New mansion of new people,
    Whom God's own love and light
Promote, increase, make holy,
    Identify, unite!

JESU, DULCIS MEMORIA

St. Bernard of Clairvaux. Tr. E. Caswall

[*1091–1153*]

Jesu, the very thought of Thee
  With sweetness fills the breast;
But sweeter far Thy Face to see,
  And in Thy Presence rest.

No voice can sing, no heart can frame,
  Nor can the memory find
A sweeter sound than Jesu's Name,
  The Saviour of mankind.

O Hope of every contrite heart,
  O Joy of all the meek,
To those who ask how kind Thou art,
  How good to those who seek!

But what to those who find? Ah! this
  Nor tongue nor pen can show;
The love of Jesus, what it is
  None but His loved ones know.

Jesu, our only Joy be Thou,
  As Thou our Prize wilt be:
In Thee be all our glory now,
  And through eternity.

JESU, DULCEDO CORDIUM

St. Bernard of Clairvaux. Tr. Ray Palmer

[*1091–1153*]

Jesus, Thou Joy of loving hearts!
  Thou Fount of Life! Thou Light of men!
From the best bliss that earth imparts,
  We turn unfill'd to Thee again.

Thy truth unchanged hath ever stood;
   Thou savest those that on Thee call;
To them that seek Thee, Thou art good,
   To them that find Thee, All in All!

We taste Thee, O Thou Living Bread,
   And long to feast upon Thee still!
We drink of Thee, the Fountain Head,
   And thirst our souls from Thee to fill!

Our restless spirits yearn for Thee,
   Where'er our changeful lot is cast;
Glad, when Thy gracious smile we see,
   Blest, when our faith can hold Thee fast.

O Jesus, ever with us stay!
   Make all our moments calm and bright!
Chase the dark night of sin away,
   Shed o'er the world Thy holy light!

DIES IRÆ, DIES ILLA

THOMAS A CELANO. TR. J. O'HAGAN

[d. *1275*]

DAY of wrath, that day whose knelling
Gives to flame this earthly dwelling;
Psalm and Sibyl thus foretelling.

Oh, what agony of trembling,
When the judge mankind assembling,
Probeth all beyond dissembling.

Pealing wondrous through the regions,
Shall the trumpet force obedience,
And the graves yield up their legions.

Startled death and nature sicken,
Thus to see the creature quicken,
Waiting judgment terror-stricken.

Open, then, with all recorded,
Stands the book from whence awarded
Doom shall pass with deed accorded.

When the judge is throned in session,
All things hid shall find confession,
Unavenged be no transgression.

Wretch, what then shall be my pleading?
Who my patron interceding?
Scarce the just securely speeding.

Thou, O king of awful splendour,
Saving grace dost freely render;
Save me, fount of pity tender.

Think, 'twas I, my lost condition,
Caused, O pitying Lord, thy mission;
Spare my soul that day's perdition.

Seeking me, thy footstep hasted;
Me to save, the cross was tasted,
Be not toil so mighty wasted.

Righteous judge of retribution,
Grant the gift of absolution
Ere the day of restitution.

Me my culprit heart accuses;
Inmost guilt my face suffuses;
Heal, O Lord, thy suppliant's bruises.

Thou who Mary's sin hast shriven,
Thou who broughtst the thief to heaven,
Hope to me hast also given.

Nothing worth is mine endeavour,
Yet, in ruth, my soul deliver
From the flame that burns for ever.

With thy sheep, thy chosen, place me,
Severed from the goats embrace me;
On thy right-hand, ransomed, place me.

When the reprobate confounded
Lie with wrathful fire surrounded,
May my call to bliss be sounded.

Crushed to dust and prostrate bending,
All my heart contrition rending;
I implore thee, guard my ending.

Oh, that awful day of mourning,
When, from earthly dust returning,

Guilty man shall bide his sentence;
Spare him, God, for his repentance.

Jesus, Lord, thy mercy lending,
Grant them rest, thy rest unending.

STABAT MATER

Jacobus de Benedictis. Tr. D. F. MacCarthy

[13th–14th Century]

By the cross, on which suspended,
With his bleeding hands extended,
Hung that Son she so adored,
Stood the mournful Mother weeping,
She whose heart, its silence keeping,
Grief had cleft as with a sword.

Oh, that Mother's sad affliction—
Mother of all benediction—
Of the sole-begotten One;
Oh, the grieving, sense-bereaving,
Of her heaving breast, perceiving
The dread sufferings of her Son.

What man is there so unfeeling,
Who, his heart to pity steeling,
   Could behold that sight unmoved?
Could Christ's Mother see there weeping,
See the pious Mother keeping
   Vigil by the Son she loved?

For his people's sins atoning,
She saw Jesus writhing, groaning,
   'Neath the scourge wherewith he bled;
Saw her loved one, her consoler,
Dying in his dreadful dolour,
   Till at length his spirit fled.

O thou Mother of election,
Fountain of all pure affection,
   Make thy grief, thy pain, my own;
Make my heart to God returning,
In the love of Jesus burning,
   Feel the fire that thine has known.

Blessed Mother of prediction,
Stamp the marks of crucifixion
   Deeply on my stony heart,
Ever leading where thy bleeding
Son is pleading for my needing,
   Let me in his wounds take part.

Make me truly, each day newly
While life lasts, O Mother, duly
   Weep with him, the Crucified.
Let me, 'tis my sole demanding,
Near the cross, where thou art standing,
   Stand in sorrow at thy side.

Queen of virgins, best and dearest,
Grant, oh, grant the prayer thou hearest,
   Let me ever mourn with thee;
Let compassion me so fashion
That Christ's wounds, his death and passion,
   Be each day renewed in me.

Oh, those wounds do not deny me;
On that cross, oh, crucify me;
   Let me drink his blood I pray:
Then on fire, enkindled, daring,
I may stand without despairing
   On that dreadful judgment-day.

May that cross be my salvation;
Make Christ's death my preservation;
   May his grace my heart make wise;
And when death my body taketh,
May my soul when it awaketh
   Ope in heaven its raptured eyes.

ADESTE FIDELES

ANONYMOUS

Called "THE PORTUGUESE CHAPEL HYMN."
Tr. J. R. BESTE

[*15th–16th Century*]

HASTEN, ye faithful, glad, joyful, and holy,
   Speed ye to Bethlem to honour the Word;
See there the King of angels is born lowly—
   Oh, come and kneel before him;
   Oh, come and all adore him;
Oh come, oh come, rejoicing to honour the Lord.

God of the Godhead, true Light unabated,
   Mary the Virgin has borne the Adored;
True God eternal, begot, uncreated—
   Oh, come and kneel before him;
   Oh, come and all adore him;
Oh come, oh come, rejoicing to honour the Lord.

Sing, all ye angels, till echoes rebounding
   Swell through your halls, for ever be heard;
'Glory to God,' through all heaven resounding—
   Oh, come and kneel before him;
   Oh, come and all adore him;
Oh come, oh come, rejoicing to honour the Lord.

Praise to the Infant, who this day descended;
Glory to thee, blessed Jesus adored;
Word, in whom two natures join, yet unblended—
Oh, come and kneel before him;
Oh, come and all adore him;
Oh come, oh come, rejoicing to honour the Lord.

O DEUS, EGO AMO TE

ATTRIBUTED TO ST. FRANCIS XAVIER. Tr. EDWARD CASWALL

[*1506–1552*]

My God, I love thee: not because
I hope for heaven thereby,
Nor because they who love thee not
Must burn eternally.

Thou, O my Jesus, Thou didst me
Upon the Cross embrace;
For me didst bear the nails and spear,
And manifold disgrace.

And grief and torments numberless,
And sweat of agony;
Yea, death itself; and all for me
Who was thine enemy.

Then why, O Blessèd Jesu Christ,
Should I not love thee well?—
Not for the hope of winning heaven,
Nor of escaping hell;

Not with the hope of gaining aught,
Not seeking a reward;
But as thyself hast lovèd me,
O ever-loving Lord!

E'en so I love thee and will love,
And in thy praise will sing,
Solely because thou art my God,
And my eternal King.

MODERN HYMNS

A MIGHTY FORTRESS IS OUR GOD

Martin Luther. Tr. Frederick Henry Hedge

[1483-1546]

A MIGHTY fortress is our God,
　　A bulwark never failing;
　　Our helper he, amid the flood
Of mortal ills prevailing.
　　For still our ancient foe
　　Doth seek to work us woe;
　　His craft and power are great;
　　And, armed with cruel hate,
On earth is not his equal.

Did we in our own strength confide,
　　Our striving would be losing,—
Were not the right man on our side,
　　The man of God's own choosing.
　　　　Dost ask who that may be?
　　　　Christ Jesus, it is he,
　　　　Lord Sabaoth his name,
　　　　From age to age the same,
　　And he must win the battle.

And though this world, with devils filled,
　　Should threaten to undo us;
We will not fear, for God hath willed
　　His truth to triumph through us.
　　　　The prince of darkness grim,—
　　　　We tremble not for him;
　　　　His rage we can endure,
　　　　For lo! his doom is sure,—
　　One little word shall fell him.

That word above all earthly powers—
No thanks to them—abideth;
The Spirit and the gifts are ours
Through him who with us sideth.
Let goods and kindred go,
This mortal life also;
The body they may kill:
God's truth abideth still,
His kingdom is forever.

NOW THANK WE ALL OUR GOD

MARTIN RINKART. Tr. CATHERINE WINKWORTH

[*1586–1649*]

Now thank we all our God,
With heart and hands and voices,
Who wondrous things hath done,
In whom his world rejoices,
Who from our mothers' arms
Hath blessed us on our way
With countless gifts of love,
And still is ours to-day.

O, may this bounteous God
Through all our life be near us,
With ever joyful hearts
And blessèd peace to cheer us,
And keep us in his grace,
And guide us when perplexed,
And free us from all ills
In this world and the next.

All praise and thanks to God,
The Father, now be given,
The Son, and him who reigns
With them in highest heaven:—
The One Eternal God,
Whom earth and heaven adore,
For thus it was, is now,
And shall be evermore!

BE NOT DISMAYED

ATTRIBUTED TO GUSTAVUS ADOLPHUS. TR. ELIZABETH CHARLES
[*1594–1632*]

Be not dismayed, thou little flock,
Although the foe's fierce battle-shock,
    Loud on all sides, assail thee.
Though o'er thy fall they laugh secure,
Their triumph cannot long endure:
    Let not thy courage fail thee.

Thy cause is God's: go at his call,
And to his hand commit thy all.
    Fear thou no ill impending.
His Gideon shall arise for thee,
God's word and people manfully,
    In God's own time, defending.

Our hope is sure in Jesus' might;
Against themselves the godless fight,
    Themselves, not us, distressing.
Shame and contempt their lot shall be;
God is with us, with him are we;
    To us belongs his blessing.

IN TEMPTATION

CHARLES WESLEY
[*1708–1788*]

Jesus, lover of my soul,
    Let me to thy bosom fly,
While the nearer waters roll,
    While the tempest still is high:
Hide me, O my Saviour, hide
    Till the storm of life is past,
Safe into the haven guide,
    O, receive my soul at last!

Other refuge have I none,
   Hangs my helpless soul on thee;
Leave, ah, leave me not alone,
   Still support and comfort me:
All my trust on thee is stayed,
   All my help from thee I bring;
Cover my defenceless head
   With the shadow of thy wing.

Wilt thou not regard my call?
   Wilt thou not accept my prayer?
Lo! I sink, I faint, I fall!
   Lo! on thee I cast my care!
Reach me out thy gracious hand
   While I of thy strength receive,
Hoping against hope I stand,
   Dying, and behold I live!

Thou, O Christ, art all I want;
   More than all in thee I find:
Raise the fallen, cheer the faint,
   Heal the sick and lead the blind!
Just and holy is thy name;
   I am all unrighteousness;
False and full of sin I am,
   Thou art full of truth and grace.

Plenteous grace with thee is found,
   Grace to cover all my sin;
Let the healing streams abound,
   Make and keep me pure within:
Thou of life the fountain art;
   Freely let me take of thee,
Spring thou up within my heart,
   Rise to all eternity!

CHRISTMAS HYMN

CHARLES WESLEY

[*1708–1788*]

Hark! how all the welkin rings
Glory to the King of kings!
Peace on earth, and mercy mild,
God and sinners reconciled!
Joyful, all ye nations, rise,
Join the triumph of the skies;
Universal nature say,
Christ the Lord is born to-day!

Christ by highest Heaven adored,
Christ, the Everlasting Lord;
Late in time behold Him come,
Offspring of a Virgin's womb:
Veiled in flesh the Godhead see;
Hail th' Incarnate Deity,
Pleased as man with men to appear,
Jesus our Immanuel here!

Hail! the heavenly Prince of Peace!
Hail! the Sun of Righteousness!
Light and life to all He brings,
Risen with healing in His wings.
Mild He lays His glory by,
Born that man no more may die,
Born to raise the sons of earth,
Born to give them second birth.

Come, Desire of nations, come,
Fix in us Thy humble home!
Rise, the Woman's conquering Seed,
Bruise in us the Serpent's head!
Now display Thy saving power,
Ruined nature now restore,
Now in mystic union join
Thine to ours, and ours to Thine!

Adam's likeness, Lord, efface;
Stamp Thy image in its place;
Second Adam from above,
Reinstate us in Thy love!
Let us Thee, though lost, regain,
Thee, the Life, the Heavenly Man:
O! to all Thyself impart,
Formed in each believing heart!

LIGHT SHINING OUT OF DARKNESS

WILLIAM COWPER

[*1731–1800*]

God moves in a mysterious way
    His wonders to perform;
He plants his footsteps in the sea,
    And rides upon the storm.

Deep in unfathomable mines
    Of never-failing skill,
He treasures up his bright designs,
    And works his sovereign will.

Ye fearful saints, fresh courage take,
    The clouds ye so much dread
Are big with mercy, and shall break
    In blessings on your head.

Judge not the Lord by feeble sense,
    But trust him for his grace;
Behind a frowning providence
    He hides a smiling face.

His purposes will ripen fast,
    Unfolding every hour;
The bud may have a bitter taste,
    But sweet will be the flower.

Blind unbelief is sure to err,
    And scan his work in vain;
God is his own interpreter,
    And he will make it plain.

THE FUTURE PEACE AND GLORY OF THE CHURCH

WILLIAM COWPER

[*1731–1800*]

HEAR what God, the Lord, hath spoken:
O my people, faint and few,
Comfortless, afflicted, broken,
Fair abodes I build for you.
Thorns of heart-felt tribulation
Shall no more perplex your ways:
You shall name your walls Salvation,
And your gates shall all be Praise.

There, like streams that feed the garden,
Pleasures without end shall flow;
For the Lord, your faith rewarding,
All his bounty shall bestow;
Still in undisturbed possession
Peace and righteousness shall reign;
Never shall you feel oppression,
Hear the voice of war again.

Ye no more your suns descending,
Waning moons no more shall see;
But your griefs, forever ending,
Find eternal noon in me.
God shall rise, and, shining o'er you,
Change to day the gloom of night;
He, the Lord, shall be your glory,
God your everlasting light.

EARLY PIETY

REGINALD HEBER

[*1783–1826*]

BY cool Siloam's shady rill
How sweet the lily grows!
How sweet the breath beneath the hill
Of Sharon's dewy rose!

Lo! such the child whose early feet
  The paths of peace have trod,
Whose secret heart with influence sweet,
  Is upward drawn to God.

By cool Siloam's shady rill
  The lily must decay;
The rose that blooms beneath the hill
  Must shortly fade away;
And soon, too soon, the wintry hour
  Of man's maturer age
Will shake the soul with sorrow's power
  And stormy passion's rage.

O Thou, whose infant feet were found
  Within Thy Father's shrine,
Whose years with changeless virtue crowned
  Were all alike divine,
Dependent on Thy bounteous breath,
  We seek Thy grace alone,
In childhood, manhood, age, and death
  To keep us still Thine own.

THE HOLY TRINITY

REGINALD HEBER

[1783–1826]

HOLY, holy, holy! Lord God Almighty!
  Early in the morning our song shall rise to Thee;
Holy, holy, holy! Merciful and Mighty!
  God in Three Persons, blessed Trinity!

Holy, holy, holy! all the saints adore Thee,
  Casting down their golden crowns around the glassy sea.
Cherubim and seraphim falling down before Thee,
  Which wert, and art, and evermore shalt be.

Holy, holy, holy! though the darkness hide Thee,
  Though the eye of sinful man Thy glory may not see,
Only Thou art holy, there is none beside Thee,
  Perfect in power, in love, and purity.

Holy, holy, holy, Lord God Almighty!
   All Thy works shall praise Thy Name in earth and sky and sea;
Holy, holy, holy! Merciful and Mighty!
   God in Three Persons, blessed Trinity!

EPIPHANY

Reginald Heber
[1783–1826]

Brightest and best of the sons of the morning,
   Dawn on our darkness, and lend us Thine aid!
Star of the East, the horizon adorning,
   Guide where our infant Redeemer is laid!

Cold on His cradle the dewdrops are shining,
   Low lies His head with the beasts of the stall;
Angels adore Him, in slumber reclining,—
   Maker, and Monarch, and Saviour of all.

Say, shall we yield Him, in costly devotion,
   Odors of Edom, and offerings divine,
Gems of the mountain, and pearls of the ocean,
   Myrrh from the forest, or gold from the mine?

Vainly we offer each ample oblation,
   Vainly with gifts would His favor secure;
Richer by far is the heart's adoration,
   Dearer to God are the prayers of the poor.

Brightest and best of the sons of the morning,
   Dawn on our darkness, and lend us Thine aid!
Star of the East, the horizon adorning,
   Guide where our infant Redeemer is laid!

SUN OF MY SOUL, THOU SAVIOUR DEAR

John Keble
[1792–1866]

Sun of my soul, Thou Saviour dear,
   It is not night if Thou be near;
Oh may no earth-born cloud arise
   To hide Thee from Thy servant's eyes!

When the soft dews of kindly sleep
  My weary eyelids gently steep,
Be my last thought how sweet to rest
  Forever on my Saviour's breast!

Abide with me from morn till eve,
  For without Thee I cannot live;
Abide with me when night is nigh,
  For without Thee I dare not die.

If some poor wandering child of Thine
  Have spurned to-day the voice divine,
Now, Lord, the gracious work begin;
  Let him no more lie down in sin.

Watch by the sick; enrich the poor
  With blessings from Thy boundless store;
Be every mourner's sleep to-night,
  Like infant slumbers, pure and light.

Come near and bless us when we wake,
  Ere through the world our way we take,
Till in the ocean of Thy love
  We lose ourselves in heaven above.

ABIDE WITH ME

Henry Francis Lyte

[*1793–1847*]

ABIDE with me! fast falls the eventide,
The darkness deepens: Lord, with me abide!
When other helpers fail, and comforts flee,
Help of the helpless, O, abide with me!

Swift to its close ebbs out life's little day;
Earth's joys grow dim, its glories pass away;
Change and decay in all around I see:
O thou who changest not, abide with me!

Not a brief glance I beg, a passing word;
But, as thou dwell'st with thy disciples, Lord,
Familiar, condescending, patient, free,
Come, not to sojourn, but abide with me!

Come not in terrors, as the King of kings;
But kind and good, with healing in thy wings;
Tears for all woes, a heart for every plea;
Come, Friend of sinners, and thus 'bide with me!

Thou on my head in early youth didst smile;
And, though rebellious and perverse meanwhile,
Thou hast not left me, oft as I left thee;
On to the close, O Lord, abide with me!

I need thy presence every passing hour:
What but thy grace can foil the tempter's power?
Who like thyself my guide and stay can be?
Through cloud and sunshine, O, abide with me!

I fear no foe, with thee at hand to bless;
Ills have no weight, and tears no bitterness:
Where is death's sting? where, grave, thy victory?
I triumph still if thou abide with me.

Hold thou thy cross before my closing eyes,
Shine through the gloom, and point me to the skies.
Heaven's morning breaks, and earth's vain shadows
    flee:
In life and death, O Lord, abide with me!

THE PILLAR OF CLOUD

JOHN HENRY NEWMAN

[1801–1890]

LEAD, kindly Light, amid the encircling gloom,
    Lead thou me on!
The night is dark, and I am far from home,—
    Lead thou me on!
Keep thou my feet! I do not ask to see
The distant scene—one step enough for me.

I was not ever thus, nor prayed that thou
    Shouldst lead me on;
I loved to choose and see my path; but now
    Lead thou me on!

I loved the garish day, and, spite of fears,
Pride ruled my will: remember not past years!

So long thy power hath blest me, sure it still
   Will lead me on,
O'er moor and fen, o'er crag and torrent, till
   The night is gone,
And with the morn those angel faces smile
Which I have loved long since, and lost awhile.

NEARER, MY GOD, TO THEE

SARAH FLOWER ADAMS

[1805–1848]

NEARER, my God, to thee,
   Nearer to thee!
E'en though it be a cross
   That raiseth me,
Still all my song would be,
Nearer, my God, to thee,
   Nearer to thee!

Though like the wanderer,
   The sun gone down,
Darkness be over me,
   My rest a stone,
Yet in my dreams I'd be
Nearer, my God, to thee,
   Nearer to thee.

There let the way appear
   Steps unto heaven;
All that thou send'st to me
   In mercy given;
Angels to beckon me
Nearer, my God, to thee,
   Nearer to thee.

Then, with my waking thoughts
   Bright with thy praise,
Out of my stony griefs
   Bethel I'll raise;

So by my woes to be
Nearer, my God, to thee,
Nearer to thee.

Or if on joyful wing
Cleaving the sky,
Sun, moon, and stars forgot,
Upwards I fly,
Still all my song shall be,
Nearer, my God, to thee,
Nearer to thee!

MY FAITH LOOKS UP TO THEE

RAY PALMER
[1808–1887]

My faith looks up to thee,
Thou Lamb of Calvary,
Saviour divine!
Now hear me while I pray,
Take all my guilt away,
O let me from this day
Be wholly thine!

May thy rich grace impart
Strength to my fainting heart
My zeal inspire!
As thou hast died for me,
O may my love to thee
Pure, warm, and changeless be,—
A living fire!

While life's dark maze I tread,
And griefs around me spread,
Be thou my guide;
Bid darkness turn to day,
Wipe sorrow's tears away,
Nor let me ever stray
From thee aside.

When ends life's transient dream,
When death's cold, sullen stream
   Shall o'er me roll,
Blest Saviour, then, in love,
Fear and distrust remove!
O bear me safe above,—
   A ransomed soul!

A SUN-DAY HYMN

Oliver Wendell Holmes

[1809–1894]

Lord of all being, throned afar,
Thy glory flames from sun and star;
Centre and soul of every sphere,
Yet to each loving heart how near!

Sun of our life, thy quickening ray
Sheds on our path the glow of day:
Star of our hope, thy softened light
Cheers the long watches of the night.

Our midnight is thy smile withdrawn;
Our noontide is thy gracious dawn;
Our rainbow arch, thy mercy's sign:
All, save the clouds of sin, are thine.

Lord of all life, below, above,
Whose light is truth, whose warmth is love;
Before thy ever-blazing throne
We ask no lustre of our own.

Grant us thy truth to make us free,
And kindling hearts that burn for thee,
Till all thy living altars claim
One holy light, one heavenly flame.

THE PILGRIMS OF THE NIGHT

Frederick William Faber

[1814-1863]

HARK, hark, my soul! angelic songs are swelling
  O'er earth's green fields and ocean's wave-beat shore:
How sweet the truth those blessèd strains are telling
  Of that new life when sin shall be no more!
    Angels of Jesus, angels of light,
      Singing to welcome the pilgrims of the night!

Darker than night life's shadows fall around us,
  And like benighted men we miss our mark:
God hides himself, and grace hath scarcely found us,
  E'er death finds out his victims in the dark.
    Angels of Jesus, etc.

Far, far away, like bells at evening pealing,
  The voice of Jesus sounds o'er land and sea,
And laden souls by thousands meekly stealing,
  Kind Shepherd, turn their weary steps to thee.
    Angels of Jesus, etc.

Onward we go, for still we hear them singing,
  "Come, weary souls, for Jesus bids you come;"
And through the dark, its echoes sweetly ringing,
  The music of the gospel leads us home.
    Angels of Jesus, etc.

Rest comes at last; though life be long and dreary,
  The day must dawn, and darksome night be past;
All journeys end in welcomes to the weary,
  And heaven, the heart's true home, will come at last.
    Angels of Jesus, etc.

Cheer up, my soul! faith's moonbeams softly glisten
  Upon the breast of life's most troubled sea,
And it will cheer thy drooping heart to listen
  To those brave songs which angels mean for thee.
    Angels of Jesus, etc.

Angels! sing on, your faithful watches keeping;
Sing us sweet fragments of the songs above,
While we toil on, and soothe ourselves with weeping,
Till life's long night shall break in endless love.
Angels of Jesus, etc.

LET THERE BE LIGHT

JOHN MARRIOTT

[1816]

THOU, Whose Almighty word
Chaos and darkness heard,
   And took their flight;
Hear us, we humbly pray;
And, where the gospel's day
Sheds not its glorious ray,
   Let there be light!

Thou, Who didst come to bring
On Thy redeeming wing
   Healing and sight,
Health to the sick in mind,
Sight to the inly blind,
Oh, now to all mankind
   Let there be light!

Spirit of truth, and love,
Life-giving, holy Dove,
   Speed forth Thy flight!
Move on the waters' face
Bearing the lamp of grace,
And in earth's darkest place
   Let there be light!

Holy and blessed Three,
Glorious Trinity,
   Wisdom, Love, Might!
Boundless as ocean's tide
Rolling in fullest pride,
Through the earth, far and wide,
   Let there be light!

BUDDHIST WRITINGS

TRANSLATED AND ANNOTATED BY
HENRY CLARKE WARREN

INTRODUCTORY NOTE

SIDDHARTHA GAUTAMA, known as Buddha, the "Awakened," was the son of the ruler of Çākya-land, a region lying to the northeast of Oude, in northern India. The date of his birth is placed about 557 B. C.

He was born a warrior prince, but at the age of twenty-nine, after having married and had a son, he determined to renounce the world. Abandoning his family and possessions, he gave himself up to asceticism and concentration of thought, under the direction of masters of this discipline. After seven years, he concluded that this method brought him no nearer to the wisdom he sought as a means of escaping rebirth into a life which he had found not worth living, and for a time he tried starvation and self-torture. This also availed him nothing; when suddenly, sitting under the sacred fig-tree at Bodhi Gayā, he became illumined and saw the Great Truths. Henceforth he was "Buddha."

Gautama's first aim had been merely his own salvation; but moved by pity for mankind he resolved to bestow on others the Four Great Truths and the eight-fold path. Beginning his ministry at Benares, he converted first five monks who had previously been his fellows in asceticism, then many of the noble youth of the city, then a thousand Brahman priests.

The rest of his life was spent in wandering about and preaching his new creed, which spread with extraordinary rapidity. He died not far from his native region about the year 477 B. C.

The foregoing outline selects what seem the most reliable main elements in a biography which has naturally become saturated with legend of later growth. The teaching of Buddha, so similar in its pessimistic view of life to that of the Book of "Ecclesiastes," is amply represented in the following writings.

CONTENTS

BUDDHIST WRITINGS

I. The Buddha   PAGE

The Story of Sumedha 577
The Birth of The Buddha 603
The Attainment of Buddhaship 613
First Events After the Attainment 625
The Buddha's Daily Habits 629
The Death of the Buddha 633

II. The Doctrine

Questions Which Tend Not to Edification 647
There Is No Ego 653
The Middle Doctrine 661
Karma . . . . , 666
Fruitful and Barren Karma 669
Good and Bad Karma 675
Rebirth is Not Transmigration 677
Death's Messengers 685
The Devoted Wife 693
The Hare-mark in the Moon 697
The Way of Purity 702
Concentration 705
The Conversion of Animals 706
Love for Animals 708
Sariputta and the Two Demons 710
The Summum Bonum 713
The Trance of Cessation 731
The Attainment of Nirvana 738

III. The Order

The Admission and Ordination Ceremonies 740
The Mendicant Ideal 748
"And Hate Not His Father and Mother" 751
The Story of Visakha 754

BUDDHIST WRITINGS

I. THE BUDDHA

THE STORY OF SUMEDHA[1]

Translated from the Introduction to the Jātaka (i.3[1]).

A HUNDRED thousand cycles vast
    And four immensities ago,
    There was a town named Amara,
A place of beauty and delights.
It had the noises ten complete[2]
And food and drink abundantly.

The noise of elephant and horse,
Of conch-shell, drum, and chariot,
And invitations to partake—
"Eat ye, and drink!"—resounded loud.

A town complete in all its parts,
Where every industry was found,
And eke the seven precious gems,[3]
And foreigners from many lands.
A prosperous city of the gods,
Full of good works and holy men.

Within this town of Amara
Sumedha lived, of Brahman caste,
Who many tens of millions had,
And grain and treasure in full store.

---

[1] This entire story is related by The Buddha to his disciples, and describes how, in his long-ago existence as the Brahman Sumedha, he first resolved to strive for the Buddhaship. In stanzas 4–5 he speaks of himself, that is, of Sumedha, in the third person, but elsewhere in the first.

[2] Only six of the ten noises indicative of a flourishing town are here mentioned. For the complete list, see The Death of The Buddha.

[3] Probably gold, silver, pearls, gems (such as sapphire and ruby), cat's-eye, diamond, and coral.

A student he, and wise in spells,
A master of the Vedas three.
He fortunes told, tradition knew,
And every duty of his caste.

In secret then I sat me down,
And thus to ponder I began:
"What misery to be born again!
And have the flesh dissolve at death!

"Subject to birth, old age, disease,
Extinction will I seek to find,
Where no decay is ever known,
Nor death, but all security.

"What if I now should rid me of
This body foul, this charnel-house,
And go my way without a care,
Or least regret for things behind!

"There is, there must be, an escape!
Impossible there should not be!
I'll make the search and find the way,
Which from existence shall release!

"Even as, although there misery is,
Yet happiness is also found;
So, though indeed existence is,
A non-existence should be sought.

"Even as, although there may be heat,
Yet grateful cold is also found;
So, though the threefold fire[4] exists,
Likewise Nirvana should be sought.

"Even as, although there evil is,
That which is good is also found;
So, though 'tis true that birth exists,
That which is not birth should be sought.

[4] Lust, hatred and infatuation.

"Even as a man befouled with dung,
Seeing a brimming lake at hand,
And nathless bathing not therein,
Were senseless should he chide the lake;

"So, when Nirvana's lake exists
To wash away corruption's stain,
Should I not seek to bathe therein,
I might not then Nirvana chide.

"Even as a man hemmed in by foes,
Seeing a certain safe escape,
And nathless seeking not to flee,
Might not the blameless pathway chide;

"So, when my passions hem me in,
And yet a way to bliss exists,
Should I not seek to follow it,
That way of bliss I might not chide.

"Even as a man who, sore diseased,
When a physician may be had,
Should fail to send to have him come,
Might the physician then not chide;

"So, when diseased with passion, sore
Oppressed, I seek the master not
Whose ghostly counsel me might cure,
The blame should not on him be laid.

"Even as a man might rid him of
A horrid corpse bound to his neck,
And then upon his way proceed,
Joyous, and free, and unconstrained;

"So must I likewise rid me of
This body foul, this charnel-house,
And go my way without a care,
Or least regret for things behind.

"As men and women rid them of
Their dung upon the refuse heap,
And go their ways without a care,
Or least regret for what they leave;

"So will I likewise rid me of
This body foul, this charnel-house,
And go my way as if I had
Cast out my filth into the draught.

"Even as the owners leave and quit
A worn-out, shattered, leaky ship,
And go their ways without a care,
Or least regret for what they leave;

"So will I likewise rid me of
This nine-holed[5] ever-trickling frame,
And go my way, as owners do,
Who ship disrupted leave behind.

"Even as a man who treasure bears,
And finds him in a robber-gang,
Will quickly flee and rid him of
The robbers, lest they steal his gold;

"So, to a mighty robber might
Be likened well this body's frame.
I'll cast it off and go my way,
Lest of my welfare I be robbed."

Thus thinking, I on rich and poor
All that I had in alms bestowed;
Hundreds of millions spent I then,
And made to Himavant[6] my way.

Not far away from Himavant,
There was a hill named Dhammaka,
And here I made and patterned well
A hermitage and hut of leaves.

[5] The two eyes, ears, and so forth.   [6] The Himalaya mountains.

A walking-place I then laid out,
Exempted from the five defects,[7]
And having all the virtues eight;[8]
And there I gained the Six High Powers.

Then ceased I cloaks of cloth to wear,
For cloaks possess the nine defects,[9]
And girded on a barken dress,
Which is with virtues twelve endued.[10]

My hut of leaves I then forsook,
So crowded with the eight defects,[11]

[7] Native gloss: Jātaka, vol. i., p. 7, l. 14: *Exempted from the five defects:* The following are the five defects in a walking-place: hardness and unevenness; trees in the midst; dense underbrush; excessive narrowness; excessive width.

[8] Ibidem, l. 30. *And having all the virtues eight:* Having the eight advantages for a monk. The following are the eight advantages for a monk: it admits of no storing-up of treasure or grain; it favors only a blameless alms-seeking; there one can eat his alms in peace and quiet, there no annoyance is experienced from the reigning families when they oppress the kingdom with their levies of the precious metals or of leaden money; no passionate desire arises for furniture and implements; there is no fear of being plundered by robbers; no intimacies are formed with kings and courtiers; and one is not shut in in any of the four directions.

[9] Native gloss: Jātaka, vol. i., p. 8, l. 27: *For cloaks possess the nine defects:* . . . For one who retires from the world and takes up the life of an anchorite, there are nine defects inherent in garments of cloth. The great cost is one defect; the fact that it is got by dependence on others is another; the fact that it is easily soiled by use is another, for when it has been soiled it must be washed and dyed; the fact that when it is much worn it must needs be patched and mended is another; the difficulty of obtaining a new one when needed is another; its unsuitableness for an anchorite who has retired from the world is another; its acceptableness to one's enemies is another, for it must needs be guarded lest the enemy take it; the danger that it may be worn for ornament is another; the temptation it affords to load one's self down with it in travelling is another.

[10] The bast, or inner bark of certain trees, was much used in India as cloth, to which indeed it bears a striking resemblance.—Native gloss: Jātaka, vol. i., p. 9, l. 2: *Which is with virtues twelve endued:* Possessing twelve advantages. For there are twelve advantages in a dress of bark. It is cheap, good, and suitable; this is one advantage. You can make it yourself; this is a second. It gets dirty but slowly by use, and hence time is not wasted in washing it; this is a third. It never needs sewing, even when much used and worn; this is a fourth. But when a new one is needed, it can be made with ease; this is a fifth. Its suitableness for an anchorite who has retired from the world is a sixth. That it is of no use to one's enemies is a seventh. That it cannot be worn for ornament is an eighth. Its lightness is a ninth. Its conducing to moderation in dress is a tenth. The irreproachableness and blamelessness of searching for bark is an eleventh. And the unimportance of its loss is a twelfth.

[11] Native gloss: Jātaka, vol. i., p. 9, l. 11: *My hut of leaves I then forsook, So crowded with the eight defects:* . . . (L. 36) For there are eight evils connected with the use of a leaf-hut. The great labor involved in searching for materials and in the putting of them together is one evil. The constant care necessary to replace the

And at the foot of trees I lived,
For such abodes have virtues ten.[12]

No sown and cultivated grain
Allowed I then to be my food;
But all the many benefits
Of wild-fruit fare I made my own.

And strenuous effort made I there,
The while I sat, or stood, or walked,
And ere seven days had passed away,
I had attained the Powers High.

When I had thus success attained,
And made me master of the Law,
A Conqueror, Lord of All the World,
Was born, by name Dīpamkara.

What time he was conceived, was born,
What time he Buddhaship attained,
When first he preached,—the Signs[13] appeared,
I saw them not, deep sunk in trance.

grass, leaves, and bits of clay that fall down is a second. Houses may do for old men, but no concentration of mind is possible when one's meditation is liable to be interrupted; thus the liability to interruption is a third. The protection afforded against heat and cold renders the body delicate, and this is a fourth. In a house all sorts of evil deeds are possible; thus the cover it affords for disgraceful practices is a fifth. The taking possession, saying, "This is mine," is a sixth. To have a house is like having a companion; this is a seventh. And the sharing of it with many others, as for instance with lice, bugs, and house-lizards, is an eighth.

[12] Ibidem, p. 10, l. 9: *And at the foot of trees I lived, For such abodes have virtues ten:* . . . The following are the ten virtues. The smallness of the undertaking is one virtue, for all that is necessary is simply to go to the tree. The small amount of care it requires is a second; for, whether swept or unswept, it is suitable for use. The freedom from interruption is a third. It affords no cover for disgraceful practices; wickedness there would be too public; thus the fact that it affords no cover for disgraceful practices is a fourth. It is like living under the open sky, for there is no feeling that the body is confined; thus the non-confinement of the body is a fifth. There is no taking possession; this is a sixth. The abandonment of all longings for household life is a seventh. When a house is shared with others, some one is liable to say, "I will look after this house myself. Begone!" Thus the freedom from eviction is an eighth. The happy contentment experienced by the occupant is a ninth. The little concern one need feel about lodgings, seeing that a man can find a tree no matter where he may be stopping,—this is a tenth.

[13] Translated from the prose of the Jātaka, vol. i., p. 10, last line but one: At his [Dīpamkara's] conception, birth, attainment of Buddhaship, and when he caused the Wheel of Doctrine to roll, the entire system of ten thousand worlds trembled, quivered, and shook, and roared with a mighty roar; also the Thirty-Two Prognostics appeared.

Then, in the distant border-land,
Invited they this Being Great,
And every one, with joyful heart,
The pathway for his coming cleared.

Now so it happened at this time,
That I my hermitage had left,
And, barken garments rustling loud,
Was passing o'er them through the air.

Then saw I every one alert,
Well-pleased, delighted, overjoyed;
And, coming downward from the sky,
The multitude I straightway asked:

"Well-pleased, delighted, overjoyed,
And all alert is every one;
For whom is being cleared the way,
The path, the track to travel on?"

When thus I asked, response was made:
"A mighty Buddha has appeared,
A Conqueror, Lord of All the World,
Whose name is called Dīpamkara.
For him is being cleared the way,
The path, the track to travel on."

This word, "The Buddha," when I heard,
Joy sprang up straightway in my heart;
"A Buddha! Buddha!" cried I then,
And publishèd my heart's content.

And standing there I pondered deep,
By joyous agitation seized:
"Here will I now some good seed sow,
Nor let this fitting season slip."

"For a Buddha do ye clear the road?
Then, pray, grant also me a place!
I, too, will help to clear the way,
The path, the track to travel on."

And so they granted also me
A portion of the path to clear,
And I gan clear, while still my heart
Said "Buddha! Buddha!" o'er and o'er.

But ere my part was yet complete,
Dīpamkara, the Mighty Sage,
The Conqueror, came that way along,
Thronged by four hundred thousand saints,
Without depravity or spot,
And having each the Six High Powers.

The people then their greetings gave,
And many kettle-drums were beat,
And men and gods, in joyous mood,
Loud shouted their applauding cries.

Then men and gods together met,
And saw each other face to face;
And all with joinèd hands upraised
Followed The Buddha and his train.

The gods, with instruments divine,
The men, with those of human make,
Triumphant music played, the while
They followed in The Buddha's train.

Celestial beings from on high
Threw broadcast over all the earth
The Erythrina flowers of heaven,
The lotus and the coral-flower.

And men abiding on the ground
On every side flung up in air
Champakas, salalas, nīpas,
Nāgas, punnāgas, ketakas.

Then loosened I my matted hair,
And, spreading out upon the mud
My dress of bark and cloak of skin,
I laid me down upon my face.

"Let now on me The Buddha tread,
With the disciples of his train;
Can I but keep him from the mire,
To me great merit shall accrue."

While thus I lay upon the ground,
Arose within me many thoughts:
"To-day, if such were my desire,
I my corruptions might consume.

"But why thus in an unknown guise
Should I the Doctrine's fruit secure?
Omniscience first will I achieve,
And be a Buddha in the world.

"Or why should I, a valorous man,
The ocean seek to cross alone?
Omniscience first will I achieve,
And men and gods convey across.

"Since now I make this earnest wish,
In presence of this Best of Men,
Omniscience sometime I'll achieve,
And multitudes convey across.

"I'll rebirth's circling stream arrest,
Destroy existence's three modes;
I'll climb the sides of Doctrine's ship,
And men and gods convey across.

"A human being, male of sex,
Who saintship gains, a Teacher meets,
As hermit lives, and virtue loves,
Nor lacks resolve, nor fiery zeal,
Can by these eight conditions joined,
Make his most earnest wish succeed."

Dīpamkara, Who Knew All Worlds,
Recipient of Offerings,
Came to a halt my pillow near,
And thus addressed the multitudes:

"Behold ye now this monk austere,
His matted locks, his penance fierce!
Lo! he, unnumbered cycles hence,
A Buddha in the world shall be.

"From the fair town called Kapila
His Great Retirement shall be made.
Then, when his Struggle fierce is o'er,
His stern austerities performed,—

"He shall in quiet sit him down
Beneath the Ajapāla-tree;
There pottage made of rice receive,
And seek the stream Nerañjarā.

"This pottage shall The Conqueror eat,
Beside the stream Nerañjarā,
And thence by road triumphal go
To where the Tree of Wisdom stands.

"Then shall the Peerless, Glorious One
Walk to the right, round Wisdom's Throne,
And there The Buddhaship achieve,
While sitting at the fig-tree's root.

"The mother that shall bring him forth,
Shall Māyā callèd be by name;
Suddhodana his father's name;
His own name shall be Gotama.

"Kolita, Upatissa too,—
These shall his Chief Disciples be;
Both undepraved, both passion-free,
And tranquil and serene of mind.

"Ananda shall be servitor
And on The Conqueror attend;
Khemā and Uppalavannā
Shall female Chief Disciples be,

"Both undepraved, both passion-free,
And tranquil and serene of mind.
The Bo-tree of this Blessed One
Shall be the tree Assattha called."

Thus spake Th' Unequalled, Mighty Sage;
And all, when they had heard his speech,
Both men and gods rejoiced, and said:
"Behold a Buddha-scion here!"

Now shouts were heard on every side,
The people clapped their arms and laughed.
Ten thousand worlds of men and gods
Paid me their homage then and said:

"If of our Lord Dīpamkara
The Doctrine now we fail to grasp,
We yet shall stand in time to come
Before this other face to face.

"Even as, when men a river cross,
And miss th' opposing landing-place,
A lower landing-place they find,
And there the river-bank ascend;

"Even so, we all, if we let slip
The present Conqueror that we have,
Yet still shall stand in time to come
Before this other, face to face."

Dīpamkara, Who All Worlds Knew,
Recipient of Offerings,
My future having prophesied,
His right foot raised and went his way.

And all who were this Conqueror's sons,
Walked to the right around me then;
And serpents, men, and demigods,
Saluting me, departed thence.

Now when The Leader of the World
Had passed from sight with all his train,
My mind with rapturous transport filled,
I raised me up from where I lay.

Then overjoyed with joy was I,
Delighted with a keen delight;
And thus with pleasure saturate
I sat me down with legs across.

And while cross-leggèd there I sat,
I thus reflected to myself:
"Behold! in trance am I adept,
And all the Powers High are mine.

"Nowhere throughout a thousand worlds
Are any seers to equal me;
Unequalled in the magic gifts
Have I this height of bliss attained."

Now while I sat with legs across,
The dwellers of ten thousand worlds
Rolled forth a glad and mighty shout:[14]
"Surely a Buddha thou shalt be!

"The presages that erst were seen,
When Future Buddhas sat cross-legged,
These presages are seen to-day—
Surely a Buddha thou shalt be!

"All cold is everywhere dispelled,
And mitigated is the heat;
These presages are seen to-day—
Surely a Buddha thou shalt be!

[14] There have been many beings who, like Sumedha here, were to become Buddhas, and who were therefore called Bodhi-sattas or "Future Buddhas." The certainty of their ultimate "Illumination," or Buddhaship, was always foretokened by certain presages. The "dwellers of ten thousand worlds" describe in the following stanzas what these presages were, declare that they are reappearing now, and announce to Sumedha their prophetic inference that he will attain Buddhaship.

"The system of ten thousand worlds
Is hushed to quiet and to peace;
These presages are seen to-day—
Surely a Buddha thou shalt be!

"The mighty winds then cease to blow,
Nor do the rivers onward glide;
These presages are seen to-day—
Surely a Buddha thou shalt be!

"All plants, be they of land or stream,
Do straightway put their blossoms forth;
Even so to-day they all have bloomed—
Surely a Buddha thou shalt be!

"And every tree, and every vine,
Is straightway laden down with fruit;
Even so to-day they're laden down—
Surely a Buddha thou shalt be!

"In sky and earth doth straightway then
Full many a radiant gem appear;
Even so to-day they shine afar—
Surely a Buddha thou shalt be!

"Then straightway music's heard to play
'Mongst men on earth and gods in heaven;
So all to-day in music join
Surely a Buddha thou shalt be!

"There falleth straightway down from heaven
A rain of many-colored flowers;
Even so to-day these flowers are seen—
Surely a Buddha thou shalt be!

"The mighty ocean heaves and roars,
And all the worlds ten thousand quake;
Even so is now this tumult heard—
Surely a Buddha thou shalt be!

"Straightway throughout the whole of hell
The fires ten thousand all die out:
Even so to-day have all expired—
Surely a Buddha thou shalt be!

"Unclouded then the sun shines forth,
And all the stars appear to view;
Even so to-day do they appear—
Surely a Buddha thou shalt be!

"Straightway, although no rain hath fallen,
Burst springs of water from the earth;
Even so to-day they gush in streams—
Surely a Buddha thou shalt be!

"And bright then shine the starry hosts
And constellations in the sky;
The moon in Libra now doth stand—
Surely a Buddha thou shalt be!

"All beasts that lurk in holes and clefts,
Then get them forth from out their lairs;
Even so to-day they've left their dens—
Surely a Buddha thou shalt be!

"Straightway content is all the world,
And no unhappiness is known;
Even so to-day are all content—
Surely a Buddha thou shalt be!

"Then every sickness vanishes,
And hunger likewise disappears;
These presages are seen to-day—
Surely a Buddha thou shalt be!

"Then lust doth dwindle and grow weak,
And hate, infatuation too;
Even so to-day they disappear—
Surely a Buddha thou shalt be!

"Then fear and danger are unknown;
All we are freed from them to-day;
And by this token we perceive—
'Surely a Buddha thou shalt be!'

"No dust upwhirleth towards the sky;
Even so to-day this thing is seen;
And by this token we perceive—
'Surely a Buddha thou shalt be!'

"All noisome odors drift away,
And heavenly fragrance fills the air;
Even so the winds now sweetness waft—
Surely a Buddha thou shalt be!

"Then all the gods appear to view,
Save those that hold the formless realm;
Even so to-day these all are seen—
Surely a Buddha thou shalt be!

"Then clearly seen are all the hells,
However many be their tale;
Even so to-day may all be seen—
Surely a Buddha thou shalt be!

"Through walls, and doors, and mountain-rocks,
One finds an easy passage then;
Even so to-day they yield like air—
Surely a Buddha thou shalt be!

"Existence then forbears its round
Of death and rebirth for a time;
Even so to-day this thing is seen—
Surely a Buddha thou shalt be!

"Do thou a strenuous effort make!
Do not turn back! Go on! Advance!
Most certainly we know this thing:
'Surely a Buddha thou shalt be!' "

When I had heard The Buddha's speech,
And what the worlds ten thousand said,
Well-pleased, delighted, overjoyed,
I thus reflected to myself:

"The Buddhas never liars are;
A Conqueror's word ne'er yet was vain;
Nothing but truth The Buddhas speak—
Surely a Buddha I shall be!

"As clods thrown upward in the air
Fall surely back upon the earth,
So what the glorious Buddhas speak
Is sure and steadfast to the end.
Nothing but truth The Buddhas speak—
Surely a Buddha I shall be!

"As also for each living thing
The approach of death is ever sure,
So what the glorious Buddhas speak
Is sure and steadfast to the end.
Nothing but truth The Buddhas speak—
Surely a Buddha I shall be!

"As at the waning of the night
The rising of the sun is sure,
So what the glorious Buddhas speak
Is sure and steadfast to the end.
Nothing but truth, *etc.*

"As, when he issues from his den,
The roaring of the lion's sure,
So what the glorious Buddhas speak
Is sure and steadfast to the end.
Nothing but truth, *etc.*

"As when a female has conceived,
Her bringing forth of young is sure,
So what the glorious Buddhas speak
Is sure and steadfast to the end.
Nothing but truth The Buddhas speak—
Surely a Buddha I shall be!

"Come now! I'll search that I may find
Conditions which a Buddha make—
Above, below, to all ten[15] points,
Where'er conditions hold their sway."

And then I searched, and saw the First
Perfection, which consists in Alms,
That highroad great whereon of old
The former seers had ever walked.

"Come now! This one as first adopt,
And practise it determinedly;
Acquire perfection in thine Alms,
If thou to Wisdom wouldst attain.

"As when a jar is brimming full,
And some one overturneth it,
The jar its water all gives forth,
And nothing for itself keeps back;

"So, when a suppliant thou dost see,
Of mean, or high, or middling rank,
Give all in Alms, in nothing stint,
E'en as the overturnèd jar.

"But now there must be more than these
Conditions which a Buddha make;
Still others will I seek to find
That shall in Buddhaship mature."

Perfection Second then I sought,
And lo! the Precepts came to view,
Which mighty seers of former times
Had practised and had follow'd.

"Come now! as second this adopt,
And practise it determinedly;
The Precepts to perfection keep,
If thou to Wisdom wouldst attain.

[15] The four cardinal points of the compass, the four intermediate points, the zenith and nadir.

"As when a Yak cow's flowing tail
Is firmly caught by bush or thorn,
She thereupon awaits her death,
But will not tear and mar her tail;

"So likewise thou in stages four,
Observe and keep the Precepts whole,
On all occasions guard them well,
As ever Yak cow does her tail.

"But now there must be more than these
Conditions which a Buddha make;
Still others will I seek to find
That shall in Buddhaship mature."

And then Perfection Third I sought,
Which is Renunciation called,
Which mighty seers of former times
Had practised and had follow'd.

"Come now! this one as third adopt,
And practise it determinedly;
Renounce, and in perfection grow,
If thou to Wisdom wouldst attain.

"Even as a man who long has dwelt
In prison, suffering miserably,
No liking for the place conceives,
But only longeth for release;

"So likewise thou must every mode
Of being as a prisoner view—
Renunciation be thy aim;
Thus from existence free thyself.

"But now there must be more than these
Conditions which a Buddha make;
Still others will I seek to find
That shall in Buddhaship mature."

And then I sought and found the Fourth
Perfection, which is Wisdom called,
Which mighty seers of former times
Had practised and had follow'd.

"Come now! this one as fourth adopt,
And practise it determinedly;
Wisdom to its perfection bring,
If thou to Wisdom wouldst attain.

"Just as a priest, when on his rounds,
Nor low, nor high, nor middling folk
Doth shun, but begs of every one,
And so his daily food receives;

"So to the learned ay resort,
And seek thy Wisdom to increase;
And when this Fourth Perfection's gained,
A Buddha's Wisdom shall be thine.

"But now there must be more than these
Conditions which a Buddha make;
Still others will I seek to find
That shall in Buddhaship mature."

And then I sought and found the Fifth
Perfection, which is Courage called,
Which mighty seers of former times
Had practised and had follow'd.

"Come now! this one as fifth adopt,
And practise it determinedly;
In Courage perfect strive to be,
If thou to Wisdom wouldst attain.

"Just as the lion, king of beasts,
In crouching, walking, standing still,
With courage ever is instinct,
And watchful always, and alert;

"So thou in each repeated birth,
Courageous energy display;
And when this Fifth Perfection's gained,
A Buddha's Wisdom shall be thine.

"But now there must be more than these
Conditions which a Buddha make;
Still others will I seek to find
That shall in Buddhaship mature."

And then I sought and found the Sixth
Perfection, which is Patience called,
Which mighty seers of former times
Had practised and had follow'd.

"Come now! this one as sixth adopt,
And practise it determinedly;
And if thou keep an even mood,
A Buddha's Wisdom shall be thine.

"Just as the earth, whate'er is thrown
Upon her, whether sweet or foul,
All things endures, and never shows
Repugnance, nor complacency;

"E'en so, or honor thou, or scorn,
Of men, with patient mood must bear;
And when this Sixth Perfection's gained,
A Buddha's Wisdom shall be thine.

"But now there must be more than these
Conditions which a Buddha make;
Still others will I seek to find
That shall in Buddhaship mature."

And then I sought and found the Seventh
Perfection, which is that of Truth,
Which mighty seers of former times
Had practised and had follow'd.

"Come now! this one as seventh adopt,
And practise it determinedly;
If thou art ne'er of double speech,
A Buddha's Wisdom shall be thine.

"Just as the morning star on high
Its balanced course doth ever keep,
And through all seasons, times, and years,
Doth never from its pathway swerve;

"So likewise thou in all thy speech
Swerve never from the path of truth;
And when this Seventh Perfection's gained,
A Buddha's Wisdom shall be thine.

"But now there must be more than these
Conditions which a Buddha make;
Still others will I seek to find
That shall in Buddhaship mature."

And then I sought and found the Eighth
Perfection, Resolution called,
Which mighty seers of former times
Had practised and had follow'd.

"Come now! this one as eighth adopt,
And practise it determinedly;
And when thou art immovable,
A Buddha's Wisdom shall be thine.

"Just as a rocky mountain-peak,
Unmovèd stands, firm-stablishèd,
Unshaken by the boisterous gales,
And always in its place abides;

"So likewise thou must ever be
In Resolution firm intrenched;
And when this Eighth Perfection's gained,
A Buddha's Wisdom shall be thine.

"But now there must be more than these
Conditions which a Buddha make;
Still others will I seek to find
That shall in Buddhaship mature."

And then I sought and found the Ninth
Perfection, which is called Good-will;
Which mighty seers of former times
Had practised and had follow'd.

"Come now! this one as ninth adopt,
And practise it determinedly;
Unequalled be in thy Good-will,
If thou to Wisdom wouldst attain.

"As water cleanseth all alike,
The righteous and the wicked, too,
From dust and dirt of every kind,
And with refreshing coolness fills;

"So likewise thou both friend and foe,
Alike with thy Good-will refresh,
And when this Ninth Perfection's gained,
A Buddha's Wisdom shall be thine.

"But now there must be more than these
Conditions which a Buddha make;
Still others will I seek to find
That shall in Buddhaship mature."

And then I sought and found the Tenth
Perfection, called Indifference;
Which mighty seers of former times
Had practised and had follow'd.

"Come now! this one as tenth adopt,
And practise it determinedly;
And when thou art of equal poise,
A Buddha's Wisdom shall be thine.

"Just as the earth, whate'er is thrown
Upon her, whether sweet or foul,
Indifferent is to all alike,
Nor hatred shows, nor amity;

"So likewise thou in good or ill,
Must even-balanced ever be;
And when this Tenth Perfection's gained,
A Buddha's Wisdom shall be thine.

"But earth no more conditions hath
That in The Buddhaship mature;
Beyond these are there none to seek;
So practise these determinedly."

Now pondering these conditions ten,
Their nature, essence, character,—
Such fiery vigor had they all,
That all the worlds ten thousand quaked.

Then shook and creaked the wide, wide earth,
As doth the sugar-mill at work;
Then quaked the ground, as doth the wheel
Of oil-mills when they're made to turn.

Th' entire assemblage that was there,
And followed in The Buddha's train,
Trembled and shook in great alarm,
And fell astonied to the ground.

And many thousand waterpots,
And many hundred earthen jars,
Were one upon another dashed,
And crushed and pounded into dust.

Excited, trembling, terrified,
Confused, and sore oppressed in mind,
The multitudes together came,
And to Dīpamkara approached.

"Oh, tell us what these signs portend.
Will good or ill betide the world?
Lo! terror seizes hold on all.
Dispel our fears, All-Seeing One!"

The Great Sage, then, Dīpamkara,
Allayed and pacified their fears:—
"Be comforted; and fear ye not
For that the world doth quake and shake.

"Of whom to-day I made proclaim—
'A glorious Buddha shall he be,'—
He now conditions pondereth,
Which former Conquerors fulfilled.

" 'Tis while on these he is intent,
As basis for The Buddhaship,
The ground in worlds ten thousand shakes,
In all the realms of gods and men."

When thus they'd heard The Buddha speak,
Their anxious minds received relief;
And all then drawing near to me,
Again they did me reverence.

Thus on the road to Buddhaship,
And firm determined in my mind,
I raised me up from off my seat,
And reverenced Dīpamkara.

Then as I raised me from my seat,
Both gods and men in unison
Sweet flowers of heaven and flowers of earth
Profusely sprinkled on my head.

And gods and men in unison
Their great delight proclaimed aloud:—
"A mighty prayer thou now hast made;
Succeed according to thy wish!

"From all misfortunes be thou free,
Let every sickness disappear!
Mayst thou no hindrance ever know,
And highest Wisdom soon achieve!

"As, when the time of spring has come,
The trees put forth their buds and flowers,
Likewise dost thou, O Hero Great,
With knowledge of a Buddha bloom.

"As all they who have Buddhas been,
The Ten Perfections have fulfilled,
Likewise do thou, O Hero Great,
The Ten Perfections strive to gain.

"As all they who have Buddhas been,
On Wisdom's Throne their insight gained,
Likewise do thou, O Hero Great,
On Conqueror's Throne thy insight gain.

"As all they who have Buddhas been,
Have made the Doctrine's Wheel to roll,
Likewise do thou, O Hero Great,
Make Doctrine's Wheel to roll once more.

"As on the mid-day of the month
The moon in full perfection shines,
Likewise do thou, with perfect mind,
Shine brightly in ten thousand worlds.

"As when the sun, by Rāhu freed,
Shines forth exceeding bright and clear,
So thou, when freed from ties of earth,
Shine forth in bright magnificence.

"Just as the rivers of all lands
Into the ocean find their way,
May gods and men from every world
Approach and find their way to thee."

Thus praised they me with glad acclaim;
And I, beginning to fulfil
The ten conditions of my quest,
Re-entered then into the wood.

END OF THE STORY OF SUMEDHA.

THE BIRTH OF THE BUDDHA

Translated from the Introduction to the Jātaka (i.47²¹)

NOW while the Future Buddha was still dwelling in the city of the Tusita gods, the "Buddha-Uproar," as it is called, took place. For there are three uproars which take place in the world,—the Cyclic-Uproar, the Buddha-Uproar, and the Universal-Monarch-Uproar. They occur as follows:—

When it is known that after the lapse of a hundred thousand years the cycle is to be renewed, the gods called Lokabyūhas, inhabitants of a heaven of sensual pleasure, wander about through the world, with hair let down and flying in the wind, weeping and wiping away their tears with their hands, and with their clothes red and in great disorder. And thus they make announcement:—

"Sirs, after the lapse of a hundred thousand years, the cycle is to be renewed; this world will be destroyed; also the mighty ocean will dry up; and this broad earth, and Sineru, the monarch of the mountains, will be burnt up and destroyed,—up to the Brahma heavens will the destruction of the world extend. Therefore, sirs, cultivate friendliness; cultivate compassion, joy, and indifference; wait on your mothers; wait on your fathers; and honor your elders among your kinsfolk."

This is called the Cyclic-Uproar.

Again, when it is known that after a lapse of a thousand years an omniscient Buddha is to arise in the world, the guardian angels of the world wander about, proclaiming:

"Sirs, after the lapse of a thousand years a Buddha will arise in the world."

This is called the Buddha-Uproar.

And lastly, when they realize that after the lapse of a hundred years a Universal Monarch is to arise, the terrestrial deities wander about, proclaiming:—

"Sirs, after the lapse of a hundred years a Universal Monarch is to arise in the world."

This is called the Universal-Monarch-Uproar. And these three are mighty uproars.

When of these three Uproars they hear the sound of the Buddha-Uproar, the gods of all ten thousand worlds come together into one place, and having ascertained what particular being is to be The Buddha, they approach him, and beseech him to become one. But it is not till after omens have appeared that they beseech him.

At that time, therefore, having all come together in one world, with the Cātum-Mahārājas, and with the Sakka, the Suyāma, the Santusita, the Paranimmita-Vasavatti, and the Mahā-Brahma of each several world, they approached the Future Buddha in the Tusita heaven, and besought him, saying,—

"Sir, it was not to acquire the glory of a Sakka, or of a Māra, or of a Brahma, or of a Universal Monarch, that you fulfilled the Ten Perfections; but it was to gain omniscience in order to save the world, that you fulfilled them. Sir, the time and fit season for your Buddhaship has now arrived."

But the Great Being, before assenting to their wish, made what is called the five great observations. He observed, namely, the time, the continent, the country, the family, and the mother and her span of life.

In the first of these observations he asked himself whether it was the right time or no. Now it is not the right time when the length of men's lives is more than a hundred thousand years. And why is it not the right time? Because mortals then forget about birth, old age, and death. And if The Buddhas, who always include in their teachings the Three Characteristics, were to attempt at such a time to discourse concerning transitoriness, misery, and the lack of substantive reality, men would not think it worth while listening to them, nor would they give them credence. Thus there would be no conversions made; and if there were no conversions, the dispensation would not conduce to salvation. This, therefore, is not the right time.

Also it is not the right time when men's lives are less than a hundred years. And why is it not the right time? Because mortals are then exceedingly corrupt; and an exhortation given to the exceedingly corrupt makes no impression, but, like a mark drawn with a stick on the surface of the water, it immediately disappears. This, therefore, also is not the right time.

But when the length of men's lives is between a hundred years and a hundred thousand years, then is it the right time. Now at that time men's lives were a hundred years; accordingly the Great Being observed that it was the right time for his birth.

Next he made the observation concerning the continent. Looking over the four continents with their attendant isles, he reflected: "In three of the continents the Buddhas are never born; only in the continent of India are they born." Thus he decided on the continent.

Next he made the observation concerning the place. "The continent of India is large," thought he, "being ten thousand leagues around. In which of its countries are The Buddhas born?" Thus he decided on the Middle Country.

The Middle Country is the country defined in the Vinaya as follows:—

"It lies in the middle, on this side of the town Kajaṅgala on the east, beyond which is Mahā-Sāla, and beyond that the border districts. It lies in the middle, on this side of the river Salalavatī on the southeast, beyond which are the border districts. It lies in the middle, on this side of the town Setakannika on the south, beyond which are the border districts. It lies in the middle, on this side of the Brahmanical town Thūna on the west, beyond which are the border districts. It lies in the middle, on this side of the hill Usīraddhaja on the north, beyond which are the border districts."

It is three hundred leagues in length, two hundred and fifty in breadth, and nine hundred in circumference. In this country are born The Buddhas, the Private Buddhas, the Chief Disciples, the Eighty Great Disciples, the Universal Monarch, and other eminent ones, magnates of the warrior caste, of the Brahman caste, and the wealthy householders. "And in it is this city called Kapilavatthu," thought he, and concluded that there he ought to be born.

Then he made the observation concerning the family. "The Buddhas," thought he, "are never born into a family of the peasant caste, or of the servile caste; but into one of the warrior caste, or of the

Brahman caste, whichever at the time is the higher in public estimation. The warrior caste is now the higher in public estimation. I
will be born into a warrior family, and king Suddhodana shall be my
father." Thus he decided on the family.

Then he made the observation concerning the mother. "The
mother of a Buddha," thought he, "is never a wanton, nor a drunkard, but is one who has fulfilled the perfections through a hundred
thousand cycles, and has kept the five precepts unbroken from the
day of her birth. Now this queen Mahā-Māyā is such a one; and she
shall be my mother."—"But what shall be her span of life?" [1] continued he. And he perceived that it was to be ten months and seven
days.

Having thus made the five great observations, he kindly made the
gods the required promise, saying,—

"Sirs, you are right. The time has come for my Buddhaship."

Then, surrounded by the gods of the Tusita heaven, and dismiss-
ing all the other gods, he entered the Nandana Grove of the Tusita
capital,—for in each of the heavens there is a Nandana Grove. And
here the gods said, "Attain in your next existence your high destiny,"
and kept reminding him that he had already paved the way to it by
his accumulated merit. Now it was while he was thus dwelling,
surrounded by these deities, and continually reminded of his accumulated merit, that he died, and was conceived in the womb of queen
Mahā-Māyā. And in order that this matter may be fully understood,
I will give the whole account in due order.

It is related that at that time the Midsummer Festival had been
proclaimed in the city of Kapilavatthu, and the multitude were enjoying the feast. And queen Mahā-Māyā, abstaining from strong
drink, and brilliant with garlands and perfumes, took part in the
festivities for the six days previous to the day of full moon. And
when it came to be the day of full moon, she rose early, bathed in
perfumed water, and dispensed four hundred thousand pieces of
money in great largess. And decked in full gala attire, she ate of
the choicest food; after which she took the eight vows, and entered

[1] That is, "How long is she to live after conceiving me?" And the answer is,
"Ten lunar [that is, the nine calendar] months of my mother's pregnancy, and
seven days after my birth."

her elegantly furnished chamber of state. And lying down on the royal couch, she fell asleep and dreamed the following dream:—

The four guardian angels came and lifted her up, together with her couch, and took her away to the Himalaya Mountains. There, in the Manosilā table-land, which is sixty leagues in extent, they laid her under a prodigious sal-tree, seven leagues in height, and took up their positions respectfully at one side. Then came the wives of these guardian angels, and conducted her to Anotatta Lake, and bathed her, to remove every human stain. And after clothing her with divine garments, they anointed her with perfumes and decked her with divine flowers. Not far off was Silver Hill, and in it a golden mansion. There they spread a divine couch with its head towards the east, and laid her down upon it. Now the Future Buddha had become a superb white elephant, and was wandering about at no great distance, on Gold Hill. Descending thence, he ascended Silver Hill, and approaching from the north, he plucked a white lotus with his silvery trunk, and trumpeting loudly, went into the golden mansion. And three times he walked round his mother's couch, with his right side towards it, and striking her on her right side, he seemed to enter her womb. Thus the conception took place in the Midsummer Festival.

On the next day the queen awoke, and told the dream to the king. And the king caused sixty-four eminent Brahmans to be summoned, and spread costly seats for them on ground festively prepared with green leaves, Dalbergia flowers, and so forth. The Brahmans being seated, he filled gold and silver dishes with the best of milk-porridge compounded with ghee, honey, and treacle; and covering these dishes with others, made likewise of gold and silver, he gave the Brahmans to eat. And not only with food, but with other gifts, such as new garments, tawny cows, and so forth, he satisfied them completely. And when their every desire had been satisfied, he told them the dream and asked them what would come of it?

"Be not anxious, great king!" said the Brahmans; "a child has planted itself in the womb of your queen, and it is a male child and not a female. You will have a son. And he, if he continue to live the household life, will become a Universal Monarch; but if he leave the household life and retire from the world, he will become a Buddha, and roll back the clouds of sin and folly of this world."

Now the instant the Future Buddha was conceived in the womb of his mother, all the ten thousand worlds suddenly quaked, quivered, and shook. And the Thirty-two Prognostics appeared, as follows: an immeasurable light spread through ten thousand worlds; the blind recovered their sight, as if from desire to see this his glory; the deaf received their hearing; the dumb talked; the hunchbacked became straight of body; the lame recovered the power to walk; all those in bonds were freed from their bonds and chains; the fires went out in all the hells; the hunger and thirst of the Manes was stilled; wild animals lost their timidity; diseases ceased among men; all mortals became mild-spoken; horses neighed and elephants trumpeted in a manner sweet to the ear; all musical instruments gave forth their notes without being played upon; bracelets and other ornaments jingled; in all quarters of the heavens the weather became fair; a mild, cool breeze began to blow, very refreshing to men; rain fell out of season; water burst forth from the earth and flowed in streams; the birds ceased flying through the air; the rivers checked their flowing; in the mighty ocean the water became sweet; the ground became everywhere covered with lotuses of the five different colors; all flowers bloomed, both those on land and those that grow in the water; trunk-lotuses bloomed on the trunks of trees, branch-lotuses on the branches, and vine-lotuses on the vines; on the ground, stalk-lotuses, as they are called, burst through the overlying rocks and came up by sevens; in the sky were produced others, called hanging-lotuses; a shower of flowers fell all about; celestial music was heard to play in the sky; and the whole ten thousand worlds became one mass of garlands of the utmost possible magnificence, with waving chowries, and saturated with the incense-like fragrance of flowers, and resembled a bouquet of flowers sent whirling through the air, or a closely woven wreath, or a superbly decorated altar of flowers.

From the time the Future Buddha was thus conceived, four angels with swords in their hands kept guard, to ward off all harm from both the Future Buddha and the Future Buddha's mother. No lustful thought sprang up in the mind of the Future Buddha's mother; having reached the pinnacle of good fortune and of glory, she felt comfortable and well, and experienced no exhaustion of body. And within her womb she could distinguish the Future Buddha, like a white thread passed through a transparent jewel. And whereas a womb that has been occupied by a Future Buddha is like the shrine of a temple, and can never be occupied or used again, therefore it was that the mother of the Future Buddha died when he was seven days old, and was reborn in the Tusita heaven.

Now other women sometimes fall short of and sometimes run over the term of ten lunar months, and then bring forth either sitting or lying down; but not so the mother of a Future Buddha. She carries the Future Buddha in her womb for just ten months, and then brings forth while standing up. This is a characteristic of the mother of a Future Buddha. So also queen Mahā-Māyā carried the Future Buddha in her womb, as it were oil in a vessel, for ten months; and being then far gone with child, she grew desirous of going home to her relatives, and said to king Suddhodana,—

"Sire, I should like to visit my kinsfolk in their city Devadaha."

"So be it," said the king; and from Kapilavatthu to the city of Devadaha he had the road made even, and garnished it with plantain-trees set in pots, and with banners, and streamers; and, seating the queen in a golden palanquin borne by a thousand of his courtiers, he sent her away in great pomp.

Now between the two cities, and belonging to the inhabitants of both, there was a pleasure-grove of sal-trees, called Lumbini Grove. And at this particular time this grove was one mass of flowers from the ground to the topmost branches, while amongst the branches and flowers hummed swarms of bees of the five different colors, and flocks of various kinds of birds flew about warbling sweetly. Throughout the whole of Lumbini Grove the scene resembled the Cittalatā Grove in Indra's paradise, or the magnificently decorated banqueting pavilion of some potent king.

When the queen beheld it she became desirous of disporting herself therein, and the courtiers therefore took her into it. And going to the foot of the monarch sal-tree of the grove, she wished to take hold of one of its branches. And the sal-tree branch, like the tip of a well-steamed reed, bent itself down within reach of the queen's hand. Then she reached out her hand, and seized hold of the branch, and immediately her pains came upon her. Thereupon the people hung a curtain about her, and retired. So her delivery took place while she was standing up, and keeping fast hold of the sal-tree branch.

At that very moment came four pure-minded Mahā-Brahma angels bearing a golden net, and, receiving the Future Buddha on this golden net, they placed him before his mother and said,—

"Rejoice, O Queen! A mighty son has been born to you."

Now other mortals on issuing from the maternal womb are smeared with disagreeable, impure matter; but not so the Future Buddha. He issued from his mother's womb like a preacher descending from his preaching-seat, or a man coming down a stair, stretching out both hands and both feet, unsmeared by any impurity from his mother's womb, and flashing pure and spotless, like a jewel thrown upon a vesture of Benares cloth. Notwithstanding this, for the sake of honoring the Future Buddha and his mother, there came two streams of water from the sky, and refreshed the Future Buddha and his mother.

Then the Brahma angels, after receiving him on their golden net, delivered him to the four guardian angels, who received him from their hands on a rug which was made of the skins of black antelopes, and was soft to the touch, being such as is used on state occasions; and the guardian angels delivered him to men who received him on a coil of fine cloth; and the men let him out of their hands on the ground, where he stood and faced the east. There, before him, lay many thousands of worlds, like a great open court; and in them, gods and men, making offerings to him of perfumes, garlands, and so on, were saying,—

"Great Being! There is none your equal, much less your superior."

When he had in this manner surveyed the four cardinal points, and the four intermediate ones, and the zenith, and the nadir, in short, all the ten directions in order, and had nowhere discovered his equal, he exclaimed, "This is the best direction," and strode forward seven paces, followed by Mahā-Brahma holding over him the white umbrella, Suyāma bearing the fan, and other divinities having the other symbols of royalty in their hands. Then, at the seventh stride, he halted, and with a noble voice, he shouted the shout of victory, beginning,—

"The chief am I in all the world."

Now in three of his existences did the Future Buddha utter words immediately on issuing from his mother's womb: namely, in his existence as Mahosadha; in his existence as Vessantara; and in this existence.

As respects his existence as Mahosadha, it is related that just as he was issuing from his mother's womb, Sakka, the king of the gods, came and placed in his hand some choice sandal-wood, and departed. And he closed his fist upon it, and issued forth.

"My child," said his mother, "what is it you bring with you in your hand?"

"Medicine, mother," said he.

Accordingly, as he was born with medicine in his hand, they gave him the name of Osadha-Dāraka [Medicine-Child]. Then they took the medicine, and placed it in an earthenware jar; and it was a sovereign remedy to heal all the blind, the deaf, and other afflicted persons who came to it. So the saying sprang up, "This is a great medicine, this is a great medicine!" And thus he received the name of Mahosadha [Great Medicine-Man].

Again, in the Vessantara existence, as he was issuing from his mother's womb, he stretched out his right hand, and said,—

"Pray, mother, is there anything in the house? I want to give alms."

Then, after he had completely issued forth, his mother said,—

"It's a wealthy family, my son, into which you are born;" and putting his hand in her own, she had them place in his a purse containing a thousand pieces of money.

Lastly, in this birth he shouted the shout of victory above-mentioned.

Thus in three of his existences did the Future Buddha utter words immediately on issuing from his mother's womb. And just as at the moment of his conception, so also at the moment of his birth appeared the Thirty-two Prognostics.

Now at the very time that our Future Buddha was born in Lumbini Grove there also came into existence the mother of Rāhula, and Channa the courtier, Kāludāyi the courtier, Kanthaka the king of horses, the Great Bo-tree, and the four urns full of treasure. Of these last, one was a quarter of a league in extent, another a half-league, the third three-quarters of a league, and the fourth a league. These seven[2] are called the Connate Ones.

Then the inhabitants of both cities took the Future Buddha, and carried him to Kapilavatthu.

[2] In making up this number the Future Buddha is to be counted as number 1, and the four urns of treasure together as number 7.

THE ATTAINMENT
OF BUDDHASHIP

Translated from the Introduction to the Jātaka (i.68[5])

NOW at that time there lived in Uruvelā a girl named Sujātā, who had been born in the family of the householder Senāni, in General's Town. On reaching maturity she made a prayer to a certain banyan-tree, saying, "If I get a husband of equal rank with myself, and my first-born is a son, I will make a yearly offering to you of the value of a hundred thousand pieces of money." And her prayer had been successful.

And wishing to make her offering on the day of full moon of the month Visākhā, full six years after the Great Being commenced his austerities, she first pastured a thousand cows in Latthimadhu Wood, and fed their milk to five hundred cows, and the milk of these five hundred cows to two hundred and fifty, and so on down to feeding the milk of sixteen cows to eight. This "working the milk in and in," as it is called, was done to increase the thickness and the sweetness and the strength-giving properties of the milk. And when it came to be the full-moon day of Visākhā, she resolved to make her offering, and rose up early in the morning, just when night was breaking into day, and gave orders to milk the eight cows. The calves had not come at the teats of the cows; yet as soon as new pails were put under the udders, the milk flowed in streams of its own accord. When she saw this miracle, Sujātā took the milk with her own hands and placed it in a new vessel, and herself made a fire and began to cook it. While the milk-rice was cooking, immense bubbles arose, and turning to the right, went round together; but not a single drop ran over the edge, and not a particle of smoke went up from the fireplace. On this occasion the four guardian angels were present, and stood guard over the fireplace; Mahā-Brahma bore aloft the canopy of state, and Sakka raked the firebrands together and made the fire blaze up brightly. And just as a man crushes honey out of a honey-comb that has formed around a stick, so the deities by their superhuman power collected an amount of vital sap sufficient for the sustenance of the gods and men of all the four great continents and their two thousand attendant isles, and infused it into the milk-rice. At other times, to be sure, the deities infuse this sap into each mouthful; but on the day of the attainment of the Buddaship, and on the day of decease, they placed it in the kettle itself.

When Sujātā had seen so many miracles appear to her in one day, she said to her slave-girl Punnā,—

"Punnā, dear girl, the deity is very graciously disposed to us to-day. I have never before seen so many marvellous things happen in so short a time. Run quickly, and get everything ready at the holy place."

"Yes, my lady," replied the slave-girl, and ran in great haste to the foot of the tree.

Now that night the Future Buddha had five great dreams, and on considering their meaning reached the conclusion, "Without doubt I shall become a Buddha this very day." And when night was over, and he had cared for his person, he came early in the morning to that tree, to await the hour to go begging. And when he sat down he illumined the whole tree with his radiance.

Then came Punnā, and saw the Future Buddha sitting at the foot of the tree, contemplating the eastern quarter of the world. And when she beheld the radiance from his body lighting up the whole tree with a golden color, she became greatly excited, saying to herself, "Our deity, methinks, has come down from the tree to-day, and has seated himself, ready to receive our offering in person." And she ran in great haste, and told Sujātā of the matter.

When Sujātā heard this news, she was overjoyed; and saying, "From this day forth be to me in the room of an eldest daughter," she decked Punnā with all the ornaments appropriate to that position. And since a Future Buddha on the day he attains the Buddhaship must needs receive a golden dish worth a hundred thousand pieces of money, therefore the idea occurred to her of putting the milk-rice in a golden dish. And bringing out a golden dish that was worth a hundred thousand, she took up the cooking-vessel and began to pour out the milk-rice. All the milk-rice rolled off like water from a lotus-leaf, and exactly filled the dish. Then, covering the dish with another, which was also made of gold, and wrapping it in a cloth, she adorned herself in all her ornaments, and with the dish on her head proceeded in state to the foot of the banyan-tree. As soon as she caught sight of the Future Buddha she was exceedingly overjoyed, supposing him to be the tree-god; and as she advanced she kept constantly bowing. And taking the pot from her head, she uncovered it, and with some flower-scented water in a golden vase, drew near and took up a position close to the Future Buddha. The earthenware bowl which the Future Buddha had kept so long, and which had been given him by Ghatīkāra, the Mahā-Brahma god, at that instant disappeared; and the Future Buddha, stretching out his right hand in an attempt to find his bowl, grasped the vase of water. Next Sujātā placed the dish of milk-rice in the hand of the Great Being. Then the Great Being looked at Sujātā; and she perceived that he was a holy man, and did obeisance, and said,—

"Lord, accept my donation, and go whithersoever it seemeth to you good." And adding, "May your wishes prosper like mine own," she departed, caring no more for her golden dish worth a hundred thousand pieces of money than if it had been a dead leaf.

The Future Buddha rose from his seat and walked round the tree with his right side towards it; and taking the dish, he proceeded to the banks of the Nerañjarā and descended into its waters, just as many thousands of Future Buddhas before him had descended on the day of their complete enlightenment.—The spot where he bathed is now a place of pilgrimage named Suppatitthita, and here he deposited the dish on the bank before descending into the water. —After bathing he dressed himself in that garb of saintship which had been the dress of many hundreds of thousands of Future Buddhas before him; and sitting down with his face to the east, he made the whole of the thick, sweet milk-rice into forty-nine pellets of the size of the fruit of the single-seeded palmyra-tree, and ate it. And he took no further nourishment until the end of the seven weeks, or forty-nine days, which he spent on the throne of wisdom after he had become a Buddha. During all that time he had no other nourishment; he neither bathed, nor rinsed his mouth, nor did he ease himself; but was wholly taken up by the delights of the Trances, of the Paths, and of the Fruits.

Now when he had consumed the milk-rice, he took the golden dish; and saying, "If I am to succeed in becoming a Buddha to-day, let this dish go up-stream; but if not, let it go down-stream," he threw it into the water. And it swam, cleaving the stream, until it came to the middle of the river, and then, like a fleet horse, it ran up-stream for a distance of eighty cubits, keeping all the while in the middle of the stream. Then it dived into a whirlpool and went to the palace of the black snake-king, and hit, "click! click!" against the dishes that had been used by the last three Buddhas, and took its place at the end of the row. When the black snake-king heard the noise, he exclaimed,—

"But yesterday a Buddha lived,
And now another has been born."

and so on, through several hundred laudatory verses. As a matter of only yesterday and to-day did the times of the snake-king's appearance above ground seem to him; and his body at such times towered up into the sky to a height of one and three quarters leagues.

Then the Future Buddha took his noonday rest on the banks of the river, in a grove of sal-trees in full bloom. And at nightfall, at the time the flowers droop on their stalks, he rose up, like a lion when he bestirs himself, and went towards the Bo-tree, along a road which the gods had decked, and which was eight usabhas wide.

The snakes, the fairies, the birds, and other classes of beings did him homage with celestial perfumes, flowers, and other offerings, and celestial choruses poured forth heavenly music; so that the ten thousand worlds were filled with these perfumes, garlands, and shouts of acclaim.

Just then there came from the opposite direction a grass-cutter named Sotthiya, and he was carrying grass. And when he saw the Great Being, that he was a holy man, he gave him eight handfuls of grass. The Future Buddha took the grass, and ascending the throne of wisdom, stood on the southern side and faced the north. Instantly the southern half of the world sank, until it seemed to touch the Avīci hell, while the northern half rose to the highest of the heavens.

"Methinks," said the Future Buddha, "this cannot be the place for the attainment of the supreme wisdom;" and walking round the tree with his right side towards it, he came to the western side and faced the east. Then the western half of the world sank, until it seemed to touch the Avīci hell, while the eastern half rose to the highest of the heavens. Wherever, indeed, he stood, the broad earth rose and fell, as though it had been a huge cart-wheel lying on its hub, and some one were treading on the rim.

"Methinks," said the Future Buddha, "this also cannot be the place for the attainment of supreme wisdom;" and walking round the tree with his right side towards it, he came to the northern side and faced the south. Then the northern half of the world sank, until it seemed to touch the Avīci hell, while the southern half rose to the highest of the heavens.

"Methinks," said the Future Buddha, "this also cannot be the place for the attainment of supreme wisdom;" and walking round the tree with his right side towards it, he came to the eastern side and faced the west. Now it is on the eastern side of their Bo-trees that all The Buddhas have sat cross-legged, and that side neither trembles nor quakes.

Then the Great Being, saying to himself, "This is the immovable spot on which all The Buddhas have planted themselves! This is the place for destroying passion's net!" took hold of his handful of grass by one end, and shook it out there. And straightway the blades of grass formed themselves into a seat fourteen cubits long, of such symmetry of shape as not even the most skilful painter or carver could design.

Then the Future Buddha turned his back to the trunk of the Bo-tree and faced the east. And making the mighty resolution, "Let my skin, and sinews, and bones become dry, and welcome! and let all the flesh and blood in my body dry up! but never from this seat will I stir, until I have attained the supreme and absolute wisdom!" he sat himself down cross-legged in an unconquerable position, from which not even the descent of a hundred thunder-bolts at once could have dislodged him.

At this point the god Māra, exclaiming, "Prince Siddhattha is desirous of passing beyond my control, but I will never allow it!" went and announced the news to his army, and sounding the Māra war-cry, drew out for battle. Now Māra's army extended in front of him for twelve leagues, and to the right and to the left for twelve leagues, and in the rear as far as to the confines of the world, and it was nine leagues high. And when it shouted, it made an earth-quake-like roaring and rumbling over a space of a thousand leagues. And the god Māra, mounting his elephant, which was a hundred and fifty leagues high, and had the name "Girded-with-mountains," caused a thousand arms to appear on his body, and with these he grasped a variety of weapons. Also in the remainder of that army, no two persons carried the same weapon; and diverse also in their appearances and countenances, the host swept on like a flood to overwhelm the Great Being.

Now deities throughout the ten thousand worlds were busy sing-ing the praises of the Great Being. Sakka, the king of the gods, was blowing the conch-shell Vijayuttara. (This conch, they say, was a hundred and twenty cubits long, and when once it had been filled with wind, it would sound for four months before it stopped.) The great black snake-king sang more than a hundred laudatory verses. And Mahā-Brahma stood holding aloft the white umbrella. But as Māra's army gradually drew near to the throne of wisdom, not one of these gods was able to stand his ground, but each fled straight before him. The black snake-king dived into the ground, and coming to the snake-abode, Mañjerika, which was five hundred leagues in extent, he covered his face with both hands and lay down. Sakka slung his conch-shell Vijayuttara over his back, and took up his position on the rim of the world. Mahā-Brahma left the white umbrella at the end of the world, and fled to his Brahma-abode. Not a single deity was able to stand his ground, and the Great Being was left sitting alone.

Then said Māra to his followers,—

"My friends, Siddhattha, the son of Suddhodana, is far greater than any other man, and we shall never be able to fight him in front. We will attack him from behind."

All the gods had now disappeared, and the Great Being looked around on three sides, and said to himself, "There is no one here." Then looking to the north, he perceived Māra's army coming on like a flood, and said,—

"Here is this multitude exerting all their strength and power against me alone. My mother and father are not here, nor my brother, nor any other relative. But I have these Ten Perfections, like old retainers long cherished at my board. It therefore behooves me to make the Ten Perfections my shield and my sword, and to strike a blow with them that shall destroy this strong array." And he remained sitting, and reflected on the Ten Perfections.

Thereupon the god Māra caused a whirlwind, thinking, "By this will I drive away Siddhattha." Straightway the east wind and all the other different winds began to blow; but although these winds could have torn their way through mountain-peaks half a league, or two leagues, or three leagues high, or have uprooted forest-shrubs and trees, or have reduced to powder and scattered in all directions, villages and towns, yet when they reached the Future Buddha, such was the energy of the Great Being's merit, they lost all power and were not able to cause so much as a fluttering of the edge of his priestly robe.

Then he caused a great rain-storm, saying, "With water will I overwhelm and drown him." And through his mighty power, clouds of a hundred strata, and clouds of a thousand strata arose, and also the other different kinds. And these rained down, until the earth became gullied by the torrents of water which fell, and until the floods had risen over the tops of every forest-tree. But on coming to the Great Being, this mighty inundation was not able to wet his priestly robes as much as a dew-drop would have done.

Then he caused a shower of rocks, in which immense mountain-peaks flew smoking and flaming through the sky. But on reaching the Future Buddha they became celestial bouquets of flowers.

Then he caused a shower of weapons, in which single-edged, and double-edged swords, spears, and arrows flew smoking and flaming through the sky. But on reaching the Future Buddha they became celestial flowers.

Then he caused a shower of live coals, in which live coals as red as kimsuka flowers flew through the sky. But they scattered themselves at the Future Buddha's feet as a shower of celestial flowers.

Then he caused a shower of hot ashes, in which ashes that glowed like fire flew through the sky. But they fell at the Future Buddha's feet as sandal-wood powder.

Then he caused a shower of sand, in which very fine sand flew smoking and flaming through the sky. But it fell at the Future Buddha's feet as celestial flowers.

Then he caused a shower of mud, in which mud flew smoking and flaming through the sky. But it fell at the Future Buddha's feet as celestial ointment.

Then he caused a darkness, thinking, "By this will I frighten Siddhattha, and drive him away." And the darkness became fourfold, and very dense. But on reaching the Future Buddha it disappeared like darkness before the light of the sun.

Māra, being thus unable with these nine storms of wind, rain, rocks, weapons, live coals, hot ashes, sand, mud, and darkness, to drive away the Future Buddha, gave command to his followers, "Look ye now! Why stand ye still? Seize, kill, drive away this prince!" And, arming himself with a discus, and seated upon the shoulders of the elephant "Girded-with-mountains," he drew near the Future Buddha, and said,—

"Siddhattha, arise from this seat! It does not belong to you, but to me."

When the Great Being heard this he said,—

"Māra, you have not fulfilled the Ten Perfections in any of their three grades; nor have you made the five great donations;[1] nor have you striven for knowledge, nor for the welfare of the world, nor for enlightenment. This seat does not belong to you, but to me."

Unable to restrain his fury, the enraged Māra now hurled his

---

[1] These are the five donations great:
The gift of treasure, gift of child,
The gift of wife, of royal rule,
And last, the gift of life and limb.
From the *Abhidhānappadīpikā*, 421.

discus. But the Great Being reflected on the Ten Perfections, and the discus changed into a canopy of flowers, and remained suspended over his head. Yet they say that this keen-edged discus, when at other times Māra hurled it in anger, would cut through solid stone pillars as if they had been the tips of bamboo shoots. But on this occasion it became a canopy of flowers. Then the followers of Māra began hurling immense mountain-crags, saying, "This will make him get up from his seat and flee." But the Great Being kept his thoughts on the Ten Perfections, and the crags also became wreaths of flowers, and then fell to the ground.

Now the gods meanwhile were standing on the rim of the world, and craning their necks to look, saying,—

"Ah, woe the day! The handsome form of prince Siddhattha will surely be destroyed! What will he do to save himself?"

Then the Great Being, after his assertion that the seat which Future Buddhas had always used on the day of their complete enlightenment belonged to him, continued, and said,—

"Māra, who is witness to your having given donations?"

Said Māra, "All these, as many as you see here, are my witnesses;" and he stretched out his hand in the direction of his army. And instantly from Māra's army came a roar, "I am his witness! I am his witness!" which was like to the roar of an earthquake.

Then said Māra to the Great Being,—

"Siddhattha, who is witness to your having given donations?"

"Your witnesses," replied the Great Being, "are animate beings, and I have no animate witnesses present. However, not to mention the donations which I gave in other existences, the great seven-hundred-fold donation which I gave in my Vessantara existence shall now be testified to by the solid earth, inanimate though she be." And drawing forth his right hand from beneath his priestly robe, he stretched it out towards the mighty earth, and said, "Are you witness, or are you not, to my having given a great seven-hundred-fold donation in my Vessantara existence?"

And the mighty earth thundered, "I bear you witness!" with a hundred, a thousand, a hundred thousand roars, as if to overwhelm the army of Māra.

Now while the Great Being was thus calling to mind the donation he gave in his Vessantara existence, and saying to himself, "Siddhattha, that was a great and excellent donation which you gave," the hundred-and-fifty-league-high elephant "Girded-with-mountains" fell upon his knees before the Great Being. And the followers of Māra fled away in all directions. No two went the same way, but leaving their head-ornaments and their cloaks behind, they fled straight before them.

Then the hosts of the gods, when they saw the army of Māra flee, cried out, "Māra is defeated! Prince Siddhattha has conquered! Let us go celebrate the victory!" And the snakes egging on the snakes, the birds the birds, the deities the deities, and the Brahma-angels the Brahma-angels, they came with perfumes, garlands, and other offerings in their hands to the Great Being on the throne of wisdom. And as they came,—

> "The victory now hath this illustrious Buddha won!
> The Wicked One, the Slayer, hath defeated been!"
> Thus round the throne of wisdom shouted joyously
> The bands of snakes their songs of victory for the Sage;
>
> "The victory now hath this illustrious Buddha won!
> The Wicked One, the Slayer, hath defeated been!"
> Thus round the throne of wisdom shouted joyously
> The flocks of birds their songs of victory for the Sage;
>
> "The victory now hath this illustrious Buddha won!
> The Wicked One, the Slayer, hath defeated been!"
> Thus round the throne of wisdom shouted joyously
> The bands of gods their songs of victory for the Sage;
>
> "The victory now hath this illustrious Buddha won!
> The Wicked One, the Slayer, hath defeated been!"
> Thus round the throne of wisdom shouted joyously
> The Brahma-angels songs of victory for the Saint.

And the remaining deities, also, throughout the ten thousand worlds, made offerings of garlands, perfumes, and ointments, and in many a hymn extolled him.

It was before the sun had set that the Great Being thus vanquished the army of Māra. And then, while the Bo-tree in homage rained red, coral-like sprigs upon his priestly robes, he acquired in the first watch of the night the knowledge of previous existences; in the middle watch of the night, the divine eye; and in the last watch of the night, his intellect fathomed Dependent Origination.

Now while he was musing on the twelve terms of Dependent Origination, forwards and backwards, round and back again, the ten thousand worlds quaked twelve times, as far as to their ocean boundaries. And when the Great Being, at the dawning of the day, had thus made the ten thousand worlds thunder with his attainment of omniscience, all these worlds became most gloriously adorned. Flags and banners erected on the eastern rim of the world let their streamers fly to the western rim of the world; likewise those erected on the western rim of the world, to the eastern rim of the world; those erected on the northern rim of the world, to the southern rim of the world; and those erected on the southern rim of the world, to the northern rim of the world; while those erected on the level of the earth let theirs fly until they beat against the Brahma-world; and those of the Brahma-world let theirs hang down to the level of the earth. Throughout the ten thousand worlds the flowering trees bloomed; the fruit trees were weighted down by their burden of fruit; trunk-lotuses bloomed on the trunks of trees; branch lotuses on the branches of trees; vine-lotuses on the vines; hanging-lotuses in the sky; and stalk-lotuses burst through the rocks and came up by sevens. The system of ten thousand worlds was like a bouquet of flowers sent whirling through the air, or like a thick carpet of flowers; in the intermundane spaces the eight-thousand-league-long hells, which not even the light of seven suns had formerly been able to illumine, were now flooded with radiance; the eighty-four-thousand-league-deep ocean became sweet to the taste; the rivers checked their flowing; the blind from birth received their sight; the deaf from birth their hearing; the cripples from birth the use of their limbs; and the bonds and fetters of captives broke and fell off.

When thus he had attained to omniscience, and was the centre of such unparalleled glory and homage, and so many prodigies were happening about him, he breathed forth that solemn utterance which has never been omitted by any of The Buddhas:—

"Through birth and rebirth's endless round,
Seeking in vain, I hastened on,
To find who framed this edifice.
What misery!—birth incessantly!

"O builder! I've discovered thee!
This fabric thou shalt ne'er rebuild!
Thy rafters all are broken now,
And pointed roof demolished lies!
This mind has demolition reached,
And seen the last of all desire!"

The period of time, therefore, from the existence in the Tusita Heaven to this attainment of omniscience on the throne of wisdom, constitutes the Intermediate Epoch.

FIRST EVENTS
AFTER THE ATTAINMENT

Translated from the Mahā-Vagga, and constituting the opening sections.
Hail to that Blessed One, that Saint, and Supreme Buddha!

AT THAT time The Buddha, The Blessed One, was dwelling at Uruvelā at the foot of the Bo-tree on the banks of the river Nerañjarā, having just attained the Buddhaship. Then The Blessed One sat cross-legged for seven days together at the foot of the Bo-tree experiencing the bliss of emancipation.

Then The Blessed One, during the first watch of the night, thought over Dependent Origination both forward and back:—

On ignorance depends karma;
On karma depends consciousness;
On consciousness depend name and form;
On name and form depend the six organs of sense;
On the six organs of sense depends contact;
On contact depends sensation;
On sensation depends desire;
On desire depends attachment;
On attachment depends existence;
On existence depends birth;
On birth depend old age and death, sorrow,
    lamentation, misery, grief, and despair.

Thus does this entire aggregation of misery arise. But on the complete fading out and cessation of ignorance ceases karma; on the cessation of karma ceases consciousness; on the cessation of consciousness cease name and form; on the cessation of name and form cease the six organs of sense; on the cessation of the six organs of sense ceases contact; on the cessation of contact ceases sensation; on the cessation of sensation ceases desire; on the cessation of desire ceases attachment; on the cessation of attachment ceases existence; on the cessation of existence ceases birth; on the cessation of birth cease old age and death, sorrow, lamentation, misery, grief, and despair. Thus does this entire aggregation of misery cease.

Then The Blessed One, concerning this, on that occasion, breathed forth this solemn utterance,—

> "When to the strenuous, meditative Brahman
> There come to light the elements of being,
> Then vanish all his doubts and eager questions,
> What time he knows THE ELEMENTS HAVE CAUSES."

Then The Blessed One, during the middle watch of the night, thought over Dependent Origination both forward and back:—On ignorance depends karma. . . . Thus does this entire aggregation of misery arise. But on the complete fading out and cessation of ignorance ceases karma. . . . Thus does this entire aggregation of misery cease.

Then The Blessed One, concerning this, on that occasion, breathed forth this solemn utterance,—

> "When to the strenuous, meditative Brahman
> There come to light the elements of being,
> Then vanish all his doubts and eager questions,
> What time he knows How CAUSES HAVE AN ENDING."

Then The Blessed One, during the last watch of the night, thought over Dependent Origination both forward and back:—On ignorance depends karma. . . . Thus does this entire aggregation of misery arise. But on the complete fading out and cessation of ignorance ceases karma. . . . Thus does this entire aggregation of misery cease.

Then The Blessed One, concerning this, on that occasion, breathed forth this solemn utterance,—

> "When to the strenuous, meditative Brahman
> There come to light the elements of being,
> Then scattereth he the hordes of Māra's army;
> Like to the sun that lightens all the heavens."

End of the account of what took place under the Bo-tree.

Then The Blessed One, after the lapse of seven days, arose from that state of exalted calm, and leaving the foot of the Bo-tree, drew near to where the Ajapāla (that is, the Goat-herd's) banyan-tree was; and having drawn near, he sat cross-legged at the foot of the Ajapāla banyan-tree for seven days together, experiencing the bliss of emancipation.

Then a certain Brahman, who was of a proud and contemptuous disposition, drew near to where The Blessed One was; and having drawn near, he exchanged greetings with The Blessed One. And having passed with him the greetings of friendship and civility, he stood respectfully at one side. And standing respectfully at one side, the Brahman spoke to The Blessed One as follows:—

"Gotama, what is it constitutes a Brahman? and what are the Brahman-making qualities?"

Then The Blessed One, concerning this, on that occasion, breathed forth this solemn utterance,—

> "The Brahman who his evil traits hath banished,
> Is free from pride, is self-restrained and spotless,
> Is learnèd, and the holy life hath followed,
> 'Tis he alone may claim the name of Brahman;
> With things of earth he hath no point of contact."

> End of the account of what took place under the Ajapāla-
> tree.

Then The Blessed One, after the lapse of seven days, arose from that state of exalted calm, and leaving the foot of the Ajapāla banyan tree, drew near to where the Mucalinda tree was; and having drawn near, he sat cross-legged at the foot of the Mucalinda tree for seven days together, experiencing the bliss of emancipation.

Now at that time a great cloud appeared out of season, and for seven days it was rainy, cloudy weather, with a cold wind. Then issued Mucalinda, the serpent-king, from his abode, and enveloping the body of The Blessed One seven times with his folds, spread his great hood above his head, saying,—

"Let neither cold nor heat, nor gnats, flies, wind, sunshine, nor creeping creatures come near The Blessed One!"

Then, when seven days had elapsed, and Mucalinda, the serpent-king, knew that the storm had broken up, and that the clouds had gone, he unwound his coils from the body of The Blessed One. And changing his natural appearance into that of a young man, he stood before The Blessed One, and with his joined hands to his forehead did reverence to The Blessed One.

Then The Blessed One, concerning this, on that occasion, breathed forth this solemn utterance,—

> "How blest the happy solitude
> Of him who hears and knows the truth!
> How blest is harmlessness towards all,
> And self-restraint towards living things!
> How blest from passion to be free,
> All sensuous joys to leave behind!
> Yet far the highest bliss of all
> To quit th' illusion false—'I am.'"

End of the account of what took place under the Mucalinda-tree.

THE BUDDHA'S DAILY HABITS

Translated from the Sumaṅgala-Vilāsinī (i.45[10]), Buddhaghosa's
Commentary on the Dīgha-Nikāya

HABITS are of two kinds, the profitable, and the unprofitable. Of these, the unprofitable habits of The Blessed One had been extirpated by his attainment of saintship at the time he sat cross-legged under the Bo-tree. Profitable habits, however, remained to The Blessed One.

These were fivefold: his before-breakfast habits; his after-breakfast habits; his habits of the first watch of the night; his habits of the middle watch of the night; his habits of the last watch of the night.

His before-breakfast habits were as follows:—

The Blessed One would rise early in the morning, and when, out of kindness to his body-servant[1] and for the sake of bodily comfort, he had rinsed his mouth and otherwise cared for his person, he would sit retired until it was time to go begging. And when it came time, he would put on his tunic, girdle, and robes, and taking his bowl, he would enter the village or the town for alms. Sometimes he went alone, sometimes surrounded by a congregation of priests; sometimes without anything especial happening, sometimes with the accompaniment of many prodigies.

While, namely, the Lord of the World is entering for alms, gentle winds clear the ground before him; the clouds let fall drops of water to lay the dust in his pathway, and then become a canopy over him; other winds bring flowers and scatter them in his path; elevations of ground depress themselves, and depressions elevate themselves; wherever he places his foot, the ground is even and pleasant to walk upon, or lotus-flowers receive his tread. No sooner has he set his right foot within the city-gate than the rays of six different colors which issue from his body race hither and thither over palaces and

[1] In order to give him a chance to acquire merit by waiting on a Buddha.

pagodas, and deck them, as it were, with the yellow sheen of gold, or with the colors of a painting. The elephants, the horses, the birds, and other animals give forth melodious sounds; likewise the tom-toms, lutes, and other musical instruments, and the ornaments worn by the people.

By these tokens the people would know, "The Blessed One has now entered for alms;" and in their best tunics and best robes, with perfumes, flowers, and other offerings, they issue forth from their houses into the street. Then, having zealously paid homage to The Blessed One with the perfumes, flowers, and other offerings, and done him obeisance, some would implore him, "Reverend Sir, give us ten priests to feed;" some, "Give us twenty;" and some, "Give us a hundred priests." And they would take the bowl of The Blessed One, and prepare a seat for him, and zealously show their reverence for him by placing food in the bowl.

When he had finished his meal, The Blessed One, with due consideration for the different dispositions of their minds, would so teach them the Doctrine that some would become established in the refuges, some in the five precepts, some would become converted, some would attain to the fruit of either once returning, or of never returning, while some would become established in the highest fruit, that of saintship, and would retire from the world. Having shown this kindness to the multitude, he would rise from his seat, and return to the monastery.

On his arrival there, he would take his seat in a pavilion, on the excellent Buddha-mat which had been spread for him, where he would wait for the priests to finish their meal. When the priests had finished their meal, the body-servant would announce the fact to The Blessed One. Then The Blessed One would enter the perfumed chamber.

These, then, were his before-breakfast habits.

Then The Blessed One, having thus finished his before-breakfast duties, would first sit in the perfumed chamber, on a seat that had been spread for him by his body-servant, and would wash his feet. Then, taking up his stand on the landing of the jeweled staircase which led to the perfumed chamber, he would exhort the congregation of the priests, saying,—

"O priests, diligently work out your salvation; for not often occur the appearance of a Buddha in the world and existence among men and the propitious moment and retirement from the world and the opportunity to hear the true Doctrine."

At this point some would ask The Blessed One for exercises in meditation, and The Blessed One would assign them exercises suited to their several characters. Then all would do obeisance to The Blessed One, and go to the places where they were in the habit of spending the night or the day—some to the forest, some to the foot of trees, some to the hills, and so on, some to the heaven of the Four Great Kings, . . . and some to Vasavatti's heaven.

Then The Blessed One, entering the perfumed chamber, would, if he wished, lie down for a while, mindful and conscious, and on his right side after the manner of a lion. And secondly, his body being now refreshed, he would rise, and gaze over the world. And thirdly, the people of the village or town near which he might be dwelling, who had given him breakfast, would assemble after breakfast at the monastery, again in their best tunics and their best robes, and with perfumes, flowers, and other offerings.

Thereupon The Blessed One, when his audience had assembled, would approach in such miraculous manner as was fitting; and taking his seat in the lecture-hall, on the excellent Buddha-mat which had been spread for him, he would teach the Doctrine, as suited the time and occasion. And when he perceived it was time, he would dismiss the audience, and the people would do obeisance to The Blessed One, and depart.

These were his after-breakfast habits.

When he had thus finished his after-breakfast duties, he would rise from the excellent Buddha-seat, and if he desired to bathe, he would enter the bath-house, and cool his limbs with water made ready by his body-servant. Then the body-servant would fetch the Buddha-seat, and spread it in the perfumed chamber. And The Blessed One, putting on a tunic of double red cloth, and binding on his girdle, and throwing his upper robe over his right shoulder, would go thither and sit down, and for a while remain solitary, and plunged in meditation. After that would come the priests from here and from there to wait on The Blessed One. And some would propound questions, some would ask for exercises in meditation, and some for a sermon; and in granting their desires The Blessed One would complete the first watch of the night.

These were his habits of the first watch of the night.

And now, when The Blessed One had finished his duties of the first watch of the night, and when the priests had done him obeisance and were departing, the deities throughout the entire system of ten thousand worlds would seize the opportunity to draw near to The Blessed One and ask him any questions that might occur to them, even such as were but four syllables long. And The Blessed One in answering their questions would complete the middle watch of the night.

These were his habits of the middle watch of the night.

The last watch of the night he would divide into three parts, and as his body would be tired from so much sitting since the morning, he would spend one part in pacing up and down to free himself from the discomfort. In the second part he would enter the perfumed chamber, and would lie down mindful and conscious, and on his right side after the manner of a lion. In the third part he would rise, and taking his seat, he would gaze over the world with the eye of a Buddha, in order to discover any individual who, under some former Buddha, with alms-giving, or keeping the precepts, or other meritorious deeds, might have made the earnest wish.

These were his habits of the last watch of the night.

THE DEATH OF THE BUDDHA

Translated from the Mahā-Parinibbāna-Sutta (v. and vi.) of the Dīgha-Nikāya

THEN The Blessed One addressed the venerable Ananda:—"Let us go hence, Ananda. To the further bank of the Hiraññavatī river, and to the city of Kusinārā and the sal-tree grove Upavattana of the Mallas will we draw near."

"Yes, Reverend Sir," said the venerable Ananda to The Blessed One in assent.

Then The Blessed One, accompanied by a large congregation of priests, drew near to the further bank of the Hiraññavatī river, and to the city of Kusinārā and the sal-tree grove Upavattana of the Mallas; and having drawn near, he addressed the venerable Ananda:—

"Be so good, Ananda, as to spread me a couch with its head to the north between twin sal-trees. I am weary, Ananda, and wish to lie down."

"Yes, Reverend Sir," said the venerable Ananda to The Blessed One in assent, and spread the couch with its head to the north between twin sal-trees. Then The Blessed One lay down on his right side after the manner of a lion, and placing foot on foot, remained mindful and conscious.

Now at that time the twin sal-trees had completely burst forth into bloom, though it was not the flowering season; and the blossoms scattered themselves over the body of The Tathāgata,[1] and strewed and sprinkled themselves in worship of The Tathāgata. Also heavenly Erythrina flowers fell from the sky; and these scattered themselves over the body of The Tathāgata, and strewed and sprin-

[1] Tathāgata is a term most commonly used by The Buddha in referring to himself. Its meaning, like that of its Jaina equivalent *Tatthagaya*, possibly is, "He who has arrived there (*tatra* or *tattha*), *i.e.* to emancipation *or* Nirvana." See "Sacred Books of the East," vol. xiii., p. 82. [Chalmers, "Journal of the Royal Asiatic Society," 1898, p. 113, takes it as "One who has come at the real truth."]

kled themselves in worship of The Tathāgata. Also heavenly sandal-wood powder fell from the sky; and this scattered itself over the body of The Tathāgata, and strewed and sprinkled itself in worship of The Tathāgata. And music sounded in the sky in worship of The Tathāgata, and heavenly choruses were heard to sing in worship of The Tathāgata.

Then The Blessed One addressed the venerable Ananda:—

"The twin sal-trees, Ananda, have completely burst forth into bloom, though it is not the flowering season; and the blossoms have scattered themselves over the body of The Tathāgata, and have strewn and sprinkled themselves in worship of The Tathāgata. Also heavenly Erythrina flowers have fallen from the sky; and these have scattered themselves over the body of The Tathāgata, and have strewn and sprinkled themselves in worship of The Tathāgata. Also heavenly sandal-wood powder has fallen from the sky; and this has scattered itself over the body of The Tathāgata, and has strewn and sprinkled itself in worship of The Tathāgata. Also music is sounding in the sky in worship of The Tathāgata, and heavenly choruses are heard to sing in worship of The Tathāgata. But it is not by all this, Ananda, that The Tathāgata is honored, esteemed, revered, worshiped, or venerated; but the priest, Ananda, or the priestess, or the lay disciple, or the female lay disciple, who shall fulfil all the greater and lesser duties, conducting himself with propriety and in accordance with the precepts, by him is The Tathāgata honored, esteemed, revered, and worshiped with the best of worship. Accordingly, Ananda, train yourselves, and fulfil all the greater and lesser duties, and conduct yourselves with propriety and in accordance with the precepts."

Now at that time the venerable Upavāna was standing in front of The Blessed One, and fanning him. Then The Blessed One was harsh to the venerable Upavāna, saying,—

"Step aside, O priest; stand not in front of me."

Then it occurred to the venerable Ananda as follows:—

"Here, this venerable Upavāna has for a long time been the body-servant of The Blessed One, and kept himself at his beck and call; yet, although his last moments are near, The Blessed One is harsh to the venerable Upavāna, saying, 'Step aside, O priest; stand not in front of me.' What, pray, was the reason, and what was the cause, that The Blessed One was harsh to the venerable Upavāna, saying, 'Step aside, O priest; stand not in front of me'?"

Then the venerable Ananda spoke to The Blessed One as follows:—

"Reverend Sir, here this venerable Upavāna has for a long time been the body-servant of The Blessed One, and kept himself at his beck and call; yet, although his last moments are near, The Blessed One is harsh to the venerable Upavāna, saying, 'Step aside, O priest; stand not in front of me.' Reverend Sir, what, pray, was the reason, and what was the cause, that The Blessed One was harsh to the venerable Upavāna, saying, 'Step aside, O priest; stand not in front of me'?"

"Ananda, almost all the deities throughout ten worlds have come together to behold The Tathāgata. For an extent, Ananda, of twelve leagues about the city Kusinārā and the sal-tree grove Upavattana of the Mallas, there is not a spot of ground large enough to stick the point of a hair into, that is not pervaded by powerful deities. And these deities, Ananda, are angered, saying, 'From afar have we come to behold The Tathāgata, for but seldom, and on rare occasions, does a Tathāgata, a saint, and Supreme Buddha arise in the world; and now, to-night, in the last watch, will The Tathāgata pass into Nirvana; but this powerful priest stands in front of The Blessed One, concealing him, and we have no chance to see The Tathāgata, although his last moments are near.' Thus, Ananda, are these deities angered."

"What are the deities doing, Reverend Sir, whom The Blessed One perceives?"

"Some of the deities, Ananda, are in the air with their minds engrossed by earthly things, and they let fly their hair and cry aloud, and stretch out their arms and cry aloud, and fall headlong to the ground and roll to and fro, saying, 'All too soon will The Blessed One pass into Nirvana; all too soon will The Happy One pass into Nirvana; all too soon will The Light of the World vanish from sight!' Some of the deities, Ananda, are on the earth with their minds engrossed by earthly things, and they let fly their hair and cry aloud, and stretch out their arms and cry aloud, and fall headlong

on the ground and roll to and fro, saying, 'All too soon will The
Blessed One pass into Nirvana; all too soon will The Happy One
pass into Nirvana; all too soon will The Light of the World vanish
from sight.' But those deities which are free from passion, mindful
and conscious, bear it patiently, saying, 'Transitory are all things.
How is it possible [that whatever has been born, has come into being,
and is organized and perishable, should not perish? That condition is not possible.]'"

. . . .

Then the venerable Ananda entered the monastery, and, leaning
against the bolt of the door, he wept, saying,—

"Behold, I am but a learner and not yet perfect, and my Teacher
is on the point of passing into Nirvana, he who was so compassionate to me."

Then The Blessed One addressed the priests:—

"Where, O priests, is Ananda?"

"Reverend Sir, the venerable Ananda has entered the monastery,
and leaning against the bolt of the door, he weeps, saying, 'Behold,
I am but a learner, and not yet perfect, and my Teacher is on the
point of passing into Nirvana, he who was so compassionate to me.'"

Then The Blessed One addressed a certain priest, saying,—

"Go, O priest, and say to the venerable Ananda from me, 'The
Teacher calleth thee, brother Ananda.'"

"Yes, Reverend Sir," said the priest to The Blessed One in assent,
and drew near to where the venerable Ananda was; and having
drawn near, he spoke to the venerable Ananda as follows:—

"The Teacher calleth thee, brother Ananda."

"Yes, brother," said the venerable Ananda to the priest in assent,
and drew near to where The Blessed One was; and having drawn
near and greeted The Blessed One, he sat down respectfully at one
side. And the venerable Ananda being seated respectfully at one
side, The Blessed One spoke to him as follows:—

"Enough, Ananda, do not grieve, nor weep. Have I not already
told you, Ananda, that it is in the very nature of all things near and
dear unto us that we must divide ourselves from them, leave them,
sever ourselves from them? How is it possible, Ananda, that what-

ever has been born, has come into being, is organized and perishable, should not perish? That condition is not possible. For a long time, Ananda, have you waited on The Tathāgata with a kind, devoted, cheerful, single-hearted, unstinted service of body, with a kind, devoted, cheerful, single-hearted, unstinted service of voice, with a kind, devoted, cheerful, single-hearted, unstinted service of mind. You have acquired much merit, Ananda; exert yourself, and soon will you be free from all depravity."

Then The Blessed One addressed the priests:—

"Priests, of all those Blessed Ones who aforetime were saints and Supreme Buddhas, all had their favorite body-servants, just as I have now my Ananda. And, priests, of all those Blessed Ones who in the future shall be saints and Supreme Buddhas, all will have their favorite body-servants, just as I have now my Ananda. Wise, O priests, is Ananda—he knows when it is a fit time to draw near to see The Tathāgata, whether for the priests, for the priestesses, for the lay disciples, for the female lay disciples, for the king, for the king's courtiers, for the leaders of heretical sects, or for their adherents.

"Ananda, O priests, has four wonderful and marvellous qualities. And what are the four? O priests, if an assembly of priests draw near to behold Ananda, it is delighted with beholding him; and if then Ananda hold a discourse on the Doctrine, it is also delighted with the discourse; and when Ananda, O priests, ceases to speak, the assembly of priests is still unsated. O priests, if an assembly of priestesses . . . an assembly of lay disciples . . . an assembly of female lay disciples draw near to behold Ananda, it is delighted with beholding him; and if then Ananda hold a discourse on the Doctrine, it is also delighted with the discourse; and when Ananda, O priests, ceases to speak, the assembly of female lay disciples is still unsated.

"A Universal Monarch, O priests, has four wonderful and marvellous qualities. And what are the four? O priests, if an assembly of men of the warrior caste . . . an assembly of men of the Brahman caste . . . an assembly of householders . . . an assembly of monks draw near to behold the Universal Monarch, it is delighted with beholding him; and if then the Universal Monarch hold a discourse, it is also delighted with the discourse; and when the Universal

Monarch, O priests, ceases to speak, the assembly of monks is still unsated.

"In exactly the same way, O priests, Ananda has four wonderful and marvellous qualities. O priests, if an assembly of priests . . . an assembly of priestesses . . . an assembly of lay disciples . . . an assembly of female lay disciples draw near to behold Ananda, it is delighted with beholding him; and if then Ananda hold a discourse on the Doctrine, it is also delighted with the discourse; and when Ananda, O priests, ceases to speak, the assembly of female lay dis- ciples is still unsated. These, O priests, are the four wonderful and marvellous qualities possessed by Ananda."

When The Blessed One had thus spoken, the venerable Ananda spoke to him as follows:—

"Reverend Sir, let not The Blessed One pass into Nirvana in this wattel-and-daub town, this town of the jungle, this branch village. For there are other great cities, Reverend Sir, to wit, Campā, Rāja- gaha, Sāvatthi, Sāketa, Kosambī, and Benares. Let The Blessed One pass into Nirvana in one of them. In them are many wealthy men of the warrior caste, many wealthy men of the Brahman caste, and many wealthy householders who are firm believers in The Tathā- gata, and they will perform the funeral rites for The Tathāgata."

"O Ananda, say not so! O Ananda, say not so, that this is a wattel- and-daub town, a town of the jungle, a branch village. There was once, Ananda, a king called Sudassana the Great, who was a Uni- versal Monarch, a virtuous king of justice, a victorious ruler of the four quarters of the earth, possessing a secure dominion over his territory, and owning the seven precious gems.[2] This city Kusinārā, Ananda, was the capital of king Sudassana the Great, and had then the name of Kusāvatī. From the east to the west it was twelve leagues in length, and from the north to the south it was seven leagues in breadth. Kusāvatī, the capital, Ananda, was prosperous and flourishing, populous and thronging with people, and well pro- vided with food. As Alakamandā, the capital of the gods, Ananda, is prosperous and flourishing, populous and thronging with gods, and is well provided with food, in exactly the same way, Ananda,

---

[2] The wheel of empire, the elephant, the horse, the gem, the empress, the treasurer, and the crown-prince.

Kusāvatī, the capital, was prosperous and flourishing, populous and thronging with people, and well provided with food. Kusāvatī, the capital, Ananda, was neither by day nor night without the ten noises,—to wit, the noise of elephants, the noise of horses, the noise of chariots, the noise of drums, the noise of tabors, the noise of lutes, the noise of song, the noise of cymbals, the noise of gongs, and the tenth noise of people crying, 'Eat ye, and drink!'

"Go thou, Ananda, and enter the city Kusinārā, and announce to the Kusinārā-Mallas:—

"'To-night, O ye Vāsetthas, in the last watch, The Tathāgata will pass into Nirvana. Be favorable, be favorable, O ye Vāsetthas, and suffer not that afterwards ye feel remorse, saying, "The Tathāgata passed into Nirvana while in our borders, but we did not avail ourselves of the opportunity of being present at the last moments of The Tathāgata.'"

"Yes, Reverend Sir," said the venerable Ananda to The Blessed One in assent; and putting on his tunic, and taking his bowl and his robes, he went to Kusinārā with another member of the Order.

Now at that time the Kusinārā-Mallas were assembled together in the town-hall on some matter of business. And the venerable Ananda drew near to the town-hall of the Kusinārā-Mallas; and having drawn near, he made announcement to the Kusinārā-Mallas, as follows:—

"To-night, O ye Vasetthas, in the last watch, The Tathāgata will pass into Nirvana. Be favorable, be favorable, O ye Vasetthas, and suffer not that afterwards ye feel remorse, saying, "The Tathāgata passed into Nirvana while in our borders, but we did not avail ourselves of the opportunity of being present at the last moments of The Tathāgata.'"

The Mallas, on hearing this speech of the venerable Ananda, and their children and their daughters-in-law and their wives were grieved and sorrowful and overwhelmed with anguish of mind, and some let fly their hair and cried aloud, and stretched out their arms and cried aloud, and fell headlong to the ground and rolled to and fro, saying, "All too soon will The Blessed One pass into Nirvana; all too soon will The Happy One pass into Nirvana; all too soon will The Light of the World vanish from sight." Then the Mallas and their children and their daughters-in-law and their wives, being grieved and sorrowful and overwhelmed with anguish of mind, drew near to the sal-tree grove Upavattana of the Mallas, and to where the venerable Ananda was.

Then it occurred to the venerable Ananda as follows:—

"If I shall cause the Kusinārā-Mallas one by one to do reverence to The Blessed One, the day will dawn ere they have finished. What if now I marshal the Mallas by families, and cause them by families to do reverence to The Blessed One, and say, 'Reverend Sir, a Malla named so-and-so, with his children, his wife, his following, and his friends, bows low in reverence at the feet of The Blessed One.'"

And the venerable Ananda marshalled the Mallas by families, and caused them by families to do reverence to The Blessed One, saying, "Reverend Sir, a Malla named so-and-so, with his children, his wife, his following, and his friends, bows low in reverence at the feet of The Blessed One." And the venerable Ananda by this device succeeded in causing all the Kusinārā-Mallas to do reverence to The Blessed One before the end of the first watch of the night.

Now at that time Subhadda, a wandering ascetic, was dwelling at Kusinārā. And Subhadda, the wandering ascetic, heard the report:—

"To-night, in the last watch, the monk Gotama will pass into Nirvana."

Then it occurred to Subhadda, the wandering ascetic, as follows:—

"I have heard wandering ascetics, that were old men, advanced in years, teachers, and teachers' teachers, declare, 'But seldom, and on rare occasions, does a Tathāgata, a saint, and Supreme Buddha arise in the world.' And to-night in the last watch, the monk Gotama will pass into Nirvana. And a certain question has arisen in my mind, and I am persuaded of the monk Gotama that he can so teach me the Doctrine that I shall be relieved of this my doubt."

Then Subhadda, the wandering ascetic, drew near to the sal-tree grove Upavattana of the Mallas, and to where the venerable Ananda was, and having drawn near, he spoke to the venerable Ananda as follows:—

"Ananda, I have heard wandering ascetics, that were old men, advanced in years, teachers, and teachers' teachers, declare, 'But seldom, and on rare occasions, does a Tathāgata, a saint, and Supreme Buddha arise in the world.' And to-night, in the last watch, the monk Gotama will pass into Nirvana. And a certain doubt has arisen in my mind, and I am persuaded of the monk Gotama that he can so teach me the Doctrine that I shall be relieved of this my doubt. Let me, then, Ananda, have an opportunity of seeing the monk Gotama."

When Subhadda, the wandering ascetic, had so spoken, the venerable Ananda spoke to him as follows:—

"Enough of that, brother Subhadda; trouble not The Tathāgata. The Blessed One is weary."

And a second time Subhadda, the wandering ascetic, . . .

And a third time Subhadda, the wandering ascetic, spoke to the venerable Ananda as follows:—

"Ananda, I have heard wandering ascetics, old men, advanced in years, teachers, and teachers' teachers, when they said, 'But seldom, and on rare occasions, does a Tathāgata, a saint, and Supreme Buddha arise in the world.' And to-night, in the last watch, the monk Gotama will pass into Nirvana. And a certain doubt has arisen in my mind, and I am persuaded of the monk Gotama that he can so teach me the Doctrine that I shall be relieved of this my doubt. Let me, then, Ananda, have an opportunity of seeing the monk Gotama."

And a third time the venerable Ananda spoke to Subhadda, the wandering ascetic, as follows:—

"Enough of that, brother Subhadda; trouble not The Tathāgata. The Blessed One is weary."

Now The Blessed One chanced to hear the conversation between the venerable Ananda and the wandering ascetic Subhadda. And The Blessed One called to the venerable Ananda:—

"Enough, Ananda; hinder not Subhadda. Let Subhadda, Ananda, have an opportunity of beholding The Tathāgata. Whatever Subhadda shall ask of me, he will ask for the sake of information, and not for the sake of troubling me, and he will quickly understand my answers to his questions."

Then the venerable Ananda spoke to Subhadda, the wandering ascetic, as follows:—

"You may come, brother Subhadda; The Blessed One grants you an audience."

Then Subhadda, the wandering ascetic, drew near to where The Blessed One was; and having drawn near, he exchanged greetings with The Blessed One; and having passed with him the greetings of friendship and civility, he sat down respectfully at one side. And seated respectfully at one side, Subhadda, the wandering ascetic, spoke to The Blessed One as follows:—

"Gotama, all those monks and Brahmans who possess a large following and crowds of hearers and disciples, and who are distinguished, renowned leaders of sects, and highly esteemed by the multitudes,—to wit, Pūrana Kassapa, Makkhali Gosāla, Ajita Kesakambali, Pakudha Kaccāyana, Sañjaya Belatthiputta, Nigantha Nāthaputta,—have they all done as they maintain, discovered the truth, or have they not? or have some of them done so, and others not?"

"Enough, O Subhadda, let us leave the question, 'Have they all done as they maintain, discovered the truth, or have they not? or have some of them done so, and others not?' The Doctrine will I teach you, Subhadda. Listen to me, and pay strict attention, and I will speak."

"Yes, Reverend Sir," said Subhadda, the wandering ascetic, to The Blessed One in assent. And The Blessed One spoke as follows:—

"Subhadda, in whatever doctrine and discipline the noble eightfold path is not found, therein also is not found the monk of the first degree, nor the monk of the second degree, nor the monk of the third degree, nor the monk of the fourth degree; and in whatever doctrine and discipline, O Subhadda, the noble eightfold path is found, therein also are found the monk of the first degree, and the monk of the second degree, and the monk of the third degree, and the monk of the fourth degree. Now in this Doctrine and Discipline, O Subhadda, the noble eightfold path is found: and therein alone, O Subhadda, are found the monk of the first degree, and the monk of the second degree, and the monk of the third degree, and the monk of the fourth degree. Destitute of true monks are all other creeds. But let these my priests, O Subhadda, live rightly, and the world will not be destitute of saints.

"What time my age was twenty-nine, Subhadda,
I left the world to seek the summum bonum.
Now fifty years and more have passed, Subhadda,
Since I renounced the world and lived ascetic
Within the Doctrine's pale, that rule of conduct
Outside of which no genuine monk existeth,

nor the monk of the second degree, nor the monk of the third degree, nor the monk of the fourth degree. Destitute of monks are all other creeds. But let these my priests, O Subhadda, live rightly, and the world will not be destitute of saints."

When The Blessed One had thus spoken, Subhadda, the wandering ascetic, spoke to him as follows:—

"O wonderful is it, Reverend Sir! O wonderful is it, Reverend Sir! It is as if, Reverend Sir, one were to set up that which was overturned, or were to disclose that which was hidden, or were to point out the way to a lost traveller, or were to carry a lamp into a dark place that they who had eyes might see forms. Even so has The Blessed One expounded the Doctrine in many different ways. Reverend Sir, I betake myself to The Blessed One for refuge, to the Doctrine, and to the Congregation of the priests. Suffer me to retire from the world under The Blessed One; suffer me to receive ordination."

"Subhadda, any one who aforetime has been an adherent of another sect and afterwards desires to retire from the world and receive ordination under this Doctrine and Discipline, must first spend four months on probation, and after the lapse of four months, strenuous-minded priests receive him into the Order and confer on him the priestly ordination. Nevertheless, in this matter of probation I recognize a difference in persons."

"Reverend Sir, if all they who aforetime have been adherents of other sects and afterwards desire to retire from the world and receive ordination under this Doctrine and Discipline, must first spend four months on probation, and after the lapse of four months strenuous-minded priests receive them into the Order, and confer on them the priestly ordination, then am I ready to spend four years on probation, and after the lapse of four years, let strenuous-minded priests receive me into the Order and confer on me the priestly ordination."

Then The Blessed One said to the venerable Ananda,

"Well, then, Ananda, receive Subhadda into the Order."

"Yes, Reverend Sir," said the venerable Ananda to The Blessed One in assent.

Then Subhadda, the wandering ascetic, spoke to the venerable Ananda as follows:—

"How fortunate you priests are, brother Ananda! How supremely fortunate, brother Ananda, that you all have been sprinkled with the sprinkling of discipleship at the hands of The Teacher himself."

And Subhadda, the wandering ascetic, retired from the world under The Blessed One, and received ordination. And without delay, after he had received ordination, the venerable Subhadda began to live solitary and retired, vigilant, strenuous, and zealous; and in no long time, and while yet alive, he came to learn for himself, and to realize, and to live in the possession of that highest good to which the holy life conducts, and for the sake of which youths of good family so nobly retire from the household life to the houseless one. And he knew that for him rebirth was exhausted, that he had lived the holy life, that he had done what it behooved him to do, and that he was no more for this world. So the venerable Subhadda became of the number of the saints, and he was the last disciple made by The Blessed One himself.

End of the Hiraññavatī Recitation, which is the Fifth.

Then The Blessed One addressed the venerable Ananda:—

"It may be, Ananda, that some of you will think, 'The word of The Teacher is a thing of the past; we have now no Teacher.' But that, Ananda, is not the correct view. The Doctrine and Discipline, Ananda, which I have taught and enjoined upon you is to be your teacher when I am gone. But whereas now, Ananda, all the priests address each other with the title of 'brother,' not so must they address each other after I am gone. A senior priest, Ananda, is to address a junior priest either by his given name, or by his family name, or by the title of 'brother;' a junior priest is to address a senior priest with the title 'reverend sir,' or 'venerable.' If the Order, Ananda, wish to do so, after I am gone they may abrogate all the lesser and minor precepts. On Channa, Ananda, after I am gone, the higher penalty is to be inflicted."

"Reverend Sir, what is this higher penalty?"

"Let Channa, Ananda, say what he likes, he is not to be spoken to nor admonished nor instructed by the priests."

Then The Blessed One addressed the priests:—

"It may be, O priests, that some priest has a doubt or perplexity respecting either The Buddha or the Doctrine or the Order or the Path or the course of conduct. Ask any questions, O priests, and suffer not that afterwards ye feel remorse, saying, 'Our Teacher was present with us, but we failed to ask him all our questions.'"

When he had so spoken, the priests remained silent.

And a second time The Blessed One, and a third time The Blessed One addressed the priests:—

"It may be, O priests, that some priest has a doubt or perplexity respecting either The Buddha or the Doctrine or the Order or the Path or the course of conduct. Ask any questions, O priests, and suffer not that afterwards ye feel remorse, saying, 'Our Teacher was present with us, but we failed to ask him all our questions.'"

And a third time the priests remained silent.

Then The Blessed One addressed the priests:—

"It may be, O priests, that it is out of respect to The Teacher that ye ask no questions. Then let each one speak to his friend."

And when he had thus spoken, the priests remained silent.

Then the venerable Ananda spoke to The Blessed One as follows:—

"It is wonderful, Reverend Sir! It is marvellous, Reverend Sir! Reverend Sir, I have faith to believe that in this congregation of priests not a single priest has a doubt or perplexity respecting either The Buddha or the Doctrine or the Order or the Path or the course of conduct."

"With you, Ananda, it is a matter of faith, when you say that; but with the Tathāgata, Ananda, it is a matter of knowledge that in this congregation of priests not a single priest has a doubt or perplexity respecting either The Buddha or the Doctrine or the Order or the Path or the course of conduct. For of all these five hundred priests, Ananda, the most backward one has become converted, and is not liable to pass into a lower state of existence, but is destined necessarily to attain supreme wisdom."

Then The Blessed One addressed the priests:—

"And now, O priests, I take my leave of you; all the constituents of being are transitory; work out your salvation with diligence."

And this was the last word of The Tathāgata.

Thereupon The Blessed One entered the first trance; and rising from the first trance, he entered the second trance; and rising from the second trance, he entered the third trance; and rising from the third trance, he entered the fourth trance; and rising from the fourth trance, he entered the realm of the infinity of space; and rising from the realm of the infinity of space, he entered the realm of the infinity of consciousness; and rising from the realm of the infinity of consciousness, he entered the realm of nothingness; and rising from the realm of nothingness, he entered the realm of neither perception nor yet non-perception; and rising from the realm of neither perception nor yet non-perception, he arrived at the cessation of perception and sensation.

Thereupon the venerable Ananda spoke to the venerable Anuruddha as follows:—

"Reverend Anuruddha, The Blessed One has passed into Nirvana."

"Nay, brother Ananda, The Blessed One has not passed into Nirvana; he has arrived at the cessation of perception and sensation."

Thereupon The Blessed One rising from the cessation of his perception and sensation, entered the realm of neither perception nor yet non-perception; and rising from the realm of neither perception nor yet non-perception, he entered the realm of nothingness; and rising from the realm of nothingness, he entered the realm of the infinity of consciousness; and rising from the realm of the infinity of consciousness, he entered the realm of the infinity of space; and rising from the realm of the infinity of space, he entered the fourth trance; and rising from the fourth trance, he entered the third trance; and rising from the third trance, he entered the second trance; and rising from the second trance, he entered the first trance; and rising from the first trance, he entered the second trance; and rising from the second trance, he entered the third trance; and rising from the third trance, he entered the fourth trance; and rising from the fourth trance, immediately The Blessed One passed into Nirvana.

BUDDHIST WRITINGS

II. THE DOCTRINE

QUESTIONS WHICH TEND NOT TO EDIFICATION

Translated from the Majjhima-Nikāya, and constituting Sutta 63

THUS have I heard.

On a certain occasion The Blessed One was dwelling at Sāvatthi in Jetavana monastery in Anāthapindika's Park. Now it happened to the venerable Māluṅkyāputta, being in seclusion and plunged in meditation, that a consideration presented itself to his mind, as follows:—

"These theories which The Blessed One has left unelucidated, has set aside and rejected,—that the world is eternal, that the world is not eternal, that the world is finite, that the world is infinite, that the soul and the body are identical, that the soul is one thing and the body another, that the saint exists after death, that the saint does not exist after death, that the saint both exists and does not exist after death, that the saint neither exists nor does not exist after death,— these The Blessed One does not elucidate to me. And the fact that The Blessed One does not elucidate them to me does not please me nor suit me. Therefore I will draw near to The Blessed One and inquire of him concerning this matter. If The Blessed One will elucidate to me, either that the world is eternal, or that the world is not eternal, or that the world is finite, or that the world is infinite, or that the soul and the body are identical, or that the soul is one thing and the body another, or that the saint exists after death, or that the saint does not exist after death, or that the saint both exists and does not exist after death, or that the saint neither exists nor does not exist after death, in that case will I lead the religious life under The Blessed One. If The Blessed One will not elucidate to me, either that the world is eternal, or that the world is not eternal, . . . or that the saint neither exists nor does not exist after death, in that case will I abandon religious training and return to the lower life of a layman."

Then the venerable Māluñkyāputta arose at eventide from his seclusion, and drew near to where The Blessed One was; and having drawn near and greeted The Blessed One, he sat down respectfully at one side. And seated respectfully at one side, the venerable Māluñkyāputta spoke to The Blessed One as follows:—

"Reverend Sir, it happened to me, as I was just now in seclusion and plunged in meditation, that a consideration presented itself to my mind; as follows: 'These theories which The Blessed One has left unelucidated, has set aside and rejected,—that the world is eternal, that the world is not eternal, . . . that the saint neither exists nor does not exist after death,—these The Blessed One does not elucidate to me. And the fact that The Blessed One does not elucidate them to me does not please me nor suit me. I will draw near to The Blessed One and inquire of him concerning this matter. If The Blessed One will elucidate to me, either that the world is eternal, or that the world is not eternal, . . . or that the saint neither exists nor does not exist after death, in that case will I lead the religious life under The Blessed One. If The Blessed One will not elucidate to me, either that the world is eternal, or that the world is not eternal, . . . or that the saint neither exists nor does not exist after death, in that case will I abandon religious training and return to the lower life of a layman.'

"If The Blessed One knows that the world is eternal, let The Blessed One elucidate to me that the world is eternal; if The Blessed One knows that the world is not eternal, let The Blessed One elucidate to me that the world is not eternal. If The Blessed One does not know either that the world is eternal or that the world is not eternal, the only upright thing for one who does not know, or who has not that insight, is to say, 'I do not know; I have not that insight.'

"If The Blessed One knows that the world is finite, . . .'

"If The Blessed One knows that the soul and the body are identical, . . .'

"If The Blessed One knows that the saint exists after death, . . .'

"If The Blessed One knows that the saint both exists and does not exist after death, let The Blessed One elucidate to me that the saint both exists and does not exist after death; if The Blessed One knows that the saint neither exists nor does not exist after death, let The Blessed One elucidate to me that the saint neither exists nor does not exist after death. If The Blessed One does not know either that the saint both exists and does not exist after death, or that the saint neither exists nor does not exist after death, the only upright thing for one who does not know, or who has not that insight, is to say, 'I do not know; I have not that insight.'"

"Pray, Māluñkyāputta, did I ever say to you, 'Come, Māluñkyā-putta, lead the religious life under me, and I will elucidate to you either that the world is eternal, or that the world is not eternal, . . . or that the saint neither exists nor does not exist after death'?"

"Nay, verily, Reverend Sir."

"Or did you ever say to me, 'Reverend Sir, I will lead the religious life under The Blessed One, on condition that The Blessed One elucidate to me either that the world is eternal, or that the world is not eternal, . . . or that the saint neither exists nor does not exist after death'?"

"Nay, verily, Reverend Sir."

"So you acknowledged, Māluñkyāputta, that I have not said to you, 'Come, Māluñkyāputta, lead the religious life under me and I will elucidate to you either that the world is eternal, or that the world is not eternal, . . . or that the saint neither exists nor does not exist after death;' and again that you have not said to me, 'Reverend Sir, I will lead the religious life under The Blessed One, on condition that The Blessed One elucidate to me either that the world is eternal, or that the world is not eternal, . . . or that the saint neither exists nor does not exist after death.' That being the case, vain man, whom are you so angrily denouncing?

"Māluñkyāputta, any one who should say, 'I will not lead the religious life under The Blessed One until The Blessed One shall elucidate to me either that the world is eternal, or that the world is not eternal, . . . or that the saint neither exists nor does not exist after death;'—that person would die, Māluñkyāputta, before The Tathāgata had ever elucidated this to him.

"It is as if, Māluñkyāputta, a man had been wounded by an arrow thickly smeared with poison, and his friends and companions, his

relatives and kinsfolk, were to procure for him a physician or sur-
geon; and the sick man were to say, 'I will not have this arrow taken
out until I have learnt whether the man who wounded me belonged
to the warrior caste, or to the Brahman caste, or to the agricultural
caste, or to the menial caste.'

"Or again he were to say, 'I will not have this arrow taken out
until I have learnt the name of the man who wounded me, and to
what clan he belongs.'

"Or again he were to say, 'I will not have this arrow taken out
until I have learnt whether the man who wounded me was tall, or
short, or of the middle height.'

"Or again he were to say, 'I will not have this arrow taken out
until I have learnt whether the man who wounded me was black,
or dusky, or of a yellow skin.'

"Or again he were to say, 'I will not have this arrow taken out
until I have learnt whether the man who wounded me was from
this or that village, or town, or city.'

"Or again he were to say, 'I will not have this arrow taken out
until I have learnt whether the bow which wounded me was a
cāpa, or a kodanda.'

"Or again he were to say, 'I will not have this arrow taken out
until I have learnt whether the bow-string which wounded me was
made from swallow-wort, or bamboo, or sinew, or maruva, or from
milk-weed.'

"Or again he were to say, 'I will not have this arrow taken out
until I have learnt whether the shaft which wounded me was a
kaccha or a ropima.'

"Or again he were to say, 'I will not have this arrow taken out
until I have learnt whether the shaft which wounded me was feath-
ered from the wings of a vulture, or of a heron, or of a falcon, or
of a peacock, or of a sithilahanu.'

"Or again he were to say, 'I will not have this arrow taken out
until I have learnt whether the shaft which wounded me was
wound round with the sinews of an ox, or of a buffalo, or of a ruru
deer, or of a monkey.'

"Or again he were to say, 'I will not have this arrow taken out
until I have learnt whether the arrow which wounded me was an

ordinary arrow, or a claw-headed arrow, or a vekanda, or an iron arrow, or a calf-tooth arrow, or a karavīrapatta.' That man would die, Māluṅkyāputta, without ever having learnt this. In exactly the same way, Māluṅkyāputta, any one who should say, 'I will not lead the religious life under The Blessed One until The Blessed One shall elucidate to me either that the world is eternal, or that the world is not eternal, . . . or that the saint neither exists nor does not exist after death;'—that person would die, Māluṅkyāputta, before The Tathāgata had ever elucidated this to him.

"The religious life, Māluṅkyāputta, does not depend on the dogma that the world is eternal; nor does the religious life, Māluṅkyāputta, depend on the dogma that the world is not eternal. Whether the dogma obtain, Māluṅkyāputta, that the world is eternal, or that the world is not eternal, there still remain birth, old age, death, sorrow, lamentation, misery, grief, and despair, for the extinction of which in the present life I am prescribing.

"The religious life, Māluṅkyāputta, does not depend on the dogma that the world is finite; . . .

"The religious life, Māluṅkyāputta, does not depend on the dogma that the soul and the body are identical; . . .

"The religious life, Māluṅkyāputta, does not depend on the dogma that the saint exists after death; . . .

"The religious life, Māluṅkyāputta, does not depend on the dogma that the saint both exists and does not exist after death; nor does the religious life, Māluṅkyāputta, depend on the dogma that the saint neither exists nor does not exist after death. Whether the dogma obtain, Māluṅkyāputta, that the saint both exists and does not exist after death, or that the saint neither exists nor does not exist after death, there still remain birth, old age, death, sorrow, lamentation, misery, grief, and despair, for the extinction of which in the present life I am prescribing.

"Accordingly, Māluṅkyāputta, bear always in mind what it is that I have not elucidated, and what it is that I have elucidated. And what, Māluṅkyāputta, have I not elucidated? I have not elucidated, Māluṅkyāputta, that the world is eternal; I have not elucidated that the world is not eternal; I have not elucidated that the world is finite; I have not elucidated that the world is infinite; I have not elucidated that the soul and the body are identical; I have not elucidated that the soul is one thing and the body another; I have not elucidated that the saint exists after death; I have not elucidated that the saint does not exist after death; I have not elucidated that the saint both exists and does not exist after death; I have not elucidated that the saint neither exists nor does not exist after death. And why, Māluṅkyāputta, have I not elucidated this? Because, Māluṅkyāputta, this profits not, nor has to do with the fundamentals of religion, nor tends to aversion, absence of passion, cessation, quiescence, the supernatural faculties, supreme wisdom, and Nirvana; therefore have I not elucidated it.

"And what, Māluṅkyāputta, have I elucidated? Misery, Māluṅkyāputta, have I elucidated; the origin of misery have I elucidated; the cessation of misery have I elucidated; and the path leading to the cessation of misery have I elucidated. And why, Māluṅkyāputta, have I elucidated this? Because, Māluṅkyāputta, this does profit, has to do with the fundamentals of religion, and tends to aversion, absence of passion, cessation, quiescence, knowledge, supreme wisdom, and Nirvana; therefore have I elucidated it. Accordingly, Māluṅkyāputta, bear always in mind what it is that I have not elucidated, and what it is that I have elucidated."

Thus spake The Blessed One; and, delighted, the venerable Māluṅkyāputta applauded the speech of The Blessed One.

The Lesser Māluṅkyāputta Sermon.

THERE IS NO EGO

1. Translated from the Milindapañha (25[1])

THEN drew near Milinda the king to where the venerable Nāgasena was; and having drawn near he greeted the venerable Nāgasena; and having passed the compliments of friendship and civility, he sat down respectfully at one side. And the venerable Nāgasena returned the greeting; by which, verily, he won the heart of king Milinda.

And Milinda the king spoke to the venerable Nāgasena as follows:—

"How is your reverence called? Bhante, what is your name?"

"Your majesty, I am called Nāgasena; my fellow-priests, your majesty, address me as Nāgasena: but whether parents give one the name Nāgasena, or Sūrasena, or Vīrasena, or Sīhasena, it is, nevertheless, your majesty, but a way of counting, a term, an appellation, a convenient designation, a mere name, this Nāgasena; for there is no Ego here to be found."

Then said Milinda the king,—

"Listen to me, my lords, ye five hundred Yonakas, and ye eighty thousand priests! Nāgasena here says thus: 'There is no Ego here to be found.' Is it possible, pray, for me to assent to what he says?"

And Milinda the king spoke to the venerable Nāgasena as follows:—

"Bhante Nāgasena, if there is no Ego to be found, who is it then furnishes you priests with the priestly requisites,—robes, food, bedding, and medicine, the reliance of the sick? who is it makes use of the same? who is it keeps the precepts? who is it applies himself to meditation? who is it realizes the Paths, the Fruits, and Nirvana? who is it destroys life? who is it takes what is not given him? who is it commits immorality? who is it tells lies? who is it drinks intoxicating liquor? who is it commits the five crimes that constitute

653

'proximate karma?'[1] In that case, there is no merit; there is no demerit; there is no one who does or causes to be done meritorious or demeritorious deeds; neither good nor evil deeds can have any fruit or result. Bhante Nāgasena, neither is he a murderer who kills a priest, nor can you priests, bhante Nāgasena, have any teacher, preceptor, or ordination. When you say, 'My fellow-priests, your majesty, address me as Nāgasena,' what then is this Nāgasena? Pray, bhante, is the hair of the head Nāgasena?"

"Nay, verily, your majesty."

"Is the hair of the body Nāgasena?"

"Nay, verily, your majesty."

"Are nails . . . teeth . . . skin . . . flesh . . . sinews . . . bones . . . marrow of the bones . . . kidneys . . . heart . . . liver . . . pleura . . . spleen . . . lungs . . . intestines . . . mesentery . . . stomach . . . faeces . . . bile . . . phlegm . . . pus . . . blood . . . sweat . . . fan . . . tears . . . lymph . . . saliva . . . snot . . . synovial fluid . . . urine . . . brain of the head Nāgasena?"

"Nay, verily, your majesty."

"Is now, bhante, form Nāgasena?"

"Nay, verily, your majesty."

"Is sensation Nāgasena?"

"Nay, verily, your majesty."

"Is perception Nāgasena?"

"Nay, verily, your majesty."

"Are the predispositions Nāgasena?"

"Nay, verily, your majesty."

"Is consciousness Nāgasena?"

"Nay, verily, your majesty."

"Are, then, bhante, form, sensation, perception, the predispositions, and consciousness unitedly Nāgasena?"

[1] Translated from the Sārasaṅgaha, as quoted in Trenckner's note to this passage: "By *proximate karma* is meant karma that ripens in the next existence. To show what this is, I [the author of the Sārasaṅgaha] give the following passage from the Atthānasutta of the first book of the Aṅguttara-Nikāya:—'It is an impossibility, O priests, the case can never occur, that an individual imbued with the correct doctrine should deprive his mother of life, should deprive his father of life, should deprive a saint of life, should in a revengeful spirit cause a bloody wound to a Tathāgata, should cause a schism in the church. This is an impossibility.'"

"Nay, verily, your majesty."

"Is it, then, bhante, something besides form, sensation, perception, the predispositions, and consciousness, which is Nāgasena?"

"Nay, verily, your majesty."

"Bhante, although I question you very closely, I fail to discover any Nāgasena. Verily, now bhante, Nāgasena is a mere empty sound. What Nāgasena is there here? Bhante, you speak a falsehood, a lie: there is no Nāgasena."

Then the venerable Nāgasena spoke to Milinda the king as follows:—

"Your majesty, you are a delicate prince, an exceedingly delicate prince; and if, your majesty, you walk in the middle of the day on hot sandy ground, and you tread on rough grit, gravel, and sand, your feet become sore, your body tired, the mind is oppressed, and the body-consciousness suffers. Pray, did you come afoot, or riding?"

"Bhante, I do not go afoot: I came in a chariot."

"Your majesty, if you came in a chariot, declare to me the chariot. Pray, your majesty, is the pole the chariot?"

"Nay, verily, bhante."

"Is the axle the chariot?"

"Nay, verily, bhante."

"Are the wheels the chariot?"

"Nay, verily, bhante."

"Is the chariot-body the chariot?"

"Nay, verily, bhante."

"Is the banner-staff the chariot?"

"Nay, verily, bhante."

"Is the yoke the chariot?"

"Nay, verily, bhante."

"Are the reins the chariot?"

"Nay, verily, bhante."

"Is the goading-stick the chariot?"

"Nay, verily, bhante."

"Pray, your majesty, are pole, axle, wheels, chariot-body, banner-staff, yoke, reins, and goad unitedly the chariot?"

"Nay, verily, bhante."

"Is it, then, your majesty, something else besides pole, axle, wheels, chariot-body, banner-staff, yoke, reins and goad which is the chariot?"

"Nay, verily, bhante."

"Your majesty, although I question you very closely, I fail to discover any chariot. Verily now, your majesty, the word chariot is a mere empty sound. What chariot is there here? Your majesty, you speak a falsehood, a lie: there is no chariot. Your majesty, you are the chief king in all the continent of India; of whom are you afraid that you speak a lie? Listen to me, my lords, ye five hundred Yonakas, and ye eighty thousand priests! Milinda the king here says thus: 'I came in a chariot;' and being requested, 'Your majesty, if you came in a chariot, declare to me the chariot,' he fails to produce any chariot. Is it possible, pray, for me to assent to what he says?"

When he had thus spoken, the five hundred Yonakas applauded the venerable Nāgasena and spoke to Milinda the king as follows:—

"Now, your majesty, answer, if you can."

Then Milinda the king spoke to the venerable Nāgasena as follows:—

"Bhante Nāgasena, I speak no lie: the word 'chariot' is but a way of counting, term, appellation, convenient designation, and name for pole, axle, wheels, chariot-body, and banner-staff."

"Thoroughly well, your majesty, do you understand a chariot. In exactly the same way, your majesty, in respect of me, Nāgasena is but a way of counting, term, appellation, convenient designation, mere name for the hair of my head, hair of my body . . . brain of the head, form, sensation, perception, the predispositions, and consciousness. But in the absolute sense there is no Ego here to be found. And the priestess Vajirā, your majesty, said as follows in the presence of The Beloved One:—

" 'Even as the word of "chariot" means
That members join to frame a whole;
So when the Groups appear to view,
We use the phrase, "A living being.²" ' "

"It is wonderful, bhante Nāgasena! It is marvellous, bhante Nāgasena! Brilliant and prompt is the wit of your replies. If The

² That is, "a living entity."

Buddha were alive, he would applaud. Well done, well done, Nāgasena! Brilliant and prompt is the wit of your replies."

2. Translated from the Visuddhi-Magga (chap. xviii)

Just as the word "chariot" is but a mode of expression for axle,
wheels, chariot-body, pole, and other constituent members, placed
in a certain relation to each other, but when we come to examine the
members one by one, we discover that in the absolute sense there
is no chariot; and just as the word "house" is but a mode of expression for wood and other constituents of a house, surrounding space
in a certain relation, but in the absolute sense there is no house;
and just as the word "fist" is but a mode of expression for the fingers,
the thumb, etc., in a certain relation; and the word "lute" for the
body of the lute, strings, etc.; "army" for elephants, horses, etc.;
"city" for fortifications, houses, gates, etc.; "tree" for trunk, branches,
foliage, etc., in a certain relation, but when we come to examine the
parts one by one, we discover that in the absolute sense there is no
tree; in exactly the same way the words "living entity" and "Ego,"
are but a mode of expression for the presence of the five attachment
groups, but when we come to examine the elements of being one by
one, we discover that in the absolute sense there is no living entity
there to form a basis for such figments as "I am," or "I"; in other
words, that in the absolute sense there is only name and form. The
insight of him who perceives this is called knowledge of the truth.

He, however, who abandons this knowledge of the truth and
believes in a living entity must assume either that this living entity
will perish or that it will not perish. If he assume that it will not
perish, he falls into the heresy of the persistence of existences; or if
he assume that it will perish, he falls into that of the annihilation of
existences. And why do I say so? Because, just as sour cream has
milk as its antecedent, so nothing here exists but what has its own
antecedents. To say, "The living entity persists," is to fall short of
the truth; to say, "It is annihilated," is to outrun the truth. Therefore has The Blessed One said:—

"There are two heresies, O priests, which possess both gods and
men, by which some fall short of the truth, and some outrun the
truth; but the intelligent know the truth.

"And how, O priests, do some fall short of the truth?

"O priests, gods and men delight in existence, take pleasure in existence, rejoice in existence, so that when the Doctrine for the cessation of existence is preached to them, their minds do not leap toward it, are not favorably disposed toward it, do not rest in it, do not adopt it.

"Thus, O priests, do some fall short of the truth."

"And how, O priests, do some outrun the truth?

"Some are distressed at, ashamed of, and loathe existence, and welcome the thought of non-existence, saying, 'See here! When they say that on the dissolution of the body this Ego is annihilated, perishes, and does not exist after death, that is good, that is excellent, that is as it should be.'

"Thus, O priests, do some outrun the truth.

"And how, O priests, do the intelligent know the truth?

"We may have, O priests, a priest who knows things as they really are, and knowing things as they really are, he is on the road to aversion for things, to absence of passion for them, and to cessation from them.

"Thus, O priests, do the intelligent know the truth."

3. Translated from the Mahā-Nidāna-Sutta (256[21]) of the Dīgha-Nikāya

"In regard to the Ego, Ananda, what are the views held concerning it?

"In regard to the Ego, Ananda, either one holds the view that sensation is the Ego, saying, 'Sensation is my Ego;'

"Or, in regard to the Ego, Ananda, one holds the view, 'Verily, sensation is not my Ego; my Ego has no sensation;'

"Or, in regard to the Ego, Ananda, one holds the view, 'Verily, neither is sensation my Ego, nor does my Ego have no sensation. My Ego has sensation; my Ego possesses the faculty of sensation.'

"In the above case, Ananda, where it is said, 'Sensation is my Ego,' reply should be made as follows: 'Brother, there are three sensations: the pleasant sensation, the unpleasant sensation, and the indifferent sensation. Which of these three sensations do you hold to be the Ego?'

"Whenever, Ananda, a person experiences a pleasant sensation, he does not at the same time experience an unpleasant sensation, nor does he experience an indifferent sensation; only the pleasant sensation does he then feel. Whenever, Ananda, a person experiences an unpleasant sensation, he does not at the same time experience a pleasant sensation, nor does he experience an indifferent sensation; only the unpleasant sensation does he then feel. Whenever, Ananda, a person experiences an indifferent sensation, he does not at the same time experience a pleasant sensation, nor does he experience an unpleasant sensation; only the indifferent sensation does he then feel.

"Now pleasant sensations, Ananda, are transitory, are due to causes, originate by dependence, and are subject to decay, disappearance, effacement, and cessation; and unpleasant sensations, Ananda, are transitory, are due to causes, originate by dependence, and are subject to decay, disappearance, effacement, and cessation; and indifferent sensations, Ananda, are transitory, are due to causes, originate by dependence, and are subject to decay, disappearance, effacement, and cessation. While this person is experiencing a pleasant sensation, he thinks, 'This is my Ego.' And after the cessation of this same pleasant sensation, he thinks, 'My Ego has passed away.' While he is experiencing an unpleasant sensation, he thinks, 'This is my Ego.' And after the cessation of this same unpleasant sensation, he thinks, 'My Ego has passed away.' And while he is experiencing an indifferent sensation, he thinks, 'This is my Ego.' And after the cessation of this same indifferent sensation, he thinks, 'My Ego has passed away.' So that he who says, 'Sensation is my Ego,' holds the view that even during his lifetime his Ego is transitory, that it is pleasant, unpleasant, or mixed, and that it is subject to rise and disappearance.

"Accordingly, Ananda, it is not possible to hold the view, 'Sensation is my Ego.'

"In the above case, Ananda, where it is said, 'Verily sensation is not my Ego; my Ego has no sensation,' reply should be made as follows: 'But, brother, where there is no sensation, is there any "I am"?' "

"Nay, verily, Reverend Sir."

"Accordingly, Ananda, it is not possible to hold the view, 'Verily, sensation is not my Ego; my Ego has no sensation.'

"In the above case, Ananda, where it is said, 'Verily, neither is sensation my Ego, nor does my Ego have no sensation. My Ego has sensation; my Ego possesses the faculty of sensation,' reply should be made as follows: 'Suppose, brother, that utterly and completely, and without remainder, all sensation were to cease—if there were nowhere any sensation, pray, would there be anything, after the cessation of sensation, of which it could be said, "This am I"?'"

"Nay, verily, Reverend Sir."

"Accordingly, Ananda, it is not possible to hold the view, 'Verily, neither is sensation my Ego, nor does my Ego have no sensation. My Ego has sensation; my Ego possesses the faculty of sensation.'

"From the time, Ananda, a priest no longer holds the view that sensation is the Ego, no longer holds the view that the Ego has no sensation, no longer holds the view that the Ego has sensation, possesses the faculty of sensation, he ceases to attach himself to anything in the world, and being free from attachment, he is never agitated, and being never agitated, he attains to Nirvana in his own person; and he knows that rebirth is exhausted, that he has lived the holy life, that he has done what it behooved him to do, and that he is no more for this world.

"Now it is impossible, Ananda, that to a mind so freed a priest should attribute the heresy that the saint exists after death, or that the saint does not exist after death, or that the saint both exists and does not exist after death, or that the saint neither exists nor does not exist after death.

"And why do I say so?

"Because, Ananda, after a priest has been freed by a thorough comprehension of affirmation and affirmation's range, of predication and predication's range, of declaration and declaration's range, of knowledge and knowledge's field of action, of rebirth and what rebirth affects, it is impossible for him to attribute such a heretical lack of knowledge and perception to a priest similarly freed."

THE MIDDLE DOCTRINE

1. Translated from the Samyutta-Nikāya (xxii. 90[16])

THE world, for the most part, O Kaccāna, holds either to a belief in being or to a belief in non-being. But for one who in the light of the highest knowledge, O Kaccāna, considers how the world arises, belief in the non-being of the world passes away. And for one who in the light of the highest knowledge, O Kaccāna, considers how the world ceases, belief in the being of the world passes away. The world, O Kaccāna, is for the most part bound up in a seeking, attachment, and proclivity [for the groups], but a priest does not sympáthize with this seeking and attachment, nor with the mental affirmation, proclivity, and prejudice which affirms an Ego. He does not doubt or question that it is only evil that springs into existence, and only evil that ceases from existence, and his conviction of this fact is dependent on no one besides himself. This, O Kaccāna, is what constitutes Right Belief.

That things have being, O Kaccāna, constitutes one extreme of doctrine; that things have no being is the other extreme. These extremes, O Kaccāna, have been avoided by The Tathāgata, and it is a middle doctrine he teaches:—

On ignorance depends karma;
On karma depends consciousness;
On consciousness depend name and form;
On name and form depend the six organs of sense;
On the six organs of sense depends contact;
On contact depends sensation;
On sensation depends desire;
On desire depends attachment;
On attachment depends existence;
On existence depends birth;
On birth depend old age and death, sorrow, lamentation, misery, grief, and despair. Thus does this entire aggregation of misery arise.

But on the complete fading out and cessation of ignorance ceases Karma;

On the cessation of karma ceases consciousness;
On the cessation of consciousness cease name and form;
On the cessation of name and form cease the six organs of sense;
On the cessation of the six organs of sense ceases contact;
On the cessation of contact ceases sensation;
On the cessation of sensation ceases desire;
On the cessation of desire ceases attachment;
On the cessation of attachment ceases existence;
On the cessation of existence ceases birth;
On the cessation of birth cease old age and death, sorrow, lamentation, misery, grief, and despair. Thus does this entire aggregation of misery cease.

2.　Translated from the Samyutta-Nikāya (xii. 35[1])

Thus have I heard.

On a certain occasion The Blessed One was dwelling at Sāvatthi in Jetavana monastery in Anāthapindika's Park. And there The Blessed One addressed the priests.

"Priests," said he.

"Lord," said the priests to The Blessed One in reply.

And The Blessed One spoke as follows:

"O priests, on ignorance depends karma; . . . Thus does this entire aggregation of misery arise."

"Reverend Sir, what are old age and death? and what is it has old age and death?"

"The question is not rightly put," said The Blessed One. "O priest to say: 'What are old age and death? and what is it has old age and death?' and to say: 'Old age and death are one thing, but it is another thing which has old age and death,' is to say the same thing in different ways. If, O priest, the dogma obtain that the soul and the body are identical, then there is no religious life; or if, O priest, the dogma obtain that the soul is one thing and the body another, then also there is no religious life. Both these extremes, O priest, have been avoided by The Tathāgata, and it is a middle doctrine he teaches: 'On birth depend old age and death.' "

"Reverend Sir, what is birth? and what is it has birth?"

"The question is not rightly put," said The Blessed One. "O priest, to say: 'What is birth? and what is it has birth?' and to say: 'Birth is one thing, but it is another thing which has birth,' is to say the same thing in different ways. If, O priest, the dogma obtain that the soul and the body are identical, then there is no religious life; or if, O priest, the dogma obtain that the soul is one thing and the body another, then also there is no religious life. Both these extremes, O priest, have been avoided by The Tathāgata, and it is a middle doctrine he teaches: 'On existence depends birth.'"

"Reverend Sir, what is existence? . . . attachment? . . . desire? . . . sensation? . . . contact? . . . the six organs of sense? . . . name and form? . . . consciousness? . . . karma? and what is it has karma?"

"The question is not rightly put," said The Blessed One. "O priest, to say: 'What is karma? and what is it has karma?' and to say: 'Karma is one thing, but it is another thing which has karma,' is to say the same thing in different ways. If, O priest, the dogma obtain that the soul and the body are identical, then there is no religious life; or if, O priest, the dogma obtain that the soul is one thing and the body another, then also there is no religious life. Both these extremes, O priest, have been avoided by The Tathāgata, and it is a middle doctrine he teaches: 'On ignorance depends karma.'

"But on the complete fading out and cessation of ignorance, O priest, all these refuges, puppet-shows, resorts, and writhings,—to wit: What are old age and death? and what is it has old age and death? or, old age and death are one thing, but it is another thing which has old age and death; or, the soul and the body are identical, or the soul is one thing, and the body another,—all such refuges of whatever kind are abandoned, uprooted, pulled out of the ground like a palmyra-tree, and become non-existent and not liable to spring up again in the future.

"But on the complete fading out and cessation of ignorance, O priest, all these refuges, puppet-shows, resorts, and writhings,—to wit: What is birth? . . . existence? . . . attachment? . . . desire? . . . sensation? . . . contact? . . . the six organs of sense? . . . name and form? . . . consciousness? . . . karma? and what is it has karma? or, karma is one thing, but it is another thing which has karma; or, the soul and the body are identical, or the soul is one thing and the body another,—all such refuges are abandoned, uprooted, pulled out of the ground like a palmyra-tree, and become non-existent and not liable to spring up again in the future."

3. Translated from the Visuddhi-Magga (chap. xvii.)

Inasmuch as it is dependently on each other and in unison and simultaneously that the factors which constitute dependence originate the elements of being, therefore did The Sage call these factors Dependent Origination.

For the ignorance etc. which have been enumerated as constituting dependence, when they originate any of the elements of being, namely, karma and the rest, can only do so when dependent on each other and in case none of their number is lacking. Therefore it is dependently on each other and in unison and simultaneously that the factors which constitute dependence originate the elements of being, not by a part of their number nor by one succeeding the other. Accordingly The Sage, skilful in the art of discovering the signification of things, calls this dependence by the name of Dependent Origination.

And in so doing, by the first of these two words is shown the falsity of such heresies as that of the persistence of existences, and by the second word, a rejection of such heresies as that existences cease to be, while by both together is shown the truth.

By the first:—The word "Dependent," as exhibiting a full complement of dependence and inasmuch as the elements of being are subject to that full complement of dependence, shows an avoidance of such heresies as that of the persistence of existences, the heresies, namely, of the persistence of existences, of uncaused existences, of existences due to an overruling power, of self-determining existences. For what have persistent existences, uncaused existences, etc., to do with a full complement of dependence?

By the second word:—The word "Origination," as exhibiting an origination of the elements of being and inasmuch as the elements of being originate by means of a full complement of dependence, shows a rejection of such heresies as that of the annihilation of existences, the heresies, namely, of the annihilation of existences, of nihilism, of the inefficacy of karma. For if the elements of being are continually originating by means of an antecedent dependence, whence can we have annihilation of existence, nihilism, and an inefficacy of karma?

By both together:—By the complete phrase "Dependent Origination," inasmuch as such and such elements of being come into existence by means of an unbroken series of their full complement of dependence, the truth, or middle course, is shown. This rejects the heresy that he who experiences the fruit of the deed is the same as the one who performed the deed, and also rejects the converse one that he who experiences the fruit of a deed is different from the one who performed the deed, and leaning not to either of these popular hypotheses, holds fast by nominalism.

KARMA

Translated from the Visuddhi-Magga (chap. xvii.)

THE kinds of karma are those already briefly mentioned, as consisting of the triplet beginning with meritorious karma and the triplet beginning with bodily karma, making six in all.

To give them here in full, however, meritorious karma consists of the eight meritorious thoughts which belong to the realm of sensual pleasure and show themselves in alms-giving, keeping the precepts, etc., and of the five meritorious thoughts which belong to the realm of form and show themselves in ecstatic meditation,— making thirteen thoughts; demeritorious karma consists of the twelve demeritorious thoughts which show themselves in the taking of life, etc.; and karma leading to immovability consists of the four meritorious thoughts which belong to the realm of formlessness and show themselves in ecstatic meditation. Accordingly these three karmas consist of twenty-nine thoughts.

As regards the other three, bodily karma consists of the thoughts of the body, vocal karma of the thoughts of the voice, mental karma of the thoughts of the mind. The object of this triplet is to show the avenues by which meritorious karma, etc., show themselves at the moment of the initiation of karma.

For bodily karma consists of an even score of thoughts, namely, of the eight meritorious thoughts which belong to the realm of sensual pleasure and of the twelve demeritorious ones. These by exciting gestures show themselves through the avenue of the body.

Vocal karma is when these same thoughts by exciting speech show themselves through the avenue of the voice. The thoughts, however, which belong to the realm of form, are not included, as they do not form a dependence for subsequent consciousness. And the case is the same with the thoughts which belong to the realm of formlessness. Therefore they also are to be excluded from the dependence of consciousness. However, all depend on ignorance.

Mental karma, however, consists of all the twenty-nine thoughts, when they spring up in the mind without exciting either gesture or speech.

Thus, when it is said that ignorance is the dependence of the karma-triplet consisting of meritorious karma, etc., it is to be understood that the other triplet is also included.

But it may be asked, "How can we tell that these karmas are dependent on ignorance?" Because they exist when ignorance exists.

For, when a person has not abandoned the want of knowledge concerning misery, etc., which is called ignorance, then by that want of knowledge concerning misery and concerning anteriority, etc., he seizes on the misery of the round of rebirth with the idea that it is happiness and hence begins to perform the threefold karma which is its cause; by that want of knowledge concerning the origin of misery and by being under the impression that thus happiness is secured, he begins to perform karma that ministers to desire, though such karma is really the cause of misery; and by that want of knowledge concerning cessation and the path and under the impression that some particular form of existence will prove to be the cessation of misery, although it really is not so, or that sacrifices, alarming the gods by the greatness of his austerities, and other like procedures are the way to cessation, although they are not such a way, he begins to perform the threefold karma.

Moreover, through this non-abandonment of ignorance in respect of the Four Truths, he does not know the fruition of meritorious karma to be the misery it really is, seeing that it is completely overwhelmed with the calamities, birth, old age, disease, death, etc.; and so to obtain it he begins to perform meritorious karma in its three divisions of bodily, vocal, and mental karma, just as a man in love with a heavenly nymph will throw himself down a precipice. When he does not perceive that at the end of that meritorious fruition considered to be such happiness comes the agonizing misery of change and disappointment, he begins to perform the meritorious karma above described, just as a locust will fly into the flame of a lamp, or a man that is greedy after honey will lick the honey-smeared edge of a knife. When he fails to perceive the calamities due to sensual gratification and its fruition, and, being under the impression that sensuality is happiness, lives enthralled by his passions, he then begins to perform demeritorious karma through the three avenues, just as a child will play with filth, or one who wishes to die will eat poison. When he does not perceive the misery of the change that takes place in the constituents of being, even in the realm of formlessness, but has a perverse belief in persistence, etc., he begins to perform mental karma that leads to immovability, just as a man who has lost his way will go after a mirage.

As, therefore, karma exists when ignorance exists but not when it does not exist, it is to be understood that this karma depends on ignorance. And it has been said as follows:

"O priests, the ignorant, uninstructed man performs meritorious karma, demeritorious karma, and karma leading to immovability. But whenever, O priests, he abandons his ignorance and acquires wisdom, he through the fading out of ignorance and the coming into being of wisdom does not even perform meritorious karma."

FRUITFUL AND BARREN
KARMA

1. Translated from the Añguttara-Nikāya (iii. 33¹).

[I. FRUITFUL KARMA]

THERE are three conditions, O priests, under which deeds are produced. And what are the three? Covetousness is a condition under which deeds are produced; hatred is a condition under which deeds are produced; infatuation is a condition under which deeds are produced.

When a man's deeds, O priests, are performed through covetousness, arise from covetousness, are occasioned by covetousness, originate in covetousness, wherever his personality may be, there those deeds ripen, and wherever they ripen, there he experiences the fruition of those deeds, be it in the present life, or in some subsequent one.

When a man's deeds, O priests, are performed through hatred, . . . are performed through infatuation, arise from infatuation, are occasioned by infatuation, originate in infatuation, wherever his personality may be, there those deeds ripen, and wherever they ripen, there he experiences the fruition of those deeds, be it in the present life, or in some subsequent one.

It is like seed, O priests, that is uninjured, undecayed, unharmed by wind or heat, and is sound, and advantageously sown in a fertile field on well-prepared soil; if then rain falls in due season, then, O priests, will that seed attain to growth, increase, and development. In exactly the same way, O priests, when a man's deeds are performed through covetousness, arise from covetousness, are occasioned by covetousness, originate in covetousness, wherever his personality may be, there those deeds ripen, and wherever they ripen, there he experiences the fruition of those deeds, be it in the present life, or in some subsequent one; when a man's deeds are performed through hatred, . . . are performed through infatuation, arise from infatuation, are occasioned by infatuation, originate in infatuation, wherever his personality may be, there those deeds ripen, and wherever they ripen, there he experiences the fruition of those deeds, be it in the present life, or in some subsequent one.

These, O priests, are the three conditions under which deeds are produced.

[II. Barren Karma]

There are three conditions, O priests, under which deeds are produced. And what are the three? Freedom from covetousness is a condition under which deeds are produced; freedom from hatred is a condition under which deeds are produced; freedom from infatuation is a condition under which deeds are produced.

When a man's deeds, O priests, are performed without covetousness, arise without covetousness, are occasioned without covetousness, originate without covetousness, then, inasmuch as covetousness is gone, those deeds are abandoned, uprooted, pulled out of the ground like a palmyra-tree, and become non-existent and not liable to spring up again in the future.

When a man's deeds, O priests, are performed without hatred, . . . are performed without infatuation, arise without infatuation, are occasioned without infatuation, originate without infatuation, then, inasmuch as infatuation is gone, those deeds are abandoned, uprooted, pulled out of the ground like a palmyra-tree, and become non-existent and not liable to spring up again in the future.

It is like seed, O priests, that is uninjured, undecayed, unharmed by wind or heat, and is sound, and advantageously sown; if some one then burn it with fire and reduce it to soot, and having reduced it to soot were then to scatter it to the winds, or throw it into a swift-flowing river, then, O priests, will that seed be abandoned, uprooted, pulled out of the ground like a palmyra-tree, and become non-existent and not liable to spring up again in the future. In exactly the same way, O priests, when a man's deeds are performed without covetousness, arise without covetousness, are occasioned without covetousness, originate without covetousness, then, inasmuch as covetousness is gone, those deeds are abandoned, uprooted, pulled out of the ground like a palmyra-tree, and become non-existent and not liable to spring up again in the future; when a man's deeds are performed without hatred, . . . without infatuation, arise without infatuation, are occasioned without infatuation, originate without infatuation, then, inasmuch as infatuation is gone, those deeds are abandoned, uprooted, pulled out of the ground like a palmyra-tree, and become non-existent and not liable to spring up again in the future.

These, O priests, are the three conditions under which deeds are produced.

> A wise priest knows he now must reap
> The fruits of deeds of former births.
> For be they many or but few,
> Deeds done in cov'tousness or hate,
> Or through infatuation's power,
> Must bear their needful consequence.
> Hence not to cov'tousness, nor hate,
> Nor to infatuation's power
> The wise priest yields, but knowledge seeks
> And leaves the way to punishment.

2. Translated from the Aṅguttara-Nikāya (iii. 99[1])

"O priests, if any one says that a man must reap according to his deeds, in that case, O priests, there is no religious life, nor is any opportunity afforded for the entire extinction of misery. But if any one says, O priests, that the reward a man reaps accords with his deeds, in that case, O priests, there is a religious life, and opportunity is afforded for the entire extinction of misery.

"We may have the case, O priests, of an individual who does some slight deed of wickedness which brings him to hell, or, again. O priests, we may have the case of another individual who does the same slight deed of wickedness, and expiates it in the present life, though it may be in a way which appears to him not slight but grievous.

"What kind of individual, O priests, is he whose slight deed of wickedness brings him to hell?—Whenever, O priests, an individual is not proficient in the management of his body, is not proficient in the precepts, is not proficient in concentration, is not proficient in wisdom, and is limited and bounded, and abides in what is finite and evil: such an individual, O priests, is he whose slight deed of wickedness brings him to hell.

"What kind of individual, O priests, is he who does the same slight deed of wickedness, and expiates it in the present life, though it may be in a way which appears to him not slight but grievous?—Whenever, O priests, an individual is proficient in the management of his body, is proficient in the precepts, is proficient in concentration, is proficient in wisdom, and is not limited, nor bounded, and abides in the universal: such an individual, O priests, is he who does the same slight deed of wickedness, and expiates it in the present life, though it may be in a way which appears to him not slight but grievous.

"It is as if, O priests, a man were to put a lump of salt into a small cup of water. What think ye, O priests? Would now the small amount of water in this cup be made salt and undrinkable by the lump of salt?"

"Yes, Reverend Sir."

"And why?"

"Because, Reverend Sir, there was but a small amount of water in the cup, and so it was made salt and undrinkable by the lump of salt."

"It is as if, O priests, a man were to throw a lump of salt into the river Ganges. What think ye, O priests? Would now the river Ganges be made salt and undrinkable by the lump of salt?"

"Nay, verily, Reverend Sir."

"And why not?"

"Because, Reverend Sir, the mass of water in the river Ganges is great, and so is not made salt and undrinkable by the lump of salt."

"In exactly the same way, O priests, we may have the case of an individual who does some slight deed of wickedness which brings him to hell; or, again, O priests, we may have the case of another individual who does the same slight deed of wickedness, and expiates it in the present life, though it may be in a way which appears to him not slight but grievous.

[Repetition of paragraphs 3 and 4, above.]

"We may have, O priests, the case of one who is cast into prison for a half-penny, for a penny, or for a hundred pence; or, again, O priests, we may have the case of one who is not cast into prison for a half-penny, for a penny, or for a hundred pence.

"Who, O priests, is cast into prison for a half-penny, for a penny, or for a hundred pence?

"Whenever, O priests, any one is poor, needy, and indigent: he, O priests, is cast into prison for a half-penny, for a penny, or for a hundred pence.

"Who, O priests, is not cast into prison for a half-penny, for a penny, or for a hundred pence?

"Whenever, O priests, any one is rich, wealthy, and affluent: he, O priests, is not cast into prison for a half-penny, for a penny, or for a hundred pence.

"In exactly the same way, O priests, we may have the case of an individual who does some slight deed of wickedness which brings him to hell; or, again, O priests, we may have the case of another individual who does the same slight deed of wickedness, and expiates it in the present life, though it may be in a way which appears to him not slight but grievous.

[Repetition of paragraphs 3 and 4, above.]

"Just as, O priests, a butcher and killer of rams will smite one man if he steal a ram, and will bind him, and burn him, and wreak his pleasure on him; and another who steals a ram, he will not attack, nor bind him, nor burn him, nor wreak his pleasure on him.

"Who is he, O priests, whom a butcher and killer of rams will smite if he steal a ram, and will bind him, and burn him, and wreak his pleasure on him?

"Whenever, O priests, the robber is poor, needy, and indigent: him, O priests, a butcher and killer of rams will smite if he steal a ram, and will bind him, and burn him, and wreak his pleasure on him.

"Who is he, O priests, whom a butcher and killer of rams will not smite if he steal a ram, nor bind him, nor burn him, nor wreak his pleasure on him?

"Whenever, O priests, the robber is rich, wealthy, and affluent, a king, or a king's minister: him, O priests, a butcher and killer of rams will not smite if he steal a ram, nor bind him, nor burn him, nor wreak his pleasure on him. On the contrary, he will stretch out his joined palms, and make supplication, saying, 'Sir, give me the ram, or the price of the ram.'

"In exactly the same way, O priests, we may have the case of an individual who does some slight deed of wickedness which brings him to hell; or, again, O priests, we may have the case of another individual who does the same slight deed of wickedness, and expiates it in the present life, though it may be in a way which appears to him not slight but grievous.

[Repetition of paragraphs 3 and 4, above.]

"O priests, if any one were to say that a man must reap according to his deeds, in that case, O priests, there is no religious life, nor is any opportunity afforded for the entire extinction of misery. But if any one says, O priests, that the reward a man reaps accords with his deeds, in that case, O priests, there is a religious life, and opportunity is afforded for the entire extinction of misery."

GOOD AND BAD KARMA

Translated from the Samyutta-Nikāya (iii. 2. 10[1])

THUS have I heard.

On a certain occasion The Blessed One was dwelling at Sāvatthi in Jetavana monastery in Anāthapindika's Park.

Then drew near king Pasenadi the Kosalan, at an unusual time of day, to where The Blessed One was; and having drawn near and greeted The Blessed One, he sat down respectfully at one side. And king Pasenadi the Kosalan being seated respectfully at one side, The Blessed One spoke to him as follows:

"Pray, whence have you come, great king, at this unusual time of day?"

"Reverend Sir, a householder who was treasurer in Sāvatthi has just died leaving no son, and I have come from transferring his property to my royal palace; and, Reverend Sir, he had ten million pieces of gold, and silver beyond all reckoning. But this householder, Reverend Sir, would eat sour gruel and kanājaka, and the clothes he wore were made of hemp . . . , and the conveyance in which he rode was a broken-down chariot with an umbrella of leaves."

"Even so, great king! Even so, great king! Formerly, great king, that householder and treasurer gave food in alms to a Private Buddha named Tagarasikkhi. But after he had given the order, saying, 'Give food to this monk,' and had risen from his seat and departed, he repented him of the gift and said to himself, 'It would have been better if my slaves or my servants had had this food.' And, moreover, he murdered his brother's only son for the sake of the inheritance. Now whereas, great king, that householder and treasurer gave food in alms to the Private Buddha Tagarasikkhi, as the fruit of this deed he was born seven times in a higher state of existence, into a heavenly world; and as a further result of this deed he has held the treasurership seven times here in Sāvatthi. And whereas, great king, that householder and treasurer repented him of the gift, and said to himself, 'It would have been better if my slaves or my servants had had this food,' as the result of this sinful thought his mind has been averse to sumptuous food, to sumptuous clothing, to sumptuous equipages, to a sumptuous gratification of the five senses. And whereas, great king, the treasurer murdered his brother's only son for the sake of the inheritance, as a result of this deed he has suffered in hell for many years, for many hundreds of years, for many thousands of years, for many hundreds of thousands of years; and as a further result of this deed he has now for the seventh time died without leaving any son and forfeited his property into the royal treasury. But now, great king, the former merit of this treasurer has become exhausted, and no new merit has been accumulated, and at the present time, great king, the treasurer is suffering in the Mahā-Roruva hell."

"Reverend Sir, has the treasurer been reborn in the Mahā-Roruva hell?"

"Yes, great king. The Treasurer has been reborn in the Mahā-Roruva hell."

> "Nor grain, nor wealth, nor store of gold and silver,
> Not one amongst his women-folk and children,
> Nor slave, domestic, hirèd man,
> Nor any one that eats his bread,
> Can follow him who leaves this life,
> But all things must be left behind.
>
> "But every deed a man performs,
> With body, or with voice, or mind,
> 'Tis this that he can call his own,
> This with him take as he goes hence.
> This is what follows after him,
> And like a shadow ne'er departs.
>
> "Let all, then, noble deeds perform,
> A treasure-store for future weal;
> For merit gained this life within,
> Will yield a blessing in the next."

REBIRTH IS
NOT TRANSMIGRATION

1. Translated from the Milindapañha (71[16])

SAID the king: "Bhante Nāgasena, does rebirth take place without anything transmigrating [passing over]?"

"Yes, your majesty. Rebirth takes place without anything transmigrating."

"How, bhante Nāgasena, does rebirth take place without anything transmigrating? Give an illustration."

"Suppose, your majesty, a man were to light a light from another light; pray, would the one light have passed over [transmigrated] to the other light?"

"Nay, verily, bhante."

"In exactly the same way, your majesty, does rebirth take place without anything transmigrating."

"Give another illustration."

"Do you remember, your majesty, having learnt, when you were a boy, some verse or other from your professor of poetry?"

"Yes, bhante."

"Pray, your majesty, did the verse pass over [transmigrate] to you from your teacher?"

"Nay, verily, bhante."

"In exactly the same way, your majesty, does rebirth take place without anything transmigrating."

"You are an able man, bhante Nāgasena."

2. Translated from the Milindapañha (46[5])

"Bhante Nāgasena," said the king, "what is it that is born into the next existence?"

"Your majesty," said the elder, "it is name and form that is born into the next existence."

"Is it this same name and form that is born into the next existence?"

"Your majesty, it is not this same name and form that is born into the next existence; but with this name and form, your majesty, one does a deed—it may be good, or it may be wicked—and by reason of this deed another name and form is born into the next existence."

"Bhante, if it is not this same name and form that is born into the next existence, is one not freed from one's evil deeds?"

"If one were not born into another existence," said the elder, "one would be freed from one's evil deeds; but, your majesty, inasmuch as one is born into another existence, therefore is one not freed from one's evil deeds."

"Give an illustration."

"Your majesty, it is as if a man were to take away another man's mangoes, and the owner of the mangoes were to seize him, and show him to the king, and say, 'Sire, this man hath taken away my mangoes;' and the other were to say, 'Sire, I did not take away this man's mangoes. The mangoes which this man planted were different mangoes from those which I took away. I am not liable to punishment.' Pray, your majesty, would the man be liable to punishment?"

"Assuredly, bhante, would he be liable to punishment."

"For what reason?"

"Because, in spite of what he might say, he would be liable to punishment for the reason that the last mangoes derived from the first mangoes."

"In exactly the same way, your majesty, with this name and form one does a deed—it may be good, or it may be wicked—and by reason of this deed another name and form is born into the next existence. Therefore is one not freed from one's evil deeds."

"Give another illustration."

"Your majesty, it is as if a man were to take away the rice of another man, . . . were to take away the sugar-cane, . . . Your majesty, it is as if a man were to light a fire in the winter-time and warm himself, and were to go off without putting it out. And then the fire were to burn another man's field, and the owner of the field were to seize him, and show him to the king, and say, 'Sire, this man has burnt up my field;' and the other were to say, 'Sire, I did not set this man's field on fire. The fire which I failed to put out was a different one from the one which has burnt up this man's field. I am not liable to punishment.' Pray, your majesty, would the man be liable to punishment?"

"Assuredly, bhante, would he be liable to punishment."

"For what reason?"

"Because, in spite of what he might say, the man would be liable to punishment for the reason that the last fire derived from the first fire."

"In exactly the same way, your majesty, with this name and form one does a deed—it may be good, or it may be wicked—and by reason of this deed another name and form is born into the next existence. Therefore is one not freed from one's evil deeds."

"Give another illustration."

"Your majesty, it is as if a man were to ascend to the top story of a house with a light, and eat there; and the light in burning were to set fire to the thatch; and the thatch in burning were to set fire to the house; and the house in burning were to set fire to the village; and the people of the village were to seize him, and say, 'Why, O man, did you set fire to the village?' and he were to say, 'I did not set fire to the village. The fire of the lamp by whose light I ate was a different one from the one which set fire to the village;' and they, quarreling, were to come to you. Whose cause, your majesty, would you sustain?"

"That of the people of the village, bhante."

"And why?"

"Because, in spite of what the man might say, the latter fire sprang from the former."

"In exactly the same way, your majesty, although the name and form which is born into the next existence is different from the name and form which is to end at death, nevertheless, it is sprung from it. Therefore is one not freed from one's evil deeds."

"Give another illustration."

"Your majesty, it is as if a man were to choose a young girl in marriage, and having paid the purchase-money, were to go off; and she subsequently were to grow up and become marriageable;

and then another man were to pay the purchase-money for her, and marry her; and the first man were to return, and say, 'O man, why did you marry my wife?' and the other were to say, 'I did not marry your wife. The young, tender girl whom you chose in marriage, and for whom you paid purchase-money, was a different person from this grown-up and marriageable girl whom I have chosen in marriage, and for whom I have paid purchase-money;' and they, quarreling, were to come to you. Whose cause, your majesty, would you sustain?"

"That of the first man."

"And why?"

"Because, in spite of what the second man might say, the grown-up girl sprang from the other."

"In exactly the same way, your majesty, although the name and form which is born into the next existence is different from the name and form which is to end at death, nevertheless, it is sprung from it. Therefore is one not freed from one's evil deeds."

"Give another illustration."

"Your majesty, it is as if a man were to buy from a cowherd a pot of milk, and were to leave it with the cowherd, and go off, thinking he would come the next day and take it. And on the next day it were to turn into sour cream; and the man were to come back, and say, 'Give me the pot of milk.' And the other were to show him the sour cream; and the first man were to say, 'I did not buy sour cream from you. Give me the pot of milk.' And the cowherd were to say, 'While you were gone, your milk turned into sour cream;' and they, quarreling, were to come to you. Whose cause, your majesty, would you sustain?"

"That of the cowherd, bhante."

"And why?"

"Because, in spite of what the man might say, the one sprang from the other."

"In exactly the same way, your majesty, although the name and form which is born into the next existence is different from the name and form which is to end at death, nevertheless, it is sprung from it. Therefore is one not freed from one's evil deeds."

"You are an able man, bhante Nāgasena."

3. Translated from the Visuddhi-Magga (chap. xvii.)

It is only elements of being possessing a dependence that arrive at a new existence: none transmigrated from the last existence, nor are they in the new existence without causes contained in the old. By this is said that it is only elements of being, with form or without, but possessing a dependence, that arrive at a new existence. There is no entity, no living principle; no elements of being transmigrated from the last existence into the present one; nor, on the other hand, do they appear in the present existence without causes in that one. This we will now make plain by considering birth and death as they occur every day among men.

For when, in any existence, one arrives at the gate of death, either in the natural course of things or through violence; and when, by a concourse of intolerable, death-dealing pains, all the members, both great and small, are loosened and wrenched apart in every joint and ligament; and the body, like a green palm-leaf exposed to the sun, dries up by degrees; and the eye-sight and the other senses fail; and the power of feeling, and the power of thinking, and vitality are making the last stand in the heart—then consciousness residing in that last refuge, the heart, continues to exist by virtue of karma, otherwise called the predispositions. This karma, however, still retains something of what it depends on, and consists of such former deeds as were weighty, much practised, and are now close at hand; or else this karma creates a reflex of itself or of the new mode of life now being entered upon, and it is with this as its object that consciousness continues to exist.

Now while the consciousness still subsists, inasmuch as desire and ignorance have not been abandoned and the evil of the object is hidden by that ignorance, desire inclines the consciousness to the object; and the karma that sprang up along with the consciousness impels it toward the object. This consciousness being in its series thus inclined toward the object by desire, and impelled toward it by karma, like a man who swings himself over a ditch by means of a rope hanging from a tree on the hither bank, quits its first resting-place and continues to subsist in dependence on objects of sense and other things, and either does or does not light on another resting-place created by karma. Here the former consciousness, from its passing out of existence, is called passing away, and the latter, from its being reborn into a new existence, is called rebirth. But it is to be understood that this latter consciousness did not come to the present existence from the previous one, and also that it is only to causes contained in the old existence,—namely, to karma called the predispositions, to inclination, an object, etc.,—that its present appearance is due.

> As illustrations here may serve
> Echoes and other similes.
> Nor sameness, nor diversity,
> Can from that series take their rise.

As illustrations of how consciousness does not come over from the last existence into the present, and how it springs up by means of causes belonging to the former existence, *here may serve echoes,* light the impressions of a seal, and reflections in a mirror. For as echoes, light, the impressions of a seal, and shadows have sound, etc., for their causes, and exist without having come from elsewhere, just so is it with this mind.

Moreover

> *Nor sameness, nor diversity,*
> *Can from that series take their rise.*

For if, in a continuous series, an absolute sameness obtained, then could sour cream not arise from milk; while, on the other hand, if there were an absolute diversity, then could not a milk-owner obtain sour cream. The same argument holds good in regard to all causes and effects. This being so, it would be more correct not to use the popular mode of stating the case, but that would not be desirable. Therefore, we must merely guard ourselves from supposing that there is here either an absolute sameness or an absolute diversity. Here some one will say,

"This explanation is not a good one. For is it not true that if there be no transmigration, and both the Groups and the fruitful karma which belong to this existence in the world of men cease, nor arrive in the new existence, the fruit of this karma would then be borne by a different thing from that which produced the karma itself? If the reaper ceased to exist, it would not be he experienced the fruit. Therefore this position is not good."

The following quotation will answer this:

> "The series which doth bear a fruit,
> Is not the same nor something else.
> The fabricating power in seeds
> Will show the meaning of this word."

For when the *fruit* arises in a *series,* as absolute sameness and absolute diversity are both excluded, it cannot be said that the fruit is borne by the *same* thing *nor* yet by *something else.*

The fabricating power in seeds will show this. For when the fabricating power in the seed of mangoes and other plants operate, inasmuch as any particular kind of fruit is dependent on the previous part of its series, it cannot come from other seeds, nor in dependence on other fabricating powers; nor yet is it those other seeds, or those other fabricating powers, which arrive at fruition. Such is to be understood to be the nature of the present case. Also when education, training, and medicaments have been applied to the body of a young person, the fruit will appear in after time in the mature body, etc. Thus is the sense to be understood.

Now as to what was said, "If the reaper ceased to exist, it would not be he experienced the fruit," consider the following:

> "As when 'tis said, 'The tree bears fruit,'
> As soon as fruit on it appears;
> Just so the Groups are reapers called,
> As soon as karma's fruit springs up."

Just as in the case of those elements of being which go under the name of tree, as soon as at any point the fruit springs up, *it is* then *said, "The tree bears fruit,"* or, "The tree has fructified"—so also in the case of those *Groups* which go under the name of "god" or "man," when a fruition of happiness or misery springs up at any point, then it is said, "That god or man is happy or miserable." Therefore is it that we have here no need of any other *reaper.*

4. Translated from the Visuddhi-Magga (chap. xvii.)

He, then, that has no clear idea of death and does not master the fact that death everywhere consists in the dissolution of the Groups, he comes to a variety of conclusions, such as, "A living entity dies and transmigrates into another body."

He that has no clear idea of rebirth and does not master the fact that the appearance of the Groups everywhere constitutes rebirth, he comes to a variety of conclusions, such as, "A living entity is born and has obtained a new body."

5. Translated from the Visuddhi-Magga (chap. xxi.)

Therefore have the ancients said:

> " 'The Groups break up, and only they,' the wise say,
> 'And death consisteth in their dissolution.'
> The thoughtful man of insight sees them vanish;
> They're like the jewel shattered by the diamond."

DEATH'S MESSENGERS

1. Translated from the Aṅguttara-Nikāya (iii. 35[1])

DEATH has three messengers, O priests. And what are the three?

Suppose, O priests, one does evil with his body, does evil with his voice, does evil with his mind. Having done evil with his body, done evil with his voice, and done evil with his mind, he arrives after the dissolution of the body, after death, at a place of punishment, a place of suffering, perdition, hell. Then, O priests, the guardians of hell seize him by the arms at every point, and they show him to Yama, the ruler of the dead, saying,

"Sire, this man did not do his duty to his friends, to his parents, to the monks, or to the Brahmans, nor did he honor his elders among his kinsfolk. Let your majesty inflict punishment upon him."

Then, O priests, king Yama questions, sounds, and addresses him touching the first of death's messengers:

"O man! Did you not see the first of death's messengers visibly appear among men?"

He replies, "Lord, I did not."

Then, O priests, king Yama says to him, "O man! Did you not see among men a woman or a man, eighty or ninety or a hundred years of age, decrepid, crooked as the curved rafter of a gable roof, bowed down, leaning on a staff, trembling as he walked, miserable, with youth long fled, broken-toothed, gray-haired and nearly bald, tottering, with wrinkled brow, and blotched with freckles?"

He replies, "Lord, I did."

Then, O priests, king Yama says to him, "O man! Did it not occur to you, being a person of mature intelligence and years, 'I also am subject to old age, and in no way exempt. Come now! I will act nobly with body, voice, and mind'?"

He replies, "Lord, I could not. Lord, I did not think."

Then, O priests, king Yama says to him, "O man! Through thoughtlessness you failed to act nobly with body, voice, and mind. Verily, it shall be done unto you, O man, in accordance with your thoughtlessness. And it was not your mother who did this wickedness, nor was it your father, nor your brother, nor your sister, nor your friends and companions, nor your relatives and kinsfolk, nor the deities, nor the monks and Brahmans; but it was you yourself who did this wickedness, and you alone shall feel its consequences."

Then, O priests, when king Yama has questioned, sounded, and addressed him touching the first of death's messengers, he questions, sounds, and addresses him touching the second of death's messengers.

"O man! Did you not see the second of death's messengers visibly appear among men?"

He replies, "Lord, I did not."

Then, O priests, king Yama says to him, "O man! Did you not see among men, women or men, diseased, suffering, grievously sick, rolling in their own filth, who when lying down had to be lifted up by others, and by others had to be laid down again?"

He replies, "Lord, I did."

Then, O priests, king Yama says to him, "O man! Did it not occur to you, being a person of mature intelligence and years, 'I also am subject to disease, and in no way exempt. Come now! I will act nobly with body, voice, and mind'?"

He replies, "Lord, I could not. Lord, I did not think."

Then, O priests, king Yama says to him, "O man! Through thoughtlessness you failed to act nobly with body, voice, and mind. Verily, it shall be done unto you, O man, in accordance with your thoughtlessness. And it was not your mother who did this wickedness, nor was it your father, nor your brother, nor your sister, nor your friends and companions, nor your relatives and kinsfolk, nor the deities, nor the monks and Brahmans; but it was you yourself who did this wickedness, and you alone shall feel its consequences."

Then, O priests, when king Yama has questioned, sounded, and addressed him touching the second of death's messengers, he questions, sounds, and addresses him touching the third of death's messengers.

"O man! Did you not see the third of death's messengers visibly appear among men?"

He replies, "Lord, I did not."

Then, O priests, king Yama says to him, "O man! Did you not see among men a woman or a man that has been one day dead, or two days dead, or three days dead, and had become swollen, black, and full of putridity?"

He replies, "Lord, I did."

Then, O priests, king Yama says to him, "O man! Did it not occur to you, being a person of mature intelligence and years, 'I also am subject to death, and in no way exempt. Come now! I will act nobly with body, voice, and mind'?"

He replies, "Lord, I could not. Lord, I did not think."

Then, O priests, king Yama says to him, "O man! Through thoughtlessness you failed to act nobly with body, voice, and mind. Verily, it shall be done unto you, O man, in accordance with your thoughtlessness. And it was not your mother who did this wickedness, nor was it your father, nor your brother, nor your sister, nor your friends and companions, nor your relatives and kinsfolk, nor the deities, nor the monks and Brahmans; but it was you yourself who did this wickedness, and you alone shall feel its consequences."

Then, O priests, when king Yama has questioned, sounded, and addressed him touching the third of death's messengers, he becomes silent.

Then, O priests, the guardians of hell inflict on him the torture called the fivefold pinion: they force a heated iron stake through his hand; they force a heated iron stake through his other hand; they force a heated iron stake through his foot; they force a heated iron stake through his other foot; they force a heated iron stake through the middle of his breast. There he experiences grievous, severe, sharp, and bitter pains; but he does not die so long as that wickedness is unexhausted.

Then, O priests, the guardians of hell lay him down, and hack him with axes. There he experiences grievous, severe, sharp, and bitter pains; but he does not die so long as that wickedness is unexhausted.

Then, O priests, the guardians of hell place him feet up, head down, and hack him with hatchets. There he experiences grievous, severe, sharp, and bitter pains; but he does not die so long as that wickedness is unexhausted.

Then, O priests, the guardians of hell harness him to a chariot, and they make him go forward and they make him go back over ground that is blazing, flaming, and glowing. There he experiences grievous, severe, sharp, and bitter pains; but he does not die so long as that wickedness is unexhausted.

Then, O priests, the guardians of hell make him ascend and make him descend an immense, blazing, flaming, and glowing mountain of live coals. There he experiences grievous, severe, sharp, and bitter pains; but he does not die so long as that wickedness is unexhausted.

Then, O priests, the guardians of hell take him feet up, head down, and throw him into a heated iron kettle that is blazing, flaming, and glowing. There he cooks and sizzles. And while he there cooks and sizzles, he goes once upwards, once downwards, and once sideways. There he experiences grievous, severe, sharp, and bitter pains; but he does not die so long as that wickedness is unexhausted.

Then, O priests, the guardians of hell throw him into the chiefest of the hells. Now this chiefest of the hells, O priests, is

> Symmetrical, and square in shape,
> Four-gated, into parts laid off.
> Of iron is its bounding wall,
> An iron roof doth close it in;
> And of its glowing iron floor
> The light with dazzling brilliancy
> Spreads for a hundred leagues around,
> And ever and for ay abides.

In former times, O priests, king Yama thought to himself, "All they, alas, who are guilty of wicked deeds in the world must suffer such horrible and manifold torture! O that I may become a man and a Tathāgata arise in the world, a holy, Supreme Buddha, and that I may sit at the feet of The Blessed One and The Blessed One teach me the Doctrine, and I come to understand the Doctrine of The Blessed One!"

Now this, O priests, that I tell you, I did not get from any one else,
be he monk or Brahman; but, O priests, what I by myself, unassisted,
have known, and seen, and learnt, that I tell you.

> All they who thoughtless are, nor heed,
> What time death's messengers appear,
> Must long the pangs of suffering feel
> In some base body habiting.
> But all those good and holy men,
> What time they see death's messengers,
> Behave not thoughtless, but give heed
> To what the Noble Doctrine says;
> And in attachment frighted see
> Of birth and death the fertile source,
> And from attachment free themselves,
> Thus birth and death extinguishing,
> Secure and happy ones are they,
> Released from all this fleeting show;
> Exempted from all sin and fear,
> All misery have they overcome.

2. Reprinted from Mrs. Piozzi's (Thrale's) Autobiography (ed. Hay-
ward, Ticknor and Fields, Boston, 1861), vol. ii. p. 247

THE THREE WARNINGS

A TALE

> The tree of deepest root is found
> Least willing still to quit the ground;
> 'Twas therefore said by ancient sages,
> That love of life increased with years.
> So much, that in our latter stages,
> When pains grow sharp and sickness rages,
> The greatest love of life appears.
> This greatest affection to believe,
> Which all confess, but few perceive,
> If old affections can't prevail,
> Be pleased to hear a modern tale.
> When sports went round, and all were gay,
> On neighbor Dobson's wedding-day,
> Death called aside the jocund groom,
> With him into another room;
> And looking grave, you must, says he,
> Quit your sweet bride, and come with me.

With you, and quit my Susan's side?
With you! the hapless husband cried:
Young as I am; 'tis monstrous hard;
Besides, in truth, I'm not prepared:
My thoughts on other matters go,
This is my wedding night, you know.
What more he urged I have not heard,
His reasons could not well be stronger,
So Death the poor delinquent spared,
And left to live a little longer.
Yet calling up a serious look,
His hour-glass trembled while he spoke,
Neighbor, he said, farewell. No more
Shall Death disturb your mirthful hour,
And further, to avoid all blame
Of cruelty upon my name,
To give you time for preparation,
And fit you for your future station,
Three several warnings you shall have
Before you're summoned to the grave:
Willing, for once, I'll quit my prey,
And grant a kind reprieve;
In hopes you'll have no more to say
But when I call again this way,
Well pleased the world will leave.
To these conditions both consented,
And parted perfectly contented.
What next the hero of our tale befell,
How long he lived, how wise, how well,
How roundly he pursued his course,
And smoked his pipe, and stroked his horse,
The willing muse shall tell:
He chaffered then, he bought, he sold,
Nor once perceived his growing old,
Nor thought of Death as near;
His friends not false, his wife no shrew,
Many his gains, his children few,
He passed his hours in peace;
But while he viewed his wealth increase,
While thus along life's dusty road
The beaten track content he trod,
Old time whose haste no mortal spares
Uncalled, unheeded, unawares,
Brought him on his eightieth year.

And now one night in musing mood,
As all alone he sate,
Th' unwelcome messenger of fate
Once more before him stood.
Half stilled with anger and surprise,
So soon returned! old Dobson cries.
So soon, d' ye call it! Death replies:
Surely, my friend, you're but in jest;
Since I was here before
'Tis six-and-thirty years at least,
And you are now fourscore.
So much the worse, the clown rejoined,
To spare the aged would be kind;
However, see your search be legal
And your authority,—Is't regal?
Else you are come on a fool's errand,
With but a secretary's warrant.
Besides, you promised me three warnings,
Which I have looked for nights and mornings;
But for that loss of time and ease
I can recover damages.
I know, cries Death, that at the best,
I seldom am a welcome guest;
But don't be captious, friend, at least;
I little thought you'd still be able
To stump about your farm and stable;
Your years have run to a great length,
I wish you joy though of your strength.
Hold, says the farmer, not so fast,
I have been lame these four years past.
And no great wonder, Death replies;
However, you still keep your eyes,
And sure to see one's loves and friends,
For legs and arms would make amends.
Perhaps, says Dobson, so it might,
But, latterly, I've lost my sight.
This is a shocking story, faith,
Yet there's some comfort still, says Death;
Each strives your sadness to amuse,
I warrant you have all the news.
There's none, cries he, and if there were,
I've grown so deaf, I could not hear.
Nay then, the spectre stern rejoined,
These are unjustifiable yearnings;

If you are lame and deaf and blind,
You've had your three sufficient warnings,
So come along, no more we'll part:
He said, and touched him with his dart;
And now old Dobson, turning pale,
Yields to his fate,—so ends my tale.

THE DEVOTED WIFE

Translated from the Dhammapada, and from Buddhaghosa's
comment

> While eagerly man culls life's flowers,
> With all his faculties intent,
> Of pleasure still insatiate—
> Death comes and overpowereth him.

"*WHILE eagerly man culls life's flowers.*" This doctrinal instruction was given by The Teacher while dwelling at Sāvatthi, and it was concerning a woman called Husband-honorer. The affair began in the Heaven of the Suite of the Thirty-three.

They say that a god of that heaven named Garland-wearer went to his pleasure-grounds in company with a thousand celestial nymphs. Five hundred of these goddesses ascended trees and threw down flowers, while five hundred picked up the flowers that were thrown down and decked the god therewith. One of these goddesses, while on the bough of a tree, fell from that existence, her body vanishing like the flame of a lamp.

Then she was conceived in a high-caste family of Sāvatthi, and was born with a reminiscence of her previous existences. And saying to herself, "I am the wife of the god Garland-wearer," she made offerings of perfumes, garlands, and the like, with the prayer that in her next rebirth she might again be with her husband. And when at the age of sixteen years she married into another family, with ticket-food, and fortnightly food, she continued to give alms, saying, "May this prove efficacious in bringing about my rebirth with my husband."

Thereupon the priests gave her the name of Husband-honorer, for they said: "She works early and late, and her only desire is for her husband."

Husband-honorer continually took care of the hall where the priests sat. She brought forward the drinking water, and spread out the mats to sit on. And when other people were desirous of giving ticket-food and other alms, they would bring it to her, and say, "Dear lady, prepare this for the congregation of the priests." And by going to and fro in this manner, she acquired the fifty-six salutary qualities, all at one time.

Then she conceived, and at the end of ten lunar months she brought forth a son; and when he was old enough to walk, another, until she had four sons.

One day, after she had given alms and offerings, and had listened to the Doctrine, and kept the precepts, she died toward night-fall from a sudden disease, and was reborn into the presence of her husband.

The other goddesses had continued to deck the god throughout the whole interval.

"We have not seen you since morning," said the god. "Where have you been?"

"I fell from this existence, my lord."

"Are you in earnest?"

"It was precisely so, my lord."

"Where were you born?"

"At Sāvatthi, in a family of high caste."

"How long were you there?"

"My lord, at the end of ten months I issued from my mother's womb, and at the age of sixteen years I married into another family; and having borne four sons, and having given gifts and done other meritorious deeds with the prayer that I might again be with you, I have been born into your presence."

"How long is the life of men?"

"Only a hundred years."

"Is that all?"

"Yes, my lord."

"If that is the length of life to which men are born, pray, now, do they pass the time asleep and reckless, or do they give gifts and do other meritorious deeds?"

"Nothing of the kind, my lord. Men are always reckless, as if they were born to a life of an incalculable number of years, and were never to grow old and die."

At this the god Garland-wearer became exceedingly agitated.

"Men, it appears, are born to a life of only one hundred years, yet they recklessly lie down and sleep away their time. When will they ever get free from misery?"

A hundred of our years make one day and night of the Gods of the Suite of the Thirty-three; thirty such days and nights their month; and twelve such months their year. And the length of their lives is a thousand such celestial years, or in human notation thirty-six million years. Thus for that god not one day has passed; but like a moment had the interval seemed to him. And thus he thought, "Recklessness for short-lived men is extremely unsuitable."

On the next day, when the priests entered the village, they found the hall had not been looked after; the mats had not been spread, and the drinking water had not been placed. Then they inquired,

"Where is Husband-honorer?"

"Reverend sirs, how could you expect to see her? Yesterday, after your worships had eaten and departed, she died at even-tide."

When the priests heard this, the unconverted among them, calling to mind her benefactions, were unable to restrain their tears, while those in whom depravity had come to an end had their elements of being agitated.

After breakfast they returned to the monastery, and made inquiry of The Teacher:

"Reverend Sir, Husband-honorer worked early and late doing many kinds of meritorious deeds, and prayed only for her husband. Now she is dead. Where, pray, has she been reborn?"

"With her husband, O priests."

"But, Reverend Sir, she is not with her husband."

"O priests, it was not this husband she was praying for. She had a husband named Garland-wearer, a God of the Suite of the Thirty-three, and fell from that existence while he was decorating himself with flowers. Now she has returned and been born again at his side."

"Reverend Sir, is it really so?"

"Assuredly, O priests."

"Alas, Reverend Sir, how very short is the life of all creatures!

In the morning she waited on us, and in the evening a disease attacked her, and she died."

"Assuredly, O priests," said The Teacher, "the life of creatures is indeed short. And thus it is that death gets creatures into his power, and drags them away howling and weeping, and still unsated in their senses and lusts."

So saying, he pronounced the following stanza:

> "While eagerly man culls life's flowers,
> With all his faculties intent,
> Of pleasure still insatiate—
> Death comes and overpowereth him."

THE HARE-MARK IN
THE MOON

Translated from the Jātaka (iii. 51^{10}), and constituting
Birth-Story 316

"*SOME red-fish have I, seven in all.*" This was related by
The Teacher while dwelling in Jetavana monastery; and
it was concerning a donation of all the requisites to the congregation of the priests.

It seems that a householder of Sāvatthi prepared a donation of all
the requisites for The Buddha and for the Order. At the door of
his house he had a pavilion built and gotten ready, and having
invited The Buddha and the congregation of the priests, he made
them sit down on costly seats which had been spread for them in
the pavilion, and gave them an excellent repast of savory dishes.
Then he invited them again for the next day, and again for the
next, until he had invited them seven times. And on the seventh
day he made the donation of all the requisites to The Buddha and
to five hundred priests.

At the end of the breakfast The Teacher returned thanks and
said,

"Layman, it is fitting that you thus manifest a hearty zeal; for
this alms-giving was also the custom of the wise of old time. For
the wise of old time surrendered their own lives to chance suppliants,
and gave their own flesh to be eaten."

Then, at the request of the householder, he related the by-gone
occurrence:—

Once upon a time, when Brahmadatta was ruling at Benares, the
Future Buddha was born as a hare, and dwelt in a wood. Now on
one side of this wood was a mountain, on another a river, and on
another a border village. And there were three other animals that
were his comrades—a monkey, a jackal, and an otter. These four

697

wise creatures dwelt together, catching their prey each in his own hunting ground, and at night resorting together. And the wise hare would exhort the other three, and teach them the Doctrine, saying, "Give alms, keep the precepts, and observe fast-days." Then the three would approve of his admonition, and go each to his own lair in the thicket, and spend the night.

Time was going by in this manner, when one day the Future Buddha looked up into the sky and saw the moon, and perceived that the next day would be fast-day. Then said he to the others,

"To-morrow is fast-day. Do you three keep the precepts and observe the day; and as alms given while keeping the precepts bring great reward, if any suppliants present themselves, give them to eat of your own food."

"Very well," said they, and passed the night in their lairs.

On the next day the otter started out early, and went to the banks of the Ganges to hunt for prey. Now a fisherman had caught seven red-fish and strung them on a vine, and buried them in the sand on the banks of the Ganges, and had then gone on downstream catching fish as he went. The otter smelt the fishy odor, and scraping away the sand, perceived the fish and drew them out. Then he called out three times, "Does any one own these?" and when he saw no owner, he bit hold of the vine with his teeth, and drew them to his lair in the thicket. There he lay down, remembering that he was keeping the precepts, and thinking, "I will eat these at the proper time."

And the jackal also went out to hunt for prey, and found in the hut of a field-watcher two spits of meat, and one iguana, and a jar of sour cream. Then he called out three times, "Does any one own these?" and when he saw no owner, he placed the cord that served as a handle for the jar of sour cream about his neck, took hold of the spits of meat and of the iguana with his teeth, and brought them home, and placed them in his lair in the thicket. Then he lay down, remembering that he was keeping the precepts, and thinking, "I will eat these at the proper time."

And the monkey also, entering the forest, fetched home a bunch of mangoes, and placed them in his lair in the thicket. Then he lay down, remembering that he was keeping the precepts, and thinking, "I will eat these at the proper time."

The Future Buddha, however, remained in his thicket, thinking, "At the proper time I will go out and eat dabba[1]-grass." Then he thought,

"If any suppliants come, they will not want to eat grass, and I have no sesamum, rice, or other such food. If any suppliant comes, I will give him of my own flesh."

Such fieriness of zeal in keeping the precepts caused the marble throne of Sakka to grow hot. Then, looking carefully, Sakka discovered the cause, and proposed to himself to try the hare. And disguised as a Brahman, he went first to the lair of the otter.

"Brahman, why stand you there?" said the otter.

Said he, "Pandit, if I could but get something to eat, I would keep fast-day vows, and perform the duties of a monk."

"Very well," said the otter; "I will give you food." And he addressed him with the first stanza:

> "Some red-fish have I, seven in all,
> Found stranded on the river bank.
> All these, O Brahman, are my own;
> Come eat, and dwell within this wood."

"I will return a little later," said the Brahman; "let the matter rest until to-morrow."

Then he went to the jackal. And the latter also asking, "Why stand you there?" the Brahman answered the same as before.

"Very well," said the jackal; "I will give you some food." And he addressed him with the second stanza:

> "A watchman guards the field close by,
> His supper have I ta'en away;
> Two spits of meat, iguana one,
> One dish of butter clarified.
> All these, O Brahman, are my own;
> Come eat, and dwell within this wood."

"I will return a little later," said the Brahman; "let the matter rest until to-morrow."

[1] Name of various kinds of grasses used for sacrificial purposes.

Then he went to the monkey. And the latter also asking, "Why stand you there?" the Brahman answered the same as before.

"Very well," said the monkey; "I will give you some food." And he addressed him with the third stanza:

> "Ripe mangoes, water clear and cold,
> And cool and pleasant woodland shade—
> All these, O Brahman, are my own;
> Come eat, and dwell within this wood."

"I will return a little later," said the Brahman; "let the matter rest until to-morrow."

Then he went to the wise hare. And he also asking, "Why stand you there?" the Brahman answered the same as before.

The Future Buddha was delighted. "Brahman," said he, "you have done well in coming to me for food. To-day I will give alms such as I never gave before; and you will not have broken the precepts by destroying life. Go, my friend, and gather wood, and when you have made a bed of coals, come and tell me. I will sacrifice my life by jumping into the bed of live coals. And as soon as my body is cooked, do you eat of my flesh, and perform the duties of a monk." And he addressed him with the fourth stanza:

> "The hare no seed of sesamum
> Doth own, nor beans, nor winnowed rice.
> But soon my flesh this fire shall roast;
> Then eat, and dwell within this wood."

When Sakka heard this speech, he made a heap of live coals by his superhuman power, and came and told the Future Buddha. The latter rose from his couch of dabba-grass, and went to the spot. And saying, "If there are any insects in my fur, I must not let them die," he shook himself three times. Then throwing his whole body into the jaws of his liberality, he jumped into the bed of coals, as delighted in mind as a royal flamingo when he alights in a cluster of lotuses. The fire, however, was unable to make hot so much as a hair-pore of the Future Buddha's body. He felt as if he had entered the abode of cold above the clouds.

Then, addressing Sakka, he said,

"Brahman, the fire you have made is exceeding cold, and is not able to make hot so much as a hair-pore of my body. What does it mean?"

"Pandit, I am no Brahman; I am Sakka, come to try you."

"Sakka, your efforts are useless; for if all beings who dwell in the world were to try me in respect of my liberality, they would not discover in me any unwillingness to give." Thus the Future Buddha thundered.

"Wise hare," said then Sakka, "let your virtue be proclaimed to the end of this world-cycle." And taking a mountain, he squeezed it, and with the juice drew the outline of a hare in the disk of the moon. Then in that wood, and in that thicket, he placed the Future Buddha on some tender dabba-grass, and taking leave of him, departed to his own celestial abode.

And these four wise creatures lived happily and harmoniously, and kept the precepts, and observed fast-days, and passed away according to their deeds.

When The Teacher had given this instruction, he expounded the truth, and identified the characters of the Birth-Story: [At the close of the exposition of the truths, the householder who had given all the requisites became established in the fruit of conversion.]

"In that existence the otter was Ananda, the jackal was Moggallāna, the monkey was Sāriputta, while the wise hare was I myself."

The Hare Birth-Story.

THE WAY OF PURITY

Translated from the Visuddhi-Magga (chap. i.)

THEREFORE has The Blessed One said:

"What man his conduct guardeth, and hath wisdom,
And thoughts and wisdom traineth well,
The strenuous and the able priest,
He disentangles all this snarl."

When it is said *hath wisdom,* there is meant a wisdom for which he does not need to strive. For it comes to him through the power of his deeds in a former existence.

The strenuous and the able priest. Perseveringly by means of the above-mentioned heroism, and intelligently through the force of his wisdom, should he *guard* his *conduct,* and *train* himself in the quiescence and insight indicated by the words *thoughts* and *wisdom.*

Thus does The Blessed One reveal the Way of Purity under the heads of conduct, concentration, and wisdom. Thus does he indicate the three disciplines, a thrice noble religion, the advent of the three-fold knowledge, etc., the avoidance of the two extremes and the adoption of the middle course of conduct, the means of escape from the lower and other states of existence, the threefold abandonment of the corruptions, the three hostilities, the purification from the three corruptions, and the attainment of conversion and of the other degrees of sanctification.

And how?

By conduct is indicated the discipline in elevated conduct; by concentration, the discipline in elevated thoughts; and by wisdom, the discipline in elevated wisdom.

By conduct, again, is indicated the nobleness of this religion in its beginning. The fact that conduct is the beginning of this religion appears from the passage, "What is the first of the meritorious qualities? Purity of conduct." And again from that other, which begins by saying, "It is the non-performance of any wickedness." And it is noble because it entails no remorse or other like evils.

By concentration is indicated its nobleness in the middle. The fact that concentration is the middle of this religion appears from the passage which begins by saying, "It is richness in merit." It is noble because it brings one into the possession of the magical powers and other blessings.

By wisdom is indicated its nobleness at the end. The fact that wisdom is the end of this religion appears from the passage,

> "To cleanse and purify the thoughts,
> 'Tis this the holy Buddhas teach,"

and from the fact that there is nothing higher than wisdom. It is noble because it brings about imperturbability whether in respect of things pleasant or unpleasant. As it is said:

> "Even as the dense and solid rock
> Cannot be stirred by wind and storm;
> Even so the wise cannot be moved
> By voice of blame or voice of praise."

By conduct, again, is indicated the advent of the threefold knowledge. For by virtuous conduct one acquires the threefold knowledge, but gets no further. By concentration is indicated the advent of the Six High Powers. For by concentration one acquires the Six High Powers, but gets no further. By wisdom is indicated the advent of the four analytical sciences. For by wisdom one acquires the four analytical sciences, and in no other way.

By conduct, again, is indicated the avoidance of the extreme called sensual gratification; by concentration, the avoidance of the extreme called self-torture. By wisdom is indicated the adoption of the middle course of conduct.

By conduct, again, is indicated the means of escape from the lower states of existence; by concentration, the means of escape from the realm of sensual pleasure; by wisdom, the means of escape from every form of existence.

By conduct, again, is indicated the abandonment of the corruption through the cultivation of their opposing virtues; by concentration, the abandonment of the corruptions through their avoidance; by wisdom, the abandonment of the corruptions through their extirpation.

By conduct, again, is indicated the hostility to corrupt acts; by concentration, the hostility to corrupt feelings; by wisdom, the hostility to corrupt propensities.

By conduct, again, is indicated the purification from the corruption of bad practices; by concentration, the purification from the corruption of desire; by wisdom, the purification from the corruption of heresy.

And by conduct, again, is indicated the attainment of conversion, and of once returning; by concentration, the attainment of never returning; by wisdom, the attainment of saintship. For the converted are described as "Perfect in the precepts," as likewise the once returning; but the never returning as "Perfect in concentration," and the saint as "Perfect in wisdom."

Thus are indicated the three disciplines, a thrice noble religion, the advent of the threefold knowledge, etc., the avoidance of the two extremes and the adoption of the middle course of conduct, the means of escape from the lower and other states of existence, the threefold abandonment of the corruptions, the three hostilities, the purification from the three corruptions, and the attainment of conversion and of the other degrees of sanctification; and not only these nine triplets, but also other similar ones.

Now although this *Way of Purity* was thus taught under the heads of conduct, concentration, and wisdom, and of the many good qualities comprised in them, yet this with excessive conciseness; and as, consequently, many would fail to be benefited, we here give its exposition in detail.

CONCENTRATION

1. Translated from the Visuddhi-Magga (chap. iii.)

WHAT is concentration? Concentration is manifold and various, and an answer which attempted to be exhaustive would both fail of its purpose and tend to still greater confusion. Therefore we will confine ourselves to the meaning here intended, and say—Concentration is an intentness of meritorious thoughts.

2. Translated from the Añguttara-Nikāya (iii. 88)

And what, O priests, is the discipline in elevated concentration? Whenever, O priests, a priest, having isolated himself from sensual pleasures, having isolated himself from demeritorious traits, and still exercising reasoning, still exercising reflection, enters upon the first trance, which is produced by isolation and characterized by joy and happiness; when, through the subsidence of reasoning and reflection, and still retaining joy and happiness, he enters upon the second trance, which is an interior tranquilization and intentness of thoughts, and is produced by concentration; when, through the paling of joy, indifferent, contemplative, conscious, and in the experience of bodily happiness—that state which eminent men describe when they say, "Indifferent, contemplative, and living happily"—he enters upon the third trance; when, through the abandonment of happiness, through the abandonment of misery, through the disappearance of all antecedent gladness and grief, he enters upon the fourth trance, which has neither misery nor happiness, but is contemplation as refined by indifference, this, O priests, is called the discipline in elevated concentration.

3. Translated from the Añguttara-Nikāya (ii. 3[10])

What advantage, O priests, is gained by training in quiescence? The thoughts are trained. And what advantage is gained by the training of the thoughts? Passion is abandoned.

THE CONVERSION OF ANIMALS

[REFLECTION ON THE BUDDHA]

Translated from the Visuddhi-Magga (chap. vii.)

THE Blessed One, moreover, was The Teacher, because he gave instruction also to animals. These, by listening to the Doctrine of The Blessed One, became destined to conversion, and in the second or third existence would enter the Paths. The frog who became a god is an illustration.

As tradition relates, The Blessed One was teaching the Doctrine to the inhabitants of the town of Campā, on the banks of Lake Gaggarā; and a certain frog, at the sound of The Blessed One's voice, obtained the mental reflex. And a certain cowherd, as he stood leaning on his staff, pinned him down fast by the head. The frog straightway died, and like a person awaking from sleep, he was reborn in the Heaven of the Thirty-three, in a golden palace twelve leagues in length. And when he beheld himself surrounded by throngs of houris, he began to consider: "To think that I should be born here! I wonder what ever I did to bring me here." And he could perceive nothing else than that he had obtained the mental reflex at the sound of the voice of The Blessed One. And straightway he came with his palace, and worshiped at the feet of The Blessed One. And The Blessed One asked him:—

> "Who is it worships at my feet,
> And flames with glorious, magic power,
> And in such sweet and winning guise,
> Lights up the quarters all around?"

> "A frog was I in former times,
> And wandered in the waters free,
> And while I listened to thy Law,
> A cowherd crushed me, and I died."

Then The Blessed One taught him the Doctrine, and the conversion of eighty-four thousand living beings took place. And the frog, who had become a god, became established in the fruit of conversion, and with a pleased smile on his face departed.

LOVE FOR ANIMALS

[SUBLIME STATE OF FRIENDLINESS]

Translated from the Culla-Vagga (v. 6.)

NOW at that time a certain priest had been killed by the bite of a snake, and when they announced the matter to The Blessed One, he said:

"Surely now, O priests, that priest never suffused the four royal families of the snakes with his friendliness. For if, O priests, that priest had suffused the four royal families of the snakes with his friendliness, that priest, O priests, would not have been killed by the bite of a snake. And what are the four royal families of the snakes? The Virūpakkhas are a royal family of snakes; the Erāpathas are a royal family of snakes; the Chabyāputtas are a royal family of snakes; the Kanhāgotamakas are a royal family of snakes. Surely, now, O priests, that priest did not suffuse the four royal families of the snakes with his friendliness. For surely, O priests, if that priest had suffused the four royal families of the snakes with his friendliness, that priest, O priests, would not have been killed by the bite of a snake. I enjoin, O priests, that ye suffuse these four royal families of the snakes with your friendliness; and that ye sing a song of defence for your protection and safeguard. After this manner, O priests, shall ye sing:

" 'Virūpakkhas, I love them all,
The Erāpathas, too, I love,
Chabyāputtas, I love them, too,
And all Kanhāgotamakas.

" 'Creatures without feet have my love,
And likewise those that have two feet,
And those that have four feet I love,
And those, too, that have many feet.

" 'May those without feet harm me not,
And those with two feet cause no hurt;
May those with four feet harm me not,
Nor those who many feet possess.

" 'Let creatures all, all things that live,
All beings of whatever kind,
See nothing that will bode them ill!
May naught of evil come to them!

" 'Infinite is The Buddha, infinite the Doctrine, infinite the Order! Finite are creeping things: snakes, scorpions, centipedes, spiders, lizards, and mice! I have now made my protection, and sung my song of defence. Let all living beings retreat! I revere The Blessed One, and the seven Supreme Buddhas!' "

SARIPUTTA AND THE
TWO DEMONS

[THE SECOND AND FIFTH HIGH POWERS]

Translated from the Udāna (iv. 4.)

THUS have I heard.

On a certain occasion The Blessed One was dwelling at
Rājagaha, in Bamboo Grove in Kalandakanivāpa. And at
that time the venerable Sāriputta and the venerable Moggallāna the
Great were dwelling in the monastery called Pigeon Glen. Now it
chanced that the venerable Sāriputta, on a moonlight night, was
seated under the open sky, with freshly shaven head, and in a state
of trance. And it chanced that two demons, who were comrades,
were passing on some errand from the northern quarter of the
heavens to the southern. And these demons saw the venerable Sāriputta, on the moonlight night, seated under the open sky, with
freshly shaven head. And at sight of him, the first demon spoke
to the second demon as follows:

"It occurs to me, comrade, that it would be a fine plan to give this
monk a blow on the head."

Hearing this, the second demon replied:

"Enough of that, comrade; do not attack the monk. Great, O
comrade, is the monk, of great magical power, and very mighty."

And a second time the first demon spoke to the second demon
as follows:

"It occurs to me, comrade, that it would be a fine plan to give
this monk a blow on the head."

And a second time the second demon replied:

"Enough of that, comrade; do not attack the monk. Great, O
comrade, is the monk, of great magical power, and very mighty."

And a third time the first demon spoke to the second demon as
follows:

"It occurs to me, comrade, that it would be a fine plan to give this monk a blow on the head."

And a third time the second demon replied:

"Enough of that, comrade; do not attack the monk. Great, O comrade, is the monk, of great magical power, and very mighty."

Then the first demon, not heeding what the other demon said, gave the venerable Sāriputta a blow on the head. With such a blow one might fell an elephant seven or seven-and-a half cubits high, or might split a mountain peak. Thereupon, with the cry, "I am burning! I am burning!" the demon fell from where he stood into hell.

And the venerable Moggallāna the Great, with his divinely clear vision surpassing that of men, saw the demon give the venerable Sāriputta the blow on the head. And when he had seen it, he drew near to where the venerable Sāriputta was; and having drawn near, he spoke to the venerable Sāriputta as follows:

"Are you comfortable, brother? Are you doing well? Does nothing trouble you?"

"I am comfortable, brother Moggallāna. I am doing well, brother Moggallāna; but my head troubles me a little."

"O wonderful is it, brother Sāriputta! O marvellous is it, brother Sāriputta! How great is the magical power, and how great is the might of the venerable Sāriputta! Just now, brother Sāriputta, a certain demon gave you a blow on the head. And a mighty blow it was! With such a blow one might fell an elephant seven or seven-and-a-half cubits high, or might split a mountain peak. But the venerable Sāriputta only says thus: 'I am comfortable, brother Moggallāna. I am doing well, brother Moggallāna; but my head troubles me a little.'"

"O wonderful is it, brother Moggallāna! O marvellous is it, brother Moggallāna! How great is the magical power, and how great is the might of the venerable Moggallāna that he should see any demon at all! I, however, have not seen so much as a mud-sprite."

Now The Blessed One, with his divinely clear hearing surpassing that of men, heard the above conversation between these two elephants among men. Then The Blessed One, on learning of this occurrence, on that occasion breathed forth this solemn utterance:

"The man whose mind, like to a rock,
Unmovèd stands, and shaketh not;
Which no delights can e'er inflame,
Or provocations rouse to wrath—
O, whence can trouble come to him,
Who thus hath nobly trained his mind?"

THE SUMMUM BONUM

Translated from the Majjhima-Nikāya, and constituting Sutta 26

THUS have I heard.

On a certain occasion The Blessed One was dwelling at Sāvatthi in Jetavana monastery in Anāthapindika's Park. Then The Blessed One, having put on his tunic in the morning, and taken his bowl and his robes, entered Sāvatthi for alms.

Then a great number of priests drew near to where the venerable Ananda was; and having drawn near, they spoke to the venerable Ananda as follows:

"It is a long time, brother Ananda, since we listened to a doctrinal discourse from the mouth of The Blessed One. Come, brother Ananda, let us obtain an opportunity to listen to a doctrinal discourse from the mouth of The Blessed One."

"Well, then, venerable sirs, draw near to the monastery of Rammaka the Brahman. Perchance you may obtain an opportunity to listen to a doctrinal discourse from the mouth of The Blessed One."

"Yes, brother," said the priests to the venerable Ananda in assent.

Then The Blessed One, when he had gone the rounds for alms in Sāvatthi, returned from his begging, and after breakfast, addressed the venerable Ananda:

"Let us go hence, Ananda, and to Eastern Monastery, and to the storied mansion of Migāra's mother will we draw near for our noon-day rest."

"Yes, Reverend Sir," said the venerable Ananda to The Blessed One in assent.

Then The Blessed One, in company with the venerable Ananda, drew near to Eastern Monastery, and to the storied mansion of Migāra's mother, for his noon-day rest. Then The Blessed One, in the afternoon, rose from meditation, and addressed the venerable Ananda:

"Let us go hence, Ananda, and to Eastern Tank will we draw near to bathe our limbs."

"Yes, Reverend Sir," said the venerable Ananda to The Blessed One in assent.

Then The Blessed One, in company with the venerable Ananda, drew near to Eastern Tank to bathe his limbs; and having bathed his limbs in Eastern Tank and come up out of the water, he stood with but a single garment on, drying his limbs.

Then the venerable Ananda spoke to The Blessed One as follows: "Reverend Sir, here is the monastery of Rammaka the Brahman, but a short way off. Delightful, Reverend Sir, is the monastery of Rammaka the Brahman; enchanting, Reverend Sir, is the monastery of Rammaka the Brahman. Reverend Sir, pray let The Blessed One be so kind as to draw near to where the monastery of Rammaka the Brahman is." And The Blessed One consented by his silence.

Then The Blessed One drew near to where the monastery of Rammaka the Brahman was. Now at that time a great number of priests were seated in the monastery of Rammaka the Brahman, engaged in doctrinal discourse. Then The Blessed One stood outside in the entrance porch, and awaited the end of the discourse. Then The Blessed One, when he perceived that the discourse had come to an end, coughed, and rattled the bolt of the door. And the priests opened the door for The Blessed One. Then The Blessed One entered the monastery of Rammaka the Brahman, and sat on the seat that was spread for him. And when The Blessed One had sat down, he addressed the priests:

"What O priests, was the subject of the present meeting? and what the discourse you were holding?"

"Reverend Sir, our doctrinal discourse was concerning The Blessed One, and then The Blessed One arrived."

"Well said, O priests! This, O priests, is worthy of you as youths of good family, who have through faith retired from the household life to the houseless one, that ye sit together in doctrinal discourse. O priests, one of two things should you do when you meet together: either hold a doctrinal discourse, or maintain a noble silence.

"There are two cravings, O priests; the noble one, and the ignoble one. And what, O priests, is the ignoble craving?

"We may have, O priests, the case of one who, himself subject to birth, craves what is subject to birth; himself subject to old age, craves what is subject to old age; himself subject to disease, . . . death, . . . sorrow, . . . corruption, craves what is subject to corruption.

"And what, O priests, should one consider as subject to birth?

"Wife and child, O priests, are subject to birth; slaves, male and female, . . . goats and sheep . . . fowls and pigs . . . elephants, cattle, horses and mares . . . gold and silver are subject to birth. All the substrata of being, O priests, are subject to birth; and enveloped, besotted, and immersed in them, this person, himself subject to birth, craves what is subject to birth.

"And what, O priests, should one consider as subject to old age . . . disease . . . death . . . sorrow . . . corruption?

"Wife and child, O priests, are subject to corruption; slaves, male and female, . . . goats and sheep . . . fowls and pigs . . . elephants, cattle, horses and mares . . . gold and silver are subject to corruption. All the substrata of being, O priests, are subject to corruption; and enveloped, besotted, and immersed in them, this person, himself subject to corruption, craves what is subject to corruption.

"This, O priests, is the ignoble craving.

"And what, O priests, is the noble craving?

"We may have, O priests, the case of one who, himself subject to birth, perceives the wretchedness of what is subject to birth, and craves the incomparable security of a Nirvana free from birth; himself subject to old age, . . . disease, . . . death, . . . sorrow, . . . corruption, perceives the wretchedness of what is subject to corruption, and craves the incomparable security of a Nirvana free from corruption.

"This, O priests, is the noble craving.

"Now I, O priests, before my Buddhaship, being not yet a Buddha, but a Future Buddha, myself subject to birth, craved what was subject to birth; myself subject to old age, . . . disease, . . . death, . . . sorrow, . . . corruption, craved what was subject to corruption. And it occurred to me, O priests, as follows:

" 'Why, myself subject to birth, do I crave what is subject to birth? myself subject to old age, . . . disease, . . . death, . . . sorrow, . . . corruption, do I crave what is subject to corruption? What if now, myself subject to birth, and perceiving the wretchedness of what is subject to birth, I were to crave the incomparable security of a

Nirvana free from birth; myself subject to old age, . . . disease, . . . death, . . . sorrow, . . . corruption, I were to crave the incomparable security of a Nirvana free from corruption?'

"Subsequently, O priests, although of tender age, with the black hair of a lad, and in the hey-day of my youth, and just entering on my prime, and although my mother and my father were unwilling, and tears streamed from their eyes, I had my hair and my beard shaved off, and put on yellow garments, and retired from the household life to the houseless one. And having thus retired from the world, and craving the summum bonum, the incomparable peaceful state, I drew near to where Alāra Kālāma was; and having drawn near, I spoke to Alāra Kālāma as follows:

" 'Brother Kālāma, I would like to lead the religious life under your doctrine and discipline.'

"When I had thus spoken, O priests, Alāra Kālāma spoke to me as follows:

" 'Let your venerable worship do so. Such is this doctrine that in no long time an intelligent man can learn for himself, realize, and live in the possession of all that his master has to teach.'

"Then I, O priests, in no long time, quickly acquired that doctrine. And I, O priests, and others with me, by a mere lip-profession, and a mere verbal assertion, claimed that we knew and had perceived the true knowledge and the orthodox doctrine. And it occurred to me, O priests, as follows:

" 'It is not through mere faith in this doctrine that Alāra Kālāma announces that he has learnt it for himself, realized it, and lives in the possession of it. Alāra Kālāma surely knows and perceives this doctrine.'

"Then, O priests, I drew near to where Alāra Kālāma was; and having drawn near, I spoke to Alāra Kālāma as follows:

" 'Brother Kālāma, how far does this doctrine conduct, concerning which you announce that you have learnt it for yourself, realized it, and entered upon it?'

"When I had thus spoken, O priests, Alāra Kālāma announced that it conducted to the realm of nothingness. And it occurred to me, O priests, as follows:

" 'Faith is not peculiar to Alāra Kālāma: I also have faith. Heroism ... contemplation ... concentration ... wisdom is not peculiar to Alāra Kālāma: I also have wisdom. What if now I were to strive for the realization of that doctrine, concerning which Alāra Kālāma announces that he has learnt it for himself, realized it, and lives in the possession of it.' Then I, O priests, in no long time, quickly learnt that doctrine for myself, realized it, and lived in the possession of it. Then, O priests, I drew near to where Alāra Kālāma was; and having drawn near, I spoke to Alāra Kālāma as follows:

" 'Brother Kālāma, is this as far as the doctrine conducts, concerning which you announce that you have learnt it for yourself, realized it, and entered upon it?'

" 'This, brother, is as far as the doctrine conducts, concerning which I announce that I have learnt it for myself, realized it, and entered upon it.'

" 'I also, brother, have learnt this doctrine for myself, realized it, and live in the possession of it.'

" 'How fortunate, brother, are we! What supreme good fortune, brother, is ours that we should light on such a co-religionist as is your venerable worship. Thus the doctrine concerning which I announce that I have learnt it for myself, realized it, and entered upon it, that doctrine you have learnt for yourself, realized, and live in the possession of; the doctrine which you have learnt for yourself, realized, and live in the possession of, concerning that doctrine I announce that I have learnt it for myself, realized it, and entered upon it. Thus you know this doctrine, and I know this doctrine. You are the same as I am, and I am the same as you are. Come, brother, let us lead this following in common.'

"Thus, O priests, did Alāra Kālāma, my teacher, take me, his pupil, and make me every whit the equal of himself, and honor me with very great honor. And it occurred to me, O priests, as follows:

" 'This doctrine does not lead to aversion, absence of passion, cessation, quiescence, knowledge, supreme wisdom, and Nirvana, but only as far as the realm of nothingness.'

"And I, O priests, did not honor that doctrine with my adhesion, and being averse to that doctrine, I departed on my journey.

"And craving, O priests, the summum bonum, the incomparable peaceful state, I drew near to where Uddaka, the disciple of Rāma, was; and having drawn near, I spoke to Uddaka, the disciple of Rāma, as follows:

" 'Brother, I would like to lead the religious life under your doctrine and discipline.'

"When I had thus spoken, O priests, Uddaka, the disciple of Rāma, spoke to me as follows:

" 'Let your venerable worship do so. Such is this doctrine that in no long time an intelligent man can learn for himself, realize, and live in the possession of all that his master has to teach.'

"Then I, O priests, in no long time, quickly acquired that doctrine. And I, O priests, and others with me, by a mere lip-profession, and a mere verbal assertion, claimed that we knew and had perceived the true knowledge and the orthodox doctrine. And it occurred to me, O priests, as follows:

" 'It was not through mere faith in this doctrine that Rāma announced that he had learnt it for himself, realized it, and lived in the possession of it. Rāma surely knew and perceived this doctrine.'

"Then, O priests, I drew near to where Uddaka, the disciple of Rāma, was; and having drawn near, I spoke to Uddaka, the disciple of Rāma, as follows:

" 'Brother, how far does this doctrine conduct, concerning which Rāma made known that he had learnt it for himself, realized it, and entered upon it?'

"When I had thus spoken, O priests, Uddaka, the disciple of Rāma, announced that it conducted to the realm of neither perception nor yet non-perception. And it occurred to me, O priests, as follows:

" 'Faith is not peculiar to Rāma: I also have faith. Heroism . . . contemplation . . . concentration . . . wisdom is not peculiar to Rāma: I also have wisdom. What if now I were to strive for that doctrine, concerning which Rāma announced that he had learnt it for himself, realized it, and lived in the possession of it.' Then I, O priests, in no long time, quickly learnt that doctrine for myself, realized it, and lived in the possession of it. Then, O priests, I drew near to where Uddaka, the disciple of Rāma, was; and having drawn near, I spoke to Uddaka, the disciple of Rāma, as follows:

" 'Brother, is this as far as the doctrine conducts, concerning which

Rāma announced that he had learnt it for himself, realized it, and entered upon it?'

" 'This, brother, is as far as the doctrine conducts, concerning which Rāma announced that he had learnt it for himself, realized, and entered upon it.'

" 'I also, brother, have learnt this doctrine for myself, realized it, and live in the possession of it.'

" 'How fortunate, brother, are we! What supreme good fortune, brother, is ours that we should light on such a co-religionist as is your venerable worship. Thus the doctrine concerning which Rāma announced that he had learnt it for himself, realized it, and entered upon it, that doctrine you have learnt for yourself, realized, and live in the possession of; the doctrine which you have learnt for yourself, realized, and live in the possession of, concerning that doctrine Rāma announced that he had learnt it for himself, realized it, and entered upon it. Thus you know this doctrine, and Rāma knew this doctrine. You are the same as Rāma was, and Rāma was the same as you are. Come, brother, lead this following.'

"Thus, O priests, did Uddaka, the disciple of Rāma, my co-religionist, make me his teacher, and honor me with very great honor. And it occurred to me, O priests, as follows:

" 'This doctrine does not lead to aversion, absence of passion, cessation, quiescence, knowledge, supreme wisdom, and Nirvana, but only as far as the realm of neither perception nor yet non-perception.'

"And I, O priests, did not honor that doctrine with my adhesion; and being averse to that doctrine, I departed on my journey.

"And craving, O priests, the summum bonum, the incomparable peaceful state, I came in the course of my journeyings among the Magadhans to Uruvelā, the General's Town. There I perceived a delightful spot with an enchanting grove of trees, and a silvery flowing river, easy of approach and delightful, and a village near by in which to beg. And it occurred to me, O priests, as follows:

" 'Truly, delightful is this spot, enchanting this grove of trees, and this silvery river flows by, easy of approach and delightful, and there is a village near by in which to beg. Truly, there is here everything necessary for a youth of good family who is desirous of struggling.'

"And there I settled down, O priests, as everything was suitable for struggling.

"And being, O priests, myself subject to birth, I perceived the wretchedness of what is subject to birth, and craving the incomparable security of a Nirvana free from birth, I attained the incomparable security of a Nirvana free from birth; myself subject to old age, . . . disease, . . . death, . . . sorrow, . . . corruption, I perceived the wretchedness of what is subject to corruption, and craving the incomparable security of a Nirvana free from corruption, I attained the incomparable security of a Nirvana free from corruption. And the knowledge and the insight sprang up within me, 'My deliverance is unshakable; this is my last existence; no more shall I be born again.' And it occurred to me, O priests, as follows:

" 'This doctrine to which I have attained is profound, recondite, and difficult of comprehension, good, excellent, and not to be reached by mere reasoning, subtile, and intelligible only to the wise. Mankind, on the other hand, is captivated, entranced, held spell-bound by its lusts; and forasmuch as mankind is captivated, entranced, and held spell-bound by its lusts, it is hard for them to understand the law of dependence on assignable reasons, the doctrine of Dependent Origination, and it is also hard for them to understand how all the constituents of being may be made to subside, all the substrata of being be relinquished, and desire be made to vanish, and absence of passion, cessation, and Nirvana be attained. If I were to teach the Doctrine, others would fail to understand me, and my vexation and trouble would be great.'

"Then, O priests, the following stanzas occurred to me, not heard of before from any one else:

> " 'This Doctrine out of toil begot
> I see 'tis useless to proclaim:
> Mankind's by lusts and hates enthralled,
> 'Tis hopeless they should master it.

> " 'Repugnant, abstruse would it prove,
> Deep, subtile, and beyond their ken;
> Th' infatuates live in clouds of lusts,
> And cannot for the darkness see.'

"Thus, O priests, did I ponder, and my mind was disinclined to action, and to any proclaiming of the Doctrine.

"Then, O priests, Brahma Sahampati perceived what was in my mind, and it occurred to him as follows:

" 'Lo, the world is lost, is ruined! For the mind of The Tathāgata, The Saint, The Supreme Buddha, is disinclined to action, and to any proclaiming of the doctrine.'

"Then, O priests, Brahma Sahampati, as quickly as a strong man might stretch out his bent arm, or might draw in his outstretched arm, even so, having vanished from the Brahma-world, appeared in my presence.

"Then, O priests, Brahma Sahampati threw his upper garment over his shoulder and, stretching out to me his joined palms, spoke as follows:

" 'Reverend Sir, let The Blessed One teach the Doctrine, let The Happy One teach the Doctrine. There are some beings having but little moral defilement, and through not hearing the Doctrine they perish. Some will be found to understand the Doctrine.'

"Thus, O priests, spoke Brahma Sahampati, and having thus spoken, he continued as follows:

> " 'The Magadhans hold hitherto a doctrine
> Impure, thought out by men themselves not spotless.
> Ope thou the door that to the deathless leadeth:
> Him let them hear who is himself unspotted.
>
> " 'As one who standeth on a rocky pinnacle,
> Might thence with wide-extended view behold mankind,
> Climb thou, Wise One, the top of Doctrine's palace,
> And thence gaze down serene on all the peoples,
> Behold how all mankind is plunged in sorrow,
> And how old age and death have overwhelmed them.
>
> " 'Rise thou, O Hero, Victor in the Battle!
> O Leader, Guiltless One, go 'mongst the nations!
> The Doctrine let The Buddha teach,
> Some will be found to master it.'

"Then I, O priests, perceiving the desire of Brahma, and having compassion on living beings, gazed over the world with the eye of a Buddha. And as I gazed over the world with the eye of a Buddha,

I saw people of every variety: some having but little moral defilement, and some having great moral defilement; some of keen faculties, and some of dull faculties; some of good disposition, and some of bad disposition; some that were docile, and some that were not docile; and also some who saw the terrors of the hereafter and of blameworthy actions. Just as in a pond of blue lotuses, of water-roses, or of white lotuses, some of the blossoms which have sprung up and grown in the water, do not reach the surface of the water but grow under water; some of the blossoms which have sprung up and grown in the water, are even with the surface of the water; and some of the blossoms which have sprung up and grown in the water, shoot up above the water and are not touched by the water; in exactly the same way, O priests, as I gazed over the world with the eye of a Buddha, I saw people of every variety: some having but little moral defilement, and some having great moral defilement; some of keen faculties, and some of dull faculties; some of good disposition, and some of bad disposition; some that were docile, and some that were not docile; and also some who saw the terrors of the hereafter and of blameworthy actions. And when I had seen this, O priests, I addressed Brahma Sahampati in the following stanza:

> " 'Let those with ears to hear come give me credence,
> For lo! the door stands open to the deathless.
> O Brahma, 'twas because I feared annoyance
> That I was loath to tell mankind the Doctrine.'

"Then, O priests, thought Brahma Sahampati, 'The Blessed One has granted my request that he should teach the Doctrine,' and saluting me, he turned his right side towards me, and straightway disappeared.

"Then, O priests, it occurred to me as follows:

" 'To whom had I best teach the Doctrine first? Who would quickly comprehend this Doctrine?'

"Then, O priests, it occurred to me as follows:

" 'Here is this Alāra Kālāma, who is learned, skilled, intelligent, and has long been a person having but little defilement. What if I teach the Doctrine to Alāra Kālāma first? He would quickly comprehend this Doctrine.'

"Then, O priests, a deity announced to me,

" 'Reverend Sir, Alāra Kālāma is dead these seven days.'

"Also in me the knowledge sprang up, 'Alāra Kālāma is dead these seven days.'

"Then, O priests, it occurred to me as follows:

" 'A noble man was Alāra Kālāma. Surely, if he could have heard this Doctrine, he would quickly have comprehended it.'

"Then, O priests, it occurred to me as follows:

" 'To whom had I best teach the Doctrine first? Who would quickly comprehend this Doctrine?'

"Then, O priests, it occurred to me as follows:

" 'Here is this Uddaka, the disciple of Rāma, who is learned, skilled, intelligent, and has long been a person having but little defilement. What if I teach the Doctrine to Uddaka, the disciple of Rāma, first? He would quickly comprehend this Doctrine.'

"Then, O priests, a deity announced to me,

" 'Reverend Sir, Uddaka, the disciple of Rāma, died yesterday at night-fall.'

"Also in me, O priests, the knowledge sprang up, 'Uddaka, the disciple of Rāma, died yesterday at night-fall.'

"Then, O priests, it occurred to me as follows:

" 'A noble man was Uddaka, the disciple of Rāma. Surely, if he could have heard this Doctrine, he would quickly have comprehended it.'

"Then, O priests, it occurred to me as follows:

" 'To whom had I best teach the Doctrine first? Who would quickly comprehend this Doctrine?'

"Then, O priests, it occurred to me as follows:

" 'Of great service has this band of five priests been, who waited upon me while I devoted myself to the struggle. What if I teach the Doctrine to the band of five priests first?'

"Then, O priests, it occurred to me as follows:

" 'Where does the band of five priests dwell at present?'

"And I, O priests, with my divinely clear vision surpassing that of men, saw the band of five priests dwelling at Benares, in the deer-park Isipatana.

"Then, O priests, having dwelt at Uruvelā as long as I wished, I

proceeded on my wanderings in the direction of Benares. And
Upaka, a naked ascetic, beheld me proceeding along the highway
between the Bo-tree and Gayā. And having seen me, he spoke to
me as follows:

" 'Placid, brother, are all your organs of sense; clear and bright is
the color of your skin. To follow whom, brother, did you retire
from the world? Who is your teacher? and whose doctrine do you
approve?'

"When, O priests, Upaka, the naked ascetic, had thus spoken, I
addressed him in the following stanzas:

> " 'All-conquering have I now become, all-knowing;
> Untainted by the elements of being.
> I've left all things, am freed through thirst's destruction
> All wisdom's mine; what teacher should I follow?
>
> " 'I have no teacher anywhere;
> My equal nowhere can be found;
> In all the world with all its gods,
> No one to rival me exists.
>
> " 'The saintship, verily, I've gained,
> I am The Teacher, unsurpassed;
> I am The Buddha, sole, supreme;
> Lust's fire is quenched, Nirvana gained.
>
> " 'To found the Doctrine's reign I seek
> Benares, chief of Kāsi's towns;
> And for this blinded world I'll cause
> The drum of deathlessness to beat.'

" 'Which is as much as to say, brother, that you profess to be a
saint, an immeasurable Conqueror.'

> " 'Yea, were The Conquerors like to me,
> Well rid of all depravity.
> I've conquered every evil trait;
> Thus, Upaka, a Conqueror I.'

" 'You may be right, brother,' replied Upaka, the naked ascetic;
and shaking his head, he took another road and departed.

"Then, O priests, I proceeded on my wanderings from place to
place, and drew near to Benares, to the deer-park Isipatana, and to

where the band of five priests was. And, O priests, the band of five priests saw me approaching from afar, and, when they had seen me, they made an agreement among themselves, saying:

" 'Here, brethren, is the monk Gotama approaching, that luxurious fellow who gave up the struggle and devoted himself to a life of luxury. Let us not salute him, nor rise and go to meet him, nor relieve him of his bowl and his robe. We will merely spread a seat for him: he can then sit down, if he is so inclined.'

"But, O priests, as I gradually approached, the band of five priests found themselves unable to hold to their agreement, and rising to meet me, one of them relieved me of my bowl and my robe, another spread a seat for me, and another brought water for washing my feet. But, O priests, they addressed me by my name, and by the title of 'Brother.'

"When, O priests, I noticed this, I spoke to the band of five priests as follows:

" 'O, priests, address not The Tathāgata by his name, nor by the title of "Brother." A saint, O priests, is The Tathāgata, a Supreme Buddha. Give ear, O priests! The deathless has been gained, and I will instruct you, and teach you the Doctrine. If ye will do according to my instructions, in no long time, and in the present life, ye shall learn for yourselves, and shall realize and live in the possession of that highest good to which the holy life conducts, and for the sake of which youths of good family so nobly retire from the household life to the houseless one.'

"When I had thus spoken, O priests, the band of five priests said to me as follows:

" 'Brother Gotama, those practices of yours, that method of procedure, those stern austerities did not enable you to transcend human limitations and attain to pre-eminence in full and sublime knowledge and insight. How, then, now that you are luxurious, and have given up the struggle and devoted yourself to a life of luxury, can you have transcended human limitations and attained to pre-eminence in full and sublime knowledge and insight?'

"When they had thus spoken, O priests, I said to the band of five priests as follows:

" 'O priests, The Tathāgata is not luxurious, and has not given up the struggle and devoted himself to a life of luxury. A saint, O priests, is The Tathāgata, a Supreme Buddha. Give ear, O priests! The deathless has been gained, and I will instruct you, and teach you the Doctrine. If ye will do according to my instructions, in no long time, and in the present life, ye shall learn for yourselves, and shall realize and live in the possession of that highest good to which the holy life conducts, and for the sake of which youths of good family so nobly retire from the household life to the houseless one.'

"And a second time, O priests, the band of five priests spoke to me as follows:

.   .   .   .

"And a second time, O priests, I replied to the band of five priests as follows:

.   .   .   .

"And a third time, O priests, the band of five priests spoke to me as follows:

.   .   .   .   .   .

"When they had thus spoken, O priests, I replied to the band of five priests as follows:

" 'Confess, O priests, have I ever before spoken to you as I have done this day?'

" 'Nay, verily, Reverend Sir.'

" 'A saint, O priests, is The Tathāgata, a Supreme Buddha. Give ear, O priests! The deathless has been gained, and I will instruct you, and teach you the Doctrine. If ye will do according to my instructions, in no long time, and in the present life, ye shall learn for yourselves, and shall realize and live in the possession of that highest good to which the holy life conducts, and for the sake of which youths of good family so nobly retire from the household life to the houseless one.'

"And I, O priests, succeeded in winning over the band of five priests.

"And I, O priests, exhorted two priests, while three priests went for alms; and the food which the three priests brought back from their begging-rounds furnished subsistence for all us six. And I, O priests, exhorted three priests, while two priests went for alms; and the food which the two priests brought back from their begging-rounds furnished subsistence for all us six.

"Then, O priests, the band of five priests, thus exhorted and instructed by me, themselves subject to birth, perceived the wretchedness of what is subject to birth, and craving the incomparable security of a Nirvana free from birth, attained the incomparable security of a Nirvana free from birth; themselves subject to old age, . . . disease, . . . death, . . . sorrow, . . . corruption, . . . perceived the wretchedness of what is subject to corruption, and craving the incomparable security of a Nirvana free from corruption, attained the incomparable security of a Nirvana free from corruption. And the knowledge and the insight sprang up within them, 'Our deliverance is unshakable; this is our last existence; no more shall we be born again.'

"There are five sensual pleasures, O priests. And what are the five? Forms perceivable by the eye, delightful, pleasant, charming, lovely, accompanied with sensual pleasure, and exciting passion; sounds perceivable by the ear, . . . odors perceivable by the nose, . . . tastes perceivable by the tongue, . . . things tangible perceivable by the body, delightful, pleasant, charming, lovely, accompanied with sensual pleasure, and exciting passion. These, O priests, are the five sensual pleasures.

"All monks and Brahmans, O priests, who partake of these sensual pleasures, and are enveloped, besotted, immersed in them, and perceive not their wretchedness, and know not the way of escape, of them is it to be understood as follows: 'They have lighted on misfortune, have lighted on destruction, and are in the power of the Wicked One.'

"Just as if, O priests, a deer of the forest were to step into a snare, and were to be caught by it. Concerning this deer it is to be understood as follows: 'It has lighted on misfortune, has lighted on destruction, and is in the power of the hunter. When the hunter shall come, it will not be able to make its escape.' In exactly the same way, O priests, all monks and Brahmans who partake of these sensual pleasures, and enveloped, besotted, and immersed in them, perceive not their wretchedness, and know not the way of escape, of them is it to be understood as follows: "They have lighted on misfortune, have lighted on destruction, and are in the power of the Wicked One.'

"On the other hand, O priests, all monks and Brahmans who partake of these sensual pleasures, and are not enveloped, besotted, and immersed in them, but perceive their wretchedness, and know the way of escape, of them is it to be understood as follows: 'They have not lighted on misfortune, have not lighted on destruction, and are not in the power of the Wicked One.'

"Just as if, O priests, a deer of the forest were to step into a snare, and were not to be caught by it. Concerning this deer it is to be understood as follows: 'It has not lighted on misfortune, has not lighted on destruction, and is not in the power of the hunter. When the hunter shall come, it will be able to make its escape.' In exactly the same way, O priests, all monks and Brahmans who do not partake of these sensual pleasures, and not enveloped, nor besotted, nor immersed in them, perceive their wretchedness, and know the way of escape, of them is it to be understood as follows: 'They have not lighted on misfortune, have not lighted on destruction, and are not in the power of the Wicked One.'

"Just as if, O priests, a deer of the forest were to roam the woods and mountain slopes; he can walk, stand, squat, and lie down in confident security. And why? Because, O priests, he is out of the reach of the hunter. In exactly the same way, O priests, a priest, having isolated himself from sensual pleasures, having isolated himself from demeritorious traits, and still exercising reasoning, still exercising reflection, enters upon the first trance which is produced by isolation, and characterized by joy and happiness. Of such a priest, O priests, is it said, 'He has blinded Māra, made useless the eye of Māra, gone out of sight of the Wicked One.'

"But again, O priests, a priest, through the subsidence of reasoning and reflection, and still retaining joy and happiness, enters upon the second trance, which is an interior tranquilization and intentness of the thoughts, and is produced by concentration. Of such a priest, O priests, is it said, 'He has blinded Māra, made useless the eye of Māra, gone out of sight of the Wicked One.'

"But again, O priests, a priest through the paling of joy, indifferent, contemplative, conscious, and in the experience of bodily happiness—that state which eminent men describe when they say, 'Indifferent, contemplative, and living happily'—enters upon the third trance. Of such a priest, O priests, is it said, 'He has blinded Māra, made useless the eye of Māra, gone out of sight of the Wicked One.'

"But again, O priests, a priest through the abandonment of happiness, through the abandonment of misery, through the disappearance of all antecedent gladness or grief, enters upon the fourth trance, which has neither misery nor happiness but is contemplation as refined by indifference. Of such a priest, O priests, is it said, 'He has blinded Māra, made useless the eye of Māra, gone out of sight of the Wicked One.'

"But again, O priests, a priest through having completely overpassed all perceptions of form, through the perishing of perceptions of inertia, and through ceasing to dwell on perceptions of diversity, says to himself, 'Space is infinite,' and dwells in the realm of the infinity of space. Of such a priest, O priests, is it said, 'He has blinded Māra, made useless the eye of Māra, gone out of sight of the Wicked One.'

"But again, O priests, a priest through having completely overpassed the realm of the infinity of space, says to himself, 'Consciousness is infinite,' and dwells in the realm of the infinity of consciousness. Of such a priest, O priests, is it said, 'He has blinded Māra, made useless the eye of Māra, gone out of sight of the Wicked One.'

"But again, O priests, a priest through having completely overpassed the realm of the infinity of consciousness, says to himself, 'Nothing exists,' and dwells in the realm of nothingness. Of such a priest, O priests, is it said, 'He has blinded Māra, made useless the eye of Māra, gone out of sight of the Wicked One.'

"But again, O priests, a priest through having completely overpassed the realm of nothingness, dwells in the realm of neither perception nor yet non-perception. Of such a priest, O priests, is it said, 'He has blinded Māra, made useless the eye of Māra, gone out of sight of the Wicked One.'

"But again, O priests, a priest through having completely overpassed the realm of neither perception nor yet non-perception, arrives at the cessation of perception and sensation, and before the clear vision of wisdom all his depravity wastes away. Of such a priest, O priests, is it said, 'He has blinded Māra, made useless the eye of Māra, gone out of sight of the Wicked One, and passed beyond all adhesion to the world.' He walks, stands, squats, and lies down in confident security. And why? Because, O priests, he is out of the reach of Māra."

Thus spake The Blessed One; and the delighted priests applauded the speech of The Blessed One.

The Noble-craving Sermon.

THE TRANCE OF CESSATION

1. Translated from the Samyutta-Nikāya (xli. 6⁵)

INSPIRATIONS and expirations, O householder, are bodily functions, therefore inspirations and expirations constitute bodily karma; first occur reasoning and reflection and afterwards articulate utterance, therefore reasoning and reflection constitute vocal karma; perception and sensation are mental functions and occur in association with the mind, therefore perception and sensation constitute mental karma.

2. Translated from the Samyutta-Nikāya (xxxvi. 11⁵)

And moreover, O priest, I have taught the gradual cessation of karma. Of one who has entered the first trance the voice has ceased; of one who has entered the second trance reasoning and reflection have ceased; of one who has entered the third trance joy has ceased; of one who has entered the fourth trance the inspirations and the expirations have ceased; of one who has entered the realm of the infinity of space the perception of form has ceased; of one who has entered the realm of the infinity of consciousness the perception of the realm of the infinity of space has ceased; of one who has entered the realm of nothingness the perception of the realm of the infinity of consciousness has ceased; of one who has entered the realm of neither perception nor yet non-perception, the perception of the realm of nothingness has ceased; of one who has entered the cessation of perception and sensation, perception and sensation have ceased. Of the priest who has lost all depravity, passion has ceased, hatred has ceased, infatuation has ceased.

3. Translated from the Visuddhi-Magga (chap. xxiii.)

What is the trance of cessation?
It is the stoppage of all mentality by a gradual cessation. . . . A

priest who is desirous of entering on cessation will take his breakfast, wash carefully his hands and his feet, and seat him cross-legged
on a well-strewn seat in some retired spot, with body erect, and
contemplative faculty active. He then enters the first trance, and
rising from it obtains insight into the transitoriness, misery, and
lack of an Ego of the constituents of being.

This insight, however, is threefold: the insight into the constituents of being, the insight belonging to the attainment of the Fruits,
and the insight belonging to the trance of cessation.

Whether the insight into the constituents of being be dull or keen,
it is in either case a preparation for the Paths.

The insight belonging to the attainment of the Fruits can only
be keen, like the realization of the Paths.

The insight, however, belonging to the trance of cessation should
not be too dull nor yet too keen. Therefore he will contemplate the
constituents of being with an insight that is neither very dull nor
very keen.

Thereupon he enters the second trance, and rising from it obtains
insight into the constituents of being in the same manner as before.
Thereupon he enters the third trance, . . . the fourth trance, . . .
the realm of the infinity of space, . . . the realm of the infinity of
consciousness, and rising from it obtains insight into the constituents
of being in the same manner as before. Then he enters the realm
of nothingness, and rising from it performs the four preliminary
duties; the protection of less intimate belongings, respect for the
Order, a summons from The Teacher, limitation of time.

The protection of less intimate belongings:—That which is not
intimately joined to the person of the priest, but is more loosely
connected, such as his bowl and his robes, his couch and his bench,
his dwelling, or any other of the requisites, should be protected
from fire, water, wind, robbers, rats, etc., by means of a firm resolve. The manner of making this firm resolve is as follows:

He makes a firm resolve, saying, "For the space of seven days let
not this and that article be burnt by fire, borne away by a flood,
blown to pieces by the wind, carried off by robbers, or eaten by rats
and the like." Then for the space of seven days no harm will touch
them, any more than it did in the case of the elder, Nāga the Great;

but if he does not make this firm resolve, they are liable to perish by fire, etc.

In regard to this elder, tradition has it that he went for alms to the village where lived his mother, a lay devotee. The lay devotee gave him some rice-gruel and asked him to sit down in a reception-hall. The elder sat down and entered on cessation. While he was sitting there, the reception-hall took fire, and all the other priests took up the several mats on which they had been sitting, and fled away. The inhabitants of the village came together, and seeing the elder, cried out, "The lazy monk! the lazy monk!" The fire blazed up in the grass, bamboo, sticks of wood, etc., completely surrounding the elder. The people brought water in pitchers and put it out, removed the ashes and made the ground neat again, and scattering flowers stood worshiping him. The elder rose from his trance, when the fixed term had elapsed, and seeing the people gazing at him, sprang up into the air, and went to the island Piyaṅgu. This is the protection of less intimate belongings.

Articles, however, which are intimately joined to the person of the priest, such as his tunic, his upper garment, or the seat on which he may be sitting, do not need any special resolve. The trance is sufficient to protect them, as in the case of the venerable Sañjīva. For it has been said as follows:

"The concentration of the venerable Sañjīva possesses magical power; the concentration of the venerable Sāriputta possesses magical power."

Respect for the Order—respect, regard for the Order. The sense is the Order cannot hold a function without his presence. Here it is not respect for the Order but reflection on the respect due it which is his preliminary duty. Therefore let him reflect as follows:

"If, during the seven days I am sitting in a trance of cessation, the Order should wish to pass a resolution, or perform some other ecclesiastical function, I will arise before a priest comes and summons me."

If he does this before entering his trance, he will rise from it at the time set; but if he does not do it, and the Order comes together and misses him, and inquires, "Where is such and such a priest?" and hearing that he has entered a trance of cessation sends some priest, saying, "Go, summon him by authority of the Order!" then he will have to rise from his trance when that priest has come within hearing and has called him, saying, "Brother, the Order sends you its respects." For such is the imperativeness of a command from the Order. Therefore he must reflect on this, and so enter his trance as to rise from it of his own accord.

A summons from The Teacher:—Here, also, it is reflection on a summons of The Teacher that is his duty. Therefore let it be reflected upon as follows:

"If, during the seven days I am sitting in a trance of cessation, The Teacher should take occasion to lay down some precept, or, apropos of some particular event, should teach the Doctrine, I will rise from my trance before any one summons me."

If he does this before sitting down, he will rise from it at the time set; but if he does not do it, and The Teacher misses him when the Order assembles, and inquires, "Where is such and such a priest?" and hearing that he has entered a trance of cessation sends some priest, saying, "Go, summon him by my authority!" then he will have to rise from his trance when that priest has come within hearing and has called him, saying, "The Teacher sends for your venerable worship." For such is the imperativeness of a summons from The Teacher. Therefore he must reflect on this, and so enter his trance as to rise from it of his own accord.

Limitation of time—limitation of the time of life. For this priest should be skilful respecting the limitation of time. He should not enter this trance without first reflecting whether his span of life is to last seven days longer or not. For if he were to enter this trance without perceiving that his vital powers were to break up within the seven-day limit, his trance of cessation would not be able to ward off death, and as death cannot take place during cessation, he would have to rise from the midst of his trance. Therefore he must enter it only after having made the above reflection. For it has been said that it is permissible to neglect the other reflections, but not this one.

When he has thus entered the realm of nothingness, and risen from it and performed these preliminary duties, he enters the realm of neither perception nor yet non-perception; and having passed beyond one or two thoughts, he stops thinking and reaches cessation. But why do I say that beyond two thoughts the thoughts cease? Because of the priest's progress in cessation. For the priest's progress in gradual cessation consists in an ascent through the eight attainments by the simultaneous use of both the quiescence and insight methods, and does not result from the trance of the realm of neither perception nor yet non-perception alone. Thus it is because of the priest's progress in cessation that beyond two thoughts the thoughts cease.

Now the priest who should rise from the realm of nothingness, and enter the realm of neither perception nor yet non-perception without having performed his preliminary duties would not be able to lose all thought, but would fall back into the realm of nothingness. In this connection I will add a simile of a man traveling on a road over which he has never passed before.

A certain man traveling on a road over which he has never passed before, comes on his way to a deep ravine containing water, or to a slough in which is a stepping-stone that has been over-heated by the sun; and essaying to descend into the ravine, without having first adjusted his tunic and his upper garment, he is obliged to retreat again to the top of the bank, through fear of wetting his requisites; or stepping upon the stone he scorches his feet so badly that he jumps back to the hither bank. In the above simile, just as the man, through not having adjusted his tunic and his upper garment, retreated to where he had started from, as soon as he had descended into the ravine, or had stepped on the heated stone; in exactly the same way the ascetic, if he have not performed the preliminary duties, as soon as he reaches the realm of neither perception nor yet non-perception, retreats again into the realm of nothingness.

As, however, another man who has traveled on that road before, when he reaches that spot, will gird his tunic tightly and cross the ravine with the other garment in his hand, or will touch the stone as little as possible in passing to the further bank; in exactly the same way a priest who has performed his preliminary duties, and entered the realm of neither perception nor yet non-perception, will pass beyond and lose all thought, and dwell in cessation.

How long will he stay in it? He who has entered it in the above-described manner will remain in it during the limit of time which he has set for it, provided that the termination of his life, or respect for the Order, or a summons from The Teacher does not interfere.

How does he rise from it? In a twofold manner. The priest who is in the path of never returning, with the attainment of the fruit of never returning, the saint with the attainment of the fruit of saintship.

When he has risen from it, to what is his mind inclined? It is inclined to Nirvana. For it has been said as follows:

"Brother Visākha, the mind of a priest who has risen from the trance of the cessation of perception and sensation is inclined to isolation, has a tendency to isolation, is impelled to isolation."

What is the difference between a dead man and one who has entered this trance? This matter also is treated of in this discourse. As it is said:

"Brother, of the man who has died and become a corpse, bodily karma has ceased and become quieted, vocal karma has ceased and become quieted, mental karma has ceased and become quieted, vitality has become exhausted, natural heat has subsided, and the senses have broken up. Of the priest who has entered on the cessation of perception and sensation, bodily karma has ceased and become quieted, vocal karma has ceased and become quieted, mental karma has ceased and become quieted, but vitality has not become exhausted, natural heat has not subsided, and the senses have not broken up."

In regard to the questions "Is the trance of cessation conditioned or unconditioned?" etc., it cannot be said either that it is conditioned or that it is unconditioned, either that it is worldly or that it is transcendent. And why not? On account of the non-existence of any positive reality. Inasmuch, however, as it can be entered upon, therefore it is correct to say that it is brought about, not that it is not brought about.

Whereas the wise who cultivate
The wisdom which doth make a saint
Are they who reach this holy trance—
This trance by saints at all times prized,

And ever by them held to be
Nirvana in the present life—
Therefore the faculty to reach
This state of trance which is conferred
By wisdom in the holy paths
A blessing of those paths is called.

THE ATTAINMENT OF NIRVANA

Translated from the Visuddhi-Magga (chap. xxiii.)

*A*CQUISITION *of honor etc.:*—The blessings to be derived from the realization of this transcendent wisdom include not only the ability to enter the trance of cessation, but also the acquisition of honor etc. For the individual who has developed his wisdom by the development of the fourfold wisdom of the paths is worthy of the worship, the veneration, the votive offerings, and the reverence of all the world of gods and men, and is an unsurpassed source of merit for the world.

To particularize:—

He who, being of weak faculties, develops the wisdom of the first path with a dull insight is reborn seven times at most; after seven rebirths in states of bliss he will make an end of misery: he who develops it with medium faculties and insight is a roamer; after two or three rebirths he will make an end of misery: he who develops it with keen faculties and insight takes root but once, only one human birth will he pass through and make an end of misery.

He who develops the wisdom of the second path returns once; once more will he return to this world and then make an end of misery.

He who develops the wisdom of the third path never returns. His destiny is fivefold, as follows: In the descending order of the worth of his faculties he passes into Nirvana in the midst, at the end, without instigation, with instigation, or passes up current to the Sublime Gods.

Here the one who passes into Nirvana *in the midst* is reborn in some one of the Pure Abodes and passes into Nirvana before attaining half the normal length of life of that heaven; he who passes into Nirvana *at the end* passes into Nirvana after attaining half the normal length of life; he who passes into Nirvana *without instigation* achieves the fourth path without instigation or urging; he who passes into Nirvana *with instigation* achieves the higher path with instigation or urging; and he who *passes up current to the Sublime Gods* starts from the particular heaven in which he may be reborn, and ascends as far as to the Sublime Gods and there passes into Nirvana.

Of those who develop the wisdom of the fourth path, one is freed by faith, another is freed by wisdom, another is doubly freed, another possesses the threefold knowledge, another the Six High Powers, but the greatest of all is he who has mastered the four analytical sciences and has lost all depravity. Concerning this last it has been said:—

"At the time he is in the paths he is disentangling the snarl, at the time he is in the fruits he has disentangled the snarl, and there is in all the world of gods and men none more worthy of votive gifts."

> Since, then, such blessings manifold
> From noble wisdom take their rise,
> Therefore the understanding man
> Should place therein his heart's delight.

The above constitutes the explanation of the development of wisdom and of its blessings in the Way of Purity as taught in the stanza,

> "What man his conduct guardeth, and hath wisdom,
> And thoughts and wisdom traineth well,
> The strenuous and the able priest,
> He disentangles all this snarl."

BUDDHIST WRITINGS

III. The Order

The Admission and Ordination Ceremonies

Reprinted from a paper by J. F. Dickson, B. A., in the Journal of the
Royal Asiatic Society for 1874

IN MAY, 1872, I was invited by my learned friend and pandit
Kewitiyāgala Unnānsē, of the Malwattē Monastery in Kandy,
to be present at an ordination service, held, according to custom,
on the full-moon day of Wesak, (May, June), being the anniversary
of the day on which Gautama Buddha attained Nirvāna, B. C. 543.
I gladly availed myself of this opportunity of witnessing the celebration of a rite of which Englishmen have but little knowledge, and
which has rarely, if ever, been witnessed by any European in Ceylon.

Nothing could be more impressive than the order and solemnity
of the proceedings. It was impossible not to feel that the ceremony
was being conducted precisely as it was more than two thousand
years ago.

The chapter house (Sinhalese, Poya-ge) is an oblong hall, with
rows of pillars forming an inner space and leaving broad aisles at
the sides. At the top of this inner space sat the aged Abbot (Sinhalese, Maha Nāyaka), as president of the chapter; on either side
of him sat the elder priests, and down the sides sat the other priests
in number between thirty and forty. The chapter or assembly thus
formed three sides of an oblong. The president sat on cushions and
a carpet; the other priests sat on mats covered with white calico.
They all sat cross-legged. On the fourth side, at the foot, stood the
candidates, behind the pillars on the right stood the deacons, the
left was given up to the visitors, and behind the candidates at the
bottom was a crowd of Buddhist laymen.

To form a chapter for this purpose not less than ten duly ordained priests are required, and the president must be not less than ten years' standing from his Upasampadā ordination. The priests attending the chapter are required to give their undivided, unremitting, and devout attention throughout the service. Every priest is instructed to join heart and mind in the exhortations, responses, formulas, etc., and to correct every error, lest the oversight of a single mistake should vitiate the efficacy of the rite. Previously to the ordination the candidates are subjected to a strict and searching examination as to their knowledge of the discourses of Buddha, the duties of a priest, etc. An examination and ordination is held on the full-moon day in Wesak, and on the three succeeding Poya days, or days of quarters of the moon.

After witnessing the celebration of this rite, I read the Upasampadā-Kammavācā or book setting forth the form and manner of ordering of priests and deacons, and I was subsequently induced to translate it. This manual was translated into Italian in 1776, by Padre Maria Percoto (missionary in Ava and Pegu), under the title of "Kammuva, ossia trattato della ordinazione dei Talapoini del secondo ordine detti Pinzi," and a portion of it was edited in 1841, in Pāli and Latin, by Professor Spiegel. Clough translated it in 1834, and Hardy has given an interesting summary of it in his Eastern Monarchism; but neither the text nor any complete translation is readily accessible, and I have therefore thought that this edition might possibly be acceptable to those who desire information respecting the practice of Buddhism in Ceylon, where, as is well pointed out by Mr. Childers, in his Pāli Dictionary, (s.v. Nibbānam, p. 272, note), "Buddhism retains almost its pristine purity."

With regard to the transliteration, I have used the system adopted (after Fausböll) by Mr. Childers in his Dictionary. In the translation I have placed in italics the rubrical directions in the text, and all explanations and amplifications of the text I have placed in square brackets. I have thus endeavoured to give a translation of the text as it stands, and, at the same time, to set out the ordination service fully and completely, precisely in the form in use in Ceylon at the present time, as I have myself witnessed it. No one who compares this form with that given in Article XV. of Hodgson's "Literature and Religion of the Buddhists in Nepaul," can fail to be struck with the purity and simplicity of the Ceylon rite as contrasted with that in use among the Northern Buddhists.

KANDY, 9th January, 1873.   J. F. D.

THE ORDINATION SERVICE

Praise be to the Blessed One, the Holy One, to him who has arrived at
the knowledge of all Truth

[The candidate, accompanied by his Tutor, in the dress of a layman, but having the yellow robes of a priest in his arms, makes the usual obeisance and offering to the President of the chapter, and standing says,]

Grant me leave to speak. Lord, graciously grant me admission to deacon's orders. *Kneels down.* Lord, I pray for admission as a deacon. Again, lord, I pray for admission as a deacon. A third time, lord, I pray for admission as a deacon. In compassion for me, lord, take these yellow robes, and let me be ordained, in order to the destruction of all sorrow, and in order to the attainment of Nirvāna. *To be repeated three times.* [The President takes the bundle of robes.] In compassion for me, lord, give me those yellow robes, and let me be ordained, in order to the destruction of all sorrow, and in order to the attainment of Nirvāna. *To be repeated three times.* [And the President then gives the bundle of robes, the yellow band of which he ties round the neck of the candidate, reciting the while the tacapañcakam, or formula of meditation on the perishable nature of the human body, as follows: kesā lomā nakhā dantā taco—taco dantā nakhā lomā kesā. Hair of the head, hair of the body, nails, teeth, skin—skin, teeth, nails, hair of the body, hair of the head. The candidate then rises up, and retires to throw off the dress of a layman, and to put on his yellow robes. While changing his dress he recites the following: In wisdom I put on the robes, as a protection against cold, as a protection against heat, as a protection against gadflies and musquitoes, wind and sun, and the touch of serpents, and to cover nakedness, *i. e.* I wear them in all humility, for use only, and not for ornament or show. Having put on the yellow robes, he returns to the side of his tutor, and says,] Grant me leave to speak. I make obeisance to my lord. Lord, forgive me all my faults. Let the merit that I have gained be shared by my lord. It is fitting to give me to share in the merit gained by my lord. It is good, it is good. I share in it. Grant me leave to speak. Graciously give me, lord, the three refuges and the precepts. [He kneels down.] Lord, I pray for the refuges and the precepts.

[The tutor gives the three refuges and the ten precepts as follows, the candidate still kneeling, and repeating them after him sentence by sentence.

I

THE THREE REFUGES

I put my trust in Buddha.
I put my trust in the Law.
I put my trust in the Priesthood.
Again I put my trust in Buddha.
Again I put my trust in the Law.
Again I put my trust in the Priesthood.
Once more I put my trust in Buddha.
Once more I put my trust in the Law.
Once more I put my trust in the Priesthood.

II

THE TEN PRECEPTS OR LAWS OF THE PRIESTHOOD

Abstinence from destroying life;
Abstinence from theft;
Abstinence from fornication and all uncleanness;
Abstinence from lying;
Abstinence from fermented liquor, spirits and strong drink which are a hindrance to merit;
Abstinence from eating at forbidden times;
Abstinence from dancing, singing, and shows;
Abstinence from adorning and beautifying the person by the use of garlands, perfumes and unguents;
Abstinence from using a high or a large couch or seat;
Abstinence from receiving gold and silver;
                        are the ten means (of leading a moral life).

[The candidate says,]
I have received these ten precepts. Permit me. [He rises up, and makes obeisance to his Tutor.] Lord, I make obeisance. Forgive me

all my faults. May the merit I have gained be shared by my lord. Give me to share in the merit of my lord. It is good, it is good. I share in it.

[This completes the ordination of a deacon, and the candidate retires.]

The foregoing ceremony is gone through previous to the ordination of a priest in all cases, even where the candidate has already been admitted as a deacon. If the candidate is duly qualified for the priestly office, he can proceed at once from deacon's to priest's orders; otherwise he must pass a term of instruction as a deacon: but a candidate who has received deacon's orders must solicit them again, and go through the above ceremony when presented for priest's orders.

The candidate being duly qualified, returns with his tutor, and goes up to the President of the chapter, presenting an offering, and makes obeisance, saying,]

Permit me to speak. Lord, graciously grant me your sanction and support. *He kneels down.* Lord, I pray for your sanction and support; a second time, lord, I pray for your sanction and support; a third time, lord, I pray for your sanction and support. Lord, be my superior. *This is repeated three times.* [The President says,] It is well. [And the candidate replies,] I am content. *This is repeated three times.* From this day forth my lord is my charge. I am charge to my lord. [This vow of mutual assistance] *is repeated three times.*

[The candidate rises up, makes obeisance, and retires alone to the foot of the assembly, where his alms-bowl is strapped on his back. His tutor then goes down, takes him by the hand, and brings him back, placing him in front of the President. One of the assembled priests stands up, and places himself on the other side of the candidate, who thus stands between two tutors. The tutors say to the assembly,] With your permission, [and then proceed to examine the candidate as to his fitness to be admitted to priest's orders]. Your name is Nāga? It is so, lord. Your superior is the venerable Tissa? It is so, lord. [The two tutors together say,] Praise be to the Blessed One, the Holy One, to him who has arrived at the knowledge of all Truth. [They then recite the following commands of Buddha.]

First it is right to appoint a superior. When the superior has been appointed, it is right to inquire whether the candidate has alms-bowl and robes [which they do as follows]. Is this your alms-bowl? It is so, lord. Is this the stole? It is so, lord. Is this the upper robe? It is so, lord. Is this the under robe? It is so, lord. Go and stand there. [The candidate here retires, going backwards in a reverential posture, and stands at the lower corner of the assembly. The tutors remain in front of the President, and one of them says,] Priests, hear me. The candidate desires ordination under the venerable Tissa. Now is the time of the assembly of priests. I will instruct the candidate. [The tutors make obeisance to the President, and go down to the foot of the assembly, and join the candidate, whom they instruct and examine as follows.] Listen, Nāga. This is the time for you to speak the truth, to state what has occurred. When asked concerning anything in the midst of the assembly, if it be true, it is meet to say so; if it be not true, it is meet to say that it is not. Do not hesitate. Conceal nothing. *They inquire of the candidate as follows.* Have you any such diseases as these? Leprosy? No, lord. Boils? No, lord. Itch? No, lord. Asthma? No, lord. Epilepsy? No, lord. Are you a human being? Yes, lord. Are you a male? Yes, lord. Are you a free man? Yes, lord. Are you free from debt? Yes, lord. Are you exempt from military service? Yes, lord. Have you come with the permission of your parents? Yes, lord. Are you of the full age of twenty years? Yes, lord. Are your alms-bowl and robes complete? Yes, lord. What is your name? Lord, I am called Nāga. What is the name of your superior? Lord, my superior is called the venerable Tissa. [The two tutors here go to the top of the assembly, and make obeisance to the President, and one of them says,] Priests, hear me. The candidate desires ordination under the venerable Tissa. He has been duly instructed by me. Now is the time of the assembly of priests. If the candidate is here, it is right to tell him to approach. [One of the tutors says.] Come hither. [The candidate comes up, and stands between the tutors, makes obeisance to the assembly, and kneels down.] Priests, I ask the assembly for ordination. Priests, have compassion on me, and lift me up. A second time, lords, I ask the assembly for ordination; lords, have compassion on me, and lift me up. A third time, lords, I ask the assembly for ordination.

Lords, have compassion on me, and lift me up. [The candidate rises up, and makes obeisance. The tutors say,] Priests, hear me. This candidate desires ordination under the venerable Tissa. Now is the time of the assembly of priests. I will examine the candidate respecting the disqualifications for the priestly office. Listen, Nāga, This is the time for you to speak the truth, to state what has occurred. I will inquire of you concerning facts. If a thing is, it is right to say it is; if a thing is not, it is right to say it is not. Have you any such diseases as these? Leprosy? No, lord. Boils? No, lord. Itch? No, lord. Asthma? No, lord. Epilepsy? No, lord. Are you a human being? Yes, lord. Are you a male? Yes, lord. Are you free from debt? Yes, lord. Are you exempt from military service? Yes, lord. Have you come with the permission of your parents? Yes, lord. Are you of the full age of twenty years? Yes, lord. Are your alms-bowl and robes complete? Yes, lord. What is your name? Lord, I am called Nāga. What is the name of your superior? My superior, lord, is called the venerable Tissa. [Here ends the examination in the midst of the assembly, and one of the tutors reports the result as follows:] This candidate desires ordination under the venerable Tissa. He is free from disqualifications. He has his alms-bowl and robes complete. The candidate asks the assembly for ordination under his superior the venerable Tissa. The assembly gives the candidate ordination under his superior the venerable Tissa. If any of the venerable assembly approves the ordination of the candidate under the venerable Tissa, let him be silent; if any objects, let him speak. A second time I state this matter. Priests, hear me. This candidate desires ordination under the venerable Tissa. He is free from disqualifications for the priestly office. His alms-bowl and robes are complete. The candidate asks the priesthood for ordination under his superior the venerable Tissa. The assembly gives the candidate ordination under his superior the venerable Tissa. If any of the venerable assembly approve the ordination of the candidate under his superior the venerable Tissa, let him be silent; if any objects, let him speak. A third time I state this matter. Priests, listen. This candidate desires ordination under the venerable Tissa. He is free from disqualifications for the priestly office. His alms-bowl and robes are complete. The candidate asks the priesthood for ordination under his superior the venerable Tissa. The assembly gives the candidate ordination under his superior the venerable Tissa. If any of the venerable assembly approves the ordination of the candidate under his superior the venerable Tissa, let him be silent; if any objects, let him speak. [The two tutors here again make obeisance to the President, and say,] The candidate has received ordination from the priesthood under his superior the venerable Tissa. The assembly approves the resolution: therefore it keeps silence. So I understand your wish.

THE MENDICANT IDEAL

Translated from the Samyutta-Nikāya (xvi. 3¹)

THUS have I heard.

On a certain occasion The Blessed One was dwelling at Sāvatthi in Jetavana monastery in Anāthapindika's Park. And there The Blessed One addressed the priests:

"Priests," said he.

"Lord," said the priests to The Blessed One in reply.

And The Blessed One spoke as follows:

"Take pattern by the moon, O priests, when ye go a-begging. Hold aloof, O priests, both in body and in mind, never weary your welcome, nor be impudent to your benefactors.

"Just as a man, O priests, would regard a dilapidated well, or a rugged mountain, or a river difficult to ford, and hold aloof both in body and in mind, in exactly the same way, O priests, take pattern by the moon when ye go a-begging, hold aloof both in body and in mind, never weary your welcome, nor be impudent to your benefactors.

"Kassapa, O priests, takes pattern by the moon when he goes a-begging. He holds aloof both in body and in mind, never wearies his welcome, nor is impudent to his benefactors.

"What do you say to this, O priests? What sort of a priest is worthy to go a-begging?"

"Reverend Sir, our beliefs derive from The Blessed One, have The Blessed One for their guide and their authority. Pray, Reverend Sir, let the answer to this find expression in the mouth of The Blessed One. Anything the priests hear from The Blessed One will be kept in mind."

Then The Blessed One waved his hand in the air: "Just as my hand, O priests, is not caught, nor seized, nor held fast by the air, in exactly the same way, O priests, when the mind of a priest who goes a-begging is not caught, nor seized, nor held fast, and when, willing that they should gain who wish for gain, and that they should acquire merit who wish to acquire merit, he is as delighted and pleased with the gains of others as with his own, such a priest, O priests, is worthy to go a-begging.

"The mind of Kassapa, O priests, when he goes a-begging is not caught, nor seized, nor held fast, and willing that they should gain who wish for gain, and that they should acquire merit who wish to acquire merit, he is as delighted and pleased with the gains of others as with his own.

"What do you say to this, O priests? What sort of a priest is an unworthy teacher of the Doctrine? And what sort of a priest is a worthy teacher of the Doctrine?"

"Reverend Sir, our beliefs derive from The Blessed One, have The Blessed One for their guide and their authority. Pray, Reverend Sir, let the meaning of this saying find expression in the mouth of The Blessed One. Anything the priests hear from The Blessed One will be kept in mind."

"Then listen, O priests, and pay strict attention, and I will speak."

"Yes, Reverend Sir," said the priests to The Blessed One in assent. And The Blessed One spoke as follows:

"Any priest, O priests, who in teaching the Doctrine to others thinks as follows: 'O that they may hear from me the Doctrine! and be won over by what they hear, and manifest delight towards me,' such a priest, O priests, is an unworthy teacher of the Doctrine.

"Any priest, O priests, who in teaching the Doctrine to others thinks as follows: 'The Doctrine has been well taught by The Blessed One, avails even in the present life, is immediate in its results, is inviting and conducive to salvation, and may be mastered by any intelligent man for himself. O that they may hear from me the Doctrine, and be enlightened by what they hear, and as a result of their enlightenment begin to act accordingly!' and thus teaches the Doctrine to others because of that Doctrine's intrinsic goodness, and because of compassion, mercy, and kindness, such a priest, O priests, is a worthy teacher of the Doctrine.

"Kassapa, O priests, in teaching the Doctrine to others, thinks as follows: 'The Doctrine has been well taught by The Blessed One, is of advantage even in the present life, is immediate in its results, is inviting and conducive to salvation, and may be mastered by any intelligent man for himself. O that they may hear from me the Doctrine, and be enlightened by what they hear, and as a result of their enlightenment begin to act accordingly!' and thus teaches the Doctrine to others because of that Doctrine's intrinsic goodness, and because of compassion, mercy, and kindness.

"I will admonish you, O priests, by the example of Kassapa, or by that of any one who may resemble Kassapa, and when you have been admonished, begin to act accordingly."

"AND HATE NOT
HIS FATHER AND MOTHER"

Translated from the Visuddhi-Magga (chap. iii.)

FOR some persons even *mother and father* are no hindrances, as in the case of the young priest, the nephew on his mother's side of an elder who dwelt in Korandaka monastery.

It is related that the young priest had gone to Rohana to hear the precepts read, and the elder's sister, who was a lay devotee, used constantly to ask the elder for news of her son. One day the elder determined to go and fetch the lad, and set out in the direction of Rohana. The youth also had left his quarters, and had issued forth from Rohana. For he said to himself, "It is a long time that I have lived here. I will go now and see my preceptor, and having learnt how the lay woman is doing, I will return again." And they both met on the banks of the Ganges. Then the young priest performed his respectful duties to the elder at the foot of a certain tree, and when the latter asked him, "Whither are you going?" he told him. Said the elder, "You do well; the lay woman is always asking after you, and it is for this very reason that I am come. By all means go, and I will stay and keep residence here." And thus he dismissed him.

The young priest arrived home at the monastery on the day for beginning residence, and they assigned to him a cell which had been built by his father. On the next day his father came, and inquired of one of the priests, "Reverend sir, to whom has my cell been assigned?" And when he heard it had been assigned to a young stranger, he drew near, and having done obeisance, he said,

"Reverend sir, any one who enters upon residence in my cell has a garment given him."

"What mean you, O layman?"

"For the next three months you must beg your food at our house, and when, after the solemnity of inviting criticism, you wish to depart, come and take leave of us."

The other assented by his silence.

Then the layman went home, and said to his wife, "A certain reverend stranger is in the dwelling I put up, and we must wait on him attentively."

"Very well," said the lay woman in assent, and prepared excellent food, both hard and soft.

At breakfast-time the lad came to the house of his mother and father, but no one recognized him. And he remained three months, and always ate his alms at their house. And when residence was over, he announced to them that he was about to depart.

Then said his mother and father, "Reverend sir, you can go on the morrow." And the next day they fed him in their house, and then filled up a measure of sesamum oil and gave it to him, and also a lump of sugar, and nine cubits' length of cloth, and said, "You can go now, reverend sir." And he returned thanks, and set out in the direction of Rohana.

And his preceptor, after the solemnity of inviting criticism, was coming in the opposite direction, and met him in the place where they had met before. The lad performed his respectful duties to the elder at the foot of a certain tree. Then said the elder,

"Well, my friend, did you see the lay woman?"

"Yes, reverend sir," said he in reply, and told him all the news. And having anointed the feet of the elder with the sesamum oil, and made him a drink with the lump of sugar, and given him the cloth, he did obeisance before him and saying, "Reverend sir, Rohana is the place for me," he departed on his way.

The elder came to the monastery, and on the next day entered the village of Korandaka. And the lay woman, who was always looking up the road, and saying, "Now, now my brother is coming with my son," saw him approaching alone, and fell at his feet, and wept, and lamented, saying, "My son, methinks, must be dead, inasmuch as the elder comes alone."

Then thought the elder, "Surely, the lad, through the moderateness of his passions, must have gone away without announcing himself." And he comforted her, and told her the whole story, and drawing forth the cloth from the scrip in which he carried his bowl, he showed it to her.

The lay woman was pleased, and lying prostrate, with her face in the direction in which her son had gone, she worshiped, saying,

"Methinks The Blessed One must have had in mind a body of priests like my son when he preached the relay course of conduct, the Nālaka course of conduct, the tuvattaka course of conduct, and the course of conduct customary with the great saints, showing how to take delight in the cultivation of content with the four reliances. This man ate for three months in the house of the mother who bore him, and never said, 'I am thy son, and thou art my mother.' O the wonderful man!"

For such a one *mother and father* are no hindrances, much less any other lay devotees.

THE STORY OF VISAKHA

Translated from the Dhammapada, and from Buddhaghosa's comment

"As flowers in rich profusion piled
Will many a garland furnish forth;
So all the years of mortal man
Should fruitful be in all good works."

"*AS flowers in rich profusion piled.*" This doctrinal instruction was given by The Teacher while dwelling near Savatthi in Eastern Monastery; and it was concerning Visākhā, a female lay disciple. She was born, we are told, in the city of Bhaddiya, in the kingdom of Bengal. Her father Dhanañjaya, son of Mendaka the treasurer, ranked also as treasurer, and her mother was the lady Sumanā, his principal wife.

When Visākhā was seven years old, The Teacher, perceiving that the Brahman Sela, and others of her city, were competent to attain to salvation, went thither on his wanderings, accompanied by a great congregation of priests.

Now at that time Mendaka, who was filling the office of treasurer in that city, was head of a household of five persons of great merit. The five persons of great merit were: Mendaka the treasurer; Padumā, his principal wife; Dhanañjaya, his eldest son; the latter's wife, Sumanā; and Mendaka's slave, Punna. Now Mendaka the treasurer was not the only person of illimitable wealth in Bimbisāra's territory. There were five of them: Jotiya, Jatila, Mendaka, Punnaka, Kākavaliya.

When Mendaka the treasurer heard of the arrival of The One Possessing the Ten Forces, he sent for the little maid Visākhā, the daughter of his son Dhanañjaya the treasurer, and said to her:

"Dear girl, this is an auspicious day for you and for me! With your five hundred girl-attendants mount five hundred chariots, and with these five hundred female slaves as your retinue go to welcome The One Possessing the Ten Forces."

"Very well," said she, and did so. But as she well knew what etiquette required, when she had gone as far in her carriage as was proper for carriages to go, she alighted, and on foot drew near to The Teacher. Then she did him obeisance, and stood respectfully at one side. Pleased with her behavior, The Teacher taught her the Doctrine, and at the end of the discourse, she attained to the fruit of conversion, together with her five hundred maidens.

Also Mendaka the treasurer drew near to The Teacher, and listening to a sermon, attained to the fruit of conversion, and invited him for the morrow to breakfast. On the next day at his own house he served The Buddha and the congregation of the priests with excellent food, both hard and soft; and thus for half a month he gave liberally. And when The Teacher had stopped in the city of Bhaddiya as long as he wished, he departed.

Now at that time Bimbisāra and Pasenadi the Kosalan were connected by marriage, being each of them the husband of the other's sister. And one day it occurred to the Kosalan king: "In Bimbisāra's territory dwell five men of illimitable wealth, while there is not one in mine. Suppose, now, I go to Bimbisāra, and ask him for one of these persons of great merit."

And going to king Bimbisāra, he was received cordially by the latter, who then asked,

"What was your purpose in coming?"

"In your territory dwell five men of illimitable wealth, persons of great merit. I have come with the intention of taking one of them back with me. Let me have one."

"It would be impossible for me to move one of those great families."

"I will not go without," was the reply.

The king took counsel with his ministers, and then said to him:

"To move such powerful personages as Joti and the others, would be like moving the world. But Mendaka the great treasurer has a son called Dhanañjaya the treasurer: I will consult with him, and then give you my reply."

Then Bimbisāra sent for Dhanañjaya the treasurer, and said to him,

"Dear friend, the king of the Kosalans says he will not return home unless you go with him. Therefore, go with him, pray."

"Sire, I will go, if you send me."

"Then make your preparations, dear friend, and go."

So he got himself ready, and the king was full of kind attentions to him, and at parting formally intrusted him to Pasenadi the king. And Pasenadi the king set out for Sāvatthi, intending to spend one night on the way. And coming to a pleasant spot, they bivouacked there.

Then said Dhanañjaya the treasurer,

"Whose territory are we on now?"

"Mine, O treasurer."

"How far is it from here to Sāvatthi?"

"Seven leagues."

"It is very crowded in a city, and my suite is a large one. Sire, if it so please you, I will dwell here."

"Very good," said the king in assent; and mapping out for him a city, he gave it to him, and went away. And from the circumstance that the settlement in that place was made in the evening [sā-yam], the city received the name of Sāketa.

Now there was dwelling at Sāvatthi a young man named Punna-vaddhana, who was the son of a treasurer named Migāra, and had just come of age. And his mother and father said to him,

"Son, choose yourself a wife from what family you please."

"Oh! I have no use for anything of that sort."

"Son, act not so! No family can last without children."

"Well, then," said he, when they continually insisted, "if I can have a girl endowed with the five beauties, I will do as you say."

"But, son, what are these five beauties?"

"Beauty of hair; beauty of flesh; beauty of bone; beauty of skin; and beauty of youth."

(The hair of a woman who is experiencing the reward of great merit is like a peacock's tail, and, when it is loosened and allowed to fall, reaches to the bottom of the tunic, where the ends turn and point upwards. This is "Beauty of hair." The lips are of a fine color, resembling a bright red gourd, and are smooth and pleasant to the touch. This is "Beauty of flesh." The teeth are white, with even interstices, resembling a row of diamonds set upright, or evenly cut mother-of-pearl. This is "Beauty of bone." The skin, even without the application of sandal-wood perfume, or any rouge, or other cosmetic, is glossy like a blue-lotus wreath, and white like a wreath of kanikāra flowers. This is "Beauty of skin." She possesses a youthfulness as fresh when she has brought forth ten times, as if she had brought forth but once. This is "Beauty of youth.")

Then his mother and father invited and entertained one hundred and eight Brahmans, and inquired of them,

"Are there any women endowed with the five beauties?"

"Assuredly there are."

"Then let eight of you go in search of a girl of this description."

And giving them a liberal present, they continued: "When you return, we will remember you again. Go, search for a girl of this description, and as soon as you find her, put on her this decoration." And with that they placed in their hands a gold wreath worth a hundred thousand pieces of money, and dismissed them.

So the eight Brahmans went searching through all the large cities, but discovered no girl endowed with the five beauties. Then they turned back, and as they were returning, they chanced to arrive at Sāketa on Public Day. "Now," thought they, "our mission will be effected."

It seems that every year in that city there was held a festival called "Public Day." Then all those ladies who are not in the habit of going out of doors issue forth from their homes with their attendants, and show themselves in public, going on foot to the banks of the river. And on the same day they do this, all the rich men's sons of the warrior and other castes station themselves alongside the paths in order to put garlands on the heads of any pretty girls they may see of equal rank with themselves.

And these Brahmans came also, and stationed themselves in a hall on the banks of the river. At that moment Visākhā, then some fifteen or sixteen years of age, came to that place on her way to bathe in the river, being decked in all her ornaments, and attended by five hundred maidens. And suddenly a cloud arose, and it began to rain. The five hundred maidens took to running, and sought refuge in the hall. The Brahmans scanned them carefully, but saw not one among them endowed with the five beauties. Then Visākhā came up at her natural gait, and entered the hall, and her garments and ornaments were wet.

The Brahmans perceived that she had four of the beauties, and being desirous of seeing her teeth, they began conversing among themselves, saying,

"Our daughter is of a lazy disposition; her husband, we must needs suppose, will have to content himself with sour gruel."

Then said Visākhā, "What is that you are saying?"

"Dear girl, we say thus and so."

(They say the sound of her voice was sweet, sounding forth like the tones of a gong of bell-metal.)

Then with a sweet voice, she asked them again,

"Why do you say that?"

"Your attendant women came running to this hall, and did not get their garments or their ornaments wet. But though it is but a little way, you did not run at all, and got your garments and ornaments wet. This is why we speak as we do."

"Good sirs, say not so. I am better able to run than they; but I had my reasons for not running."

"What were they, dear girl?"

"Good sirs, there are four things which do not appear to advantage when running. And there is another reason."

"Dear girl, what are the four things?"

"Good sirs, an anointed and richly dressed king does not appear to advantage when he binds up his loin-cloth, and runs in the royal court. Every one finds fault, saying, 'How is it this great king rushes around like any householder?' He appears to advantage when walking at a slow gait. The king's caparisoned state elephant does not appear to advantage when running. He appears to advantage when marching at an elephant's natural dignified pace. A man who has retired from the world does not appear to advantage when running. Every one finds fault, saying, 'How is it this monk rushes about like any layman?' He appears to advantage when adopting a tranquil gait. No woman appears to advantage when running. People justly find fault with her, saying, 'How is it this woman rushes about like a man?' These four do not appear to advantage when running."

"But what, dear girl, was your other reason?"

"Good sirs, a daughter is brought up by her mother and father, who put a value on every limb in her body. For we are goods for sale. They bring us up in order to marry us into another family. If we should run and stumble, either over our skirts or over some obstacle on the ground, and in falling should break either a hand or a foot, we should remain as burdens on our families. But articles of ornament, if they get wet, can dry. This, good sirs, was my reason for not running."

All the while she was talking, the Brahmans were beholding the splendor of her teeth, such splendor as they felt they had never seen before. And having applauded her speech, they took the gold wreath, and placed it on her head, and said:

"You, dear girl, are the one whom this befits."

Then she asked them: "Good sirs, from what city are you come?"

"From Sāvatthi, dear girl."

"The treasurer, the head of the family, what is his name?"

"His name, dear girl, is Migāra the treasurer."

"And my young master, what is his name?"

"He is the young Punnavaddhana, dear girl."

Having thus ascertained that the family was of equal caste to her own, she sent a message to her father to send the chariot. For although she had come on foot, it is not allowed to maidens to return in that manner when once they have been decorated with the wreath. The daughters of influential families return in chariots and the like; others, either mount ordinary carriages, or walk under a palm-leaf parasol, or, if that is lacking, they raise the skirts of their cloaks and throw them over their shoulders. In the present instance, her father sent her five hundred chariots, and she and her attendants mounted and returned home, while the Brahmans accompanied them.

Then said the treasurer to the Brahmans,

"Whence are ye come?"

"From Sāvatthi, great treasurer."

"The treasurer, what is his name?"

"Migāra the treasurer."

"What is the son's name?"

"Young Punnavaddhana."

"The riches, how great are the riches?"

"Four hundred millions, great treasurer."

"His riches, by the side of ours, are but as a farthing. However, from the time one obtains a protector for a maiden, why look for anything else?" Thus he gave his consent.

After a day or two of hospitable entertainment, he dismissed them. And they returned to Sāvatthi, and announced to Migāra the treasurer:

"We have found the girl."

"Whose daughter is she?"

"Dhanañjaya the treasurer's."

"That is a powerful personage whose daughter you have secured for us. We must go quickly to fetch her." Then he went and announced to the king the circumstances of the case, and that he must needs absent himself for a while.

And the king thought to himself: "This is the great personage whom I removed from before Bimbisāra and settled in Sāketa. I ought to pay him some attention." And he said to Migāra the treasurer,

"I, too, will go."

"Very good, sire," replied the other, and sent the following message to Dhanañjaya the treasurer: "When I come, the king will come also, and the king's army is large. Shall you be able to take care of so many people, or not?"

The return message came: "Let ten kings come, if they wish."

Then Migāra the treasurer took all the inhabitants of that large city, leaving barely enough to guard the houses, and when he had come within half a league of Sāketa, he halted, and sent a message announcing his arrival.

Then Dhanañjaya the treasurer, after sending out to them a large present, consulted with his daughter:

"My dear," said he, "I hear that your father-in-law has come with the king of the Kosalans. Which house shall we get ready for him, which for the king, and which ones for the deputy kings?"

Now clever was the treasurer's daughter, with a fully matured and keen intellect, the result of longing expressed and aspiration cherished through a hundred thousand world-cycles. And she gave orders: "Let such and such a house be got ready for my father-in-law, such another for the king, and such others for the deputy kings." After making these arrangements, she next summoned the slaves and servants, and said to them: "Let so many of you wait on the king, and so many on the deputy kings; and do you who are hostlers and the like take care of the elephants, horses, and other beasts; for our guests must have a merry time while they are here." Such were her orders. And why? So that none might say: "We came to Visākhā's merrymaking and got nothing for our pains, but spent our time looking after our beasts."

That same day, Visākhā's father sent for five hundred goldsmiths, and giving them a thousand nikkhas of red gold, besides silver, gems, pearls, coral, diamonds, etc., enough to go with it, he said: "Make for my daughter what is called the great creeper parure."

After remaining a few days, the king sent a message to Dhanañjaya the treasurer, saying,

"It is too great a load for a simple treasurer to feed and take care of us. Be pleased to appoint a time for the maiden's departure."

But Dhanañjaya the treasurer returned word to the king:

"The rainy season is now come, and you can well afford to remain four months. Let everything pertaining to your army be my care. It will be time enough for your majesty to go when I dismiss you."

From that time on it was like a continual festival for the city of Sāketa. From the king down, every one was provided with garlands, perfumes, garments, and other gifts, so that each one felt himself the especial object of the treasurer's hospitality.

Thus three months went by, but the parure was not yet finished.

Then came the masters of ceremonies, and announced to the treasurer:

"There is no lack of anything else, but the army has not sufficient wood to cook its meals."

"Go, my dear sirs, take all the tumble-down elephant stables, and other buildings of the kind in the city, and all the dilapidated houses, and use them for cooking-fuel."

This wood did the cooking for half a month, and thereupon they again announced to the treasurer:

"There is no wood."

"At this time in the year one cannot go for wood. But open the store-houses where stuffs are kept, and make wicks of the coarse cloths, dip them in vessels of oil, and so cook your meals."

They did so for half a month, and thus four months had gone by, and the parure was finished. There was no thread in this parure; silver was used instead. When this parure was on, it extended from head to foot. At the latter place were bunches of gold medals, and silver dies. On the crown of the head was a medal, at the top of the ears two, at the throat one, at the knees two, at the elbows two, and at the sides of the waist two.

Now a part of this parure consisted of a peacock, and there were five hundred feathers of red gold in the wing on the right side, and five hundred in the one on the left side. The beak was of coral, the eyes were of jewels, and likewise the neck and the tail-feathers. The midribs of the feathers were of silver, and likewise the shanks of the legs. When placed in position on Visākhā's head, it appeared like a peacock dancing on the summit of a mountain, and the sound which came from the thousand midribs rolled forth like the tones of celestial choruses and orchestras. And it was only when people had come quite close that they knew it was not a real peacock.

This parure was worth ninety millions, and a hundred thousand was spent on the workmanship. But what was the deed in a previous existence which caused her to obtain this parure? They say that in the time of Kassapa Buddha she gave cloth for robes to twenty thousand priests, also thread and needles and dyeing material, all her own property; and the parure was the result of this liberality. For the giving of robes by a woman attains its fruition in the great creeper parure; by a man, in the supernatural bowl and robes.

When the great treasurer had thus spent four months in getting ready his daughter's trousseau, he began giving her the dowry. He gave five hundred carts full of money, five hundred carts full of gold dishes, five hundred full of silver dishes, five hundred full of copper dishes, five hundred full of silk garments, five hundred full of clarified butter, five hundred full of husked rice, and five hundred full of plow-shares and other implements. They say the reason why he thus gave her all manner of implements was for fear that his daughter in her new home might need something, and be obliged to send to a neighbor's for it. And he gave fifteen hundred waiting-maids whose duties were to bathe, feed, and dress her,—all of them handsome slaves, and richly dressed, and riding in five hundred chariots, three to each several chariot.

Then he determined to give his daughter some cattle, and gave orders to his men:

"Look you now! Go and open the door of my lesser cattle-fold, and post yourselves for a distance of three quarters of a league, and at every quarter-league have a drum. And let the space across from side to side be a hundred and forty cubits, and let not the cows transgress those limits. And as soon as you get them in position, sound your drums."

They did so. When the cows passed out of the fold, and had gone a quarter-league, the men gave a signal with the drum, and again at the end of the second quarter-league, and again at the third quarter-league. And they hemmed them in at the sides. Thus, for a space of three-quarters of a league in length, and a hundred and forty cubits across, the cows stood so close that they chafed one another.

Then said the great treasurer, "That is enough cows for my daughter. Shut the door." So they shut the door of the fold; but, notwithstanding the door was shut, such was the effect of Visākhā's merit that the vigorous bulls and the milch cows leaped up and got out. And in spite of all the men could do to prevent them, sixty thousand vigorous bulls and sixty thousand milch cows got out, and behind the milch cows followed vigorous bull calves.

What was the deed in a previous existence by reason of which the cattle thus got out? Because once she kept on giving, in spite of the efforts people made to stop her. As tradition has it, in the time of The Supreme Buddha Kassapa, she was the youngest of the seven daughters of king Kiki, and her name was Servant-of-the-Congregation. And as she was once giving the five products of the cow in alms to twenty thousand priests, the young priests and the novices cried, "Enough, enough!" and closed their hands up tight. But, notwithstanding their efforts to prevent her, she kept on giving, saying, "Here is a sweet bit; here is a dainty morsel." This was the reason the cattle kept on coming out, notwithstanding the efforts made to prevent them.

When the treasurer had got thus far in his giving, his wife said to him,

"You have assigned goods to my daughter, but no male and female vassals to do her bidding. Why is this?"

"Because I want to find out who are fond of her, and who are not. Of course, I shall send vassals with her to do her bidding. When she comes to mount her chariot to depart, I shall make proclamation: 'Let all who wish to go with my daughter, do so; and let all others stay at home.' "

Now the day before she was to depart, the treasurer sat in his room and had his daughter sit by him, and he admonished her, telling her what rules of conduct she should adopt when she came to dwell in her husband's family. And it happened that Migāra the treasurer was seated in the next room, and overheard the admonition of Dhanañjaya the treasurer, which was as follows:

"My child, as long as you dwell in your father-in-law's family, the in-door fire is not to be taken out of doors; out-door fire is not to be brought within doors; give only to him who gives; give not to him who does not give; give both to him who gives, and to him who does not give; sit happily; eat happily; sleep happily; wait upon the fire; and reverence the household divinities." This was the tenfold admonition.

On the next day he assembled the different guilds of artisans, and in the presence of the royal army he appointed eight householders to be sponsors for his daughter, saying, "You are to try any charge of sin that may be brought against my daughter in her new home." Next he had his daughter put on her great creeper parure that was worth ninety millions, and gave her besides five hundred and forty millions with which to buy aromatic powders for her bath. And causing her to mount a chariot, he took her about in the neighborhood of Sāketa as far as to Anurādhapura, through fourteen villages that were subject to him; and as he went through one after another, he caused proclamation to be made: "Let all who wish to go with

my daughter, go." On hearing the proclamation all the inhabitants
of the fourteen villages, without exception, issued forth, saying,
"When our mistress is on the point of leaving, why stay we here?"
Then Dhanañjaya the treasurer, full of polite attentions to the king
and Migāra the treasurer, accompanied them a short distance on
their way; and having intrusted his daughter into their hands, he
there took leave of them.

And Migāra the treasurer rode in a conveyance behind the others,
and beholding a great crowd of people following, he asked,

"Pray, who are these?"

"They are male and female vassals to do the bidding of your
daughter-in-law."

"Who could ever feed so many? Beat and drive them away and
keep only those who do not run."

"Hold!" cried Visākhā; "do not drive them away! The one army
can feed the other."

But the treasurer persisted, saying, "My dear girl, we have no
use for them. Who is there to feed them?" And he caused his men
to fling clods of earth at them, and to beat them with sticks, and
all those who did not run he took with him, saying, "These are a
plenty."

When Visākhā approached the gate of the city of Sāvatthi, she
began to reflect, "Shall I enter seated in a covered conveyance, or
standing erect in a chariot?" Then she thought, "If I am in a
covered conveyance when I enter, no one will see the elegance of
my great creeper parure." So she entered the city standing in her
chariot, and showing herself to the whole town. And when the
inhabitants of Sāvatthi beheld the magnificence of Visākhā, they
said, "This, then, is Visākhā. Truly, her magnificence becomes her
well!" And thus it was in great pomp she entered the treasurer's
house.

Then all the inhabitants of the city sent gifts to her, according
to their power, and according to their ability; for they thought,
"Dhanañjaya the treasurer was exceedingly hospitable to us when
we went to his city." But Visākhā took all the gifts that were sent
her, and distributed them to the different families everywhere
throughout the city. And in sending, she accompanied each gift

with an affectionate message: "This is for my mother, this for my father, this for my brother, and this for my sister;" thus treating each one according to age, and making, as it were, all the inhabitants of the city her relatives.

Now towards the end of the night, her thoroughbred mare gave birth to a foal. And Visākhā, accompanied by her female slaves bearing torches, went to the stable, and superintended while they washed the mare with warm water, and anointed her with oil. Then she returned to her own quarters.

Now Migāra the treasurer had for a long time been favorably disposed to the sect of naked ascetics. And urged by this feeling, though The Buddha was dwelling in a neighboring monastery, he neglected him in the festivities of his son's wedding, but determined to do the naked ascetics an honor. So, on a certain day, he had some rice porridge cooked in several hundred new dishes, and extended an invitation to five hundred of the unclothed. And when he had got them all into his house he sent a message to Visākhā, saying, "Let my daughter-in-law come and do reverence to the saints."

When Visākhā heard the word "saints" she was greatly delighted, for she had been converted, and was a noble disciple. But when she came to the place where they were eating, and beheld them, she was angry with the treasurer, and returned to her own quarters, saying reproachfully, "These persons so devoid of shame and fear of sinning cannot be saints. Why did my father-in-law have me summoned?"

When the unclothed caught sight of her, they all with one mouth reproached the treasurer:

"Why, O householder, did you not find some one else for a daughter-in-law? You have introduced into your house an arrant misfortune-breeder, a disciple of the monk Gotama. Make haste and have her expelled from the house."

"It is out of the question," thought the treasurer, "for me to expel her just because these men tell me to do so. She is from too powerful a family." And he dismissed them, saying,

"Your reverences, young people sometimes act without knowing what they are about. Hold your peace!"

Then he sat down on a costly seat, and began to eat the sweet rice porridge from a golden bowl. At that moment a [Buddhist]

elder on his begging rounds entered the house. Visākhā was standing fanning her father-in-law, and saw him. And thinking, "It would not be fitting for me to announce him to my father-in-law," she moved off in such a way as to call his attention to the elder. But the foolish, unconverted man, although he saw the elder, made as if he did not see him, and with head bent down, he kept on eating.

"Pass on, reverend sir," said Visākhā, when she perceived that her father-in-law made no sign, notwithstanding he had seen the elder; "my father-in-law is eating stale fare."

The treasurer, although he had borne with the talk of the naked ascetics, the moment she said, "He is eating stale fare," removed his hand from his bowl, and exclaimed,

"Take away this rice porridge, and turn the girl out of the house! To think that she should accuse *me,* and in a time of festivity, too, of eating anything unclean!"

But all the slaves and servants in the house belonged to Visākhā. Who was there to seize her by hand or foot? There was not one who dared so much as open his mouth.

"Father," said Visākhā, after listening to him; "I'll not leave so easily as you seem to think. I am not a common prostitute, picked up at some river bathing-place; and daughters whose parents are still living are not turned out so easily. Now my father has provided for this very case. When I was starting to come hither, he summoned eight householders, and put me in their charge, saying, 'If any charge of sin be made against my daughter, investigate it.' Have these men summoned, and establish my guilt or innocence."

"She speaks well," said the treasurer, and had the eight householders summoned.

Said he: "This young girl, when I was seated, in a time of festivity, eating rice porridge from a golden bowl, said I was eating what was unclean. Find her guilty and turn her out."

"Dear girl, is it so, as he says?"

"That is not as *I* say:—but when a certain elder on his begging-rounds came and stood in the door-way, my father-in-law, who was eating sweet rice porridge, paid no attention to him. Then I thought: 'My father-in-law is not acquiring any merit in this existence, but is consuming old, stale merit.' So I said: 'Pass on, reverend sir; my father-in-law is eating stale fare.' Now, what fault is there here of mine?"

"There is none. Our daughter speaks justly. Why are you angry with her?"

"Sirs, granted that this is no fault: but one night in the middle watch, she went out behind the house, accompanied by her male and female slaves."

"Dear girl, is it so, as he says?"

"Good sirs, I went for no other reason but that I thought when a thoroughbred mare was bringing forth in this very house, it would not do to sit still and make no sign. So I had my slave-girls take torches, and went and caused the mare to receive the attentions suitable for a time of foaling."

"Sir, our daughter does in your house work that is unfit even for slave-girls. What fault can you discover here?"

"Sirs, granted that here also there is no fault. Her father, however, was admonishing her at the time she was starting to come hither, and gave her ten admonitions of a deeply hidden meaning; and I do not understand them. Let her tell me their meaning. For instance, her father said, 'The in-door fire is not to be taken out of doors.' Is it possible, pray, for us to get on with our neighbors, without ever sending fire to their households?"

"Is it so, as he says, dear girl?"

"Good sirs, my father did not mean that by what he said; but this is what he meant: 'Dear girl, if you notice any fault in your mother-in-law, or your father-in-law, or your husband, do not tell of it outside in some one else's house. There is no worse fire than this.'"

"Sirs, so be it: but her father said: 'Out-door fire is not to be brought within doors.' Would it be possible, if our in-door fire were to go out, for us not to fetch fire from outside?"

"Is it so, as he says, dear girl?"

"Good sirs, my father did not mean that by what he said; but this is what he meant: 'If any of your neighbors, whether male or female, speak ill of your father-in-law, or of your husband, do not bring their talk home, and repeat it saying. "So and so has this or that to say of you." For there is no fire comparable to this fire.'"

Thus, in this point also she was guiltless. And as in this case, so also in the others; and the following is their purport:—

"When her father said to her: 'Give only to him who gives,' he meant, 'Give only to those who give borrowed articles back again.'"

And "Give not to him who does not give," meant, "Give not to those who do not give back again what they borrow."

"Give both to him who gives, and to him who does not give," meant, "When your needy relatives and friends come to you, you should give to them, whether they are able to repay you or not."

"Sit happily," meant, "When you see your mother-in-law, or your father-in-law, or your husband, you should rise, and not keep your seat."

"Eat happily," meant, "You should not eat before your mother-in-law, or your father-in-law, or your husband. You must eat after you have waited on them, and they have been helped to everything they wish."

"Sleep happily," meant, "Do not ascend your couch to lie down to sleep before your mother-in-law, or your father-in-law, or your husband; but when you have done for them all the different services which should be done, you can afterwards yourself lie down to sleep."

"Wait upon the fire," meant, "You should look upon your mother-in-law, your father-in-law, and your husband, as if they were a flame of fire, or a royal serpent."

"Reverence the household divinities," meant, "You should look upon your mother-in-law, your father-in-law, and your husband, as your divinities."

When thus the treasurer had heard the meaning of the ten admonitions, he was unable to find any reply, and sat with downcast eyes. The householders then said to him,

"Treasurer, is there any other sin in our daughter?"

"Sirs, there is none."

"Then, if she is guiltless, why did you attempt without cause to turn her out of doors?"

"Good sirs," said Visākhā, at this point in the discussion, "although at first it was not fitting that I should leave at the command of my father-in-law, yet now that you whom my father appointed to try charges which might be brought against me, have found me guilt-less, it is a good time to go."

So saying, she gave orders to her male and female slaves to get ready the carriages and make the other necessary preparations.

"Dear girl, I spoke in ignorance; pardon me," said then the treas-urer, speaking half to the householders.

"Good sir, I do pardon you all there is to pardon. I am, however, daughter in a family that has studied and has faith in the religion of The Buddha, and to see something of the congregation of the priests is necessary to us. If I can be allowed to wait on the congre-gation of the priests at my pleasure, I will stay."

"Dear girl, wait on your monks as much as you please," was the reply.

Visākhā, accordingly, sent an invitation to The One Possessing the Ten Forces, and on the next day received him at her house. And the naked monks, when they heard that The Teacher had gone to the house of Migāra the treasurer, went also, and sat down outside the house encompassing it. Visākhā, having given the water of dona-tion, sent a message to her father-in-law:

"All the arrangements for the entertainment are ready. Let my father-in-law come and wait on The One Possessing the Ten Forces."

But as he was about to go, the naked ascetics restrained him, say-ing,

"O householder, go not near the monk Gotama."

So he sent back word: "Let my daughter-in-law wait on him her-self."

When she had waited on The Buddha and on the congregation of the priests that followed him, and the meal was now at an end, she again sent a message:

"Let my father-in-law come and hear the sermon."

"If I were not to go now, it would not do at all," said then the treasurer; for he was very desirous of hearing the Doctrine.

"Well, then," said the naked monks, when they saw he was bent on going, "you may listen to the Doctrine of the monk Gotama, if you will sit outside of a curtain." Then they went ahead of him, and drew a curtain around, and he went and sat down outside of the curtain.

But The Teacher thought, "Sit outside of a curtain, if you will, or beyond a wall, or beyond a mountain, or at the end of the world. I am The Buddha, and can make you hear my voice." And marching as it were with a mighty Jambu trunk held aloft, and showering down as it were showers of ambrosia, he began to teach the Doctrine in consecutive discourse.

Now when a Supreme Buddha teaches the Doctrine, those in front, and those behind, and those beyond a hundred or a thousand worlds, and those, even, who inhabit the abode of the Sublime Gods, exclaim: "The Teacher is looking at me; The Teacher is teaching the Doctrine to me." To each one it seems as if The Teacher were beholding and addressing him alone. The Buddhas, they say, resemble the moon: as the moon in the midst of the heavens appears to every living being as if over his head, so The Buddhas appear to every one as if standing in front of him. This gift is said to be their reward for liberality in previous existences, when, for the benefit of others, they cut off their own garlanded heads, gouged out their own eyes, tore out their own hearts, and gave away to be slaves sons such as Jāli, daughters such as Kanhājinā, and wives such as Maddī.

And Migāra the treasurer, as he sat outside the curtain, and turned over and over in his mind the teaching of The Tathāgata, became established in the thousandfold ornamented fruit of conversion, and acquired an immovable and unquestioning faith in the three refuges. Then, raising the curtain, he approached his daughter-in-law, and taking her breast in his hand, he said: "From this day forth you are my mother," thus giving her the position of mother. And henceforth she was known as "Migāra's mother"; and when, later on, she had a son, she named him Migāra.

The great treasurer then let go his daughter-in-law's breast, and went and fell at the feet of The Blessed One, and stroking them with his hands, and kissing them with his lips, he three times proclaimed his own name, "Reverend Sir, I am Migāra."

"Reverend Sir," continued he, "all this time have I been without knowing that on you should one bestow alms to obtain great reward. But now I have learnt it, thanks to my daughter-in-law, and am released from all danger of being reborn in a lower state of existence. Truly, it was for my advantage and for my welfare that my daughter-in-law came to my house." So saying, he pronounced the following stanza:

"Now have I learnt where rich reward
Will surely follow every gift!
Truly a happy day for me,
When first my daughter sought my home!"

Visākhā invited The Teacher again for the next day on her own account, and on the day after her mother-in-law also attained to the fruit of conversion. And henceforth that house kept open doors for the religion of The Buddha.

Then thought the treasurer, "My daughter-in-law is a great benefactress to me; I must make her a present. And, truly, her present parure is too heavy for every-day wear. I will have a very light one made, which she can wear both by day and by night in all the four postures."

And he had made what is called a highly polished parure, worth a thousand pieces of money: and when it was finished, he invited The Buddha, and the congregation of the priests, and assiduously waited on them at breakfast. And causing Visākhā to bathe herself with sixteen pitcherfuls of perfumed water, he placed her in front of The Teacher, and putting her parure upon her, he had her do obeisance. Then The Teacher, after giving thanks for the repast, returned to the monastery.

And Visākhā continued to give alms, and do other deeds of merit, and she received the eight boons from The Teacher. And as the crescent of the moon waxes great in the sky, so did she increase in sons and daughters. They say she had ten sons and ten daughters, and of these each had ten sons and ten daughters, and of these also each had ten sons and ten daughters. Thus the children and children's children which had sprung from her numbered eight thousand and four hundred and twenty persons.

She lived to be a hundred and twenty years old, but there was not a single gray hair on her head,—always she appeared as if about sixteen. When people saw her on her way to the monastery, surrounded by her children and children's children, there were al-

ways those who inquired: "Which of these is Visākhā?" Those
who saw her as she walked would think: "I hope she will walk a
little further; our lady looks well when she walks." And those who
saw her stand, or sit, or lie, would think: "I hope she will lie a little
longer now; our lady looks well when she is lying down." Thus
in respect of the four postures, it could not be charged against her
that there was any one posture in which she did not look well.

Moreover, she was as strong as five elephants. And the king,
hearing that Visākhā was currently reported to be as strong as five
elephants, was desirous of testing her strength; and one day, as
she was on her way back from the monastery where she had been
to hear a sermon, he let loose an elephant against her. The elephant,
lifting his trunk, came on to meet Visākhā. Of her five hundred
attendant women, some fled away, while others threw their arms
about her. And when she asked what the matter was, they replied:
"They say the king is desirous of testing your iron strength, and
has let loose an elephant against you." When Visākhā saw the
elephant, she thought, "What is the need of my running away? It
is only a question how I shall take hold of him." And, being afraid
that if she seized him roughly it might kill him, she took hold of
his trunk with two fingers, and pressed him back. The elephant
was unable either to resist or to keep his feet, and fell back on his
haunches in the royal court. Thereupon the crowd shouted "Bravo!"
and she and her attendants reached home in safety.

Now at that time Visākhā, Migāra's mother, lived at Sāvatthi,
and had many children and many children's children, and the children were free from disease, and the children's children were free
from disease, and she was considered to bring good luck. Among
her thousands of children and children's children not one had died.
And when the inhabitants of Sāvatthi had their festivals and holi-
days, Visākhā was always the first to be invited, and the first to be
feasted.

Now on a certain day of merry-making, the populace were going
in their fine clothes and ornaments to the monastery to listen to the
Doctrine. And Visākhā, having come from a place of entertainment, and wearing the great creeper parure, was likewise proceed-

ing with the populace to the monastery. There she took off her ornaments, and gave them to her slave-girl. Concerning which it is said,

"Now at that time there was a merry-making at Sāvatthi; and the people in gorgeous array went to the park. Visākhā, also, Migāra's mother, in gorgeous array went to the monastery. Then Visākhā, Migāra's mother, took off her ornaments, and tying them up in a bundle in her cloak, gave them to her slave-girl, saying, 'Here, take this bundle.' "

It would appear that she thought it not seemly to enter the monastery wearing such an extremely costly and showy parure,— a decoration which, when put on, adorned her from head to foot. Thus it was that, as she was proceeding to the monastery, she took it off, and made of it a bundle, and gave it to a slave-girl, who had been born with the strength of five elephants as the result of former good deeds, and hence was able to carry it. Thus her mistress could say to her, "Dear girl, take this parure. I will put it on when I return from The Teacher."

Having put on her highly polished parure, she drew near The Teacher, and listened to the Doctrine. And at the close of the sermon she rose, did obeisance to The Blessed One, and went forth from his presence. The slave-girl, however, forgot the parure. Now it was the custom of Ananda the elder, when the assembly had listened to the Doctrine, and had departed, to put away anything that had been forgotten. And so this day he noticed the great creeper parure, and announced to The Teacher,

"Reverend Sir, Visākhā has gone forgetting her parure."

"Lay it aside, Ananda."

The elder lifted it up, and hung it on the side of the staircase.

And Visākhā, in company with her friend Suppiyā, wandered about the monastery to see what could be done for the in-coming, for the out-going, for the sick, and others. Now it was the custom of the young priests and novices, when they saw the devout ladies bringing clarified butter, honey, oil, and other medicaments, to draw near with basins of various kinds. And on that day also they did so.

Thereupon Suppiyā saw a certain sick priest, and asked him,

"Sir, of what do you stand in need?"

"Meat broth," was the reply.

"Very well, sir; I will send you some.

But as she failed on the next day to obtain any suitable meat, she made the preparation with flesh from her own thigh; and afterwards by the favor of The Teacher her body was made whole.

When Visākhā had attended to the sick and to the young priests, she issued forth from the monastery. But before she had gone far, she stopped and said,

"Dear girl, bring me the parure; I will put it on."

Instantly the slave-girl remembered that she had forgotten it, and had left it behind. And she said,

"Mistress, I forgot it."

"Go, then, and get it, and bring it hither. But if my master, Ananda the elder, has taken it up and laid it away anywhere, then do not fetch it. It is a present to my master." It appears she knew that the elder was in the habit of putting away valuables which highborn personages had forgotten; and this was why she spoke as she did.

When the elder saw the slave-girl, he said to her,

"Why have you returned?"

"I went away forgetting my mistress's parure," said she.

"I have put it by the staircase," said the elder; "go and get it."

"My lord," said the slave-girl, "an article which has been touched by your hand is not to be reclaimed by my mistress." And so she returned empty-handed.

"How was it, dear girl?" said Visākhā. And she told her.

"Dear girl, never will I wear an article which my master has touched. I make him a present of it. Nevertheless, it would be troublesome for my masters to take care of it. I will sell it, and give them things which are more suitable. Go fetch it."

And the slave-girl went and fetched it.

Visākhā did not put it on, but sent for some goldsmiths and had it appraised.

"It is worth ninety millions," said they; "and the workmanship is worth a hundred thousand."

"Then put the parure in a wagon," said Visākhā, "and sell it."

"There is no one who is able to take it at such a price, and a woman worthy to wear such a parure is difficult to find. For in all the circuit of the earth only three women have the great creeper parure: Visākhā, the great female lay disciple; the wife of Bandhula, the general of the Mallas; and Mallikā, daughter of a treasurer of Benares."

So Visākhā paid the price herself; and, putting ninety millions and a hundred thousand into a cart, she took the amount to the monastery.

"Reverend Sir," said she, when she had made her obeisance to The Teacher, "my master, Ananda the elder, has touched with his hand my parure, and from the time he has touched it, it is impossible for me to wear it again. I have endeavored to sell it, thinking that with the amount I should get for it, I would give things suitable for priests. But when I saw there was no one else able to buy it, I made up the price myself, and have now brought the money with me. Reverend Sir, which one of the four reliances shall I give?"

"Visākhā, a dwelling-place at the east gate for the congregation of the priests would be fitting."

"The very thing, Reverend Sir!"

And Visākhā, with a joyous mind, bought a site for ninety millions, and with another ninety millions she began constructing a monastery.

Now one day, as The Teacher at dawn was gazing over the world, he perceived that a son, Bhaddiya, had been born from heaven into the family of a treasurer of the city of Bhaddiya, and was competent to attain to salvation. And after taking breakfast at the house of Anāthapindika, he directed his steps towards the north gate of the city. Now it was the custom of The Teacher, if he took alms at the house of Visākhā, to issue forth from the city by the south gate and lodge at Jetavana monastery. If he took alms at the house of Anāthapindika, he would issue forth by the east gate, and lodge in Eastern Park; but if The Blessed One was perceived at sunrise making his way to the north gate, then people knew that he was setting out on his travels.

So when Visākhā heard on that day that he had gone in the direction of the north gate, she hastened to him, and making an obeisance, said,

"Reverend Sir, are you desirous of going traveling?"

"Yes, Visākhā."

"Reverend Sir, at this vast expense am I having a monastery built for you. Reverend Sir, turn back."

"Visākhā, this journey admits not of my turning back."

"Assuredly," thought Visākhā, "The Blessed One has some special reason in all this." Then she said, "Reverend Sir, in that case, before you go, command some priest to stay behind who will know how the work should be done."

"Visākhā, take the bowl of any one you wish."

Then Visākhā, though fond of Ananda, thought of the magical power of the elder, Moggallāna the Great, and how swiftly the work would progress with him to assist, and took his bowl.

The elder then looked at The Teacher.

"Moggallāna," said The Teacher, "take five hundred priests in your train and turn back."

And he did so: and by his supernatural power they would go a distance of fifty or sixty leagues for logs and stones; and having secured logs and stones of tremendous size, they would bring them home on the same day. And they who placed the logs and stones on the carts were not exhausted, nor did the axles break. And in no long time they had erected a two-story building on high foundations and approached by steps. The building contained a thousand apartments,—five hundred apartments being in the lower story, and the same number in the upper.

After traveling about for nine months, The Teacher came again to Sāvatthi; and in these nine months Visākhā had put up her building, and was now at work on the peak, which was intended to hold the water-pots, and was finished in solid, beaten, red gold.

And Visākhā, hearing that The Teacher was proceeding towards Jetavana monastery, went to meet him; and, conducting him to her monastery, she exacted of him a promise:

"Reverend Sir, dwell here for four months with the congregation of the priests, and I will have the building completed."

The Teacher consented; and thenceforth she gave alms to The Buddha, and to the congregation of the priests in the monastery.

And it came to pass that a certain female friend of Visākhā came to her with a piece of stuff that was worth a thousand pieces of money.

"Dear friend," said she, "I want to replace some of the floor covering in your pavilion, and spread this instead. Tell me a place in which to spread it."

"Dear friend, if I were to tell you there was no place left, you would think, 'She does not want to let me have a place.' But look through the two floors of the pavilion and the thousand apartments yourself, and find a place in which to spread it."

Then the other took the piece of stuff worth a thousand pieces of money, and went through the building; but finding no stuff there of less value than hers, she was overcome with grief; for she thought: "I shall have no share in the merit of this building." And stopping still, she wept.

And Ananda the elder happened to see her, and said, "Why do you weep?" And she told him the matter.

"Let not that trouble you," said the elder; "I will tell you a place in which to spread it. Make a door-mat of it, and spread it between the place for washing the feet and the staircase. The priests, after washing their feet, will wipe them upon the mat before they enter the building: thus will your reward be great." This spot, it appears, had been overlooked by Visākhā.

For four months did Visākhā give alms in her monastery to The Buddha and to the congregation which followed him; and at the end of that time she presented the congregation of the priests with stuff for robes, and even that received by the novices was worth a thousand pieces of money. And of medicines, she gave the fill of every man's bowl. Ninety millions were spent in this donation. Thus ninety millions went for the site of the monastery, ninety for the construction of the monastery, and ninety for the festival at the opening of the monastery, making two hundred and seventy millions in all that were expended by her on the religion of The Buddha. No other woman in the world was as liberal as this one who lived in the house of a heretic.

On the day the monastery was completed, when the shadows of eventide were lengthening, she walked with her children and her children's children round and round the building, delighted with the thought that her prayer of a former existence had now attained its complete fruition. And with a sweet voice, in five stanzas, she breathed forth this solemn utterance:—

> " 'O when shall I a mansion give,
> Plastered with mud and stuccoed o'er,
> A pleasing monastery-gift?'—
> O this my prayer is now fulfilled!

> " 'O when shall I give household goods,
> Benches and stools to sit upon,
> And bolsters, pillows for the couch?'—
> O this my prayer is now fulfilled!

> " 'O when shall I provisions give,
> The ticket-food so pure and good,
> Smothered in broths of various meats?'—
> O this my prayer is now fulfilled!

> " 'O when shall I give priestly robes,
> Garments of fine Benares cloth,
> And linen, cotton goods as well?'—
> O this my prayer is now fulfilled!

> " 'O when shall I give medicines,
> Fresh butter, butter clarified,
> And honey, treacle, purest oil?'—
> O this my prayer is now fulfilled! "

When the priests heard her, they brought word to The Teacher: "Reverend Sir, in all this time we have never known Visākhā to sing; but now, surrounded by her children and her children's children, she walks singing round and round the building. Pray, is her bile out of order? or has she become mad?"

"Priests," said The Teacher, "my daughter is not singing; but the desire of her heart having come to pass, in her delight she breathes forth a solemn utterance."

"But when was it, Reverend Sir, she made the prayer?"

"Priests, will you listen?"

"Reverend Sir, we will."

Whereupon he related a tale of ancient times—

"Priests, a hundred thousand cycles ago, a Buddha was born into the world by the name of Padumuttara. His term of life was a hundred thousand years; his retinue of those in whom depravity had become extinct was a hundred thousand; his city was Hamsavatī; his father, king Sunanda; and his mother, queen Sujātā. The chief benefactress of this Teacher, a lay devotee, had obtained the eight boons and held the position of mother, and used to provide him with the four reliances. Every evening and morning she used to wait on him at the monastery, and a certain female friend constantly accompanied her.

"When this friend saw on what intimate terms she conversed with The Teacher, and how much she was beloved, she began to consider: 'What do people do to be beloved by The Buddhas?' And she said to The Teacher:

" 'Reverend Sir, what is this woman to you?'

" 'She is the chief of my benefactresses.'

" 'Reverend Sir, by what means does one thus become chief benefactress?'

" 'By praying for a hundred thousand world-cycles to become one.'

" 'Reverend Sir, could I become one, if I now made my prayer?'

" 'Assuredly, you could.'

" 'In that case, Reverend Sir, come with your hundred thousand priests and take alms of me for seven days.'

"The Teacher consented; and for seven days she gave alms of food, and on the last day stuff for robes. Then she did obeisance to The Teacher, and, falling at his feet, made her prayer:

" 'Reverend Sir, I do not pray for rule among the gods, or any other such reward as the fruit of this alms-giving; but that from some Buddha like yourself I may obtain the eight boons, and have the position of mother, and be chief of those able to provide the four reliances.'

"The Teacher looked into the future for a hundred thousand cycles to see if her prayer would be fulfilled, and said:

" 'At the end of a hundred thousand cycles a Buddha named Gotama shall arise, and you shall be a female lay disciple of his, and have the name Visākhā. From him you shall obtain the eight boons,

and obtain the position of mother, and become chief of the benefactresses who shall provide the four reliances.'

". . . and after a life of meritorious deeds, she was reborn in the
world of the gods. And continuing to be reborn in the world of the
gods and the world of men, she was born in the time of The Supreme
Buddha Kassapa as the youngest of the seven daughters of Kiki,
king of Benares. In this existence she was called Servant-of-the-
Congregation; and having married, and with her sisters for a long
time given alms and done other meritorious deeds, she fell at the feet
of The Supreme Buddha Kassapa, and prayed: 'At a future time
may I hold the position of mother to a Buddha such as you, and
become chief of the female givers of the four reliances.' Now, after
further rebirths in the world of the gods and the world of men, she
has been born in this existence as the daughter of Dhanañjaya the
treasurer, the son of Mendaka the treasurer, and has done many
meritorious deeds for my religion. Thus it is, O priests, that I say
my daughter is not singing, but that, at the realization of her prayer,
she breathes forth a solemn utterance."

And The Teacher continued his instruction, and said,

"Priests, just as a skilful garland-maker, if he obtain a large heap
of various kinds of flowers, will go on and on making all manner
of garlands, even so does the mind of Visākhā incline to do all manner of noble deeds." So saying, he pronounced this stanza:

"As flowers in rich profusion piled
Will many a garland furnish forth;
So all the years of mortal man
Should fruitful be in all good works."

(HINDUISM)

THE BHAGAVAD-GITA

OR

SONG CELESTIAL

TRANSLATED BY
SIR EDWIN ARNOLD

INTRODUCTORY NOTE

DURING the centuries in which Buddhism was establishing itself in the east of India, the older Brahmanism in the west was undergoing the changes which resulted in the Hinduism which is now the prevailing religion of India. The main ancient sources of information with regard to these Hindu beliefs and practises are the two great epics, the "Rāmā-yana" and the Mahā Bhārata. The former is a highly artificial production based on legend and ascribed to one man, Vālmīki. The latter, a "huge conglomeration of stirring adventure, legend, myth, history, and super-stition," is a composite production, begun probably as early as the fourth or fifth century before Christ, and completed by the end of the sixth century of our era. It represents many strata of religious belief.

The "Bhagavad-Gîtâ," of which a translation is here given, occurs as an episode in the Mahā-Bhārata, and is regarded as one of the gems of Hindu literature. The poem is a dialogue between Prince Arjuna, the brother of King Yudhisthira, and Vishnu, the Supreme God, incarnated as Krishna, and wearing the disguise of a charioteer. The conversation takes place in a war-chariot, stationed between the armies of the Kauravas and Pāndavas, who are about to engage in battle.

To the Western reader much of the discussion seems childish and illogical; but these elements are mingled with passages of undeniable sublimity. Many of the more puzzling inconsistencies are due to inter-polations by later re-writers. "It is," says Hopkins, "a medley of beliefs as to the relation of spirit and matter, and other secondary matters; it is uncertain in its tone in regard to the comparative efficacy of action and inaction, and in regard to the practical man's means of salvation; but it is at one with itself in its fundamental thesis, that all things are each a part of one Lord, that men and gods are but manifestations of the One Divine Spirit."

THE BHAGAVAD-GITA

OR

SONG CELESTIAL

CHAPTER I

Dhritirashtra:

RANGED thus for battle on the sacred plain—
On Kurukshetra—say, Sanjaya! say
What wrought my people, and the Pandavas?

SANJAYA:

When he beheld the host of Pandavas
Raja Duryôdhana to Drona drew,
And spake these words: "Ah, Guru! see this line,
How vast it is of Pandu fighting-men,
Embattled by the son of Drupada,
Thy scholar in the war! Therein stand ranked
Chiefs like Arjuna, like to Bhîma chiefs,
Benders of bows; Virâta, Yuyudhân,
Drupada, eminent upon his car,
Dhrishtaket, Chekitân, Kasi's stout lord,
Purujit, Kuntibhôj, and Saivya,
With Yudhâmanyu, and Uttamanj
Subhadra's child; and Drupadi's;—all famed!
All mounted on their shining chariots!
On our side, too,—thou best of Brahmans! see
Excellent chiefs, commanders of my line,
Whose names I joy to count: thyself the first,
Then Bhishma, Karna, Kripa fierce in fight,
Vikarna, Aswatthâman; next to these
Strong Saumadatti, with full many more
Valiant and tried, ready this day to die

For me their king, each with his weapon grasped,
Each skilful in the field. Weakest—meseems—
Our battle shows where Bhishma holds command,
And Bhima, fronting him, something too strong!
Have care our captains nigh to Bhishma's ranks
Prepare what help they may! Now, blow my shell!"

Then, at the signal of the aged king,
With blare to wake the blood, rolling around
Like to a lion's roar, the trumpeter
Blew the great Conch; and, at the noise of it,
Trumpets and drums, cymbals and gongs and horns
Burst into sudden clamor; as the blasts
Of loosened tempest, such the tumult seemed!
Then might be seen, upon their car of gold
Yoked with white steeds, blowing their battle-shells,
Krishna the God, Arjuna at his side:
Krishna, with knotted locks, blew his great conch
Carved of the "Giant's bone;" Arjuna blew
Indra's loud gift; Bhima the terrible—
Wolf-bellied Bhima—blew a long reed-conch;
And Yudhisthira, Kunti's blameless son,
Winded a mighty shell, "Victory's Voice;"
And Nakula blew shrill upon his conch
Named the "Sweet-sounding," Sahadev on his
Called "Gem-bedecked," and Kasi's Prince on his.
Sikhandi on his car, Dhrishtadyumn,
Virâta, Sâtyaki the Unsubdued,
Drupada, with his sons, (O Lord of Earth!)
Long-armed Subhadra's children, all blew loud,
So that the clangor shook their foemen's hearts,
With quaking earth and thundering heav'n.
                                        Then 'twas—
Beholding Dhritirashtra's battle set,
Weapons unsheathing, bows drawn forth, the war
Instant to break—Arjun, whose ensign-badge
Was Hanuman the monkey, spake this thing

To Krishna the Divine, his charioteer:
"Drive, Dauntless One! to yonder open ground
Betwixt the armies; I would see more nigh
These who will fight with us, those we must slay
To-day, in war's arbitrament; for, sure,
On bloodshed all are bent who throng this plain,
Obeying Dhritirashtra's sinful son."

Thus, by Arjuna prayed (O Bharata!)
Between the hosts that heavenly Charioteer
Drove the bright car, reining its milk-white steeds
Where Bhishma led, and Drona, and their Lords.
"See!" spake he to Arjuna, "where they stand,
Thy kindred of the Kurus:" and the Prince
Marked on each hand the kinsmen of his house,
Grandsires and sires, uncles and brothers and sons,
Cousins and sons-in-law and nephews, mixed
With friends and honored elders; some this side,
Some that side ranged: and, seeing those opposed,
Such kith grown enemies—Arjuna's heart
Melted with pity, while he uttered this.

ARJUNA:

Krishna! as I behold, come here to shed
Their common blood, yon concourse of our kin,
My members fail, my tongue dries in my mouth,
A shudder thrills my body, and my hair
Bristles with horror; from my weak hand slips
Gandîv, the goodly bow; a fever burns
My skin to parching; hardly may I stand;
The life within me seems to swim and faint;
Nothing do I foresee save woe and wail!
It is not good, O Keshav! nought of good
Can spring from mutual slaughter! Lo, I hate
Triumph and domination, wealth and ease,
Thus sadly won! *Aho!* what victory
Can bring delight, Govinda! what rich spoils

Could profit; what rule recompense; what span
Of life itself seem sweet, bought with such blood?
Seeing that these stand here, ready to die,
For whose sake life was fair, and pleasure pleased,
And power grew precious:—grandsires, sires, and sons.
Brothers, and fathers-in-law, and sons-in-law,
Elders and friends! Shall I deal death on these
Even though they seek to slay us? Not one blow,
O Madhusudan! will I strike to gain
The rule of all Three Worlds; then, how much less
To seize an earthly kingdom! Killing these
Must breed but anguish, Krishna! If they be
Guilty, we shall grow guilty by their deaths;
Their sins will light on us, if we shall slay
Those sons of Dhritirashtra, and our kin;
What peace could come of that, O Madhava?
For if indeed, blinded by lust and wrath,
These cannot see, or will not see, the sin
Of kingly lines o'erthrown and kinsmen slain,
How should not we, who see, shun such a crime—
We who perceive the guilt and feel the shame—
Oh, thou Delight of Men, Janârdana?
By overthrow of houses perisheth
Their sweet continuous household piety,
And—rites neglected, piety extinct—
Enters impiety upon that home;
Its women grow unwomaned, whence there spring
Mad passions, and the mingling-up of castes,
Sending a Hell-ward road that family,
And whoso wrought its doom by wicked wrath.
Nay, and the souls of honored ancestors
Fall from their place of peace, being bereft
Of funeral-cakes and the wan death-water.[1]
So teach our holy hymns. Thus, if we slay
Kinsfolk and friends for love of earthly power,
Ahovat! what an evil fault it were!

---

[1] Some repetitionary lines are here omitted.

Better I deem it, if my kinsmen strike,
To face them weaponless, and bare my breast
To shaft and spear, than answer blow with blow.

So speaking, in the face of those two hosts,
Arjuna sank upon his chariot-seat,
And let fall bow and arrows, sick at heart.

*Here endeth Chapter I. of the Bhagavad-Gîtâ, entitled
"Arjun-Vishâd," or "The Book of the
Distress of Arjuna."*

CHAPTER II

SANJAYA:

HIM, filled with such compassion and such grief,
With eyes tear-dimmed, despondent, in stern words
The Driver, Madhusudan, thus addressed:

KRISHNA:

How hath this weakness taken thee? Whence springs
The inglorious trouble, shameful to the brave,
Barring the path of virtue? Nay, Arjun!
Forbid thyself to feebleness! it mars
Thy warrior-name! cast off the coward-fit!
Wake! Be thyself! Arise, Scourge of thy foes!

ARJUNA:

How can I, in the battle, shoot with shafts
On Bhishma, or on Drona—oh, thou Chief!—
Both worshipful, both honorable men?

Better to live on beggar's bread
    With those we love alive,
Than taste their blood in rich feasts spread,
    And guiltily survive!
Ah! were it worse—who knows?—to be
    Victor or vanquished here,
When those confront us angrily
    Whose death leaves living drear?
In pity lost, by doubtings tossed,
    My thoughts—distracted—turn
To Thee, the Guide I reverence most,
    That I may counsel learn:

I know not what would heal the grief
  Burned into soul and sense,
If I were earth's unchallenged chief—
  A god—and these gone thence!

SANJAYA:

So spake Arjuna to the Lord of Hearts,
And sighing, "I will not fight!" held silence then.
To whom, with tender smile (O Bharata!)
While the Prince wept despairing 'twixt those hosts,
Krishna made answer in divinest verse:

KRISHNA:

Thou grievest where no grief should be! thou speak'st
Words lacking wisdom! for the wise in heart
Mourn not for those that live, nor those that die.
Nor I, nor thou, nor any one of these,
Ever was not, nor ever will not be,
For ever and for ever afterwards.
All, that doth live, lives always! To man's frame
As there come infancy and youth and age,
So come there raisings-up and layings-down
Of other and of other life-abodes,
Which the wise know, and fear not. This that irks—
Thy sense-life, thrilling to the elements—
Bringing thee heat and cold, sorrows and joys,
'Tis brief and mutable! Bear with it, Prince!
As the wise bear. The soul which is not moved,
The soul that with a strong and constant calm
Takes sorrow and takes joy indifferently,
Lives in the life undying! That which is
Can never cease to be; that which is not
Will not exist. To see this truth of both
Is theirs who part essence from accident,
Substance from shadow. Indestructible,
Learn thou! the Life is, spreading life through all;

It cannot anywhere, by any means,
Be anywise diminished, stayed, or changed.
But for these fleeting frames which it informs
With spirit deathless, endless, infinite,
They perish. Let them perish, Prince! and fight!
He who shall say, "Lo! I have slain a man!"
He who shall think, "Lo! I am slain!" those both
Know naught! Life cannot slay. Life is not slain!
Never the spirit was born; the spirit shall cease to be never;
   Never was time it was not; End and Beginning are
    dreams!
Birthless and deathless and changeless remaineth the spirit
   for ever;
   Death hath not touched it at all, dead though the house
   of it seems!

Who knoweth it exhaustless, self-sustained,
Immortal, indestructible,—shall such
Say, "I have killed a man, or caused to kill?"

      Nay, but as when one layeth
       His worn-out robes away,
      And, taking new ones, sayeth,
       "These will I wear to-day!"
      So putteth by the spirit
       Lightly its garb of flesh,
      And passeth to inherit
       A residence afresh.

   I say to thee weapons reach not the Life,
Flame burns it not, waters cannot o'erwhelm,
Nor dry winds wither it. Impenetrable,
Unentered, unassailed, unharmed, untouched,
Immortal, all-arriving, stable, sure,
Invisible, ineffable, by word
And thought uncompassed, ever all itself,
Thus is the Soul declared! How wilt thou, then,

Knowing it so,—grieve when thou shouldst not grieve?
How, if thou hearest that the man new-dead
Is, like the man new-born, still living man—
One same, existent Spirit—wilt thou weep?
The end of birth is death; the end of death
Is birth: this is ordained! and mournest thou,
Chief of the stalwart arm! for what befalls
Which could not otherwise befall? The birth
Of living things comes unperceived; the death
Comes unperceived; between them, beings perceive:
What is there sorrowful herein dear Prince?
Wonderful, wistful, to contemplate!
   Difficult, doubtful, to speak upon!
Strange and great for tongue to relate,
   Mystical hearing for every one!
Nor wotteth man this, what a marvel it is,
   When seeing, and saying, and hearing are done!

   This Life within all living things, my Prince!
Hides beyond harm; scorn thou to suffer, then,
For that which cannot suffer. Do thy part!
Be mindful of thy name, and tremble not!
Nought better can betide a martial soul
Than lawful war; happy the warrior
To whom comes joy of battle—comes, as now,
Glorious and fair, unsought; opening for him
A gateway unto Heav'n. But, if thou shunn'st
This honorable field—a Kshattriya—
If, knowing thy duty and thy task, thou bidd'st
Duty and task go by—that shall be sin!
And those to come shall speak thee infamy
From age to age; but infamy is worse
For men of noble blood to bear than death!
The chiefs upon their battle-chariots
Will deem 'twas fear that drove thee from the fray.
Of those who held thee mighty-souled the scorn
Thou must abide, while all thine enemies

Will scatter bitter speech of thee, to mock
The valor which thou hadst; what fate could fall
More grievously than this? Either—being killed—
Thou wilt win Swarga's safety, or—alive
And victor—thou wilt reign an earthly king.
Therefore, arise, thou Son of Kunti! brace
Thine arm for conflict, nerve thy heart to meet—
As things alike to thee—pleasure or pain,
Profit or ruin, victory or defeat:
So minded, gird thee to the fight, for so
Thou shalt not sin!

      Thus far I speak to thee
As from the "Sânkhya"—unspiritually—
Hear now the deeper teaching of the Yôg,
Which holding, understanding, thou shalt burst
Thy Karmabandh, the bondage of wrought deeds.
Here shall no end be hindered, no hope marred
No loss be feared: faith—yea, a little faith—
Shall save thee from the anguish of thy dread.
Here, Glory of the Kurus! shines one rule—
One steadfast rule—while shifting souls have laws
Many and hard. Specious, but wrongful deem
The speech of those ill-taught ones who extol
The letter of their Vedas, saying, "This
Is all we have, or need;" being weak at heart
With wants, seekers of Heaven: which comes—they say—
As "fruit of good deeds done;" promising men
Much profit in new births for works of faith;
In various rites abounding; following whereon
Large merit shall accrue towards wealth and power;
Albeit, who wealth and power do most desire
Least fixity of soul have such, least hold
On heavenly meditation. Much these teach,
From Veds, concerning the "three qualities;"
But thou, be free of the "three qualities,"

Free of the "pairs of opposites," [1] and free
From that sad righteousness which calculates;
Self-ruled, Arjuna! simple, satisfied! [2]
Look! like as when a tank pours water forth
To suit all needs, so do these Brahmans draw
Texts for all wants from tank of Holy Writ.
But thou, want not! ask not! Find full reward
Of doing right in right! Let right deeds be
Thy motive, not the fruit which comes from them.
And live in action! Labor! Make thine acts
Thy piety, casting all self aside,
Contemning gain and merit; equable
In good or evil: equability
Is Yôg, is piety!

        Yet, the right act
Is less, far less, than the right-thinking mind.
Seek refuge in thy soul; have there thy heaven!
Scorn them that follow virtue for her gifts!
The mind of pure devotion—even here—
Casts equally aside good deeds and bad,
Passing above them. Unto pure devotion
Devote thyself: with perfect meditation
Comes perfect act, and the right-hearted rise—
More certainly because they seek no gain—
Forth from the bands of body, step by step,
To highest seats of bliss. When thy firm soul
Hath shaken off those tangled oracles
Which ignorantly guide, then shall it soar
To high neglect of what's denied or said,
This way or that way, in doctrinal writ.
Troubled no longer by the priestly lore
Safe shall it live, and sure; steadfastly bent
On meditation. This is Yôg—and Peace!

[1] Technical phrases of Vedic religion.
[2] The whole of this passage is highly involved and difficult to render.

ARJUNA:

What is his mark who hath that steadfast heart,
Confirmed in holy meditation? How
Know we his speech, Kesava? Sits he, moves he
Like other men?

KRISHNA:

         When one, O Prithâ's Son!—
Abandoning desires which shake the mind—
Finds in his soul full comfort for his soul,
He hath attained the Yôg—that man is such!
In sorrows not rejected, and in joys
Not overjoyed; dwelling outside the stress
Of passion, fear, and anger; fixed in calms
Of lofty contemplation;—such an one
Is Muni, is the Sage, the true Recluse!
He, who to none and nowhere overbound
By ties of flesh, takes evil things and good
Neither desponding nor exulting, such
Bears wisdom's plainest mark! He who shall draw,
As the wise tortoise draws its four feet safe
Under its shield, his five frail senses back
Under the spirit's buckler from the world
Which else assails them, such an one, my Prince!
Hath wisdom's mark! Things that solicit sense
Hold off from the self-governed; nay, it comes,
The appetites of him who lives beyond
Depart,—aroused no more. Yet may it chance
O Son of Kunti! that a governed mind
Shall some time feel the sense-storms sweep, and wrest
Strong self-control by the roots. Let him regain
His kingdom! let him conquer this, and sit
On Me intent. That man alone is wise
Who keeps the mastery of himself! If one
Ponders on objects of the sense, there springs
Attraction; from attraction grows desire,

Desire flames to fierce passion, passion breeds
Recklessness; then the memory—all betrayed—
Lets noble purpose go, and saps the mind,
Till purpose, mind, and man are all undone.
But, if one deals with objects of the sense
Not loving and not hating, making them
Serve his free soul, which rests serenely lord,
Lo, such a man comes to tranquillity;
And out of that tranquillity shall rise
The end and healing of his earthly pains,
Since the will governed sets the soul at peace.
The soul of the ungoverned is not his,
Nor hath he knowledge of himself; which lacked,
How grows serenity? and, wanting that,
Whence shall he hope for happiness?
         The mind
That gives itself to follow shows of sense
Seeth its helm of wisdom rent away,
And, like a ship in waves of whirlwind, drives
To wreck and death. Only with him, great Prince!
Whose senses are not swayed by things of sense
Only with him who holds his mastery,
Shows wisdom perfect. What is midnight-gloom
To unenlightened souls shines wakeful day
To his clear gaze; what seems as wakeful day
Is known for night, thick night of ignorance,
To his true-seeing eyes. Such is the Saint!

And like the ocean, day by day receiving
 Floods from all lands, which never overflows;
Its boundary-line not leaping, and not leaving,
 Fed by the rivers, but unswelled by those;—

So is the perfect one! to his soul's ocean
 The world of sense pours streams of witchery;
They leave him as they find, without commotion,
 Taking their tribute, but remaining sea.

Yea! whoso, shaking off the yoke of flesh,
Lives lord, not servant, of his lusts; set free
From pride, from passion, from the sin of "Self,"
Toucheth tranquillity! O Prithâ's son!
That is the state of Brahm! There rests no dread
When that last step is reached! Live where he will,
Die when he may, such passeth from all 'plaining,
To blest Nirvâna, with the Gods, attaining.

*Here endeth Chapter II. of the Bhagavad-Gîtâ,
entitled "Sânkhya-Yôg," or "The Book of
Doctrines"*

CHAPTER III

ARJUNA:

THOU whom all mortals praise, Janârdana!
If meditation be a nobler thing
Than action, wherefore, then, great Kesava!
Dost thou impel me to this dreadful fight?
Now am I by thy doubtful speech disturbed!
Tell me one thing, and tell me certainly;
By what road shall I find the better end?

KRISHNA:

I told thee, blameless Lord! there be two paths
Shown to this world; two schools of wisdom. First
The Sânkhya's, which doth save in way of works
Prescribed[1] by reason; next, the Yôg, which bids
Attain by meditation, spiritually:
Yet these are one! No man shall 'scape from act
By shunning action; nay, and none shall come
By mere renouncements unto perfectness.
Nay, and no jot of time, at any time,
Rests any actionless; his nature's law
Compels him, even unwilling, into act;
[For thought is act in fancy]. He who sits
Suppressing all the instruments of flesh,
Yet in his idle heart thinking on them,
Plays the inept and guilty hypocrite:
But he who, with strong body serving mind,
Gives up his mortal powers to worthy work,
Not seeking gain, Arjuna! such an one
Is honorable. Do thine allotted task!
Work is more excellent than idleness;

---

[1] I feel convinced *sânkhyânân* and *yoginân* must be transposed here in sense.

The body's life proceeds not, lacking work.
There is a task of holiness to do,
Unlike world-binding toil, which bindeth not
The faithful soul; such earthly duty do
Free from desire, and thou shalt well perform
Thy heavenly purpose. Spake Prajâpati—
In the beginning, when all men were made,
And, with mankind, the sacrifice—"Do this!
Work! sacrifice! Increase and multiply
With sacrifice! This shall be Kamadûk,
Your 'Cow of Plenty,' giving back her milk
Of all abundance. Worship the gods thereby;
The gods shall yield ye grace. Those meats ye crave
The gods will grant to Labor, when it pays
Tithes in the altar-flame. But if one eats
Fruits of the earth, rendering to kindly Heaven
No gift of toil, that thief steals from his world."

Who eat of food after their sacrifice
Are quit of fault, but they that spread a feast
All for themselves, eat sin and drink of sin.
By food the living live; food comes of rain,
And rain comes by the pious sacrifice,
And sacrifice is paid with tithes of toil;
Thus action is of Brahmâ, who is One,
The Only, All-pervading; at all times
Present in sacrifice. He that abstains
To help the rolling wheels of this great world,
Glutting his idle sense, lives a lost life,
Shameful and vain. Existing for himself,
Self-concentrated, serving self alone,
No part hath he in aught; nothing achieved,
Nought wrought or unwrought toucheth him; no hope
Of help for all the living things of earth
Depends from him.[2] Therefore, thy task prescribed
With spirit unattached gladly perform,

[2] I am doubtful of accuracy here.

Since in performance of plain duty man
Mounts to his highest bliss. By works alone
Janak, and ancient saints reached blessedness!
Moreover, for the upholding of thy kind,
Action thou should'st embrace. What the wise choose
The unwise people take; what best men do
The multitude will follow. Look on me,
Thou Son of Prithâ! in the three wide worlds
I am not bound to any toil, no height
Awaits to scale, no gift remains to gain,
Yet I act here! and, if I acted not—
Earnest and watchful—those that look to me
For guidance, sinking back to sloth again
Because I slumbered, would decline from good,
And I should break earth's order and commit
Her offspring unto ruin, Bharata!
Even as the unknowing toil, wedded to sense,
So let the enlightened toil, sense-freed, but set
To bring the world deliverance, and its bliss;
Not sowing in those simple, busy hearts
Seed of despair. Yea! let each play his part
In all he finds to do, with unyoked soul.
All things are everywhere by Nature wrought
In interaction of the qualities.
The fool, cheated by self, thinks, "This I did"
And "That I wrought;" but—ah, thou strong-armed
      Prince!—
A better-lessoned mind, knowing the play
Of visible things within the world of sense,
And how the qualities must qualify,
Standeth aloof even from his acts. Th' untaught
Live mixed with them, knowing not Nature's way,
Of highest aims unwitting, slow and dull.
Those make thou not to stumble, having the light;
But all thy dues discharging, for My sake,
With meditation centred inwardly,
Seeking no profit, satisfied, serene,

Heedless of issue—fight! They who shall keep
My ordinance thus, the wise and willing hearts,
Have quittance from all issue of their acts;
But those who disregard my ordinance,
Thinking they know, know nought, and fall to loss,
Confused and foolish. 'Sooth, the instructed one
Doth of his kind, following what fits him most;
And lower creatures of their kind; in vain
Contending 'gainst the law. Needs must it be
The objects of the sense will stir the sense
To like and dislike, yet th' enlightened man
Yields not to these, knowing them enemies.
Finally, this is better, that one do
His own task as he may, even though he fail,
Than take tasks not his own, though they seem good
To die performing duty is no ill;
But who seeks other roads shall wander still.

ARJUNA:

Yet tell me, Teacher! by what force doth man
Go to his ill, unwilling; as if one
Pushed him that evil path?

KRISHNA:

                     Kama it is!
Passion it is! born of the Darknesses,
Which pusheth him. Mighty of appetite,
Sinful, and strong is this!—man's enemy!
As smoke blots the white fire, as clinging rust
Mars the bright mirror, as the womb surrounds
The babe unborn, so is the world of things
Foiled, soiled, enclosed in this desire of flesh.
The wise fall, caught in it; the unresting foe
It is of wisdom, wearing countless forms,
Fair but deceitful, subtle as a flame.
Sense, mind, and reason—these, O Kunti's son!

Are booty for it; in its play with these
It maddens man, beguiling, blinding him.
Therefore, thou noblest child of Bharata!
Govern thy heart! Constrain th' entangled sense!
Resist the false, soft sinfulness which saps
Knowledge and judgment! Yea, the world is strong,
But what discerns it stronger, and the mind
Strongest; and high o'er all the ruling Soul.
Wherefore, perceiving Him who reigns supreme,
Put forth full force of Soul in thy own soul!
Fight! vanquish foes and doubts, dear Hero! slay
What haunts thee in fond shapes, and would betray!

Here endeth Chapter III. of the Bhagavad-Gîtâ
entitled "Karma-Yôg," or "The Book
of Virtue in Work"

CHAPTER IV

KRISHNA:

THIS deathless Yoga, this deep union,
I taught Vivaswata,[1] the Lord of Light;
Vivaswata to Manu gave it; he
To Ikshwâku; so passed it down the line
Of all my royal Rishis. Then, with years,
The truth grew dim and perished, noble Prince!
Now once again to thee it is declared—
This ancient lore, this mystery supreme—
Seeing I find thee votary and friend.

ARJUNA:

Thy birth, dear Lord, was in these later days,
And bright Vivaswata's preceded time!
How shall I comprehend this thing thou sayest,
"From the beginning it was I who taught?"

KRISHNA:

Manifold the renewals of my birth
Have been, Arjuna! and of thy births too!
But mine I know, and thine thou knowest not,
O slayer of thy Foes! Albeit I be
Unborn, undying, indestructible,
The Lord of all things living; not the less—
By Maya, by my magic which I stamp
On floating Nature-forms, the primal vast—
I come, and go, and come. When Righteousness
Declines, O Bharata! when Wickedness
Is strong, I rise, from age to age, and take

[1] A name of the sun.

Visible shape, and move a man with men,
Succoring the good, thrusting the evil back,
And setting Virtue on her seat again.
Who knows the truth touching my births on earth
And my divine work, when he quits the flesh
Puts on its load no more, falls no more down
To earthly birth: to Me he comes, dear Prince!

Many there be who come! from fear set free,
From anger, from desire; keeping their hearts
Fixed upon me—my Faithful—purified
By sacred flame of Knowledge. Such as these
Mix with my being. Whoso worship me,
Them I exalt; but all men everywhere
Shall fall into my path; albeit, those souls
Which seek reward for works, make sacrifice
Now, to the lower gods. I say to thee
Here have they their reward. But I am He
Made the Four Castes, and portioned them a place
After their qualities and gifts. Yea, I
Created, the Reposeful; I that live
Immortally, made all those mortal births:
For works soil not my essence, being works
Wrought uninvolved.[2] Who knows me acting thus
Unchained by action, action binds not him;
And, so perceiving, all those saints of old
Worked, seeking for deliverance. Work thou
As, in the days gone by, thy fathers did.

Thou sayst, perplexed, It hath been asked before
By singers and by sages, "What is act,
And what inaction?" I will teach thee this,
And, knowing, thou shalt learn which work doth save.
Needs must one rightly meditate those three—
Doing,—not doing,—and undoing. Here
Thorny and dark the path is! He who sees

[2] Without desire of fruit.

How action may be rest, rest action—he
Is wisest 'mid his kind; he hath the truth!
He doeth well, acting or resting. Freed
In all his works from prickings of desire,
Burned clean in act by the white fire of truth,
The wise call that man wise; and such an one,
Renouncing fruit of deeds, always content,
Always self-satisfying, if he works,
Doth nothing that shall stain his separate soul,
Which—quit of fear and hope—subduing self—
Rejecting outward impulse—yielding up
To body's need nothing save body, dwells
Sinless amid all sin, with equal calm
Taking what may befall, by grief unmoved,
Unmoved by joy, unenvyingly; the same
In good and evil fortunes; nowise bound
By bond of deeds. Nay, but of such an one,
Whose crave is gone, whose soul is liberate,
Whose heart is set on truth—of such an one
What work he does is work of sacrifice,
Which passeth purely into ash and smoke
Consumed upon the altar! All's then God!
The sacrifice is Brahm, the ghee and grain
Are Brahm, the fire is Brahm, the flesh it eats
Is Brahm, and unto Brahm attaineth he
Who, in such office, meditates on Brahm.
Some votaries there be who serve the gods
With flesh and altar-smoke; but other some
Who, lighting subtler fires, make purer rite
With will of worship. Of the which be they
Who, in white flame of continence, consume
Joys of the sense, delights of eye and ear,
Foregoing tender speech and sound of song:
And they who, kindling fires with torch of Truth,
Burn on a hidden altar-stone the bliss
Of youth and love, renouncing happiness:
And they who lay for offering there their wealth,

Their penance, meditation, piety,
Their steadfast reading of the scrolls, their lore
Painfully gained with long austerities:
And they who, making silent sacrifice,
Draw in their breath to feed the flame of thought,
And breathe it forth to waft the heart on high,
Governing the ventage of each entering air
Lest one sigh pass which helpeth not the soul:
And they who, day by day denying needs,
Lay life itself upon the altar-flame,
Burning the body wan. Lo! all these keep
The rite of offering, as if they slew
Victims; and all thereby efface much sin
Yea! and who feed on the immortal food
Left of such sacrifice, to Brahma pass
To The Unending. But for him that makes
No sacrifice, he hath nor part nor lot
Even in the present world. How should he share
Another, O thou Glory of thy Line.

In sight of Brahma all these offerings
Are spread and are accepted! Comprehend
That all proceed by act; for knowing this,
Thou shalt be quit of doubt. The sacrifice
Which Knowledge pays is better than great gifts
Offered by wealth, since gifts' worth—O my Prince!
Lies in the mind which gives, the will that serves:
And these are gained by reverence, by strong search,
By humble heed of those who see the Truth
And teach it. Knowing Truth, thy heart no more
Will ache with error, for the Truth shall show
All things subdued to thee, as thou to Me.
Moreover, Son of Pandu! wert thou worst
Of all wrong-doers, this fair ship of Truth
Should bear thee safe and dry across the sea
Of thy transgressions. As the kindled flame
Feeds on the fuel till it sinks to ash,

So unto ash, Arjuna! unto nought
The flame of Knowledge wastes works' dross away!
There is no purifier like thereto
In all this world, and he who seeketh it
Shall find it—being grown perfect—in himself.
Believing, he receives it when the soul
Masters itself, and cleaves to Truth, and comes—
Possessing knowledge—to the higher peace,
The uttermost repose. But those untaught,
And those without full faith, and those who fear
Are shent; no peace is here or other where,
No hope, nor happiness for whoso doubts.
He that, being self-contained, hath vanquished doubt,
Disparting self from service, soul from works,
Enlightened and emancipate, my Prince!
Works fetter him no more! Cut then atwain
With sword of wisdom, Son of Bharata!
This doubt that binds thy heart-beats! cleave the bond
Born of thy ignorance! Be bold and wise!
Give thyself to the field with me! Arise!

*Here endeth Chapter IV. of the Bhagavad-Gîtâ,
entitled "Jnana-Yôg," or "The Book of
the Religion of Knowledge"*

CHAPTER V

ARJUNA:

YET, Krishna! at the one time thou dost laud
Surcease of works, and, at another time,
Service through work. Of these twain plainly tell
Which is the better way?

KRISHNA:

To cease from works
Is well, and to do works in holiness
Is well; and both conduct to bliss supreme;
But of these twain the better way is his
Who working piously refraineth not.

That is the true Renouncer, firm and fixed,
Who—seeking nought, rejecting nought—dwells proof
Against the "opposites." [1] O valiant Prince!
In doing, such breaks lightly from all deed:
'Tis the new scholar talks as they were two,
This Sânkhya and this Yôga: wise men know
Who husbands one plucks golden fruit of both!
The region of high rest which Sânkhyans reach
Yogins attain. Who sees these twain as one
Sees with clear eyes! Yet such abstraction, Chief!
Is hard to win without much holiness.
Whoso is fixed in holiness, self-ruled,
Pure-hearted, lord of senses and of self,
Lost in the common life of all which lives—
A "Yôgayukt"—he is a Saint who wends
Straightway to Brahm. Such an one is not touched
By taint of deeds. "Nought of myself I do!"
Thus will he think—who holds the truth of truths—

[1] That is, "joy and sorrow, success and failure, heat and cold," &c.

In seeing, hearing, touching, smelling; when
He eats, or goes, or breathes; slumbers or talks,
Holds fast or loosens, opes his eyes or shuts;
Always assured "This is the sense-world plays
With senses." He that acts in thought of Brahm,
Detaching end from act, with act content,
The world of sense can no more stain his soul
Than waters mar th' enamelled lotus-leaf.
With life, with heart, with mind,—nay, with the help
Of all five senses—letting selfhood go—
Yogins toil ever towards their souls' release.
Such votaries, renouncing fruit of deeds,
Gain endless peace: the unvowed, the passion-bound,
Seeking a fruit from works, are fastened down.
The embodied sage, withdrawn within his soul,
At every act sits godlike in "the town
Which hath nine gateways,"[2] neither doing aught
Nor causing any deed. This world's Lord makes
Neither the work, nor passion for the work,
Nor lust for fruit of work; the man's own self
Pushes to these! The Master of this World
Takes on himself the good or evil deeds
Of no man—dwelling beyond! Mankind errs here
By folly, darkening knowledge. But, for whom
That darkness of the soul is chased by light,
Splendid and clear shines manifest the Truth
As if a Sun of Wisdom sprang to shed
Its beams of dawn. Him meditating still,
Him seeking, with Him blended, stayed on Him,
The souls illuminated take that road
Which hath no turning back—their sins flung off
By strength of faith. [Who will may have this Light;
Who hath it sees.] To him who wisely sees,
The Brahman with his scrolls and sanctities,
The cow, the elephant, the unclean dog,
The Outcast gorging dog's meat, are all one.

2 *i. e.,* the body.

The world is overcome—aye! even here!
By such as fix their faith on Unity.
The sinless Brahma dwells in Unity,
And they in Brahma. Be not over-glad
Attaining joy, and be not over-sad
Encountering grief, but, stayed on Brahma, still
Constant let each abide! The sage whose soul
Holds off from outer contacts, in himself
Finds bliss; to Brahma joined by piety,
His spirit tastes eternal peace. The joys
Springing from sense-life are but quickening wombs
Which breed sure griefs: those joys begin and end!
The wise mind takes no pleasure, Kunti's Son!
In such as those! But if a man shall learn,
Even while he lives and bears his body's chain,
To master lust and anger, he is blest!
He is the *Yukta;* he hath happiness,
Contentment, light, within: his life is merged
In Brahma's life; he doth Nirvâna touch!
Thus go the Rishis unto rest, who dwell
With sins effaced, with doubts at end, with hearts
Governed and calm. Glad in all good they live,
Nigh to the peace of God; and all those live
Who pass their days exempt from greed and wrath,
Subduing self and senses, knowing the Soul!

The Saint who shuts outside his placid soul
All touch of sense, letting no contact through;
Whose quiet eyes gaze straight from fixëd brows,
Whose outward breath and inward breath are drawn
Equal and slow through nostrils still and close;
That one—with organs, heart, and mind constrained,
Bent on deliverance, having put away
Passion, and fear, and rage;—hath, even now,
Obtained deliverance, ever and ever freed.
Yea; for he knows Me Who am He that heeds
The sacrifice and worship, God revealed;

And He who heeds not, being Lord of Worlds,
Lover of all that lives, God unrevealed,
Wherein who will shall find surety and shield!

Here ends Chapter V. of the Bhagavad-Gîtâ, entitled
"Karmasanyâsayog," or "The Book of Religion
by Renouncing Fruit of Works"

CHAPTER VI

KRISHNA:

THEREFORE, who doeth work rightful to do,
Not seeking gain from work, that man, O Prince!
Is Sânyasi and Yôgi—both in one!
And he is neither who lights not the flame
Of sacrifice, nor setteth hand to task.

   Regard as true Renouncer him that makes
Worship by work, for who renounceth not
Works not as Yôgin. So is that well said
"By works the votary doth rise to saint,
And saintship is the ceasing from all works;"
Because the perfect Yôgin acts—but acts
Unmoved by passions and unbound by deeds,
Setting result aside.

                    Let each man raise
The Self by Soul, not trample down his Self,
Since Soul that is Self's friend may grow Self's foe.
Soul is Self's friend when Self doth rule o'er Self
But self turns enemy if Soul's own self
Hates Self as not itself.[1]
                    The sovereign soul
Of him who lives self-governed and at peace
Is centered in itself, taking alike
Pleasure and pain; heat, cold; glory and shame.
He is the Yôgi, he is *Yûkta,* glad
With joy of light and truth; dwelling apart
Upon a peak, with senses subjugate

[1] The Sanskrit has this play on the double meaning of *Atman*.

Whereto the clod, the rock, the glistering gold
Show all as one. By this sign is he known
Being of equal grace to comrades, friends,
Chance-comers, strangers, lovers, enemies,
Aliens and kinsmen; loving all alike,
Evil or good.

     Sequestered should he sit,
Steadfastly meditating, solitary,
His thoughts controlled, his passions laid away,
Quit of belongings. In a fair, still spot
Having his fixed abode,—not too much raised,
Nor yet too low,—let him abide, his goods
A cloth, a deerskin, and the Kusa-grass.
There, setting hard his mind upon The One,
Restraining heart and senses, silent, calm,
Let him accomplish Yôga, and achieve
Pureness of soul, holding immovable
Body and neck and head, his gaze absorbed
Upon his nose-end,[2] rapt from all around,
Tranquil in spirit, free of fear, intent
Upon his Brahmacharya vow, devout,
Musing on Me, lost in the thought of Me.
That Yôjin, so devoted, so controlled,
Comes to the peace beyond,—My peace, the peace
Of high Nirvana!   But for earthly needs
Religion is not his who too much fasts
Or too much feasts, nor his who sleeps away
An idle mind; nor his who wears to waste
His strength in vigils. Nay, Arjuna! call
That the true piety which most removes
Earth-aches and ills, where one is moderate
In eating and in resting, and in sport;
Measured in wish and act; sleeping betimes,
Waking betimes for duty.

             [2] So in original.

When the man,
So living, centres on his soul the thought
Straitly restrained—untouched internally
By stress of sense—then is he *Yûkta*. See!
Steadfast a lamp burns sheltered from the wind;
Such is the likeness of the Yôgi's mind
Shut from sense-storms and burning bright to Heaven.
When mind broods placid, soothed with holy wont;
When Self contemplates self, and in itself
Hath comfort; when it knows the nameless joy
Beyond all scope of sense, revealed to soul—
Only to soul! and, knowing, wavers not,
True to the farther Truth; when, holding this,
It deems no other treasure comparable,
But, harbored there, cannot be stirred or shook
By any gravest grief, call that state "peace,"
That happy severance Yôga, call that man
The perfect Yôgin!
                              Steadfastly the will
Must toil thereto, till efforts end in ease,
And thought has passed from thinking. Shaking off
All longings bred by dreams of fame and gain,
Shutting the doorways of the senses close
With watchful ward; so, step by step, it comes
To gift of peace assured and heart assuaged,
When the mind dwells self-wrapped, and the soul broods
Cumberless. But, as often as the heart
Breaks—wild and wavering—from control, so oft
Let him re-curb it, let him rein it back
To the soul's governance! for perfect bliss
Grows only in the bosom tranquillized,
The spirit passionless, purged from offence,
Vowed to the Infinite. He who thus vows
His soul to the Supreme Soul, quitting sin,
Passes unhindered to the endless bliss
Of unity with Brahma. He so vowed,
So blended, sees the Life-Soul resident

In all things living, and all living things
In that Life-Soul contained. And whoso thus
Discerneth Me in all, and all in Me,
I never let him go; nor looseneth he
Hold upon Me; but, dwell he where he may,
Whate'er his life, in Me he dwells and lives
Because he knows and worships Me, Who dwell
In all which lives, and cleaves to Me in all.
Arjuna! if a man sees everywhere—
Taught by his own similitude—one Life,
One Essence in the Evil and the Good,
Hold him a Yôgi, yea! well-perfected!

ARJUNA:

Slayer of Madhu! yet again, this Yôg,
This Peace, derived from equanimity,
Made known by thee—I see no fixity
Therein, no rest, because the heart of men
Is unfixed, Krishna! rash, tumultuous,
Wilful and strong. It were all one, I think,
To hold the wayward wind, as tame man's heart.

KRISHNA:

Hero long-armed! beyond denial, hard
Man's heart is to restrain, and wavering;
Yet may it grow restrained by habit, Prince!
By wont of self-command. This Yôg, I say,
Cometh not lightly to th' ungoverned ones;
But he who will be master of himself
Shall win it, if he stoutly strive thereto.

ARJUNA:

And what road goeth he who, having faith,
Fails, Krishna! in the striving; falling back
From holiness, missing the perfect rule?
Is he not lost, straying from Brahma's light,
Like the vain cloud, which floats 'twixt earth and Heaven

When lightning splits it, and it vanisheth?
Fain would I hear thee answer me herein,
Since, Krishna! none save thou can clear the doubt.

KRISHNA:

He is not lost, thou Son of Prithâ! No!
Nor earth, nor heaven is forfeit, even for him,
Because no heart that holds one right desire
Treadeth the road of loss! He who should fail,
Desiring righteousness, cometh at death
Unto the Region of the Just; dwells there
Measureless years, and being born anew,
Beginneth life again in some fair home
Amid the mild and happy. It may chance
He doth descend into a Yôgin house
On Virtue's breast; but that is rare! Such birth
Is hard to be obtained on this earth, Chief!
So hath he back again what heights of heart
He did achieve, and so he strives anew
To perfectness, with better hope, dear Prince!
For by the old desire he is drawn on
Unwittingly; and only to desire
The purity of Yôga is to pass
Beyond the *Sabdabrahm,* the spoken Ved.
But, being Yôgi, striving strong and long,
Purged from transgressions, perfected by births
Following on births, he plants his feet at last
Upon the farther path. Such an one ranks
Above ascetics, higher than the wise,
Beyond achievers of vast deeds! Be thou
Yôgi, Arjuna! And of such believe,
Truest and best is he who worships Me
With inmost soul, stayed on My Mystery!

*Here endeth Chapter VI. of the Bhagavad-Gîtâ,
entitled "Atmasanyamayôg," or "The
Book of Religion by Self-Restraint"*

CHAPTER VII

KRISHNA:

LEARN now, dear Prince! how, if thy soul be set
Ever on Me—still exercising Yôg,
Still making Me thy Refuge—thou shalt come
Most surely unto perfect hold of Me.
I will declare to thee that utmost lore,
Whole and particular, which, when thou knowest
Leaveth no more to know here in this world.

Of many thousand mortals, one, perchance,
Striveth for Truth; and of those few that strive—
Nay, and rise high—one only—here and there—
Knoweth Me, as I am, the very Truth.

Earth, water, flame, air, ether, life, and mind,
And individuality—those eight
Make up the showing of Me, Manifest.

These be my lower Nature; learn the higher,
Whereby, thou Valiant One! this Universe
Is, by its principle of life, produced;
Whereby the worlds of visible things are born
As from a *Yoni*. Know! I am that womb:
I make and I unmake this Universe:
Than me there is no other Master, Prince!
No other Maker! All these hang on me
As hangs a row of pearls upon its string.
I am the fresh taste of the water; I
The silver of the moon, the gold o' the sun,
The word of worship in the Veds, the thrill
That passeth in the ether, and the strength

Of man's shed seed. I am the good sweet smell
Of the moistened earth, I am the fire's red light,
The vital air moving in all which moves,
The holiness of hallowed souls, the root
Undying, whence hath sprung whatever is;
The wisdom of the wise, the intellect
Of the informed, the greatness of the great,
The splendor of the splendid. Kunti's Son!
These am I, free from passion and desire;
Yet am I right desire in all who yearn,
Chief of the Bhâratas! for all those moods,
Soothfast, or passionate, or ignorant,
Which Nature frames, deduce from me; but all
Are merged in me—not I in them! The world—
Deceived by those three qualities of being—
Wotteth not Me Who am outside them all,
Above them all, Eternal! Hard it is
To pierce that veil divine of various shows
Which hideth Me; yet they who worship Me
Pierce it and pass beyond.

                      I am not known
To evil doers, nor to foolish ones,
Nor to the base and churlish; nor to those
Whose mind is cheated by the show of things,
Nor those that take the way of Asuras.[1]

Four sorts of mortals know me: he who weeps,
Arjuna! and the man who yearns to know;
And he who toils to help; and he who sits
Certain of me, enlightened.

                     Of these four,
O Prince of India! highest, nearest, best
That last is, the devout soul, wise, intent
Upon "The One." Dear, above all, am I
To him; and he is dearest unto me!

    [1] Beings of low and devilish nature.

All four are good, and seek me; but mine own,
The true of heart, the faithful—stayed on me,
Taking me as their utmost blessedness,
They are not "mine," but I—even I myself!
At end of many births to Me they come!
Yet hard the wise Mahatma is to find,
That man who sayeth, "All is Vâsudev!" [2]

There be those, too, whose knowledge, turned aside
By this desire or that, gives them to serve
Some lower gods, with various rites, constrained
By that which mouldeth them. Unto all such—
Worship what shrine they will, what shapes, in faith—
'Tis I who give them faith! I am content!
The heart thus asking favor from its God,
Darkened but ardent, hath the end it craves,
The lesser blessing—but 'tis I who give!
Yet soon is withered what small fruit they reap
Those men of little minds, who worship so,
Go where they worship, passing with their gods.
But Mine come unto me! Blind are the eyes
Which deem th' Unmanifested manifest,
Not comprehending Me in my true Self!
Imperishable, viewless, undeclared,
Hidden behind my magic veil of shows,
I am not seen by all; I am not known—
Unborn and changeless—to the idle world.
But I, Arjuna! know all things which were,
And all which are, and all which are to be,
Albeit not one among them knoweth Me!

By passion for the "pairs of opposites,"
By those twain snares of Like and Dislike, Prince!
All creatures live bewildered, save some few
Who, quit of sins, holy in act, informed,

[2] Krishna.

Freed from the "opposites," and fixed in faith,
Cleave unto Me.

Who cleave, who seek in Me
Refuge from birth[3] and death, those have the Truth!
Those know Me BRAHMA; know Me Soul of Souls,
The ADHYATMAN; know KARMA, my work;
Know I am ADHIBHUTA, Lord of Life,
And ADHIDAIVA, Lord of all the Gods,
And ADHIYAJNA, Lord of Sacrifice;
Worship Me well, with hearts of love and faith,
And find and hold Me in the hour of death.

*Here endeth Chapter VII. of the Bhagavad-Gîtâ,
entitled "Vijnânayôg," or "The Book
of Religion by Discernment"*

[3] I read here *janma*, "birth;" not *jara*, "age."

CHAPTER VIII

ARJUNA:

WHO is that BRAHMA? What that Soul of Souls,
The ADHYATMAN? What, Thou Best of All!
Thy work, the KARMA? Tell me what it is
Thou namest ADHIBHUTA? What again
Means ADHIDAIVA? Yea, and how it comes
Thou canst be ADHIYAJNA in thy flesh?
Slayer of Madhu! Further, make me know
How good men find thee in the hour of death?

KRISHNA:

I BRAHMA am! the One Eternal GOD,
And ADHYATMAN is My Being's name,
The Soul of Souls! What goeth forth from Me,
Causing all life to live, is KARMA called:
And, Manifested in divided forms,
I am the ADHIBHUTA, Lord of Lives;
And ADHIDAIVA, Lord of all the Gods,
Because I am PURUSHA, who begets.
And ADHIYAJNA, Lord of Sacrifice,
I—speaking with thee in this body here—
Am, thou embodied one! (for all the shrines
Flame unto Me!) And, at the hour of death,
He that hath meditated Me alone,
In putting off his flesh, comes forth to Me,
Enters into My Being—doubt thou not!
But, if he meditated otherwise
At hour of death, in putting off the flesh,
He goes to what he looked for, Kunti's Son!
Because the Soul is fashioned to its like.

Have Me, then, in thy heart always! and fight!
Thou too, when heart and mind are fixed on Me,
Shalt surely come to Me! All come who cleave
With never-wavering will of firmest faith,
Owning none other Gods: all come to Me,
The Uttermost, Purusha, Holiest!

Whoso hath known Me, Lord of sage and singer,
    Ancient of days; of all the Three Worlds Stay,
Boundless,—but unto every atom Bringer
    Of that which quickens it: whoso, I say,

Hath known My form, which passeth mortal knowing;
    Seen my effulgence—which no eye hath seen—
Than the sun's burning gold more brightly glowing,
    Dispersing darkness,—unto him hath been

Right life! And, in the hour when life is ending,
    With mind set fast and trustful piety,
Drawing still breath beneath calm brows unbending,
    In happy peace that faithful one doth die,—

In glad peace passeth to Purusha's heaven,
    The place which they who read the Vedas name
AKSHARAM, "Ultimate;" whereto have striven
    Saints and ascetics—their road is the same.

That way—the highest way—goes he who shuts
The gates of all his senses, locks desire
Safe in his heart, centres the vital airs
Upon his parting thought, steadfastly set;
And, murmuring OM, the sacred syllable—
Emblem of BRAHM—dies, meditating Me.

For who, none other Gods regarding, looks
Ever to Me, easily am I gained
By such a Yôgi; and, attaining Me,
They fall not—those Mahatmas—back to birth,
To life, which is the place of pain, which ends,
But take the way of utmost blessedness.

The worlds, Arjuna!—even Brahma's world—
Roll back again from Death to Life's unrest;
But they, O Kunti's Son! that reach to Me,
Taste birth no more. If ye know Brahma's Day
Which is a thousand Yugas; if ye know
The thousand Yugas making Brahma's Night,
Then know ye Day and Night as He doth know!
When that vast Dawn doth break, th' Invisible
Is brought anew into the Visible;
When that deep Night doth darken, all which is
Fades back again to Him Who sent it forth;
Yea! this vast company of living things—
Again and yet again produced—expires
At Brahma's Nightfall; and, at Brahma's Dawn,
Riseth, without its will, to life new-born.
But—higher, deeper, innermost—abides
Another Life, not like the life of sense,
Escaping sight, unchanging. This endures
When all created things have passed away:
This is that Life named the Unmanifest,
The Infinite! the All! the Uttermost.
Thither arriving none return. That Life
Is Mine, and I am there! And, Prince! by faith
Which wanders not, there is a way to come
Thither. I, the PURUSHA, I Who spread
The Universe around me—in Whom dwell
All living Things—may so be reached and seen!

. . . . [1]

Richer than holy fruit on Vedas growing,
    Greater than gifts, better than prayer or fast,
Such wisdom is! The Yôgi, this way knowing,
    Comes to the Utmost Perfect Peace at last.

Here endeth Chapter VIII. of the Bhagavad-Gîtâ, entitled
"Aksharaparabrahmayôg," or "The Book of
Religion by Devotion to the One Supreme God"

[1] I have discarded ten lines of Sanskrit text here as an undoubted interpolation by some Vedantist.

CHAPTER IX

Krishna:

Now will I open unto thee—whose heart
Rejects not—that last lore, deepest-concealed,
That farthest secret of My Heavens and Earths,
Which but to know shall set thee free from ills,—
A Royal lore! a Kingly mystery!
Yea! for the soul such light as purgeth it
From every sin; a light of holiness
With inmost splendor shining; plain to see;
Easy to walk by, inexhaustible!

They that receive not this, failing in faith
To grasp the greater wisdom, reach not Me,
Destroyer of thy foes! They sink anew
Into the realm of Flesh, where all things change!

By Me the whole vast Universe of things
Is spread abroad;—by Me, the Unmanifest!
In Me are all existences contained;
Not I in them!

Yet they are not contained,
Those visible things! Receive and strive to embrace
The mystery majestical! My Being—
Creating all, sustaining all—still dwells
Outside of all!

See! as the shoreless airs
Move in the measureless space, but are not space,
[And space were space without the moving airs];
So all things are in Me, but are not I.

825

At closing of each Kalpa, Indian Prince!
All things which be back to My Being come:
At the beginning of each Kalpa, all
Issue newborn from Me.

               By Energy
And help of Prakritî, my outer Self,
Again, and yet again, I make go forth
The realms of visible things—without their will—
All of them—by the power of Prakritî.

Yet these great makings, Prince! involve Me not,
Enchain Me not! I sit apart from them,
Other, and Higher, and Free; nowise attached!

Thus doth the stuff of worlds, moulded by Me,
Bring forth all that which is, moving or still,
Living or lifeless! Thus the worlds go on!

The minds untaught mistake Me, veiled in form;—
Naught see they of My secret Presence, nought
Of My hid Nature, ruling all which lives.
Vain hopes pursuing, vain deeds doing; fed
On vainest knowledge, senselessly they seek
An evil way, the way of brutes and fiends.
But My Mahatmas, those of noble soul
Who tread the path celestial, worship Me
With hearts unwandering,—knowing Me the Source,
Th' Eternal Source, of Life. Unendingly
They glorify Me; seek Me; keep their vows
Of reverence and love, with changeless faith
Adoring Me. Yea, and those too adore,
Who, offering sacrifice of wakened hearts,
Have sense of one pervading Spirit's stress,
One Force in every place, though manifold!
I am the Sacrifice! I am the Prayer!
I am the Funeral-Cake set for the dead!

I am the healing herb! I am the ghee,
The Mantra, and the flame, and that which burns!
I am—of all this boundless Universe—
The Father, Mother, Ancestor, and Guard!
The end of Learning! That which purifies
In lustral water! I am OM! I am
Rig-Veda, Sama-Veda, Yajur-Ved;
The Way, the Fosterer, the Lord, the Judge,
The Witness; the Abode, the Refuge-House,
The Friend, the Fountain and the Sea of Life
Which sends, and swallows up; Treasure of Worlds
And Treasure-Chamber! Seed and Seed-Sower,
Whence endless harvests spring! Sun's heat is mine;
Heaven's rain is mine to grant or to withhold;
Death am I, and Immortal Life I am,
Arjuna! SAT and ASAT, Visible Life,
And Life Invisible!

Yea! those who learn
The threefold Veds, who drink the Soma-wine,
Purge sins, pay sacrifice—from Me they earn
Passage to Swarga; where the meats divine

Of great gods feed them in high Indra's heaven.
Yet they, when that prodigious joy is o'er,
Paradise spent, and wage for merits given,
Come to the world of death and change once more.

They had their recompense! they stored their treasure,
Following the threefold Scripture and its writ;
Who seeketh such gaineth the fleeting pleasure
Of joy which comes and goes! I grant them it!

But to those blessèd ones who worship Me,
Turning not otherwhere, with minds set fast,
I bring assurance of full bliss beyond.

Nay, and of hearts which follow other gods
In simple faith, their prayers arise to me,
O Kunti's Son! though they pray wrongfully:
For I am the Receiver and the Lord
Of every sacrifice, which these know not
Rightfully; so they fall to earth again!
Who follow gods go to their gods; who vow
Their souls to Pitris go to Pitris; minds
To evil Bhûts given o'er sink to the Bhûts;
And whoso loveth Me cometh to Me.
Whoso shall offer Me in faith and love
A leaf, a flower, a fruit, water poured forth,
That offering I accept, lovingly made
With pious will. Whate'er thou doest, Prince!
Eating or sacrificing, giving gifts,
Praying or fasting, let it all be done
For Me, as Mine. So shalt thou free thyself
From *Karmabandh,* the chain which holdeth men
To good and evil issue, so shalt come
Safe unto Me—when thou art quit of flesh—
By faith and abdication joined to Me!

I am alike for all! I know not hate,
I know not favor! What is made is Mine!
But them that worship Me with love, I love;
They are in Me, and I in them!

Nay, Prince!
If one of evil life turn in his thought
Straightly to Me, count him amidst the good;
He hath the highway chosen; he shall grow
Righteous ere long; he shall attain that peace
Which changes not. Thou Prince of India!
Be certain none can perish, trusting Me!
O Prithâ's Son! whoso will turn to Me,
Though they be born from the very womb of Sin,

Woman or man; sprung of the Vaisya caste
Or lowly disregarded Sudra,—all
Plant foot upon the highest path; how then
The holy Brahmans and My Royal Saints?
Ah! ye who into this ill world are come—
Fleeting and false—set your faith fast on Me!
Fix heart and thought on Me! Adore Me! Bring
Offerings to Me! Make Me prostrations! Make
Me your supremest joy! and, undivided,
Unto My rest your spirits shall be guided.

*Here ends Chapter IX. of the Bhagavad-Gîtâ, entitled
"Rajavidyârajaguhyayôg," or "The Book of
Religion by the Kingly Knowledge and
the Kingly Mystery"*

CHAPTER X

Krishna:[1]

Hear farther yet thou Long-Armed Lord! these latest words I say—
Uttered to bring thee bliss and peace, who lovest Me alway—
Not the great company of gods nor kingly Rishis know
My Nature, who have made the gods and Rishis long ago;
He only knoweth—only he is free of sin, and wise,
Who seeth Me, Lord of the Worlds, with faith-enlightened eyes,
Unborn, undying, unbegun. Whatever Natures be
To mortal men distributed, those natures spring from Me!
Intellect, skill, enlightenment, endurance, self-control,
Truthfulness, equability, and grief or joy of soul,
And birth and death, and fearfulness, and fearlessness, and shame,
And honor, and sweet harmlessness,[2] and peace which is the same
Whate'er befalls, and mirth, and tears, and piety, and thrift,
And wish to give, and will to help,—all cometh of My gift!
The Seven Chief Saints, the Elders Four, the Lordly Manus set—
Sharing My work—to rule the worlds, these too did I beget;
And Rishis, Pitris, Manus, all, by one thought of My mind;
Thence did arise, to fill this world, the races of mankind;
Wherefrom who comprehends My Reign of mystic Majesty—
That truth of truths—is thenceforth linked in faultless faith to Me:
Yea! knowing Me the source of all, by Me all creatures wrought,
The wise in spirit cleave to Me, into My Being brought;
Hearts fixed on Me; breaths breathed to Me; praising Me, each to
    each,
So have they happiness and peace, with pious thought and speech;
And unto these—thus serving well, thus loving ceaselessly—
I give a mind of perfect mood, whereby they draw to Me;
And, all for love of them, within their darkened souls I dwell,
And, with bright rays of wisdom's lamp, their ignorance dispel.

[1] The Sanskrit poem here rises to an elevation of style and manner which I have endeavored to mark by change of metre.   [2] Ahinsâ.

ARJUNA:

Yes! Thou art Parabrahm! The High Abode!
The Great Purification! Thou art God
Eternal, All-creating, Holy, First,
Without beginning! Lord of Lords and Gods!
Declared by all the Saints—by Narada,
Vyâsa, Asita, and Devalas;
And here Thyself declaring unto me!
What Thou hast said now know I to be truth,
O Kesava! that neither gods nor men
Nor demons comprehend Thy mystery
Made manifest, Divinest! Thou Thyself
Thyself alone dost know, Maker Supreme!
Master of all the living! Lord of Gods!
King of the Universe! To Thee alone
Belongs to tell the heavenly excellence
Of those perfections wherewith Thou dost fill
These worlds of Thine; Pervading, Immanent!
How shall I learn, Supremest Mystery!
To know Thee, though I muse continually?
Under what form of Thine unnumbered forms
Mayst Thou be grasped? Ah! yet again recount,
Clear and complete, Thy great appearances,
The secrets of Thy Majesty and Might,
Thou High Delight of Men! Never enough
Can mine ears drink the Amrit[3] of such words!

KRISHNA:

Hanta! So be it! Kuru Prince! I will to thee unfold
Some portions of My Majesty, whose powers are manifold!
I am the Spirit seated deep in every creature's heart;
From Me they come; by Me they live; at My word they depart!
Vishnu of the Adityas I am, those Lords of Light;
Marîtchi of the Maruts, the Kings of Storm and Blight;
By day I gleam, the golden Sun of burning cloudless Noon;

[3] The nectar of immortality.

By Night, amid the asterisms I glide, the dappled Moon!
Of Vedas I am Sâma-Ved, of gods in Indra's Heaven
Vâsava; of the faculties to living beings given
The mind which apprehends and thinks; of Rudras Sankara;
Of Yakshas and of Râkshasas, Vittesh; and Pâvaka
Of Vasus, and of mountain-peaks Meru; Vrihaspati
Know Me 'mid planetary Powers; 'mid Warriors heavenly
Skanda; of all the water-floods the Sea which drinketh each,
And Bhrigu of the holy Saints, and Om of sacred speech;
Of prayers the prayer ye whisper;[4] of hills Himâla's snow,
And Aswattha, the fig-tree, of all the trees that grow;
Of the Devarshis, Narada; and Chitrarath of them
That sing in Heaven, and Kapila of Munis, and the gem
Of flying steeds, Uchchaisravas, from Amrit-wave which burst;
Of elephants Airâvata; of males the Best and First;
Of weapons Heav'n's hot thunderbolt; of cows white Kâmadhuk,
From whose great milky udder-teats all hearts' desires are strook;
Vâsuki of the serpent-tribes, round Mandara entwined;
And thousand-fanged Ananta, on whose broad coils reclined
Leans Vishnu; and of water-things Varuna; Aryam
Of Pitris, and, of those that judge, Yama the Judge I am;
Of Daityas dread Prahlâda; of what metes days and years,
Time's self I am; of woodland-beasts—buffaloes, deers, and bears—
The lordly-painted tiger; of birds the vast Garûd,
The whirlwind 'mid the winds; 'mid chiefs Rama with blood im-
brued,
Makar 'mid fishes of the sea, and Ganges 'mid the streams;
Yea! First, and Last, and Centre of all which is or seems
I am, Arjuna! Wisdom Supreme of what is wise,
Words on the uttering lips I am, and eyesight of the eyes,
And "A" of written characters, Dwandwa[5] of knitted speech,
And Endless Life, and boundless Love, whose power sustaineth
each;
And bitter Death which seizes all, and joyous sudden Birth,
Which brings to light all beings that are to be on earth;

[4] Called "The Jap."
[5] The compound form of Sanskrit words.

And of the viewless virtues, Fame, Fortune, Song am I,
And Memory, and Patience; and Craft, and Constancy:
Of Vedic hymns the Vrihatsâm, of metres Gayatrî,
Of months the Mârgasirsha, of all the seasons three
The flower-wreathed Spring; in dicer's-play the conquering
    Double-Eight;
The splendor of the splendid, and the greatness of the great,
Victory I am, and Action! and the goodness of the good,
And Vâsudev of Vrishni's race, and of this Pandu brood
Thyself!—Yea, my Arjuna! thyself; for thou art Mine!
Of poets Usana, of saints Vyâsa, sage divine;
The policy of conquerors, the potency of kings, ⎫
The great unbroken silence in learning's secret things; ⎬
The lore of all the learnèd, the seed of all which springs. ⎭
Living or lifeless, still or stirred, whatever beings be,
None of them is in all the worlds, but it exists by Me!
Nor tongue can tell, Arjuna! nor end of telling come
Of these My boundless glories, whereof I teach thee some;
For wheresoe'er is wondrous work, and majesty, and might,
From Me hath all proceeded. Receive thou this aright!
Yet how shouldst thou receive, O Prince! the vastness of this word?
I, who am all, and made it all, abide its separate Lord!

*Here endeth Chapter X. of the Bhagavad-Gîtâ,
entitled "Vibhuti Yôg," or "The Book of
Religion by the Heavenly Perfections"*

CHAPTER XI

ARJUNA:

THIS, for my soul's peace, have I heard from Thee,
The unfolding of the Mystery Supreme
Named Adhyâtman; comprehending which,
My darkness is dispelled; for now I know—
O Lotus-eyed![1]—whence is the birth of men,
And whence their death, and what the majesties
Of thine immortal rule. Fain would I see,
As thou Thyself declar'st it, Sovereign Lord!
The likeness of that glory of Thy Form
Wholly revealed. O Thou Divinest One!
If this can be, if I may bear the sight,
Make Thyself visible, Lord of all prayers!
Show me Thy very self, the Eternal God!

KRISHNA:

Gaze, then, thou Son of Prithâ! I manifest for thee
Those hundred thousand thousand shapes that clothe my Mystery:
I show thee all my semblances, infinite, rich, divine,
My changeful hues, my countless forms. See! in this face of mine,
Adityas, Vasus, Rudras, Aswins, and Maruts; see
Wonders unnumbered, Indian Prince! revealed to none save thee.
Behold! this is the Universe!—Look! what is live and dead
I gather all in one—in Me! Gaze, as thy lips have said,
On GOD ETERNAL, VERY GOD! See ME! see what thou prayest!

.   .   .   .

Thou canst not!—nor, with human eyes, Arjuna! ever mayest
Therefore I give thee sense divine. Have other eyes, new light!
And, look! This is My glory, unveiled to mortal sight!

[1] "Kamalapatrâksha."

834

SANJAYA:

Then, O King! the God, so saying,
Stood, to Prithâ's Son displaying
All the splendor, wonder, dread
Of His vast Almighty-head.
Out of countless eyes beholding,
Out of countless mouths commanding,
Countless mystic forms enfolding
In one Form: supremely standing
Countless radiant glories wearing,
Countless heavenly weapons bearing,
Crowned with garlands of star-clusters,
Robed in garb of woven lustres,
Breathing from His perfect Presence
Breaths of all delicious essence
Of all sweetest odors; shedding
Blinding brilliance, overspreading—
Boundless, beautiful—all spaces
From His all-regarding faces;
So He showed! If there should rise
Suddenly within the skies
Sunburst of a thousand suns
Flooding earth with rays undeemed-of,
Then might be that Holy One's
Majesty and glory dreamed of!

So did Pandu's Son behold
All this universe enfold
All its huge diversity
Into one great shape, and be
Visible, and viewed, and blended
In one Body—subtle, splendid,
Nameless—th' All-comprehending
God of Gods, the Never-Ending
Deity!

But, sore amazed,
Thrilled, o'erfilled, dazzled, and dazed,
Arjuna knelt, and bowed his head,
And clasped his palms, and cried, and said:

ARJUNA:

Yea! I have seen! I see!
Lord! all is wrapped in Thee!
The gods are in Thy glorious frame! the creatures
Of earth, and heaven, and hell
In Thy Divine form dwell,
And in Thy countenance show all the features

Of Brahma, sitting lone
Upon His lotus-throne;
Of saints and sages, and the serpent races
Ananta, Vâsuki.
Yea! mightiest Lord! I see
Thy thousand thousand arms, and breasts, and faces,

And eyes,—on every side
Perfect, diversified;
And nowhere end of Thee, nowhere beginning,
Nowhere a centre! Shifts
Wherever soul's gaze lifts
Thy central Self, all-willing, and all-winning!

Infinite King! I see
The anadem on Thee,
The club, the shell, the discus; see Thee burning
In beams insufferable,
Lighting earth, heaven, and hell
With brilliance blinding, glorious, flashing, turning

Darkness to dazzling day,
Look I whichever way.
Ah, Lord! I worship Thee, the Undivided,

The Uttermost of thought,
The Treasure-Palace wrought
To hold the wealth of the worlds; the shield provided

To shelter Virtue's laws;
The Fount whence Life's stream draws
All waters of all rivers of all being:
The One Unborn, Unending:
Unchanging and unblending!
With might and majesty, past thought, past seeing!

Silver of moon and gold
Of sun are glances rolled
From Thy great eyes; Thy visage beaming tender
Over the stars and skies,
Doth to warm life surprise
Thy Universe. The worlds are filled with wonder

Of Thy perfections! Space
Star-sprinkled, and the place
From pole to pole of the heavens, from bound to bound,
Hath Thee in every spot,
Thee, Thee!—Where Thou art not
O Holy, Marvellous Form! is nowhere found!

O Mystic, Awful One!
At sight of Thee, made known,
The Three Worlds quake; the lower gods draw nigh Thee;
They fold their palms, and bow
Body, and breast, and brow,
And, whispering worship, laud and magnify Thee!

Rishis and Siddhas cry
"Hail! Highest Majesty!"
From sage and singer breaks the hymn of glory
In holy melody,
Sounding the praise of Thee,
While countless companies take up the story,

Rudras, who rides the storms,
Th' Adityas' shining forms,
Vasus and Sâdhyas, Viswas, Ushmapas,
Maruts, and those great Twins,
The heavenly, fair, Aswins,
Gandharvas, Rakshasas, Siddhas, Asuras,—

These see Thee, and revere
In silence-stricken fear;
Yea! the Worlds,—seeing Thee with form stupendous,
With faces manifold,
With eyes which all behold,
Unnumbered eyes, vast arms, members tremendous,

Flanks, lit with sun and star,
Feet planted near and far,
Tushes of terror, mouths wrathful and tender;—
The Three wide Worlds before Thee
Adore, as I adore Thee,
Quake, as I quake, to witness so much splendor!

I mark Thee strike the skies
With front in wondrous wise
Huge, rainbow-painted, glittering; and thy mouth
Opened, and orbs which see
All things, whatever be,
In all Thy worlds, east, west, and north and south.

O Eyes of God! O Head!
My strength of soul is fled,
Gone is heart's force, rebuked is mind's desire!
When I behold Thee so,
With awful brows a-glow,
With burning glance, and lips lighted with fire,

Fierce as those flames which shall
Consume, at close of all,
Earth, Heaven! Ah me! I see no Earth and Heaven!

Thee, Lord of Lords! I see,
Thee only—only Thee!
Ah! let Thy mercy unto me be given!

Thou Refuge of the World!
Lo! to the cavern hurled
Of Thy wide-opened throat, and lips white-tushed,
I see our noblest ones,
Great Dhritarashtra's sons,
Bhishma, Drona, and Karna, caught and crushed!

The Kings and Chiefs drawn in,
That gaping gorge within;
The best of all both armies torn and riven!
Between Thy jaws they lie
Mangled fell bloodily,
Ground into dust and death! Like streams down driven

With helpless haste, which go
In headlong furious flow
Straight to the gulfing maw of th' unfilled ocean,
So to that flaming cave
These heroes great and brave
Pour, in unending streams, with helpless motion!

Like moths which in the night
Flutter towards a light,
Drawn to their fiery doom, flying and dying,
So to their death still throng,
Blind, dazzled, borne along
Ceaselessly, all these multitudes, wild flying!

Thou, that hast fashioned men,
Devourest them agen,
One with another, great and small, alike!
The creatures whom Thou mak'st,
With flaming jaws Thou tak'st,
Lapping them up! Lord God! Thy terrors strike

From end to end of earth,
Filling life full, from birth
To death, with deadly, burning, lurid dread!
Ah, Vishnu! make me know
Why is Thy visage so?
Who art Thou, feasting thus upon Thy dead?

Who? awful Deity!
I bow myself to Thee,
Nâmostu Tê Devavara! Prasîd![2]
O Mightiest Lord! rehearse
Why hast Thou face so fierce?
Whence did this aspect horrible proceed?

KRISHNA:

Thou seest Me as Time who kills, Time who brings all to doom,
The Slayer Time, Ancient of Days, come hither to consume;
Excepting thee, of all these hosts of hostile chiefs arrayed,
There shines not one shall leave alive the battlefield! Dismayed
No longer be! Arise! obtain renown! destroy thy foes!
Fight for the kingdom waiting thee when thou hast vanquished those.
By Me they fall—not thee! the stroke of death is dealt them now,
Even as they stand thus gallantly; My instrument art thou!
Strike, strong-armed Prince! at Drona! at Bhishma strike! deal death
To Karna, Jyadratha; stay all this warlike breath!
'Tis I who bid them perish! Thou wilt but slay the slain.
Fight! they must fall, and thou must live, victor upon this plain!

SANJAYA:

Hearing mighty Keshav's word,
Tremblingly that helmèd Lord
Clasped his lifted palms, and—praying
Grace of Krishna—stood there, saying,
With bowed brow and accents broken,
These words, timorously spoken:

[2] "Hail to Thee, God of Gods! Be favorable!"

Arjuna:

Worthily, Lord of Might!
The whole world hath delight
In Thy surpassing power, obeying Thee;
The Rakshasas, in dread
At sight of Thee, are sped
To all four quarters; and the company

Of Siddhas sound Thy name.
How should they not proclaim
Thy Majesties, Divinest, Mightiest?
Thou Brahm, than Brahma greater!
Thou Infinite Creator!
Thou God of gods, Life's Dwelling-place and Rest!

Thou, of all souls the Soul!
The Comprehending Whole!
Of Being formed, and formless Being the Framer;
O Utmost One! O Lord!
Older than eld, Who stored
The worlds with wealth of life. O Treasure-claimed.

Who wottest all, and art
Wisdom Thyself! O Part
In all, and all, for all from Thee have risen!
Numberless now I see
The aspects are of Thee!
Vayu[3] Thou art, and He who keeps the prison

Of Narak, Yama dark,
And Agni's shining spark.
Varuna's waves are Thy waves. Moon and star-light
Are Thine! Prajâpati
Art Thou, and 'tis to Thee
Men kneel in worshipping the old world's far light,

[3] The wind.

The first of mortal men.
Again, Thou God! again
A thousand thousand times be magnified!
Honor and worship be—
Glory and praise,—to Thee
Namô, Namastê, cried on every side.

Cried here, above, below,
Uttered when Thou dost go,
Uttered when Thou dost come! *Namô!* we call.
Namôstu! God adored!
Namôstu! Nameless Lord!
Hail to Thee! Praise to Thee! Thou One in all.

For Thou art All! Yea, Thou!
Ah! if in anger now
Thou shouldst remember I did think Thee Friend,
Speaking with easy speech,
As men use each to each;
Did call Thee "Krishna," "Prince," nor comprehend

Thy hidden majesty,
The might, the awe of Thee;
Did, in my heedlessness, or in my love,
On journey, or in jest,
Or when we lay at rest,
Sitting at council, straying in the grove,

Alone, or in the throng,
Do Thee, most Holy wrong,
Be Thy grace granted for that witless sin!
For Thou art now I know,
Father of all below,
Of all above, of all the worlds within,

Guru of Gurus, more
To reverence and adore
Than all which is adorable and high!

How, in the wide worlds three
Should any equal be?
Shall any other share Thy majesty?

Therefore, with body bent
And reverent intent,
I praise, and serve, and seek Thee, asking grace.
As father to a son,
As friend to friend, as one
Who loveth to his lover, turn Thy face

In gentleness on me!
Good is it I did see
This unknown marvel of Thy Form! But fear
Mingles with joy! Retake,
Dear Lord! for pity's sake
Thine earthly shape, which earthly eyes may bear!

Be merciful, and show
The visage that I know;
Let me regard Thee, as of yore, arrayed
With disc and forehead-gem,
With mace and anedem,
Thou who sustainest all things! Undismayed

Let me once more behold
The form I loved of old,
Thou of the thousand arms and countless eyes!
My frightened heart is fain
To see restored again
The Charioteer, my Krishna's kind disguise.

KRISHNA:

Yea! thou hast seen, Arjuna! because I loved thee well,
The secret countenance of Me, revealed by mystic spell,
Shining, and wonderful, and vast, majestic, manifold,
Which none save thou in all the years had favor to behold:

For not by Vedas cometh this, nor sacrifice, nor alms,
Nor works well-done, nor penance long, nor prayers nor chaunted
   psalms,
That mortal eyes should bear to view the Immortal Soul unclad,
Prince of the Kurus! This was kept for thee alone! Be glad!
Let no more trouble shake thy heart because thine eyes have seen
My terror with My glory. As I before have been
So will I be again for thee; with lightened heart behold!
Once more I am thy Krishna, the form thou knew'st of old!

SANJAYA:

These words to Arjuna spake
Vâsudev, and straight did take
Back again the semblance dear
Of the well-loved charioteer;
Peace and joy it did restore
When the Prince beheld once more
Mighty BRAHMA's form and face
Clothed in Krishna's gentle grace.

ARJUNA:

Now that I see come back, Janardana!
This friendly human frame, my mind can think
Calm thoughts once more; my heart beats still again!

KRISHNA:

Yea! it was wonderful and terrible
To view me as thou didst, dear Prince! The gods
Dread and desire continually to view!
Yet not by Vedas, nor from sacrifice,
Nor penance, nor gift-giving, nor with prayer
Shall any so behold, as thou hast seen!
Only by fullest service, perfect faith,
And uttermost surrender am I known
And seen, and entered into, Indian Prince!

Who doeth all for Me; who findeth Me
In all; adoreth always; loveth all
Which I have made, and Me, for Love's sole end,
That man, Arjuna! unto Me doth wend.

*Here endeth Chapter XI. of the Bhagavad-Gîtâ,
entitled "Viswarupdarsanam," or "The Book
of the Manifesting of the One
and Manifold".*

CHAPTER XII

ARJUNA:

LORD! of the men who serve Thee—true in heart—
As God revealed; and of the men who serve,
Worshipping Thee Unrevealed, Unbodied, far,
Which take the better way of faith and life?

KRISHNA:

Whoever serve Me—as I show Myself—
Constantly true, in full devotion fixed,
These hold I very holy. But who serve—
Worshipping Me The One, The Invisible,
The Unrevealed, Unnamed, Unthinkable,
Uttermost, All-pervading, Highest, Sure—
Who thus adore Me, mastering their sense,
Of one set mind to all, glad in all good,
These blessed souls come unto Me.

                                        Yet, hard
The travail is for whoso bend their minds
To reach th' Unmanifest. That viewless path
Shall scarce be trod by man bearing his flesh!
But whereso any doeth all his deeds,
Renouncing self in Me, full of Me, fixed
To serve only the Highest, night and day
Musing on Me—him will I swiftly lift
Forth from life's ocean of distress and death
Whose soul clings fast to Me. Cling thou to Me!
Clasp Me with heart and mind! so shalt thou dwell
Surely with Me on high. But if thy thought
Droops from such height; if thou be'st weak to set
Body and soul upon Me constantly,
Despair not! give Me lower service! seek

To read Me, worshipping with steadfast will;
And, if thou canst not worship steadfastly,
Work for Me, toil in works pleasing to Me!
For he that laboreth right for love of Me
Shall finally attain! But, if in this
Thy faint heart fails, bring Me thy failure!
    find
Refuge in Me! let fruits of labor go,
Renouncing all for Me, with lowliest heart,
So shalt thou come; for, though to know is more
Than diligence, yet worship better is
Than knowing, and renouncing better still
Near to renunciation—very near—
Dwelleth Eternal Peace!
                Who hateth nought
Of all which lives, living himself benign,
Compassionate, from arrogance exempt,
Exempt from love of self, unchangeable
By good or ill; patient, contented, firm
In faith, mastering himself, true to his word,
Seeking Me, heart and soul; vowed unto Me,—
That man I love! Who troubleth not his kind,
And is not troubled by them; clear of wrath,
Living too high for gladness, grief, or fear,
That man I love! Who, dwelling quiet-eyed,[1]
Stainless, serene, well-balanced, unperplexed,
Working with Me, yet from all works detached,
That man I love! Who, fixed in faith on Me,
Dotes upon none, scorns none; rejoices not,
And grieves not, letting good and evil hap
Light when it will, and when it will depart,
That man I love! Who, unto friend and foe
Keeping an equal heart, with equal mind
Bears shame and glory, with an equal peace
Takes heat and cold, pleasure and pain; abides
Quit of desires, hears praise or calumny

---

[1] "Not peering about,"—*anapeksha*.

In passionless restraint, unmoved by each,
Linked by no ties to earth, steadfast in Me,
That man I love! But most of all I love
Those happy ones to whom 'tis life to live
In single fervid faith and love unseeing,
Eating the blessèd Amrit of my Being!

*Here endeth Chapter XII. of the Bhagavad-Gîtâ,
entitled "Bhakityôgô," or "The Book of
the Religion of Faith"*

CHAPTER XIII

ARJUNA:

Now would I hear, O gracious Kesava![1]
Of Life which seems, and Soul beyond, which sees,
And what it is we know—or seem to know.

KRISHNA:

Yea! Son of Kunti! for this flesh ye see
Is *Kshetra,* is the field where Life disports;
And that which views and knows it is the Soul,
Kshetrajna. In all "fields," thou Indian prince!
I am *Kshetrajna.* I am what surveys!
Only that knowledge knows which knows the known
By the knower![2] What it is, that "field" of life,
What qualities it hath, and whence it is,
And why it changeth, and the faculty
That wotteth it, the mightiness of this,
And how it wotteth—hear these things from Me!

. . . . [3]

The elements, the conscious life, the mind,
The unseen vital force, the nine great gates
Of the body, or the five domains of sense,
Desire, dislike, pleasure and pain, and thought
Deep-woven, and persistency of being;
These all are wrought on matter by the Soul!

Humbleness, truthfulness, and harmlessness,
Patience and honor, reverence for the wise,
Purity, constancy, control of self,

---

[1] The Calcutta edition of the Mahábhárata has these opening lines.
[2] This is the nearest possible version of
    Kshetrakshetrajnayojnánan yat tagjnán matan mama.
[3] I omit two lines of the Sanskrit here, evidently interpolated by some Vedantist.

Contempt of sense-delights, self-sacrifice,
Perception of the certitude of ill
In birth, death, aye, disease, suffering, and sin;
Detachment, lightly holding unto home,
Children, and wife, and all that bindeth men;
An ever-tranquil heart in fortunes good
And fortunes evil, with a will set firm
To worship Me—Me only! ceasing not;
Loving all solitudes, and shunning noise
Of foolish crowds; endeavors resolute
To reach perception of the Utmost Soul,
And grace to understand what gain it were
So to attain,—this is true Wisdom, Prince!
And what is otherwise is ignorance!

Now will I speak of knowledge best to know—
That Truth which giveth man Amrit to drink,
The Truth of HIM, the Para-Brahm, the All,
The Uncreated; not *Asat,* not *Sat,*
Not Form, nor the Unformed; yet both, and more;—
Whose hands are everywhere, and everywhere
Planted His feet, and everywhere His eyes
Beholding, and His ears in every place
Hearing, and all His faces everywhere
Enlightening and encompassing His worlds.
Glorified by the senses He hath given,
Yet beyond sense He is; sustaining all,
He dwelleth unattached: of forms and modes
Master, yet neither form nor mode hath He;
He is within all beings—and without—
Motionless, yet still moving; not discerned
For subtlety of instant presence; close
To all, to each, yet measurelessly far!
Not manifold, and yet subsisting still
In all which lives; for ever to be known
As the Sustainer, yet, at the End of Times,
He maketh all to end—and re-creates.

The Light of Lights He is, in the heart of the
   Dark
Shining eternally. Wisdom He is
And Wisdom's way, and Guide of all the wise,
Planted in every heart.
                  So have I told
Of Life's stuff, and the moulding, and the lore
To comprehend. Whoso, adoring Me,
Perceiveth this, shall surely come to Me!

  Know thou that Nature and the Spirit both
Have no beginning! Know that qualities
And changes of them are by Nature wrought;
That Nature puts to work the acting frame,
But Spirit doth inform it, and so cause
Feeling of pain and pleasure. Spirit, linked
To moulded matter, entereth into bond
With qualities by Nature framed, and, thus
Married to matter, breeds the birth again
In good or evil *yonis*.[4]
              Yet is this—
Yea! in its bodily prison!—Spirit pure,
Spirit supreme; surveying, governing,
Guarding, possessing; Lord and Master still
PURUSHA, Ultimate, One Soul with Me.

  Whoso thus knows himself, and knows his soul
PURUSHA, working through the qualities
With Nature's modes, the light hath come for him!
Whatever flesh he bears, never again
Shall he take on its load. Some few there be
By meditation find the Soul in Self
Self-schooled; and some by long philosophy
And holy life reach thither; some by works.
Some, never so attaining, hear of light
From other lips, and seize, and cleave to it

        [4] Wombs.

Worshipping; yea! and those—to teaching true—
Overpass Death!

Wherever, Indian Prince!
Life is—of moving things, or things unmoved,
Plant or still seed—know, what is there hath grown
By bond of Matter and of Spirit: Know
He sees indeed who sees in all alike
The living, lordly Soul; the Soul Supreme,
Imperishable amid the Perishing:
For, whoso thus beholds, in every place,
In every form, the same, one, Living Lord,
Doth no more wrongfulness unto himself,
But goes the highest road which brings to bliss.
Seeing, he sees, indeed, who sees that works
Are Nature's wont, for Soul to use, not love,
Acting, yet not the actor; sees the mass
Of separate living things—each of its kind—
Issue from One, and blend again to One:
Then hath he BRAHMA, he attains!

O Prince!
That Ultimate, High Spirit, Uncreate,
Unqualified, even when it entereth flesh
Taketh no stain of acts, worketh in nought!
Like to th' ethereal air, pervading all,
Which, for sheer subtlety, avoideth taint,
The subtle Soul sits everywhere, unstained:
Like to the light of the all-piercing sun
[Which is not changed by aught it shines upon,]
The Soul's light shineth pure in every place;
And they who, by such eye of wisdom see
How matter, and what deals with it, divide;
And how the Spirit and the flesh have strife,
These wise ones go the way which leads to Life!

*Here ends Chapter XIII. of the Bhagavad-Gîtâ,
entitled "Kshetrakshetrajnavibhâgayôgô,"
or "The Book of Religion by Separation of Matter and Spirit"*

CHAPTER XIV

KRISHNA:

YET farther will I open unto thee
This wisdom of all wisdoms, uttermost,
The which possessing, all My saints have passed
To perfectness. On these high verities
Reliant, rising into fellowship
With Me, they are not born again at birth
Of *Kalpas,* nor at *Pralyas* suffer change!

This Universe the Womb is where I plant
Seed of all lives! Thence, Prince of India comes
Birth to all beings! Whoso, Kunti's Son!
Mothers each mortal form, Brahma conceives,
And I am He that fathers, sending seed!

Sattwan, Rajas, and *Tamus,* so are named,
The qualities of Nature, "Soothfastness,"
"Passion," and "Ignorance." These three bind down
The changeless Spirit in the changeful flesh.
Whereof sweet "Soothfastness"—by purity
Living unsullied and enlightened—binds
The sinless Soul to happiness and truth;
And Passion, being kin to appetite,
And breeding impulse and propensity,
Binds the embodied Soul, O Kunti's Son!
By tie of works. But Ignorance, the child
Of Darkness, blinding mortal men, binds down
Their souls to stupor, sloth, and drowsiness.
Yea, Prince of India! Soothfastness binds souls
In pleasant wise to flesh; and Passion binds
By toilsome strain; but Ignorance, which blots

The beams of wisdom, binds the soul to sloth
Passion and Ignorance, once overcome,
Leave Soothfastness, O Bharata! Where this
With Ignorance are absent, Passion rules;
And Ignorance in hearts not good nor quick.
When at all gateways of the Body shines
The Lamp of Knowledge, then may one see well
Soothfastness settled in that city reigns;
Where longing is, and ardor, and unrest,
Impulse to strive and gain, and avarice,
Those spring from Passion—Prince!—engrained; and
     where
Darkness and dulness, sloth and stupor are,
'Tis Ignorance hath caused them, Kuru Chief!

Moreover, when a soul departeth, fixed
In Soothfastness, it goeth to the place—
Perfect and pure—of those that know all Truth
If it departeth in set hebetude
Of impulse, it shall go into the world
Of spirits tied to works; and, if it dies
In hardened Ignorance, that blinded soul
Is born anew in some unlighted womb.

The fruit of Soothfastness is true and sweet;
The fruit of lusts is pain and toil; the fruit
Of Ignorance is deeper darkness. Yea!
For Light brings light, and Passion ache to have.
Blindness, bewilderments, and ignorance
Grow forth from Ignorance. Those of the first
Rise ever higher; those of the second mode
Take a mid place; the darkened souls sink back
To lower deeps, loaded with witlessness!

When, watching life, the living man perceives
The only actors are the Qualities,

And knows what lives beyond the Qualities,
Then is he come nigh unto Me!
                              The Soul,
Thus passing forth from the Three Qualities—
Whereof arise all bodies—overcomes
Birth, Death, Sorrow, and Age; and drinketh deep
The undying wine of Amrit.

ARJUNA:

                              Oh, my Lord!
Which be the signs to know him that hath gone
Past the Three Modes? How liveth he? What way
Leadeth him safe beyond the threefold modes?

KRISHNA:

He who with equanimity surveys
Lustre of goodness, strife of passion, sloth
Of ignorance, not angry if they are,
Not angry when they are not: he who sits
A sojourner and stranger in their midst
Unruffled, standing off, saying—serene—
When troubles break, "These are the Qualities!"
He unto whom—self-centred—grief and joy
Sound as one word; to whose deep-seeing eyes
The clod, the marble, and the gold are one;
Whose equal heart holds the same gentleness
For lovely and unlovely things, firm-set,
Well-pleased in praise and dispraise; satisfied
With honor or dishonor; unto friends
And unto foes alike in tolerance,
Detached from undertakings,—he is named
Surmounter of the Qualities!

                              And such—
With single, fervent faith adoring Me,
Passing beyond the Qualities, conforms
To Brahma, and attains Me!

For I am
That whereof Brahma is the likeness! Mine
The Amrit is; and Immortality
Is mine; and mine perfect Felicity!

*Here ends Chapter XIV. of the Bhagavad-Gîtâ,
entitled "Gunatrayavibhâgayôgô," or "The
Book of Religion by Separation
from the Qualities"*

CHAPTER XV

KRISHNA:

MEN call the Aswattha,—the Banyan-tree,—
Which hath its boughs beneath, its roots on high,—
The ever-holy tree. Yea! for its leaves
Are green and waving hymns which whisper Truth!
Who knoweth well the Aswattha, knows all.

Its branches shoot to heaven and sink to earth,[1]
Even as the deeds of men, which take their birth
    From qualities: its silver sprays and blooms,
And all the eager verdure of its girth,

Leap to quick life at touch of sun and air,
As men's lives quicken to the temptings fair
    Of wooing sense: its hanging rootlets seek
The soil beneath, helping to hold it there,

As actions wrought amid this world of men
Bind them by ever-tightening bonds again.
    If ye knew well the teaching of the Tree,
What its shape saith; and whence it springs; and, then

How it must end, and all the ills of it,
The axe of sharp Detachment ye would whet,
    And cleave the clinging snaky roots, and lay
This Aswattha of sense-like low,—to set

New growths upspringing to that happier sky,—
Which they who reach shall have no day to die,
    Nor fade away, nor fall—to Him, I mean,
FATHER and FIRST, Who made the mystery

---

[1] I do not consider these verses—which are somewhat freely rendered here—"an
attack on the authority of the Vedas," but a beautiful lyrical episode, a new "Parable
of the fig-tree."

Of old Creation; for to Him come they
From passion and from dreams who break away;
  Who part the bonds constraining them to flesh,
And,—Him, the Highest, worshipping alway—

No longer grow at mercy of what breeze
Of summer pleasure stirs the sleeping trees,
  What blast of tempest tears them, bough and stem
To the eternal world pass such as these!

  Another Sun gleams there! another Moon!
Another Light,—a Light which none shall lack
Whose eyes once see; for those return no more
They have attained My Uttermost Abode!

  When, in this world of manifested life,
The undying Spirit, setting forth from Me,
Taketh on form, it draweth to itself
From Being's storehouse,—which containeth all,—
Senses and intellect. The Sovereign Soul

Thus entering the flesh, or quitting it,
Gathers these up, as the wind gathers scents,
Blowing above the flower-banks. Ear and Eye,
And Touch and Taste, and Smelling, these it takes,—
Yea, and a sentient mind;—linking itself
To sense-things so.

            The unenlightened ones
Mark not that Spirit when he goes or comes,
Nor when he takes his pleasure in the form,
Conjoined with qualities; but those see plain
Who have the eyes to see. Holy souls see
Which strive thereto. Enlightened, they behold
That Spirit in themselves; but foolish ones,
Even though they strive, discern not, having hearts
Unkindled, ill-informed!

Know, too, from Me
Shineth the gathered glory of the sun
Which lightens all the world: from Me the moon
Draws silvery beams, and fire fierce loveliness.
I penetrate the clay, and lend all shapes
Their living force; I glide into the plant—
Its root, leaf, bloom—to make the woodland green
With springing sap. Becoming vital warmth,
I glow in glad, respiring frames, and pass
With outward and with inward breath to feed
The body with all meats.[2]

For in this world
Being is twofold: the Divided, one;
The Undivided, one. All things that live
Are "the Divided." That which sits apart,
"The Undivided."

Higher still is ONE,
The Highest, holding all whose Name is LORD,
The Eternal, Sovereign, First! Who fills all worlds,
Sustaining them. And—dwelling thus beyond
Divided Life and Undivided—I
Am called of men and Vedas, God Supreme,
The PURUSHOTTAMA.

Who knows Me thus,
With mind unclouded, knoweth all, dear Prince!
And with his whole soul ever worshippeth Me.

Now is the sacred secret Mystery
Declared to thee! Who comprehendeth this
Hath wisdom! He is quit of works in bliss!

*Here ends Chapter XV. of the Bhagavad-Gîtâ
entitled "Purushottamapraptiyôgô,"
or "The Book of Religion by
attaining the Supreme"*

[2] I omit a verse here, evidently interpolated.

CHAPTER XVI

KRISHNA:

FEARLESSNESS, singleness of soul, the will
Always to strive for wisdom; opened hand
And governed appetites; and piety
And love of lonely study; humbleness,
Uprightness, heed to injure nought which lives,
Truthfulness, slowness unto wrath, a mind
That lightly letteth go what others prize;
And equanimity, and charity
Which spieth no man's faults; and tenderness
Towards all that suffer; a contented heart,
Fluttered by no desires; a bearing mild,
Modest, and grave, with manhood nobly mixed
With patience, fortitude, and purity;
An unrevengeful spirit, never given
To rate itself too high;—such be the signs,
O Indian Prince! of him whose feet are set
On that fair path which leads to heavenly birth!

Deceitfulness, and arrogance, and pride,
Quickness to anger, harsh and evil speech,
And ignorance, to its own darkness blind,—
These be the signs, My Prince! of him whose birth
Is fated for the regions of the vile.[1]

The Heavenly Birth brings to deliverance,
So should'st thou know! The birth with Asuras
Brings into bondage. Be thou joyous, Prince
Whose lot is set apart for heavenly Birth.

[1] "Of the Asuras," lit.

Two stamps there are marked on all living men,
Divine and Undivine; I spake to thee
By what marks thou shouldst know the Heavenly Man,
Hear from me now of the Unheavenly!

They comprehend not, the Unheavenly,
How souls go forth from Me; nor how they come
Back unto Me: nor is there Truth in these,
Nor purity, nor rule of Life. "This world
Hath not a Law, nor Order, nor a Lord,"
So say they: "nor hath risen up by Cause
Following on Cause, in perfect purposing,
But is none other than a House of Lust."
And, this thing thinking, all those ruined ones—
Of little wit, dark-minded—give themselves
To evil deeds, the curses of their kind.
Surrendered to desires insatiable,
Full of deceitfulness, folly, and pride,
In blindness cleaving to their errors, caught
Into the sinful course, they trust this lie
As it were true—this lie which leads to death—
Finding in Pleasure all the good which is,
And crying "Here it finisheth!"

                                        Ensnared
In nooses of a hundred idle hopes,
Slaves to their passion and their wrath, they buy
Wealth with base deeds, to glut hot appetites;
"Thus much, to-day," they say, "we gained! thereby
Such and such wish of heart shall have its fill;
And this is ours! and th' other shall be ours!
To-day we slew a foe, and we will slay
Our other enemy to-morrow! Look!
Are we not lords? Make we not goodly cheer?
Is not our fortune famous, brave, and great?
Rich are we, proudly born! What other men
Live like to us? Kill, then, for sacrifice!

Cast largesse, and be merry!" So they speak
Darkened by ignorance; and so they fall—
Tossed to and fro with projects, tricked, and bound
In net of black delusion, lost in lusts—
Down to foul Naraka. Conceited, fond,
Stubborn and proud, dead-drunken with the wine
Of wealth, and reckless, all their offerings
Have but a show of reverence, being not made
In piety of ancient faith. Thus vowed
To self-hood, force, insolence, feasting, wrath,
These My blasphemers, in the forms they wear
And in the forms they breed, my foemen are,
Hateful and hating; cruel, evil, vile,
Lowest and least of men, whom I cast down
Again, and yet again, at end of lives,
Into some devilish womb, whence—birth by birth—
The devilish wombs re-spawn them, all beguiled;
And, till they find and worship Me, sweet Prince!
Tread they that Nether Road.

     The Doors of Hell
Are threefold, whereby men to ruin pass,—
The door of Lust, the door of Wrath, the door
Of Avarice. Let a man shun those three!
He who shall turn aside from entering
All those three gates of Narak, wendeth straight
To find his peace, and comes to Swarga's gate.
. . . . [2]

*Here endeth Chapter XVI. of the Bhagavad-Gîtâ,
entitled "Daivasarasaupadwibhâgayôg," or
"The Book of the Separateness of the
Divine and Undivine"*

[2] I omit the ten concluding shlokas, with Mr. Davies.

CHAPTER XVII

ARJUNA:

IF men forsake the holy ordinance,
Heedless of Shastras, yet keep faith at heart
And worship, what shall be the state of those,
Great Krishna! *Sattwan, Rajas, Tamas?* Say!

KRISHNA:

Threefold the faith is of mankind, and springs
From those three qualities,—becoming "true,"
Or "passion-stained," or "dark," as thou shalt hear!

    The faith of each believer, Indian Prince!
Conforms itself to what he truly is.
Where thou shalt see a worshiper, that one
To what he worships lives assimilate,
[Such as the shrine, so is the votary,]
The "soothfast" souls adore true gods; the souls
Obeying *Rajas* worship Rakshasas[1]
Or Yakshas; and the men of Darkness pray
To Pretas and to Bhutas.[2] Yea, and those
Who practise bitter penance, not enjoined
By rightful rule—penance which hath its root
In self-sufficient, proud hypocrisies—
Those men, passion-beset, violent, wild,
Torturing—the witless ones—My elements
Shut in fair company within their flesh,
(Nay, Me myself, present within the flesh!)
Know them to devils devoted, not to Heaven!
For like as foods are threefold for mankind
In nourishing, so is there threefold way

[1] Rakshasas and Yakshas are unembodied but capricious beings of great power, gifts, and beauty, sometimes also of benignity.
[2] These are spirits of evil, wandering ghosts.

Of worship, abstinence, and almsgiving!
Hear this of Me! there is a food which brings
Force, substance, strength, and health, and joy to live,
Being well-seasoned, cordial comforting,
The "Soothfast" meat. And there be foods which bring
Aches and unrests, and burning blood, and grief,
Being too biting, heating, salt, and sharp,
And therefore craved by too strong appetite
And there is foul food—kept from over-night,[3]
Savorless, filthy, which the foul will eat,
A feast of rottenness, meet for the lips
Of such as love the "Darkness."

Thus with rites;—
A sacrifice not for rewardment made,
Offered in rightful wise, when he who vows
Sayeth, with heart devout, "This I should do!"
Is "Soothfast" rite. But sacrifice for gain,
Offered for good repute, be sure that this,
O Best of Bharatas! is Rajas-rite,
With stamp of "passion." And a sacrifice
Offered against the laws, with no due dole
Of food-giving, with no accompaniment
Of hallowed hymn, nor largesse to the priests,
In faithless celebration, call it vile.
The deed of "Darkness!"—lost!

Worship of gods
Meriting worship; lowly reverence
Of Twice-borns, Teachers, Elders; Purity,
Rectitude, and the Brahmacharya's vow,
And not to injure any helpless thing,—
These make a true religiousness of Act.

Words causing no man woe, words ever true,
Gentle and pleasing words, and those ye say

[3] *Yâtayaman,* food which has remained after the watches of the night. In India this would probably "go bad."

In murmured reading of a Sacred Writ,—
These make the true religiousness of Speech.

Serenity of soul, benignity,
Sway of the silent Spirit, constant stress
To sanctify the Nature,—these things make
Good rite, and true religiousness of Mind.

Such threefold faith, in highest piety
Kept, with no hope of gain, by hearts devote,
Is perfect work of *Sattwan,* true belief.

Religion shown in act of proud display
To win good entertainment, worship, fame,
Such—say I—is of *Rajas,* rash and vain.

Religion followed by a witless will
To torture self, or come at power to hurt
Another,—'tis of *Tamas,* dark and ill.

The gift lovingly given, when one shall say
"Now must I gladly give!" when he who takes
Can render nothing back; made in due place,
Due time, and to a meet recipient,
Is gift of *Sattwan,* fair and profitable.

The gift selfishly given, where to receive
Is hoped again, or when some end is sought,
Or where the gift is proffered with a grudge,
This is of *Rajas,* stained with impulse, ill.

The gift churlishly flung, at evil time,
In wrongful place, to base recipient,
Made in disdain or harsh unkindliness,
Is gift of *Tamas,* dark; it doth not bless![4]

*Here endeth Chapter XVII. of the Bhagavad-Gîtâ,
entitled "Sraddhatrayavibhâgayôg," or
"The Book of Religion by the Threefold Kinds of Faith"*

---

[4] I omit the concluding shlokas, as of very doubtful authenticity.

CHAPTER XVIII

ARJUNA:

FAIN would I better know, Thou Glorious One!
The very truth—Heart's Lord!—of *Sannyâs,*
Abstention; and Renunciation, Lord!
Tyâga; and what separates these twain!

KRISHNA:

The poets rightly teach that *Sannyâs*
Is the foregoing of all acts which spring
Out of desire; and their wisest say
Tyâga is renouncing fruit of acts.

There be among the saints some who have held
All action sinful, and to be renounced;
And some who answer "Nay! the goodly acts—
As worship, penance, alms—must be performed!"
Hear now My sentence, Best of Bharatas!

'Tis well set forth, O Chaser of thy Foes!
Renunciation is of threefold form,
And Worship, Penance, Alms, not to be stayed;
Nay, to be gladly done; for all those three
Are purifying waters for true souls!

Yet must be practised even those high works
In yielding up attachment, and all fruit
Produced by works. This is My judgment, Prince!
This My insuperable and fixed decree!

Abstaining from a work by right prescribed
Never is meet! So to abstain doth spring

From "Darkness," and Delusion teacheth it.
Abstaining from a work grievous to flesh,
When one saith " 'Tis unpleasing!" this is null!
Such an one acts from "passion;" nought of gain
Wins his Renunciation! But, Arjun!
Abstaining from attachment to the work,
Abstaining from rewardment in the work,
While yet one doeth it full faithfully,
Saying, " 'Tis right to do!" that is "true" act
And abstinence! Who doeth duties so,
Unvexed if his work fail, if it succeed
Unflattered, in his own heart justified,
Quit of debates and doubts, his is "true" act:
For, being in the body, none may stand
Wholly aloof from act; yet, who abstains
From profit of his acts is abstinent.

The fruit of labors, in the lives to come,
Is threefold for all men,—Desirable,
And Undesirable, and mixed of both;
But no fruit is at all where no work was.

Hear from me, Long-armed Lord! the makings five
Which go to every act, in Sânkhya taught
As necessary. First the force; and then
The agent; next, the various instruments;
Fourth, the especial effort; fifth, the God.
What work soever any mortal doth
Of body, mind, or speech, evil or good,
By these five doth he that. Which being thus,
Whoso, for lack of knowledge, seeth himself
As the sole actor, knoweth nought at all
And seeth nought. Therefore, I say, if one—
Holding aloof from self—with unstained mind
Should slay all yonder host, being bid to slay,
He doth not slay; he is not bound thereby!

Knowledge, the thing known, and the mind which knows,
These make the threefold starting-ground of act.
The act, the actor, and the instrument,
These make the threefold total of the deed.
But knowledge, agent, act, are differenced
By three dividing qualities. Hear now
Which be the qualities dividing them.

There is "true" Knowledge. Learn thou it is this!
To see one changeless Life in all the Lives,
And in the Separate, One Inseparable.
There is imperfect Knowledge: that which sees
The separate existences apart,
And, being separated, holds them real.
There is false Knowledge: that which blindly clings
To one as if 'twere all, seeking no Cause,
Deprived of light, narrow, and dull, and "dark."

There is "right" Action: that which—being enjoined—
Is wrought without attachment, passionlessly,
For duty, not for love, nor hate, nor gain.
There is "vain" Action: that which men pursue
Aching to satisfy desires, impelled
By sense of self, with all-absorbing stress:
This is of *Rajas*—passionate and vain.
There is "dark" Action: when one doth a thing
Heedless of issues, heedless of the hurt
Or wrong for others, heedless if he harm
His own soul—'tis of *Tamas,* black and bad!

There is the "rightful" doer. He who acts
Free from selfseeking, humble, resolute,
Steadfast, in good or evil hap the same,
Content to do aright—he "truly" acts.
There is th' "impassioned" doer. He that works
From impulse seeking profit, rude and bold
To overcome, unchastened; slave by turns

Of sorrow and of joy: of *Rajas* he!
And there be evil doers; loose of heart,
Low-minded, stubborn, fraudulent, remiss,
Dull, slow, despondent—children of the "dark."

Hear, too, of Intellect and Steadfastness
The threefold separation, Conqueror-Prince!
How these are set apart by Qualities.

Good is the Intellect which comprehends
The coming forth and going back of life,
What must be done, and what must not be done,
What should be feared, and what should not be feared,
What binds and what emancipates the soul:
That is of *Sattwan*, Prince! of "soothfastness."
Marred is the Intellect which, knowing right
And knowing wrong, and what is well to do
And what must not be done, yet understands
Nought with firm mind, nor as the calm truth is:
This is of *Rajas*, Prince! and "passionate!"
Evil is Intellect which, wrapped in gloom,
Looks upon wrong as right, and sees all things
Contrariwise of Truth. O Pritha's Son!
That is of *Tamas*, "dark" and desperate!

Good is the steadfastness whereby a man
Masters his beats of heart, his very breath
Of life, the action of his senses; fixed
In never-shaken faith and piety:
That is of *Sattwan*, Prince! "soothfast" and fair!
Stained is the steadfastness whereby a man
Holds to his duty, purpose, effort, end,
For life's sake, and the love of goods to gain,
Arjuna! 'tis of *Rajas*, passion-stamped!
Sad is the steadfastness wherewith the fool
Cleaves to his sloth, his sorrow, and his fears,
His folly and despair. This—Pritha's Son!—
Is born of *Tamas*, "dark" and miserable!

Hear further, Chief of Bharatas! from Me
The threefold kinds of Pleasure which there be.

Good Pleasure is the pleasure that endures,
Banishing pain for aye; bitter at first
As poison to the soul, but afterward
Sweet as the taste of Amrit. Drink of that!
It springeth in the Spirit's deep content.
And painful Pleasure springeth from the bond
Between the senses and the sense-world. Sweet
As Amrit is its first taste, but its last
Bitter as poison. 'Tis of *Rajas,* Prince!
And foul and "dark" the Pleasure is which springs
From sloth and sin and foolishness; at first
And at the last, and all the way of life
The soul bewildering. 'Tis of *Tamas,* Prince!

For nothing lives on earth, nor 'midst the gods
In utmost heaven, but hath its being bound
With these three Qualities, by Nature framed.

The work of Brahmans, Kshatriyas, Vaisyas,
And Sudras, O thou Slayer of thy Foes!
Is fixed by reason of the Qualities
Planted in each:

                A Brahman's virtues, Prince!
Born of his nature, are serenity,
Self-mastery, religion, purity,
Patience, uprightness, learning, and to know
The truth of things which be. A Kshatriya's pride,
Born of his nature, lives in valor, fire,
Constancy, skilfulness, spirit in fight,
And open-handedness and noble mien,
As of a lord of men. A Vaisya's task,
Born with his nature, is to till the ground,
Tend cattle, venture trade. A Sudra's state,
Suiting his nature, is to minister.

Whoso performeth—diligent, content—
The work allotted him, whate'er it be,
Lays hold of perfectness! Hear how a man
Findeth perfection, being so content:
He findeth it through worship—wrought by work—
Of HIM that is the Source of all which lives,
Of HIM by Whom the universe was stretched.

Better thine own work is, though done with fault,
Than doing other's work, ev'n excellently.
He shall not fall in sin who fronts the task
Set him by Nature's hand! Let no man leave
His natural duty, Prince! though it bear blame!
For every work hath blame, as every flame
Is wrapped in smoke! Only that man attains
Perfect surcease of work whose work was wrought
With mind unfettered, soul wholly subdued,
Desires for ever dead, results renounced.

Learn from me, Son of Kunti! also this,
How one, attaining perfect peace, attains
BRAHM, the supreme, the highest height of all!

Devoted—with a heart grown pure, restrained
In lordly self-control, foregoing wiles
Of song and senses, freed from love and hate,
Dwelling 'mid solitudes, in diet spare,
With body, speech, and will tamed to obey,
Ever to holy meditation vowed,
From passions liberate, quit of the Self,
Of arrogance, impatience, anger, pride;
Freed from surroundings, quiet, lacking nought—
Such an one grows to oneness with the BRAHM;
Such an one, growing one with BRAHM, serene,
Sorrows no more, desires no more; his soul,
Equally loving all that lives, loves well
Me, Who have made them, and attains to Me.

By this same love and worship doth he know
Me as I am, how high and wonderful,
And knowing, straightway enters into Me.
And whatsoever deeds he doeth—fixed
In Me, as in his refuge—he hath won
For ever and for ever by My grace
Th' Eternal Rest! So win thou! In thy thoughts
Do all thou dost for Me! Renounce for Me!
Sacrifice heart and mind and will to Me!
Live in the faith of Me! In faith of Me
All dangers thou shalt vanquish, by My grace,
But, trusting to thyself and heeding not,
Thou can'st but perish! If this day thou say'st
Relying on thyself, "I will not fight!"
Vain will the purpose prove! thy qualities
Would spur thee to the war. What thou dost shun,
Misled by fair illusions, thou wouldst seek
Against thy will, when the task comes to thee
Waking the promptings in thy nature set.
There lives a Master in the hearts of men
Maketh their deeds, by subtle pulling-strings,
Dance to what tune HE will. With all thy soul
Trust Him, and take Him for thy succor, Prince!
So—only so, Arjuna!—shall thou gain—
By grace of Him—the uttermost repose,
The Eternal Place!

        Thus hath been opened thee
This Truth of Truths, the Mystery more hid
Than any secret mystery. Meditate!
And—as thou wilt—then act!

        Nay! but once more
Take My last word, My utmost meaning have!
Precious thou art to Me; right well-beloved!
Listen! I tell thee for thy comfort this.
Give Me thy heart! adore Me! serve Me! cling

In faith and love and reverence to Me!
So shalt thou come to Me! I promise true,
For thou art sweet to Me!

              And let go those—
Rites and writ duties! Fly to Me alone!
Make Me thy single refuge! I will free
Thy soul from all its sins! Be of good cheer!

[Hide, the holy Krishna saith,
This from him that hath no faith,
Him that worships not, nor seeks
Wisdom's teaching when she speaks:
Hide it from all men who mock;
But, wherever, 'mid the flock
Of My lovers, one shall teach
This divinest, wisest, speech—
Teaching in the faith to bring
Truth to them, and offering
Of all honor unto Me—
Unto Brahma cometh he!
Nay, and nowhere shall ye find
Any man of all mankind
Doing dearer deed for Me;
Nor shall any dearer be
In My earth. Yea, furthermore,
Whoso reads this converse o'er
Held by Us upon the plain,
Pondering piously and fain,
He hath paid Me sacrifice!
(Krishna speaketh in this wise!)
Yea, and whoso, full of faith,
Heareth wisely what it saith,
Heareth meekly,—when he dies,
Surely shall his spirit rise
To those regions where the Blest,
Free of flesh, in joyance rest.]

Hath this been heard by thee, O Indian Prince!
With mind intent? hath all the ignorance—
Which bred thy trouble—vanished, My Arjun?

ARJUNA:

Trouble and ignorance are gone! the Light
Hath come unto me, by Thy favor, Lord!
Now am I fixed! my doubt is fled away!
According to Thy word, so will I do!

SANJAYA:

Thus gathered I the gracious speech of Krishna, O my King!
Thus have I told, with heart a-thrill, this wise and wondrous thing
By great Vyâsa's learning writ, how Krishna's self made known
The Yôga, being Yôga's Lord. So is the high truth shown!
And aye, when I remember, O Lord my King, again
Arjuna and the God in talk, and all this holy strain,
Great is my gladness: when I muse that splendor, passing speech,
Of Hari, visible and plain, there is no tongue to reach
My marvel and my love and bliss. O Archer-Prince! all hail!
O Krishna, Lord of Yôga! surely there shall not fail
Blessing, and victory, and power, for Thy most mighty sake,
Where this song comes of Arjun, and how with God he spake.

*Here ends, with Chapter XVIII. entitled "Mokshasan-
yâsayôg," or "The Book of Religion by
Deliverance and Renunciation,"*

THE BHAGAVAD-GITA

Subhamastu Sarvajagatân

(MOHAMMEDAN)

CHAPTERS FROM THE KORAN

TRANSLATED AND ANNOTATED BY
E. H. PALMER

INTRODUCTORY NOTE

THE ancient religion of the Arabs was the worship of the stars, but long before the birth of Mohammed, it had become greatly corrupted, and a multifarious idolatry had come to prevail. By the sixth century even this had become perfunctory, and most of the population had ceased to believe in anything, though pilgrimages and sacrifices were to some extent kept up. The chief seat of this degraded worship was the city of Mecca, where was situated the Kaabah, the most ancient shrine of the country; and it was from the family of the princes of Mecca and guardians of the Kaabah that the prophet was descended.

Mohammed was born in 571 A. D. His father died before he was born, and his mother when he was only six. In his youth he tended sheep and goats, and at twenty-four he was employed to drive caravans of camels by a rich widow, 'Hadīgah, whom he married.

When he was forty, while wandering alone on a desolate mountain near Mecca, he had a vision. An angel appeared to him and told him to read, and recited certain verses. From youth he had suffered from a kind of hysteria, and this vision seems to have increased his tendency to hallucinations and ecstasy. There was an intermission of two or three years before the vision reappeared, after which revelations came rapidly. He became convinced of his prophetic mission, and began to make converts, the first being the women of his own family.

For years, however, the new religion made little progress, and the prophet underwent great hardships, finally having to flee from Mecca to Medinah. From this "Flight," which took place in 622 A. D., the Mohammedan era dates. Two years later began the Holy War, and from this time on Mohammedanism was extended largely by the sword. When its founder died in 632, it was firmly established as a great political power as well as a religion; and it is now said to be the belief of about a hundred and seventy millions of people.

From the Qur'ân or Koran, in which are collected Mohammed's revelations, the following chapters are selected to give a view of all the more important elements of the faith he taught.

CONTENTS

MOHAMMEDAN

Chapters from The Koran

Mecca Suras

PAGE

The Chapter of Congealed Blood 879
The Chapter of the 'Covered' 879
The Chapter of the Enwrapped 881
The Chapter of the Forenoon 882
The Opening Chapter 882
The Chapter of Misbelievers 883
The Chapter of Unity 883
The Chapter of 'Necessaries' 883
The Chapter of the Night 883
The Chapter of the Land 884
The Chapter 'He Frowned' 885
The Chapter of the Smiting 886
The Chapter of the Cleaving Asunder 886
The Chapter of the Folding Up 886
The Chapter of Those who Tear Out 887
The Chapter of Those Sent 889
The Chapter of the Resurrection 890
The Chapter of the Infallible 891
The Chapter of the Mount 893
The Chapter of the Inevitable 895
The Chapter of the Star 897
The Chapter of the Merciful 899
The Chapter of the Poets 902
The Chapter of Mary 908
The Chapter of the Night Journey 913
The Chapter of Joseph (peace be on him!) 922
The Chapter of the Believer 931
The Chapter of Thunder 936

Medina Suras

The Chapter of the Congregation 942
The Chapter of the Spoils 943

CONTENTS

878

PAGE

The Chapter of Imran's Family 949
The Chapter of the Ranks 966
The Chapter of Women 967
The Chapter of the Confederates 985
The Chapter of Prohibition 992
The Chapter of the Table 994

CHAPTERS FROM THE KORAN

MECCA SURAS

The Chapter of Congealed Blood[1]

IN the name of the merciful and compassionate God.
READ, in the name of thy Lord!
Who created man from congealed blood!
Read, for thy Lord is most generous!
Who taught the pen!
Taught man what he did not know!
Nay, verily, man is indeed outrageous at seeing himself get rich!
Verily, unto thy Lord is the return!
Hast thou considered him who forbids a servant[2] when he prays[3]?
Hast thou considered if he were in guidance or bade piety?
Hast thou considered if he said it was a lie, and turned his back?
Did he not know that God can see?
Nay, surely, if he do not desist we will drag him by the forelock!
—the lying sinful forelock!
So let him call his counsel: we will call the guards of hell!
Nay, obey him not, but adore and draw nigh!

The Chapter of the 'Covered'[4]

IN the name of the merciful and compassionate God.
O thou who art covered! rise up and warn!
And thy Lord magnify!
And thy garments purify!
And abomination shun!

[1] The five opening verses of this chapter are generally allowed to have been the first that were revealed.
[2] I. e. Mohammed.
[3] The allusion is to Abu Ghal, who threatened to set his foot on Mohammed's neck if he caught him in the act of adoration.
[4] The first five verses of this chapter form the second revelation by the angel Gabriel in person, and the first after the Fatrah, or period of 'Intermission.'

And grant not favours to gain increase!

And for thy Lord await!

And when the trump is blown,—for that day is a difficult day! for the misbelievers aught but easy!

Leave me alone with him I have created and for whom I have made extensive wealth[5] and sons that he may look upon, and for whom I have smoothed things down. Then he desires that I should increase! nay, verily, he is hostile to our signs! I will drive him up a hill! Then he reflected and planned! May he be killed,—how he planned! Again, may he be killed,—how he planned! Then he looked; then he frowned and scowled; then he retreated and was big with pride and said, 'This is only magic exhibited! this is only mortal speech!'—I will broil him in hell-fire! and what shall make thee know what hell-fire is? It will not leave and will not let alone. It scorches the flesh; over it are nineteen (angels).

We have made only angels guardians of the fire, and we have only made their number a trial to those who misbelieve; that those who have been given the Book may be certain, and that those who believe may be increased in faith; and that those who have been given the Book and the believers may not doubt; and that those in whose hearts is sickness, and the misbelievers may say, 'What does God mean by this as a parable?'

Thus God leads astray whom He pleases, and guides him He pleases: and none knows the hosts of thy Lord save Himself; and it is only a reminder to mortals!

Nay, by the moon!

And the night when it retires!

And the morning when it brightly dawns!

Verily, it is one of the greatest misfortunes; a warning to mortals; for him amongst you who wishes to press forward or to tarry!

Every soul is pledged[6] for what it earns; except the fellows of the right: in gardens shall they ask each other about the sinners!—'What drove you into hell-fire?'

They shall say, 'We weren't of those who prayed; we didn't feed the poor; but we did plunge into discussion with those who plunged,

[5] The person meant is generally supposed to be Walîd ibn Mughâirah, one of the chiefs of the Qurâis.   [6] See note 3, Chapter of the Mount.

and we called the judgment day a lie until the certainty[7] did come to us!'

But there shall not profit them the intercession of the intercessors.

What ailed them that they turned away from the memorial as though they were timid asses fleeing from a lion?

Nay, every man of them wished that he might have given him books spread open!

Nay, but they did not fear the hereafter!

Nay, it is a memorial! and let him who will remember it; but none will remember it except God please. He is most worthy of fear; and he is most worthy to forgive!

THE CHAPTER OF THE ENWRAPPED

In the name of the merciful and compassionate God.

O thou who art enwrapped! rise by night except a little—the half, or deduct therefrom a little, or add thereto, and chant the Qur'ân chanting. Verily, we will cast on thee a heavy speech.

Verily, the early part of the night is stronger in impressions and more upright in speech!

Verily, thou hast by day a long employment; but mention the name of thy Lord and devote thyself thoroughly to Him, the Lord of the east and the west; there is no god but He; then take Him for a guardian!

And endure patiently what they say, and flee from them with a decorous flight.

And leave me and those who say it is a lie, who are possessed of comfort; and let them bide for a while.

Verily, with us are heavy fetters and hell-fire, and food that chokes, and mighty woe!

On the day when the earth and the mountains shall tremble and the earth shall be as a crumbling sand-hill!

Verily, we have sent unto you an apostle bearing witness against you, as we sent an apostle unto Pharaoh.

But Pharaoh rebelled against the apostle, and we seized him with an overpowering punishment.

Then how will ye shield yourselves if ye misbelieve from the day

[7] I. e. death.

which shall make children grey-headed, whereon the heaven cleaves
—its promise shall be fulfilled!

Verily, this is a memorial, and whoso will, let him take unto his
Lord a way.[1]

Verily, thy Lord knows that thou dost stand up to pray nearly
two-thirds of the night, or the half of it or the third of it, as do part
of those who are with thee; for God measures the night and the day;
He knows that ye cannot calculate it, and He turns relentant towards
you.

So read what is easy of the Qur'ân. He knows that there will be
of you some who are sick and others who beat about in the earth
craving the grace of God, and others who are fighting in the cause
of God. Then read what is easy of it and be steadfast in prayer, and
give alms, and lend to God a goodly loan, for what ye send forward
for yourselves of good ye will find it with God. It is better and a
greater hire; and ask ye pardon of God; verily, God is forgiving,
merciful!

THE CHAPTER OF THE FORENOON

In the name of the merciful and compassionate God.

By the forenoon!

And the night when it darkens!

Thy Lord has not forsaken thee, nor hated thee! and surely the
hereafter is better for thee than the former; and in the end thy Lord
will give thee, and thou shalt be well pleased!

Did He not find thee an orphan, and give thee shelter? and find
thee erring, and guide thee? and find thee poor with a family, and
nourish thee?

But as for the orphan oppress him not; and as for the beggar drive
him not away; and as for the favour of thy Lord discourse thereof.

THE OPENING CHAPTER

In the name of the merciful and compassionate God.

Praise belongs to God, the Lord of the worlds, the merciful, the
compassionate, the ruler of the day of judgment! Thee we serve and

---

[1] From verse 20 the rest of the sûrah seems from its style to belong to the Medînah
period; and there is a tradition ascribed to 'Ayeshah that it was revealed a year
later than the earlier part of the chapter.

Thee we ask for aid. Guide us in the right path, the path of those Thou art gracious to; not of those Thou art wroth with; nor of those who err.

THE CHAPTER OF MISBELIEVERS

In the name of the merciful and compassionate God.

Say, 'O ye misbelievers! I do not serve what ye serve; nor will ye serve what I serve; nor will I serve what ye serve; nor will ye serve what I serve;—ye have your religion, and I have my religion!'

THE CHAPTER OF UNITY

In the name of the merciful and compassionate God.

Say, 'He is God alone!

God the Eternal!

He begets not and is not begotten!

Nor is there like unto Him any one!'

THE CHAPTER OF 'NECESSARIES'

In the name of the merciful and compassionate God.

Hast thou considered him who calls the judgment a lie? He it is who pushes the orphan away; and urges not (others) to feed the poor.

But woe to those who pray and who are careless in their prayers, Who pretend and withhold necessaries.[1]

THE CHAPTER OF THE NIGHT

In the name of the merciful and compassionate God.

By the night when it veils!

And the day when it is displayed!

And by what created male and female!

Verily, your efforts are diverse!

But as for him who gives alms and fears God,

And believes in the best,

We will send him easily to ease!

But as for him who is niggardly,

---

[1] Or, 'alms.' The word might be rendered 'resources.'

And longs for wealth,
And calls the good a lie,
We will send him easily to difficulty!
And his wealth shall not avail him
When he falls down (into hell)!
Verily, it is for us to guide;
And, verily, ours are the hereafter and the former life!
And I have warned you of a fire that flames!

None shall broil thereon, but the most wretched, who says it is a lie and turns his back.

But the pious shall be kept away from it, he who gives his wealth in alms, and who gives no favour to any one for the sake of reward, but only craving the face of his Lord most High; in the end he shall be well pleased!

The Chapter of the Land

In the name of the merciful and compassionate God.

I need not swear by the Lord of this land,[1] and thou a dweller in this land[2]!

Nor by the begetter and what he begets!

We have surely created man in trouble.

Does he think that none can do aught against him?

He says, 'I have wasted wealth in plenty;' does he think that no one sees him?

Have we not made for him two eyes and a tongue, and two lips? and guided him in the two highways? but he will not attempt the steep!

And what shall make thee know what the steep is? It is freeing captives, or feeding on the day of famine, an orphan who is akin, or a poor man who lies in the dust; and again (it is) to be of these who believe and encourage each other to patience, and encourage each other to mercy,—these are the fellows of the right!

But those who disbelieve in our signs, they are the fellows of the left, for them is fire that closes in!

---

[1] I. e. the sacred territory of Mecca.
[2] Or, 'art at liberty to act as thou pleasest.'

THE CHAPTER 'HE FROWNED'

In the name of the merciful and compassionate God.

He frowned and turned his back, for that there came to him a blind man[1]!

But what should make thee know whether haply he may be purified? or may be mindful and the reminder profit him?

But as for him who is wealthy, thou dost attend to him; and thou dost not care that he is not purified; but as for him who comes to thee earnestly fearing the while, from him thou art diverted!

Nay! verily, it is a memorial; and whoso pleases will remember it.

In honored pages exalted, purified, in the hands of noble, righteous scribes!

May man be killed! how ungrateful he is!

Of what did He create him? Of a clot. He created him and fated him; then the path He did make easy for him; then He killed him, and laid him in the tomb; then when He pleases will He raise him up again.

Nay, he has not fulfilled his bidding!

But let man look unto his foods. Verily, we have poured the water out in torrents: then we have cleft the earth asunder, and made to grow therefrom the grain, and the grape, and the hay, and the olive, and the palm, and gardens closely planted, and fruits, and grass,—a provision for you and for your cattle!

But when the stunning noise shall come, on the day when man shall flee from his brother and his mother and his father and his spouse and his sons! Every man among them on that day shall have a business to employ him.

Faces on that day shall be bright,—laughing, joyous! and faces shall have dust upon them,—darkness shall cover them! those are the wicked misbelievers!

---

[1] One Abdallah ibn Umm Maktûm, a poor blind man, once interrupted Mohammed while the latter was in conversation with Walîd ibn Mug͟hâirah and some others of the Qurâis chiefs. The prophet taking no notice of him, the blind man raised his voice and earnestly begged for religious instruction, but Mohammed, annoyed at the interruption, frowned and turned away. This passage is a reprimand to the prophet for his conduct on the occasion. Afterwards, whenever he saw the blind Abdallah, Mohammed used to say, 'Welcome to him on whose account my Lord reproved me!' and subsequently made him governor of Medînah.

The Chapter of the Smiting

In the name of the merciful and compassionate God.

The smiting!

What is the smiting?

And what shall make thee know what the smiting is?

The day when men shall be like scattered moths; and the mountains shall be like flocks of carded wool!

And as for him whose balance is heavy, he shall be in a well-pleasing life.

But as for him whose balance is light, his dwelling shall be the pit of hell.

And who shall make thee know what it is?—a burning fire!

The Chapter of the Cleaving Asunder

In the name of the merciful and compassionate God.

When the heaven is cleft asunder,

And when the stars are scattered,

And when the seas gush together,

And when the tombs are turned upside down,

The soul shall know what it has sent on or kept back!

O man! what has seduced thee concerning thy generous Lord, who created thee, and fashioned thee, and gave thee symmetry, and in what form He pleased composed thee?

Nay, but ye call the judgment a lie! but over you are guardians set,[1]—noble, writing down! they know what ye do!

Verily, the righteous are in pleasure, and, verily, the wicked are in hell; they shall broil therein upon the judgment day; nor shall they be absent therefrom!

And what shall make thee know what is the judgment day? Again, what shall make thee know what is the judgment day? a day when no soul shall control aught for another; and the bidding on that day belongs to God!

The Chapter of the Folding up

In the name of the merciful and compassionate God.

When the sun is folded up,

[1] The recording angels.

And when the stars do fall,
And when the mountains are moved,
And when the she-camels ten months gone with young shall be
neglected,[1]
And when the beasts shall be crowded together,[2]
And when the seas shall surge up,
And when souls shall be paired with bodies,
And when the child who was buried alive shall be asked for what
sin she was slain,
And when the pages shall be spread out,
And when the heaven shall be flayed,
And when hell shall be set ablaze,
And when Paradise shall be brought nigh.
The soul shall know what it has produced!
I need not swear by the stars that slink back, moving swiftly, slink-
ing into their dens!
Nor by the night when darkness draws on!
Nor by the morn when it first breathes up!
Verily, it is the speech of a noble apostle, mighty, standing sure
with the Lord of the throne, obeyed and trusty too!
Your comrade is not mad; he saw him[3] on the plain horizon, nor
does he grudge to communicate the unseen.
Nor is it the speech of a pelted devil.[4]
Then whither do ye go?
It is but a reminder to the worlds, to whomsoever of you pleases to
go straight:—but ye will not please, except God, the Lord of the
world, should please.

THE CHAPTER OF THOSE WHO TEAR OUT

In the name of the merciful and compassionate God.
By those who tear out violently!
And by those who gaily release[5]!

---

[1] Such camels being among the most valuable of an Arab's possessions, neglect
of them must imply some terribly engrossing calamity.
[2] The terrors of the judgment day will drive all the wild beasts together for
mutual shelter.   [3] Gabriel.
[4] See note 5, Chapter of Imrân's Family.
[5] Referring to the angel of death and his assistants, who tear away the souls of
the wicked violently, and gently release the souls of the good.

And by those who float through the air!

And the preceders who precede[6]!

And those who manage the affair!

On the day when the quaking[7] quakes which the following one shall succeed! Hearts on that day shall tremble; eyes thereon be humbled!

They say, 'Shall we be sent back to our old course?—What! when we are rotten bones?' they say, 'That then were a losing return!'

But it will only be one scare, and lo! they will be on the surface!

Has the story of Moses come to you? when his Lord addressed him in the holy valley of Tuvâ, 'Go unto Pharaoh, verily, he is outrageous; and say, "Hast thou a wish to purify thyself, and that I may guide thee to thy Lord, and thou mayest fear?"'

So he showed him the greatest signs; but he called him a liar and rebelled. Then he retreated hastily, and gathered, and proclaimed, and said, 'I am your Lord most High!' but God seized him with the punishment of the future life and of the former.

Verily, in that is a lesson to him who fears!

Are ye harder to create or the heaven that He has built? He raised its height and fashioned it; and made its night to cover it, and brought forth its noonday light; and the earth after that He did stretch out. He brings forth from it its water and its pasture.

And the mountains He did firmly set, a provision for you and for your cattle.

And when the great predominant calamity shall come, on the day when man shall remember what he strove after, and hell shall be brought out for him who sees!

And as for him who was outrageous and preferred the life of this world, verily, hell is the resort!

But as for him who feared the station of his Lord, and prohibited his soul from lust, verily, Paradise is the resort!

They shall ask thee about the Hour, for when it is set. Whereby canst thou mention it? Unto thy Lord its period belongs.

Thou art only a warner to him who fears it.

---

[6] The angels who precede the souls of the righteous to Paradise.

[7] The trumpet blast at the last day, which shall make the universe quake.

On the day they see it, it will be as though they had only tarried an evening or the noon thereof.

THE CHAPTER OF THOSE SENT

IN the name of the merciful and compassionate God.

By those sent in a series[1]!

And by those who speed swiftly!

And by the dispensers abroad!

And by the separators apart!

And by those who instil the reminder, as an excuse or warning!

Verily, what ye are threatened with shall surely happen!

And when the stars shall be erased!

And when the heavens shall be cleft!

And when the mountains shall be winnowed!

And when the apostles shall have a time appointed for them!

For what day is the appointment made?

For the day of decision! and what shall make thee know what the decision is?

Woe on that day for those who say it is a lie!

Have we not destroyed those of yore, and then followed them up with those of the latter day?

Thus do we with the sinners.

Woe on that day for those who say it is a lie!

Did we not create you from contemptible water, and place it in a sure depository unto a certain decreed term? for we are able and well able too!

Woe on that day for those who say it is a lie!

Have we not made for them the earth to hold the living and the dead? and set thereon firm mountains reared aloft? and given you to drink water in streams?

Woe on that day for those who say it is a lie!

Go off to that which ye did call a lie! Go off to the shadow of three columns, that shall not shade nor avail against the flame! Verily, it throws off sparks like towers,—as though they were yellow camels!

Woe on that day for those who say it is a lie!

[1] Either angels or winds, or as some interpret the passage, the verses of the Qur'ân.

This is the day when they may not speak,—when they are not permitted to excuse themselves!

Woe on that day for those who say it is a lie!

This is the day of decision! We have assembled you with those of yore; if ye have any stratagem employ it now!

Woe on that day for those who say it is a lie!

Verily, the pious are amid shades and springs and fruit such as they love.—'Eat and drink with good digestion, for that which ye have done!'

Verily, thus do we reward those who do well.

Woe on that day for those who say it is a lie!

'Eat and enjoy yourselves for a little; verily, ye are sinners!'

Woe on that day for those who say it is a lie!

And when it is said to them bow down, they bow not down.

Woe on that day for those who say it is a lie!

And in what new discourse after it will they believe?

The Chapter of the Resurrection

In the name of the merciful and compassionate God.

I need not swear by the resurrection day!

Nor need I swear by the self-accusing soul!

Does man think that we shall not collect his bones? Able are we to arrange his finger tips!

Nay, but man wishes to be wicked henceforward! he asks, When is the resurrection day?

But when the sight shall be dazed, and the moon be eclipsed, and the sun and the moon be together, and man shall say upon that day, 'Where is a place to flee to?'— nay, no refuge! and to thy Lord that day is the sure settlement: He will inform man on that day of what He has sent forward or delayed!

Nay, man is an evidence against himself, and even if he thrusts forward his excuses—.

Do not move thy tongue thereby to hasten it.[1] It is for us to collect it and to read it; and when we read it then follow its reading. And again it is for us to explain it.

---

[1] I. e. the revelation. The words are addressed to Mohammed by the angel Gabriel.

Nay, indeed, but ye love the transient life, and ye neglect the hereafter!

Faces on that day shall be bright, gazing on their Lord!

And faces on that day shall be dismal!

Thou wilt think that a back-breaking calamity has happened to them!

Nay, but when the [soul] comes up into the throat, and it is said, 'Who will charm it back?' and he will think that it is his parting [hour]. And leg shall be pressed on leg;[2] unto thy Lord on that day shall the driving be.

For he did not believe[3] and did not pray; but he said it was a lie, and turned his back! Then he went to his people haughtily—woe to thee, and woe to thee! again woe to thee, and woe to thee!

Does man think that he shall be left to himself?

Wasn't he a clot of emitted seed? Then he was congealed blood, and (God) created him, and fashioned him, and made of him pairs, male and female.

Is not He able to quicken the dead?

THE CHAPTER OF THE INFALLIBLE

In the name of the merciful and compassionate God.

The Infallible, what is the Infallible? and what should make thee know what the Infallible is?

Thamûd and 'Ad called the Striking Day a lie; but as for Thamûd they perished by the shock; and as for 'Ad they perished with the violent cold blast of wind, which He subjected against them for seven nights and eight days consecutively. Thou mightest see the people therein prostrate as though they were palm stumps thrown down, and canst thou see any of them left?

And Pharaoh and those before him of the overturned cities[1] committed sins, and they rebelled against the apostle of their Lord, and He seized them with an excessive punishment.

Verily, we, when the water surged, bore you on it in a sailing ship, to make it a memorial for you, and that the retentive ear might hold it.

---

[2] I. e. in the death struggle.   [3] Or did not give in charity.
[1] Sodom and Gomorrah.

And when the trumpet shall be blown with one blast, and the earth shall be borne away, and the mountains too, and both be crushed with one crushing; on that day shall the inevitable happen; and the heaven on that day shall be cleft asunder, for on that day shall it wane! and the angels upon the sides thereof; and above them on that day shall eight bear the throne of thy Lord!

On the day when ye shall be set forth no hidden thing of yours shall be concealed.

And as for him who is given his book in his right hand, he shall say, 'Here! take and read my book. Verily, I thought that I should meet my reckoning'; and he shall be in a pleasing life, in a lofty garden, whose fruits are nigh to cull—'Eat ye and drink with good digestion, for what ye did aforetime in the days that have gone by!'

But as for him who is given his book in his left hand he shall say, 'O, would that I had not received my book! I did not know what my account would be. O, would that it² had been an end of me! my wealth availed me not! my authority has perished from me!' 'Take him and fetter him, then in hell broil him! then into a chain whose length is seventy cubits force him! verily, he believed not in the mighty God, nor was he particular to feed the poor: therefore he has not here to-day any warm friend, nor any food except foul ichor, which none save sinners shall eat!'

I need not swear by what ye see or what ye do not see, verily, it is the speech of a noble apostle; and it is not the speech of a poet:— little is it ye believe!

And it is not the speech of a soothsayer,—little is it that ye mind! —a revelation from the Lord of the worlds.

Why if he had invented against us any sayings, we would have seized him by the right hand, then we would have cut his jugular vein; nor could any one of you have kept us off from him.

Verily, it is a memorial to the pious; and, verily, we know that there are amongst you those who say it is a lie; and, verily, it is a source of sighing to the misbelievers; and, verily, it is certain truth!

Therefore celebrate the name of thy mighty Lord!

² I. e. death.

THE CHAPTER OF THE MOUNT

IN the name of the merciful and compassionate God.

By the mount! by the Book inscribed upon an outstretched vellum! by the frequented house[1]! by the elevated roof[2]! by the swelling sea! verily, the torment of thy Lord will come to pass;—there is none to avert it!

The day when the heavens shall reel about, and the mountains shall move about,—then woe upon that day to those who call (the apostles) liars, who plunge into discussion for a sport!

On the day when they shall be thrust away into the fire of hell,— 'This is the fire, the which ye used to call a lie!—Is it magic, this? or can ye not see?—broil ye therein, and be patient thereof or be not patient, it is the same to you: ye are but rewarded for that which ye did do!'

Verily, the pious (shall be) in gardens and pleasure, enjoying what their Lord has given them; for their Lord will save them from the torment of hell.

'Eat and drink with good digestion, for that which ye have done!'

Reclining on couches in rows; and we will wed them to large-eyed maids.

And those who believe and whose seed follows them in the faith, we will unite their seed with them; and we will not cheat them of their work at all;—every man is pledged for what he earns.[3]

And we will extend to them fruit and flesh such as they like. They shall pass to and fro therein a cup in which is neither folly nor sin.

And round them shall go boys of theirs, as though they were hidden pearls.

And they shall accost each other and ask questions, and shall say, 'Verily, we were before amidst our families shrinking with terror,[4] but God has been gracious to us and saved us from the torment of the hot blast.

'Verily, we used to call on Him before; verily, He is the righteous, the compassionate!'

[1] I. e. either the Kaabah itself or the model of it, said to exist in the heavens and to be frequented by the angels.   [2] I. e. of heaven.

[3] Every man is pledged to God for his conduct, and, if he does well, redeems himself.   [4] At the thought of the next life.

Wherefore do thou[5] remind them: for thou art, by the favour of thy Lord, neither a soothsayer nor mad!

Will they say, 'A poet; we wait for him the sad accidents of fate?' Say, 'Wait ye then; for I too am of those who wait!'

Do their dreams bid them this? or are they an outrageous people? Or will they say, 'He has invented it?'—nay, but they do not believe!

But let them bring a discourse like it, if they tell the truth!

Or were they created of nothing, or were they the creators? Or did they create the heavens and the earth?—nay, but they are not sure!

Or have they the treasures of thy Lord? or are they the governors supreme?

Or have they a ladder whereon they can listen[6]?—then let their listener bring obvious authority.

Has He daughters, while ye have sons?

Or dost thou ask them a hire, while they are borne down by debt?

Or have they the unseen, so that they write it down?

Or do they desire a plot?—but those who misbelieve it is who are plotted against!

Or have they a god beside God? celebrated be God's praises above what they join with Him!

But if they should see a fragment of the sky falling down, they would say, 'Clouds in masses!'

But leave them till they meet that day of theirs whereon they shall swoon[7]; the day when their plotting shall avail them naught, and they shall not be helped!

And, verily, there is a torment beside that[8] for those who do wrong; but most of them do not know!

But wait thou patiently for the judgment of thy Lord, for thou art in our eyes. And celebrate the praises of thy Lord what time thou risest, and in the night, and at the fading of the stars!

[5] Addressed to Mohammed.

[6] I. e. a ladder reaching to the gates of heaven, upon which they may stand and listen to the angels discoursing, as the devils do.

[7] At the sound of the last trumpet.

[8] I. e. beside the torment of the judgment day they shall be punished with defeat and loss here.

THE CHAPTER OF THE INEVITABLE

In the name of the merciful and compassionate God.

When the inevitable[1] happens; none shall call its happening a lie!—abasing—exalting!

When the earth shall quake, quaking! and the mountains shall crumble, crumbling, and become like motes dispersed!

And ye shall be three sorts;

And the fellows of the right hand—what right lucky fellows!

And the fellows of the left hand—what unlucky fellows!

And the foremost foremost[2]!

These are they who are brought nigh,

In gardens of pleasure!

A crowd of those of yore,

And a few of those of the latter day!

And gold-weft couches, reclining on them face to face.

Around them shall go eternal youths, with goblets and ewers and a cup of flowing wine; no headache shall they feel therefrom, nor shall their wits be dimmed!

And fruits such as they deem the best;

And flesh of fowl as they desire;

And bright and large-eyed maids like hidden pearls;

A reward for that which they have done!

They shall hear no folly there and no sin;

Only the speech, 'Peace, Peace!'

And the fellows of the right—what right lucky fellows!

Amid thornless lote trees.

And tal'h[3] trees with piles of fruit;

And outspread shade,

And water out-poured;

And fruit in abundance, neither failing nor forbidden;

And beds upraised!

Verily, we have produced them[4] a production.

[1] I. e. the day of judgment.
[2] I. e. the foremost in professing the faith on earth shall be the foremost then.
[3] The mimosa gummifera is generally so called in Arabia; but the banana is said to be meant in this passage.   [4] The celestial damsels.

And made them virgins, darlings of equal age (with their spouses)
for the fellows of the right!
A crowd of those of yore, and a crowd of those of the latter day!
And the fellows of the left—what unlucky fellows!
In hot blasts and boiling water;
And a shade of pitchy smoke,
Neither cool nor generous!
Verily, they were affluent ere this, and did persist in mighty crime;
and used to say, 'What, when we die and have become dust and
bones, shall we then indeed be raised? or our fathers of yore?'
Say, 'Verily, those of yore and those of the latter day shall surely be
gathered together unto the tryst of the well-known day.'
Then ye, O ye who err! who say it is a lie! shall eat of the Zaqqûm
tree! and fill your bellies with it! and drink thereon of boiling
water! and drink as drinks the thirsty camel.
This is their entertainment on the judgment day!
We created you, then why do ye not credit?
Have ye considered what ye emit?
Do we create it, or are we the creators?
We have decreed amongst you death; but we are not forestalled from
making the likes of you in exchange, or producing you as ye know
not of.
Ye do know the first production—why then do ye not mind?
Have ye considered what ye till?
Do ye make it bear seed, or do we make it bear seed?
If we pleased we could make it mere grit, so that ye would pause to
marvel:
'Verily, we have got into debt[5] and we are excluded.'[6]
Have ye considered the water which ye drink?
Do ye make it come down from the clouds, or do we make it come
down?
If we pleased we could make it pungent—why then do ye not give
thanks?
Have ye considered the fire which ye strike?
Do ye produce the tree that gives it,[7] or do we produce it?

---

[5] I. e. for seed and labour. [6] From reaping the fruits of it.

[7] The ancient Arabs produced fire by the friction of a stick in a hollow piece
of wood.

We have made it a memorial and a chattel for the traveller of the waste?

Then celebrate the grand name of thy Lord!

So I will not swear by the positions of the stars; and, verily, it is a grand oath if ye did but know—that, verily, this is the honourable Qur'ân—in the laid-up Book!

Let none touch it but the purified!

A revelation from the Lord of the worlds.

What! this new discourse will ye despise?

And make for your provision, that you call it a lie?

Why then—when it[8] comes up to the throat, and ye at that time look on, though we are nearer to him than you are, but ye cannot see,—why, if ye are not to be judged, do ye not send it back, if ye do tell the truth?

But either, if he be of those brought nigh to God,—then rest and fragrance and the garden of pleasure!

Or, if he be of the fellows of the right! then 'Peace to thee!' from the fellows of the right!

Or, if he be of those who say it is a lie,—who err! then an entertainment of boiling water! and broiling in hell!

Verily, this is surely certain truth!

So celebrate the grand name of thy Lord!

THE CHAPTER OF THE STAR

In the name of the merciful and compassionate God.

By the star when it falls, your comrade errs not, nor is he deluded! nor speaks he out of lust! It is but an inspiration inspired! One mighty in power[1] taught him, endowed with sound understanding and appeared, he being in the loftiest tract.

Then drew he near and hovered o'er! until he was two bows length off or nigher still! Then he inspired his servant what he inspired him; the heart belies not what he saw! What, will ye dispute with him on what he saw?

And he saw him another time, by the lote tree none may pass; near which is the garden of the Abode! When there covered the

---

[8] The soul of a dying man.　[1] The angel Gabriel, who appeared twice to Mohammed in his natural form, namely, on the occasion of the 'Night Journey,' to which this passage refers, and on the first revelation of the Qur'ân.

lote tree what did cover it! The sight swerved not nor wandered. He saw then the greatest of the signs of his Lord.

Have ye considered Allât and Al 'Huzzâ, and Manât the other third? Shall there be male offspring for Him and female for you? That were an unfair division! They are but names which ye have named, ye and your fathers! God has sent down no authority for them! They do but follow suspicion and what their souls lust after! —And yet there has come to them guidance from their Lord.

Shall man have what he desires? But God's is the hereafter and the present!

How many an angel in the heaven!—their intercession avails not at all, save after God has given permission to whomsoever He will and is pleased with!

Verily, those who believe not in the hereafter do surely name the angels with female names!—but they have no knowledge thereof; they do but follow suspicion, and, verily, suspicion shall not avail against the truth at all!

But turn aside from him who turns his back upon our remembrance and desires naught but this world's life! This is their sum of knowledge; verily, thy Lord knows best who has erred from His way, and He knows best who is guided!

God's is what is in the heavens and what is in the earth, that He may reward those who do evil for what they have done; and may reward those who do good with good! those who shun great sins and iniquities,—all but venial faults,—verily, thy Lord is of ample forgiveness; He knows best about you, when He produced you from the earth, and when ye were embryos in the wombs of your mothers.

Make not yourselves out, then, to be pure; He knows best who it is that fears.

Hast thou considered him who turns his back? who gives but little and then stops[2]? Has he then the knowledge of the unseen, so that he can see?

---

[2] This passage refers to one El Walîd ibn Mughâirah, who being abused for following Mohammed and forsaking the religion of the Qurâis, answered that he had done so to escape divine vengeance. Thereupon an idolater offered to take on himself El Walîd's sin for a certain sum of money. The offer was accepted, and Walîd apostatized from El Islâm, paying down a portion of the amount agreed upon at the time. Later on he refused to pay the balance on the ground that he had already paid enough.

Has he not been informed of what is in the pages of Moses and Abraham who fulfilled his word?—that no burdened soul shall bear the burden of another? and that man shall have only that for which he strives; and that his striving shall at length be seen? Then shall he be rewarded for it with the most full reward; and that unto thy Lord is the limit; and that it is He who makes men laugh and weep; and that it is He who kills and makes alive; and that He created pairs, male and female, from a clot when it is emitted; and that for Him is the next production[3]; and that He enriches and gives possession; and that He is the Lord of the Dog-star,[4] and that He it was who destroyed 'Ad of yore, and Thamûd, and left none of them; and the people of Noah before them,—verily, they were most unjust and outrageous!

And the overthrown (cities)[5] He threw down; and there covered them what did cover them!

Which then of your Lord's benefits do ye dispute?

This is a warner, one of the warners of yore!

The approaching day approaches; there is none to discover it but God.

At this new discourse then do ye wonder? and do ye laugh and not weep? and ye divert yourselves the while!

But adore God and serve (Him).[6]

THE CHAPTER OF THE MERCIFUL

In the name of the merciful and compassionate God.

The Merciful taught the Qur'ân;
He created man, taught him plain speech.
The sun and the moon have their appointed time;
The herbs and the trees adore;
And the heavens, He raised them and set the balance, that ye should
    not be outrageous in the balance;
But weigh ye aright, and stint not the balance.

[3] I. e. the resurrection.
[4] Sirius, or the Dog-star, was an object of worship amongst the ancient Arabs.
[5] Sodom, Gomorrah, &c.
[6] At this verse the Quarâis, who were present at the first reading of this chapter when their gods were spoken well of, fell down adoring with Mohammed.

And the earth He has set it for living creatures; therein are fruits and palms, with sheaths; and grain with chaff and frequent shoots; Then which of your Lord's bounties will ye twain deny?

He created men of crackling clay like the potters. And He created the ginn from smokeless fire.

Then which of your Lord's bounties will ye twain deny?

The Lord of the two easts[1] and the Lord of the two wests!

Then which of your Lord's bounties will ye twain deny?

He has let loose the two seas that meet together; between them is a barrier they cannot pass!

Then which of your Lord's bounties will ye twain deny?

He brings forth from each pearls both large and small!

Then which of your Lord's bounties will ye twain deny?

His are the ships which rear aloft in the sea like mountains.

Then which of your Lord's bounties will ye twain deny?

Every one upon it[2] is transient, but the face of thy Lord endowed with majesty and honour shall endure.

Then which of your Lord's bounties will ye twain deny?

Of Him whosoever is in the heaven and the earth does beg; every day He is in (some fresh) business!

Then which of your Lord's bounties will ye twain deny?

We shall be at leisure for you, O ye two weighty ones[3]!

Then which of your Lord's bounties will ye twain deny?

O assembly of ginns and mankind! if ye are able to pass through the confines of heaven and earth then pass through them!—ye cannot pass through save by authority!

Then which of your Lord's bounties will ye twain deny?

There shall be sent against you a flash of fire, and molten copper, and ye shall not be helped!

Then which of your Lord's bounties will ye twain deny?

And when the heaven is rent asunder and become rosy red[4]—(melting) like grease!

Then which of your Lord's bounties will ye twain deny?

On that day neither man nor ginn shall be asked about his crime!

Then which of your Lord's bounties will ye twain deny?

---

[1] I. e. the east and west, though some understand it of the two solstices.
[2] The earth.
[3] I. e. mankind and the ginn; the meaning is, that God will have leisure to judge them both.   [4] The word is also said to mean red leather.

The sinners shall be known by their marks, and shall be seized by
the forelock and the feet!
Then which of your Lord's bounties will ye twain deny?
'This is hell, which the sinners did call a lie! they shall circulate
between it and water boiling quite!'
Then which of your Lord's bounties will ye twain deny?
But for him who fears the station of his Lord are gardens twain!
Then which of your Lord's bounties will ye twain deny?
Both furnished with branching trees.
Then which of your Lord's bounties will ye twain deny?
In each are flowing springs.
Then which of your Lord's bounties will ye twain deny?
In each are, of every fruit, two kinds.
Then which of your Lord's bounties will ye twain deny?
Reclining on beds the linings of which are of brocade, and the fruit
of the two gardens within reach to cull.
Then which of your Lord's bounties will ye twain deny?
Therein are maids of modest glances whom no man nor ginn has
deflowered before.
Then which of your Lord's bounties will ye twain deny?
As though they were rubies and pearls.
Then which of your Lord's bounties will ye twain deny?
Is the reward of goodness aught but goodness?
Then which of your Lord's bounties will ye twain deny?
And besides these are gardens twain,[5]
Then which of your Lord's bounties will ye twain deny?
With dark green foliage.
Then which of your Lord's bounties will ye twain deny?
In each two gushing springs.
Then which of your Lord's bounties will ye twain deny?
In each fruit and palms and pomegranates.
Then which of your Lord's bounties will ye twain deny?
In them maidens best and fairest!
Then which of your Lord's bounties will ye twain deny?
Bright and large-eyed maids kept in their tents.
Then which of your Lord's bounties will ye twain deny?
Whom no man nor ginn has deflowered before them.

[5] For the inferior inhabitants of Paradise.

Then which of your Lord's bounties will ye twain deny?
Reclining on green cushions and beautiful carpets.
Then which of your Lord's bounties will ye twain deny?
Blessed be the name of thy Lord possessed of majesty and honour!

THE CHAPTER OF THE POETS

IN the name of the merciful and compassionate God.
T. S. M. Those are the signs of the perspicuous Book; haply thou
art vexing thyself to death that they will not be believers!

If we please we will send down upon them from the heaven a
sign, and their necks shall be humbled thereto. But there comes not
to them any recent Reminder from the Merciful One that they do
not turn away from. They have called (thee) liar! but there shall
come to them a message of that at which they mocked.

Have they not looked to the earth, how we caused to grow therein
of every noble kind? verily, in that is a sign; but most of them will
never be believers! but, verily, thy Lord He is mighty and merciful.

And when thy Lord called Moses (saying), 'Come to the unjust
people, to the people of Pharaoh, will they not fear?' Said he, 'My
Lord! verily, I fear that they will call me liar; and my breast is
straitened, and my tongue is not fluent; send then unto Aaron,[1] for
they have a crime against me, and I fear that they may kill me.'[2] Said
He, 'Not so; but go with our signs, verily, we are with you listening.

'And go to Pharaoh and say, "Verily, we are the apostles of the
Lord of the worlds (to tell thee to) send with us the children of
Israel."'

And he said, 'Did we not bring thee up amongst us as a child? and
thou didst dwell amongst us for years of thy life; and thou didst do
thy deed which thou hast done, and thou art of the ungrateful!'

Said he, 'I did commit this, and I was of those who erred.

'And I fled from you when I feared you, and my Lord granted
me judgment, and made me one of His messengers; and this is the
favour thou hast obliged me with, that thou hast enslaved the children of Israel!'

Said Pharaoh, 'Who is the Lord of the worlds?' Said he, 'The

---

[1] That he may be my minister.   [2] The slaying of the Egyptian.

Lord of the heavens and the earth and what is between the two, if ye are but sure.'

Said he to those about him, 'Do ye not listen?' Said he, 'Your Lord and the Lord of your fathers of yore!'

Said he, 'Verily, your apostle who is sent to you is surely mad!'

Said he, 'The Lord of the east and of the west, and of what is between the two, if ye had but sense!'

Said he, 'If thou dost take a god besides Me I will surely make thee one of the imprisoned!'

Said he, 'What, if I come to thee with something obvious?'

Said he, 'Bring it, if thou art of those who tell the truth!'

And he threw down his rod, and, behold, it was an obvious serpent! and he plucked out his hand, and, behold, it was white to the spectators!

He[3] said to the chiefs around him, 'Verily, this is a knowing sorcerer, he desires to turn you out of your land! what is it then ye bid?'

They said, 'Give him and his brother some hope, and send into the cities to collect and bring to thee every knowing sorcerer.'

And the sorcerers assembled at the appointed time on a stated day, and it was said to the people, 'Are ye assembled? haply we may follow the sorcerers if we gain the upper hand.'

And when the sorcerers came they said to Pharaoh, 'Shall we, verily, have a hire if we gain the upper hand?' Said he, 'Yes; and, verily, ye shall then be of those who are nigh (my throne).' And Moses said to them, 'Throw down what ye have to throw down.' So they threw down their ropes and their rods and said, 'By Pharaoh's might, verily, we it is who shall gain the upper hand!'

And Moses threw down his rod, and, lo, it swallowed up what they falsely devised!

And the sorcerers threw themselves down, adoring. Said they, 'We believe in the Lord of the worlds, the Lord of Moses and Aaron!' Said he, 'Do ye believe in Him ere I give you leave? Verily, he is your chief who has taught you sorcery, but soon ye shall know. I will surely cut off your hands and your feet from opposite sides, and I will crucify you all together!'

[3] Pharaoh.

They said, 'No harm; verily, unto our Lord do we return! verily, we hope that our Lord will forgive us our sins, for we are the first of believers!'

And we inspired Moses, 'Journey by night with my servants; verily, ye are pursued.'

And Pharaoh sent into the cities to collect; 'Verily, these are a small company. And, verily, they are enraged with us; but we are a multitude, wary!

'Turn them out of gardens and springs, and treasuries, and a noble station!'—thus,—and we made the children of Israel to inherit them.

And they followed them at dawn; and when the two hosts saw each other, Moses' companions said, 'Verily, we are overtaken!' Said he, 'Not so; verily, with me is my Lord, He will guide me.'

And we inspired Moses, 'Strike with thy rod the sea;' and it was cleft asunder, and each part was like a mighty mountain. And then we brought the others. And we saved Moses and those with him all together; then we drowned the others; and that is a sign: but most of them will never be believers! And, verily, thy Lord He is mighty, merciful.

And recite to them the story of Abraham; when he said to his father and his people, 'What do ye serve?' They said, 'We serve idols, and we are still devoted to them. He said, 'Can they hear you when ye call, or profit you, or harm?'

They said, 'No; but we found our fathers doing thus.' He said, 'Have ye considered what ye have been serving, ye and your fathers before you? Verily, they are foes to me, save only the Lord of the worlds, who created me and guides me, and who gives me food and drink. And when I am sick He heals me; He who will kill me, and then bring me to life; and who I hope will forgive me my sins on the day of judgment! Lord, grant me judgment, and let me reach the righteous; and give me a tongue of good report amongst posterity; and make me of the heirs of the paradise of pleasure; and pardon my father, verily, he is of those who err; and disgrace me not on the day when they are raised up again; the day when wealth shall profit not, nor sons, but only he who comes to God with a sound heart. And paradise shall be brought near to the pious; and hell shall be brought forth to those who go astray, and it shall be said to them,

"Where is what ye used to worship beside God? can they help you, or get help themselves?" And they shall fall headlong into it, they and those who have gone astray, and the hosts of Iblîs all together!

'They shall say, while they quarrel therein, "By God! we were surely in an obvious error, when we made you equal to the Lord of the worlds! but it was only sinners who led us astray. But we have no intercessors and no warm friend; but had we a turn we would be of the believers." '—Verily, in that is a sign, but most of them will never be believers; and, verily, thy Lord He is mighty and merciful.

The people of Noah said the apostles were liars, when their brother Noah said to them, 'Will ye not fear? verily, I am a faithful apostle to you; then fear God and obey me. I do not ask you for it any hire; my hire is only with the Lord of the worlds. So fear God and obey me.' They said, 'Shall we believe in thee, when the reprobates follow thee?' He said, ' I did not know what they were doing; their account is only with my Lord, if ye but perceive. And I am not one to drive away the believers, I am only a plain warner.'

They said, 'Verily, if thou desist not, O Noah! thou shalt surely be of those who are stoned!' Said he, 'My Lord! verily, my people call me liar; open between me and between them an opening, and save me and those of the believers who are with me!'

So we saved him and those with him in the laden ark, then we drowned the rest; verily, in that is a sign, but most of them will never be believers; and, verily, thy Lord He is mighty and merciful.

And 'Ad called the apostles liars; when their brother Hûd said to them, 'Will ye not fear? Verily, I am to you a faithful apostle; then fear God and obey me. I do not ask you for it any hire; my hire is only with the Lord of the worlds. Do ye build on every height a landmark in sport, and take to works that haply ye may be immortal?

'And when ye assault ye assault like tyrants; but fear God and obey me; and fear Him who hath given you an extent of cattle and sons, and gardens and springs. Verily, I fear for you the torment of a mighty day!'

They said, 'It is the same to us if thou admonish or art not of those who do admonish; this is nothing but old folks' fictions, for we shall not be tormented!'

And they called him liar! but we destroyed them. Verily, in that is a sign, but most of them will never be believers. And, verily, thy Lord is mighty, merciful.

Thamûd called the apostles liars; when their brother Zâli'h said to them, 'Do ye not fear? verily, I am to you a faithful apostle; so fear God and obey me. I do not ask you for it any hire; my hire is only with the Lord of the worlds. Shall ye be left here in safety with gardens and springs, and corn-fields and palms, the spathes whereof are fine? and ye hew out of the mountains houses skilfully. But fear God and obey me; and obey not the bidding of the extravagant, who do evil in the earth and do not act aright!'

They said, 'Thou art only of the infatuated; thou art but mortal like ourselves; so bring us a sign, if thou be of those who speak the truth!'

He said, 'This she-camel shall have her drink and you your drink on a certain day; but touch her not with evil, or there will seize you the torment of a mighty day!'

But they hamstrung her, and on the morrow they repented; and the torment seized them; verily, in that is a sign; but most of them will never be believers: but verily, thy Lord He is mighty, merciful.

The people of Lot called the apostles liars; when their brother Lot said to them, 'Do ye not fear? verily, I am to you a faithful apostle; then fear God and obey me. I do not ask you for it any hire; my hire is only with the Lord of the worlds. Do ye approach males of all the world and leave what God your Lord has created for you of your wives? nay, but ye are people who transgress!'

They said, 'Surely, if thou dost not desist, O Lot! thou shalt be of those who are expelled!'

Said he, 'Verily, I am of those who hate your deed; my Lord! save me and my people from what they do.'

And we saved him and his people all together, except an old woman amongst those who lingered. Then we destroyed the others; and we rained down upon them a rain; and evil was the rain of those who were warned. Verily, in that is a sign; but most of them will never be believers. And, verily, thy Lord He is mighty, merciful, compassionate.

The fellows of the Grove[4] called the apostles liars; Sho'hâib said to them, 'Will ye not fear? verily, I am to you a faithful apostle, then fear God and obey me. I do not ask you for it any hire; my hire is only with the Lord of the worlds. Give good measure, and be not of those who diminish; and weigh with a fair balance, and do not cheat men of their goods; and waste not the land, despoiling it; and fear Him who created you and the races of yore!' Said they, 'Thou art only of the infatuated; and thou art only a mortal like ourselves; and, verily, we think that thou art surely of the liars; so make a portion of the heaven to fall down upon us, if thou art of those who tell the truth!'

Said he, 'My Lord knows best what ye do!' but they called him liar, and the torment of the day of the shadow seized them; for it was the torment of a mighty day: verily, in that is a sign; but most of them will never be believers; but, verily, thy Lord He is mighty, merciful!

And, verily, it[5] is a revelation from the Lord of the worlds; the Faithful Spirit came down with it[6] upon thy heart, that thou shouldst be of those who warn;—in plain Arabic language, and, verily, it is (foretold) in the scriptures of yore! Have they not a sign, that the learned men of the children of Israel recognize it[7]? Had we sent it down to any barbarian, and he had read it to them, they would not have believed therein. Thus have we made for it[8] a way into the hearts of the sinners; they will not believe therein until they see the grievous woe! and it shall come to them suddenly while they do not perceive! They will say, 'Shall we be respited?—What! do they wish to hasten on our torment?'

What thinkest thou? if we let them enjoy themselves for years, and then there come to them what they are threatened, that will not avail them which they had to enjoy! But we do not destroy any city without its having warners as a reminder, for we are never unjust.

The devils did not descend therewith; it is not fit work for them; nor are they able to do it. Verily, they are deposed from listening[9]; call not then with God upon other gods, or thou wilt be of the tormented; but warn thy clansmen who are near of kin. And lower[10]

---

[4] The Midianites.   [5] The Qur'ân.   [6] The angel Gabriel.   [7] The Qur'ân.
[8] Infidelity.   [9] See note 5, Chapter of Imrân's Family.
[10] Behave with humility and gentleness.

thy wing to those of the believers who follow thee; but if they rebel against thee, say, 'Verily, I am clear of what ye do,' and rely thou upon the mighty, merciful One, who sees thee when thou dost stand up, and thy posturing amongst those who adore.[11] Verily, He both hears and knows!

Shall I inform you upon whom the devils descend? they descend upon every sinful liar, and impart what they have heard[12]; but most of them are liars.

And the poets do those follow who go astray! Dost thou not see that they wander distraught in every vale? and that they say that which they do not do? save those who believe, and do right, and remember God much, and defend themselves after they are wronged; but those who do wrong shall know with what a turn they shall be turned.[13]

THE CHAPTER OF MARY

IN the name of the merciful and compassionate God.

K. H. Y. 'H. Z. The mention of thy Lord's mercy to His servant Zachariah, when he called on his Lord with a secret calling. Said he, 'My Lord! verily, my bones are weak, and my head flares with hoariness;—and I never was unfortunate in my prayers to Thee, my Lord! But I fear my heirs after me, and my wife is barren; then grant me from Thee a successor, to be my heir and the heir of the family of Jacob, and make him, my Lord! acceptable.'

'O Zachariah! verily, we give thee glad tidings of a son, whose name shall be John. We never made a namesake of his before.' [1]

Said he, 'My Lord! how can I have a son, when my wife is barren, and I have reached through old age to decrepitude?'

He said, 'Thus says thy Lord, It is easy for Me, for I created thee at first when yet thou wast nothing.'

Said he, 'O my Lord! make for me a sign.' He said, 'Thy sign is

---

[11] Or, it may be thy going to and fro amongst believers, as Mohammed is reported to have done one night, to see what they were about, and he found the whole settlement 'buzzing like a hornet's nest with the sound of the recitation of the Qur'ân and of their prayers.'

[12] That is, by listening at the door of heaven.

[13] That is, in what condition they shall be brought before God.

[1] Cf. Luke i. 61, where, however, it is said that none of Zachariah's kindred was ever before called by that name. Some commentators avoid the difficulty by interpreting the word samîyyun to mean 'deserving of the name.'

that thou shalt not speak to men for three nights (through) sound.'

Then he went forth unto his people from the chamber, and he made signs to them: 'Celebrate (God's) praises morning and evening!'

'O John! take the Book with strength;' and we gave him judgment when a boy, and grace from us, and purity; and he was pious and righteous to his parents, and was not a rebellious tyrant.

So peace upon him the day he was born, and the day he died, and the day he shall be raised up alive.

And mention, in the Book, Mary; when she retired from her family into an eastern place; and she took a veil (to screen herself) from them; and we sent unto her our spirit; and he took for her the semblance of a well-made man. Said she, 'Verily, I take refuge in the Merciful One from thee, if thou art pious.' Said he, 'I am only a messenger of Thy Lord to bestow on thee a pure boy.'

Said she, 'How can I have a boy when no man has touched me, and when I am no harlot?' He said, 'Thus says thy Lord, It is easy for Me! and we will make him a sign unto man, and a mercy from us; for it is a decided matter.'

So she conceived him, and she retired with him into a remote place. And the labour pains came upon her at the trunk of a palm tree, and she said 'O that I had died before this, and been forgotten out of mind!' and he called[2] to her from beneath her, 'Grieve not, for thy Lord has placed a stream beneath thy feet; and shake towards thee the trunk of the palm tree, it will drop upon thee fresh dates fit to gather; so eat, and drink, and cheer thine eye; and if thou shouldst see any mortal say, "Verily, I have vowed to the Merciful One a fast, and I will not speak to-day with a human being."'

Then she brought it to her people, carrying it; said they, 'O Mary! thou hast done an extraordinary thing! O sister of Aaron[3]! thy father was not a bad man, nor was thy mother a harlot!'

And she pointed to him, and they said, 'How are we to speak with one who is in the cradle a child?' He said, 'Verily, I am a servant of God; He has brought me the Book, and He has made me a prophet, and He has made me blessed wherever I be; and He has required of

[2] Either the infant himself or the angel Gabriel; or the expression 'beneath her' may be rendered 'beneath it,' and may refer to the palm tree.

[3] See note 4, Chapter of Imrân's Family.

me prayer and almsgiving so long as I live, and piety towards my mother, and has not made me a miserable tyrant; and peace upon me the day I was born, and the day I die, and the day I shall be raised up alive.'

That is, Jesus the son of Mary,—by the word of truth whereon ye do dispute!

God could not take to himself any son! celebrated be His praise! when He decrees a matter He only says to it 'BE,' and it is; and, verily, God is my Lord and your Lord, so worship Him; this is the right way.

And the parties have disagreed amongst themselves, but woe to those who disbelieve, from the witnessing of the mighty day! they can hear and they can see, on the day when they shall come to us; but the evildoers are to-day in obvious error!

And warn them of the day of sighing, when the matter is decreed while they are heedless, and while they do not believe.

Verily, we will inherit the earth and all who are upon it, and unto us shall they return!

And mention, in the Book, Abraham; verily, he was a confessor,— a prophet. When he said to his father, 'O my sire! why dost thou worship what can neither hear nor see nor avail thee aught? O my sire! verily, to me has come knowledge which has not come to thee; then follow me, and I will guide thee to a level way.

'O my sire! serve not Satan; verily, Satan is ever a rebel against the Merciful. O my sire! verily, I fear that there may touch thee torment from the Merciful, and that thou mayest be a client of Satan.'

Said he, 'What! art thou averse from my gods, O Abraham? verily, if thou dost not desist I will certainly stone thee; but get thee gone from me for a time!'

Said he, 'Peace be upon thee! I will ask forgiveness for thee from my Lord; verily, He is very gracious to me: but I will part from you and what ye call on beside God, and will pray my Lord that I be not unfortunate in my prayer to my Lord.'

And when he had parted from them and what they served beside God, we granted him Isaac and Jacob, and each of them we made a prophet; and we granted them of our mercy, and we made the tongue of truth lofty for them.[4]

And mention, in the Book, Moses; verily, he was sincere, and was an apostle,—a prophet. We called him from the right side of the mountain; and we made him draw nigh unto us to commune with him, and we granted him, of our mercy, his brother Aaron as a prophet.

And mention, in the Book, Ishmael; verily, he was true to his promise, and was an apostle,—a prophet; and he used to bid his people prayers and almsgiving, and was acceptable in the sight of his Lord.

And mention, in the Book, Idrîs[5]; verily, he was a confessor,—a prophet; and we raised him to a lofty place.

These are those to whom God has been gracious, of the prophets of the seed of Adam, and of those whom we bore with Noah, and of the seed of Abraham and Israel, and of those we guided and elected; when the signs of the Merciful are read to them, they fall down adoring and weeping.

And successors succeeded them, who lost sight of prayer and followed lusts, but they shall at length find themselves going wrong, except such as repent and believe and act aright; for these shall enter Paradise, and shall not be wronged at all,—gardens of Eden, which the Merciful has promised to His servants in the unseen; verily, His promise ever comes to pass!

They shall hear no empty talk therein, but only 'peace;' and they shall have their provision therein, morning and evening; that is Paradise which we will give for an inheritance to those of our servants who are pious!

We do not descend[6] save at the bidding of thy Lord; His is what is before us, and what is behind us, and what is between those; for thy Lord is never forgetful,—the Lord of the heavens and the earth, and of what is between the two; then serve Him and persevere in His service. Dost thou know a namesake of His?

[4] That is, 'gave them great renown.'   [5] Generally identified with Enoch.

[6] Amongst various conjectures the one most usually accepted by the Mohammedan commentators is, that these are the words of the angel Gabriel, in answer to Mohammed's complaint of long intervals elapsing between the periods of revelation.

Man will say, 'What! when I have died shall I then come forth alive? Does not man then remember that we created him before when he was naught?'

And by thy Lord! we will surely gather them together, and the devils too; then we will surely bring them forward around hell, on their knees!

Then we will drag off from every sect whichever of them has been most bold against the Merciful.

Then we know best which of them deserves most to be broiled therein.

There is not one of you who will not go down to it,—that is settled and decided by thy Lord.[7]

Then we will save those who fear us; but we will leave the evil-doers therein on their knees.

And when our signs are recited to them manifest, those who misbelieve say to those who believe, 'Which of the two parties is best placed and in the best company?'

And how many generations before them have we destroyed who were better off in property and appearance?

Say, 'Whosoever is in error, let the Merciful extend to him length of days!—until they see what they are threatened with, whether it be the torment or whether it be the Hour, then they shall know who is worse placed and weakest in forces!'

And those who are guided God will increase in guidance.

And enduring good works are best with thy Lord for a reward, and best for restoration.

Hast thou seen him who disbelieves in our signs, and says, 'I shall surely be given wealth and children[8]?'

Has he become acquainted with the unseen, or has he taken a compact with the Merciful? Not so! We will write down what he says, and we will extend to him a length of torment, and we will make him inherit what he says, and he shall come to us alone. They

[7] This is interpreted by some to mean that all souls, good and bad, must pass through hell, but that the good will not be harmed. Others think it merely refers to the passage of the bridge of el Aarâf.

[8] 'Hâsîy ibn Wâil, being indebted to 'Habbâb, refused to pay him unless he renounced Mohammed. This 'Habbâb said he would never do alive or dead, or when raised again at the last day. El 'Hâsîy told him to call for his money on the last day, as he should have wealth and children then.

take other gods besides God to be their glory! Not so! They[9] shall deny their worship and shall be opponents of theirs!

Dost thou not see that we have sent the devils against the misbelievers, to drive them on to sin? but, be not thou hasty with them. Verily, we will number them a number (of days),—the day when we will gather the pious to the Merciful as ambassadors, and we will drive the sinners to hell like (herds) to water! They shall not possess intercession, save he who has taken a compact with the Merciful.

They say, 'The Merciful has taken to Himself a son:'—ye have brought a monstrous thing! The heavens well-nigh burst asunder thereat, and the earth is riven, and the mountains fall down broken, that they attribute to the Merciful a son! but it becomes not the Merciful to take to Himself a son! there is none in the heavens or the earth but comes to the Merciful as a servant; He counts them and numbers them by number, and they are all coming to Him on the resurrection day singly.

Verily, those who believe and act aright, to them the Merciful will give love.

We have only made it easy for thy tongue that thou mayest thereby give glad tidings to the pious, and warn thereby a contentious people.

How many a generation before them have we destroyed? Canst thou find any one of them, or hear a whisper of them?

The Chapter of the Night Journey[1]

In the name of the merciful and compassionate God.

Celebrated be the praises of Him who took His servant a journey by night from the Sacred Mosque[2] to the Remote Mosque,[3] the precinct of which we have blessed, to show him of our signs! verily, He both hears and looks.

And we gave Moses the Book and made it a guidance to the children of Israel: 'Take ye to no guardian but me.'

Seed of those we bore with Noah (in the ark)! verily, he was a thankful servant!

And we decreed to the children of Israel in the Book, 'Ye shall

---

[9] That is, the false gods.
[1] Also called 'The Children of Israel.'
[2] The Kaabah at Mecca.
[3] The Temple at Jerusalem.

verily do evil in the earth twice,[4] and ye shall rise to a great height (of pride).'

And when the threat for the first (sin) of the two came, we sent over them servants of ours, endued with violence, and they searched inside your houses; and it was an accomplished threat.

Then we rallied you once more against them, and aided you with wealth and sons, and made you a numerous band.

'If ye do well, ye will do well to your own souls; and if ye do ill, it is against them!

'And when the threat for the last came[5]—to harm your faces and to enter the mosque as they entered it the first time, and to destroy what they had got the upper-hand over with utter destruction.'

It may be that thy Lord will have mercy on you;—but if ye return we will return, and we have made hell a prison for the misbelievers.

Verily, this Qur'ân guides to the straightest path, and gives the glad tidings to the believers who do aright that for them is a great hire; and that for those who believe not in the hereafter, we have prepared a mighty woe.

Man prays for evil as he prays for good; and man was ever hasty.

We made the night and the day two signs; and we blot out the sign of the night and make the sign of the day visible, that ye may seek after plenty from your Lord, and that ye may number the years and the reckoning; and we have detailed everything in detail.

And every man's augury[6] have we fastened on his neck; and we will bring forth for him on the resurrection day a book offered to him wide open.

'Read thy book, thou art accountant enough against thyself to-day!'

He who accepts guidance, accepts it only for his own soul: and he who errs, errs only against it; nor shall one burdened soul bear the burden of another.

---

[4] The Mohammedan commentators interpret this as referring the first to either Goliath, Sennacherib, or Nebuchadnezzar, and the latter to a second Persian invasion. The two sins committed by the Jews, and for which these punishments were threatened and executed, were, first, the murder of Isaiah and the imprisonment of Jeremiah, and the second, the murder of John the Baptist. Mohammedan views of ancient history are, however, vague.   [5] Supply, 'we sent foes.'

[6] I. e. 'fortune' or 'fate,' literally, 'bird;' the Arabs, like the ancient Romans, having been used to practise divination from the flight of birds.

Nor would we punish until we had sent an apostle. And when we desired to destroy a city we bade[7] the opulent ones thereof; and they wrought abomination therein; and its due sentence was pronounced; and we destroyed it with utter destruction.

How many generations have we destroyed after Noah! but thy Lord of the sins of his servant is well aware, and sees enough.

Whoso is desirous of this life that hastens away, we will hasten on for him therein what we please,—for whom we please. Then we will make hell for him to broil in—despised and outcast.

But whoso desires the next life, and strives for it and is a believer—these, their striving shall be gratefully received.

To all—these and those—will we extend the gifts of thy Lord; for the gifts of thy Lord are not restricted.

See how we have preferred some of them over others, but in the next life are greater degrees and greater preference.

Put not with God other gods, or thou wilt sit despised and forsaken.

Thy Lord has decreed that ye shall not serve other than Him; and kindness to one's parents, whether one or both of them reach old age with thee; and say not to them, 'Fie!' and do not grumble at them, but speak to them a generous speech. And lower to them the wing of humility out of compassion, and say, 'O Lord! have compassion on them as they brought me up when I was little!' Your Lord knows best what is in your souls if ye be righteous, and, verily, He is forgiving unto those who come back penitent.

And give thy kinsman his due and the poor and the son of the road; and waste not wastefully, for the wasteful were ever the devil's brothers; and the devil is ever ungrateful to his Lord.

But if thou dost turn away from them to seek after mercy from thy Lord,[8] which thou hopest for, then speak to them an easy speech.

Make not thy hand fettered to thy neck, nor yet spread it out quite open, lest thou shouldst have to sit down blamed and straitened in means. Verily, thy Lord spreads out provision to whomsoever He will or He doles it out. Verily, He is ever well aware of and sees His servants.

[7] Bade them obey the Apostle.
[8] I. e. if you are compelled to leave them in order to seek your livelihood; or if your present means are insufficient to enable you to relieve others.

And slay not your children for fear of poverty; we will provide for them; beware! for to slay them is ever a great sin!

And draw not near to fornication; verily, it is ever an abomination, and evil is the way thereof.

And slay not the soul that God has forbidden you, except for just cause; for he who is slain unjustly we have given his next of kin authority; yet let him not exceed in slaying; verily, he is ever helped.

And draw not near to the wealth of the orphan, save to improve it, until he reaches the age of puberty, and fulfil your compacts; verily, a compact is ever enquired of.

And give full measure when ye measure out, and weigh with a right balance; that is better and a fairer determination.

And do not pursue that of which thou hast no knowledge; verily, the hearing, the sight, and the heart, all of these shall be enquired of.

And walk not on the earth proudly; verily, thou canst not cleave the earth, and thou shalt not reach the mountains in height.

All this is ever evil in the sight of your Lord and abhorred.

That is something of what thy Lord has inspired thee with of wisdom; do not then put with God other gods, or thou wilt be thrown into hell reproached and outcast. What! has your Lord chosen to give you sons, and shall He take for Himself females from among the angels? verily, ye are speaking a mighty speech.

Now have we turned it in various ways in this Qur'ân, so let them bear in mind; but it will only increase them in aversion.

Say, 'Were there with Him other gods, as ye say, then would they seek a way against the Lord of the throne.'

Celebrated be His praises, and exalted be He above what they say with a great exaltation!

The seven heavens and the earth celebrate His praises, and all who therein are; nor is there aught but what celebrates His praise: but ye cannot understand their celebration;—verily, He is clement and forgiving.

And when thou readest the Qur'ân we place between thee and those who believe not in the hereafter a covering veil. And we place covers upon their hearts, lest they should understand, and dulness in their ears.

And when thou dost mention in the Qur'ân thy Lord by Himself they turn their backs in aversion.

We know best for what they listen when they listen to thee; and when they whisper apart—when the wrong-doers say, 'Ye only follow a man enchanted.'

Behold, how they strike out for you parables, and err, and cannot find the way!

They say, 'What! when we have become bones and rubbish are we to be raised up a new creature?' Say, 'Be ye stones, or iron, or a creature, the greatest your breasts can conceive—!' Then they shall say, 'Who is to restore us?' Say, 'He who originated you at first;' and they will wag their heads and say, 'When will that be?' Say, 'It may, perhaps, be nigh.'

The day when He shall call on you and ye shall answer with praise to Him, and they will think that they have tarried but a little.

And say to my servants that they speak in a kind way[9]; verily, Satan makes ill-will between them; verily, Satan was ever unto man an open foe.

Your Lord knows you best; if He please He will have mercy upon you, or if He please He will torment you: but we have not sent thee to take charge of them.

And thy Lord best knows who is in the heavens and the earth; we did prefer some of the prophets over the others, and to David did we give the Psalms.

Say, 'Call on those whom ye pretend other than God'; but they shall not have the power to remove distress from you, nor to turn it off.

Those on whom they call,[10] seek themselves for a means of approaching their Lord, (to see) which of them is nearest: and they hope for His mercy and they fear His torment; verily, the torment of thy Lord is a thing to beware of.

[9] I. e. they are not to provoke the idolaters by speaking too roughly to them so as to exasperate them.

[10] Sale interprets this to mean 'the angels and prophets.' Rodwell remarks that it is an 'obvious allusion to the saint worship of the Christians.' As, however, precisely the same expression is used elsewhere in the Qur'ân for the false gods of the Arabs, and the existence of those ginns and angels whom they associated with God is constantly recognised, their divinity only being denied, I prefer to follow the Moslem commentators, and refer the passage to the gods of the Arabian pantheon at Mecca.

There is no city but we will destroy it before the day of judgment, or torment it with keen torment;—that is in the Book inscribed.

Naught hindered us from sending thee with signs, save that those of yore said they were lies; so we gave Thamûd the visible she-camel, but they treated her unjustly! for we do not send (any one) with signs save to make men fear.

And when we said to thee, 'Verily, thy Lord encompasses men!' and we made the vision which we showed thee only a cause of sedition unto men, and the cursed tree[11] as well; for we will frighten them, but it will only increase them in great rebellion.

And when we said to the angels, 'Adore Adam'; and they adored, save Iblîs, who said, 'Am I to adore one whom Thou hast created out of clay?'

Said he, 'Dost thou see now? this one whom Thou hast honoured above me, verily, if Thou shouldst respite me until the resurrection day, I will of a surety utterly destroy his seed except a few.'

Said He, 'Begone! and whoso of them follows thee—verily, hell is your recompense, an ample recompense. Entice away whomsoever of them thou canst with thy voice; and bear down upon them with thy horse and with thy foot; and share with them in their wealth and their children; and promise them,—but Satan promises them naught but deceit. Verily, my servants, thou hast no authority over them; thy Lord is guardian enough over them!'

It is your Lord who drives the ships for you in the sea that ye may seek after plenty from Him; verily, He is ever merciful to you. And when distress touches you in the sea, those whom ye call on, except Him, stray away from you; but when He has brought you safe to shore, ye turn away; for man is ever ungrateful.

Are ye sure that He will not cleave with you the side of the shore, or send against you a heavy sand-storm? then ye will find no guardian for yourselves.

Or are ye sure that He will not send you back therein another time, and send against you a violent wind, and drown you for your misbelief? then ye will find for yourselves no protector against us.

[11] The Zaqqûm. The vision referred to is the night journey to heaven, although those commentators who believe this to have been an actual fact suppose another vision to account for this passage.

But we have been gracious to the children of Adam, and we have borne them by land and sea, and have provided them with good things, and have preferred them over many that we have created.

The day when we will call all men by their high priest; and he whose book is given in his right hand—these shall read their book, nor shall they be wronged a straw. But he who in this life is blind shall be blind in the next too, and err farther from the way.

They had well-nigh beguiled thee from what we inspired thee with, that thou shouldst forge against us something else, and then they would have taken thee for a friend; and had it not been that we stablished thee, thou wouldst have well-nigh leant towards them a little: then would we have made thee taste of torment both of life and death, then thou wouldst not have found against us any helper.[12]

And they well-nigh enticed thee away from the land, to turn thee out therefrom; but then—they should not have tarried after thee except a little.

[This is] the course of those of our prophets whom we have sent before thee; and thou shalt find no change in our course.

Be thou steadfast in prayer from the declining of the sun until the dusk of the night, and the reading of the dawn; verily, the reading of the dawn is ever testified to.

And for the night, watch thou therein as an extra service. It may be that thy Lord will raise thee to a laudable station.

And say, 'O my Lord! make me enter with a just entry; and make me come forth with a just coming forth; and grant me from Thee authority to aid.'

And say, 'Truth has come, and falsehood has vanished! verily, falsehood is transient.'

And we will send down of the Qur'ân that which is a healing and a mercy to the believers, but it will only increase the wrong-doers in loss.

And when we favour man he turns away and retires aside, but when evil touches him he is ever in despair. Say, 'Every one acts

---

[12] The commentators say that this refers to a treaty proposed by the tribe of THaqîf, who insisted, as a condition of their submission, that they should be exempt from the more irksome duties of Muslims, and should be allowed to retain their idol Allât for a certain time, and that their territory should be considered sacred, like that of Mecca.

after his own manner, but your Lord knows best who is most guided in the way.'

They will ask thee of the spirit.[13] Say, 'The spirit comes at the bidding of my Lord, and ye are given but a little knowledge thereof.'

If we had wished we would have taken away that with which we have inspired thee; then thou wouldst have found no guardian against us, unless by a mercy from thy Lord; verily, His grace towards thee is great!

Say, 'If mankind and ginns united together to bring the like of this Qur'ân, they could not bring the like, though they should back each other up!'

We have turned about for men in this Qur'ân every parable; but most men refuse to accept it, save ungratefully.

And they say, 'We will by no means believe in thee, until there gush forth for thee a fountain from the earth; or there be made for thee a garden of palms and grapes, and rivers come gushing out amidst them; or thou make the sky to fall down upon us in pieces; or thou bring us God and the angels before us; or there be made for thee a house of gold; or thou climb up into the heaven; and even then we will not believe in thy climbing there, until thou send down on us a book that we may read!'

Say, 'Celebrated be the praises of my Lord! was I aught but a mortal apostle?'

Naught prohibited men from believing when the guidance came to them, save their saying, 'God has sent a mortal for an apostle.'

Say, 'Were there angels on the earth walking in quiet, we had surely sent them an angel as an apostle.'

Say, 'God is witness enough between me and you; verily, He is ever of His servants well aware, and sees.'

He whom God guides, he is guided indeed; and he whom God leads astray, thou shalt never find patrons for them beside Him; and we will gather them upon the resurrection day upon their faces, blind, and dumb, and deaf; their resort is hell; whenever it grows dull we will give them another blaze!

---

[13] According to some, the soul generally; but according to others, and more probably, the angel Gabriel as the agent of revelation.

That is their reward for that they disbelieved in our signs, and said, 'What! when we are bones and rubbish, shall we then be raised up a new creation?'

Could they not see that God who created the heavens and the earth is able to create the like of them, and to set for them an appointed time; there is no doubt therein, yet the wrong-doers refuse to accept it, save ungratefully!

Say, 'Did ye control the treasuries of the mercy of my Lord, then ye would hold them through fear of expending; for man is ever niggardly!'

And we did bring Moses nine manifest signs; then ask the children of Israel (about) when he came to them, and Pharaoh said to him, 'Verily, I think thee, O Moses! enchanted.'

He said, 'Well didst thou know that none sent down these save the Lord of the heavens and the earth as visible signs; and, verily, I think thee, O Pharaoh! ruined.'

And he desired to drive them out of the land; but we drowned him and those with him, one and all.

And after him we said to the children of Israel, 'Dwell ye in the land; and when the promise of the hereafter comes to pass, we will bring you in a mixed crowd (to judgment).

'In truth have we sent it down, and in truth has it come down; and we have not sent thee as aught but a herald of glad tidings and a warner.

'And a Qur'ân which we have divided, that thou mayst read it to mankind leisurely, and we sent it down, sending it down.[14]

Say, 'Believe ye therein, or believe not; verily, those who were given the knowledge before it, when it is read to them fall down upon their beards adoring! and they say, "Celebrated be the praises of our Lord! verily, the promise of our Lord is ever fulfilled"—they fall down upon their beards weeping, and it increases their humility.'

Say, 'Call on God, or call on the Merciful One, whichever ye may call on Him by; for His are the best of names.'

And do not say thy prayers openly, nor yet murmur them, but seek a way between these.

[14] As occasion required.

And say, 'Praise belongs to God, who has not taken to Himself a son, and has not had a partner in His kingdom, nor had a patron against (such) abasement.' And magnify Him greatly!

THE CHAPTER OF JOSEPH, (PEACE BE ON HIM!)

IN the name of the merciful and compassionate God.

A. L. R. Those are the signs of the perspicuous Book. Verily, we have revealed it, an Arabic Qur'ân; haply ye may understand.

We tell thee the best of stories, in inspiring thee with this Qur'ân, though thou wert before it among the heedless.

When Joseph said to his father, 'O my sire! verily, I saw eleven stars, and the sun, and the moon,—I saw them adoring me!'

He said, 'O my boy! tell not thy vision to thy brethren, for they will plot a plot against thee; verily, the devil is to man an open foe.'

Thus does thy Lord choose thee, and teach thee the interpretation of sayings, and fulfil His favour upon thee, and upon Jacob's people, as He fulfilled it upon thy two forefathers before thee, Abraham and Isaac,—verily, thy Lord is knowing, wise!

In Joseph and his brethren were signs to those who enquire!

When they said, 'Surely, Joseph and his brother are dearer to our father than we, a band[1] although we be; verily, our father is in obvious error.

'Slay Joseph, or cast him in some land; that your father's face may be free for you, and ye may be, after he is gone, a people who do right.'

A speaker from amongst them spake, 'Slay not Joseph, but throw him into the bottom of the pit; some of the travellers may pick him up, if so ye do.'

Said they, 'O our father! what ails thee that thou wilt not trust us with Joseph while we are unto him sincere? Send him with us to-morrow to revel and to play, and, verily, we over him will keep good guard.'

Said he, 'Verily, it grieves me that ye should go off with him, for I fear lest the wolf devour him while ye of him do take no heed.'

Said they, 'Why, if the wolf should devour him while we are (such) a band, verily, we then should deserve to lose!'

---

[1] The word means a band of between twenty and forty persons.

And when they had gone off with him and agreed to put him in the depths of the pit, and we inspired him, 'Thou shalt surely inform them of this affair of theirs and they shall not perceive.' [2]

And they came to their father at eve and weeping said, 'O our father! verily, we went forth to race and left Joseph by our goods, and the wolf devoured him,—but thou wilt not believe us, truth tellers though we be.'

And they brought his shirt with lying blood upon it. Said he, 'Nay, but your souls have induced you to do this; but patience is fair! and God is He whom I ask for aid against that which ye describe.'

And travellers came and sent their water-drawer; and he let down his bucket. Said he, 'O glad tidings! this is a youth.' And they kept him secret, as a chattel; but God knew what they were doing.

And they sold him for a mean price,—drachmæ counted out,—and they parted with him cheaply.

And the man from Egypt who had bought him said to his wife, 'Honour his abiding here; it may be he will be of use to us, or we may adopt him as a son.'

Thus did we stablish Joseph in the land; and we did surely teach him the interpretation of sayings; for God can overcome His affairs, though most men do not know.

And when he had reached his strength[3] we brought him judgment and knowledge, for thus do we reward those who do good.

And she in whose house he was desired him for his person; and she locked the doors and said, 'Come along with thee!' Said he, 'Refuge in God! verily, my Lord has made good my abiding here; verily, the wrong-doers shall not prosper.'

And she was anxious for him, and he would have been anxious for her, had it not been that he saw the demonstration[4] of his Lord; thus did we turn evil and fornication from him; verily, he was of our sincere servants.

And they raced to the door and she rent his shirt from behind; and they met her master at the door. Said she, 'What is the recom-

---

[2] This is a prophetic intimation to Joseph of his future interview with his brethren in Egypt.   [3] The age of puberty.

[4] The angel Gabriel in the form of his father appeared with a warning gesture, according to the Muslim commentators.

pense of him who wishes evil for thy family, but that imprisonment or a grievous torment?'

Said he, 'She desired me for my person.' And a witness from among her family bore witness: 'If his shirt be rent from in front, then she speaks the truth and he is of the liars; but if his shirt be rent from behind, then she lies and he is of the truth tellers.'

And when he saw his shirt rent from behind he said, 'This is one of your tricks; verily, your tricks are mighty! Joseph! turn aside from this. And do thou, woman, ask pardon for thy fault; verily, thou wert of the sinners.'

And women in the city said, 'The wife of the prince desires her young man for his person; he has infatuated her with love: verily, we see her in obvious error.' And when she heard of their craftiness, she sent to them and prepared for them a banquet, and gave each of them a knife; and she said, 'Come forth to them!' And when they saw him they said, 'Great God!' and cut their hands[5] and said, 'God forbid! This is no mortal, this is nothing but an honourable angel.' Said she, 'This is he concerning whom ye blamed me. I did desire him for his person, but he was too continent. But if he do not what I bid him he shall surely be imprisoned and shall surely be among the small!' Said he, 'My lord! Prison is dearer to me than what they call on me to do; and unless Thou turn from me their craftiness I shall feel a passion for them and shall be among the ignorant!' And his Lord answered him and turned from him their craftiness; verily, He both hears and knows!

Then it appeared good to them, even after they had seen the signs,[6] to imprison him until a time.

And there entered the prison with him two young men. Said one of them, 'Verily, I see myself[7] pressing wine.' And the other said, 'Verily, I see myself bearing on my head loaves from which the birds do eat; inform us of the interpretation thereof; verily, we see that thou art of those who do good.'

He said, 'There shall not come to you any food with which ye are provided, but I will inform you both of its interpretation before it comes to you. That is (some) of what my Lord has taught me; verily, I have left the faith of a people who do not believe in God,

---

[5] In their sudden emotion at his beauty. [6] Of his innocence. [7] In a dream.

while in the future too they disbelieve. And I have followed the faith of my fathers, Abraham and Isaac and Jacob; we could not associate aught with God; that is from God's grace upon us and upon men: but most men give not thanks. O ye twain fellow-prisoners! Are manifold lords better, or God, the one, the dominant? What ye worship beside Him are naught but names which ye have named, ye and your fathers, for which God has sent down no authority. Judgment is only God's; He bids you worship only Him. That is the standard of religion,—but most men do not know. O ye twain fellow-prisoners! as for one of you, he shall pour out wine for his lord: and as for the other, he shall be crucified, and the birds shall eat of his head. The matter is decreed whereon ye asked me for a decision!'

And he said to him whom he thought would escape of those two, 'Remember me with thy lord!' But Satan made him[8] forget the remembrance of his lord, so he tarried in prison a few years.

Then said the king, 'Verily, I see seven fat kine which seven lean kine devoured; and seven green ears of corn and others dry. O ye chiefs! Explain to me my vision, if a vision ye can expound!'

Said they, 'Confused dreams, and naught of the exposition of such dreams know we!'

Then he who had escaped of those twain said,—remembering after a while,—'Verily, I will inform you of the interpretation thereof, so send me.'

'Joseph! O thou truth teller! explain to us the seven fat kine which seven lean devoured; and the seven green ears of corn and others dry. Haply I may go back to the men, haply they then may know!'

He said, 'Ye shall sow for seven years, as is your wont; but what ye reap, let it remain in the ear, except a little whereof ye shall eat. Then there shall come after that seven severe (years) which shall devour what ye have put by before for them, save a little of what ye shall preserve. Then there will come after that a year in which men shall have rain and in which they shall press.'[9]

---

[8] The application of the pronoun is vague in the text of this passage, which is variously interpreted, either that Satan made the butler forget to mention Joseph to his lord Pharaoh, or that Satan made Joseph forget for the moment his Lord God, and place his trust on the man rather than on Him.   [9] I. e. press wine and oil.

Then said the king, 'Bring him to me.'

And when the messenger came to him, he said, 'Go back to thy lord, and ask him, "What meant the women who cut their hands? Verily, my lord knows their craftiness!"'

He said, 'What was your design when ye desired Joseph for his person?' They said, 'God forbid! we know no bad of him.' Said the wife of the prince, 'Now does the truth appear! I desired him for his person and, verily, he is of those who tell the truth.'

'That' (said Joseph) 'was that he might know that I did not betray him in his absence, and that God guides not the craft of those who do betray! Yet I do not clear myself, for the soul is very urgent to evil, save what my Lord has had mercy on; verily, my Lord is forgiving and merciful!'

And the king said, 'Bring him to me. I will take him specially for myself.' And when he had spoken with him he said, 'Verily, to-day thou art with us in a permanent place of trust.'

He said, 'Place me over the treasures of the land; verily, I will be a knowing keeper.'

Thus did we stablish Joseph in the land that he might settle in what part thereof he pleased—we overtake with our mercy whom we will, nor do we waste the hire of those who do good; and surely the hire of the future life is better for those who believe and who have feared.

And his brethren came to Joseph, and they entered in unto him and he knew them, but they recognised not him.

And when he had equipped them with their equipment he said, 'Bring me a brother that ye have from your father; do ye not see that I give good measure, and that I am the best of entertainers? But if ye bring him not to me, no measure shall ye have with me, nor shall ye come nigh me.'

They said, 'We will desire him of our father, and we will surely do it.'

Then he said to his young men, 'Put their chattels[10] in their packs, haply they may know it when they are come back to their family; haply they may return.'

And when they returned to their father, they said, 'O our father!

---

[10] The goods which they had brought to barter, or the money they had paid for the corn.

Measure is withheld from us; so send with us our brother that we may get measure, and, verily, him we will keep!'

He said, 'Shall I entrust you with him, save as I entrusted you with his brother before? but God is the best of keepers, and He is the most merciful of the merciful.'

And when they opened their goods they found their chattels restored to them. Said they, 'O our father! What more can we crave? Here are our chattels restored to us, and we shall guard our brother, and shall have an additional measure beside that—a small measure.' [11]

He said, 'I will by no means send him with you until you give me a compact from God that ye will surely bring him to me, unless ye be encompassed.' [12]

So when they had given him their compact he said, 'God over what ye say has charge.'

And he said, 'O my sons! enter not by one gate, but enter by several gates; but I cannot avail you aught against God. Judgment is only God's; upon Him do I rely, and on Him do the reliant rely.'

And when they had entered as their father bade them, it availed them nothing against God, save for a want in Jacob's soul which it fulfilled; for, verily, he was possessed of knowledge, for that we had taught him;—but most men do not know.

And when they entered in unto Joseph, he took his brother to stay with him, and said, 'Verily, I am thy brother—then take not ill that which they have been doing.'

And when he had equipped them with their equipment he placed the drinking cup in his brother's pack; then a crier cried out, 'O ye caravan! verily, ye are thieves!'

They said, approaching them, 'What is it that ye miss?'

Said they, 'We miss the goblet of the king, and whoso brings it shall have a camel-load, and I am guarantee thereof.'

They said, 'By God! Ye knew we came not to do evil in the land, and that we were not thieves.'

They said, 'And what shall be the recompense thereof if ye be liars?'

[11] Commentators differ as to whether this means that what they had brought was insufficient, or whether the additional measure was a small quantity for Pharaoh to bestow, or whether Jacob utters the words meaning that it is not enough to induce him to part with his son.   [12] By some unavoidable hindrance.

They said, 'The recompense thereof is he in whose pack it is found—he shall be the recompense thereof; thus do we recompense the unjust.'

And he began with their sacks before the sacks of his brother; then he drew it forth from his brother's sack. Thus did we devise a stratagem for Joseph. He could not take his brother by the king's religion[13] except God pleased;—we raise the degrees of whomsoever we please, and over every possessor of knowledge is one who knows.

They said, 'If he has stolen, a brother of his has stolen before him.'

But Joseph kept it secret in his soul and disclosed it not to them. Said he, 'Ye are in a bad case, and God knows best about what ye describe.'

They said, 'O prince! Verily, he has a father, a very old man; take then one of us instead of him; verily, we can see that thou art of those who do good.'

Said he, '(I seek) refuge in God from taking any save him with whom we found our property; verily, we should then be certainly unjust.'

And when they despaired of him they retired to consult privately. Said the eldest of them, 'Do ye not know that your father has taken a compact from God against you? Aforetime ye exceeded in the matter of Joseph—I will surely not quit the land until my father give me leave, or God judge for me, for He is the best of judges.

'Return ye to your father and say, "O our father! verily, thy son has committed theft, and we bore testimony to naught but what we knew; for of the unforeseen we were not keepers!"

'Ask then in the city where we were, and of the caravan in which we approached it, for, verily, we tell the truth.'

Said he, 'Nay, your souls have induced you to do this thing. But patience is fair. It may be that God will give me them all together; —verily, He is knowing, wise.'

And he turned away from them and said, 'O my lament for Joseph!' and his eyes grew white with grief, for he repressed (his woe).

---

[13] I. e. by the law of Egypt it was not lawful for Joseph to take his brother for a bondsman as a punishment for theft.

They said, 'By God! thou wilt not cease to remember Joseph till thou art at the point of death, or art of those who perish!'

Said he, 'I only complain of my emotion and my grief to God, for I know that from God which ye know nothing of.

'O my sons! go and enquire concerning Joseph and his brother, and despair not of God's comfort; for, verily, none need despair of God's comfort save a misbelieving people!'

And when they entered in unto him they said, 'O prince! distress has touched both us and our families, and we have brought trifling chattels. So give us full measure and bestow upon us in charity; verily, God rewards the charitable.'

He said, 'Do ye know what ye did with Joseph and his brother, while ye were ignorant?'

They said, 'Art thou then indeed Joseph?' He said, 'I am Joseph, and this is my brother; God has been gracious towards us. Verily, whoso fears God and is patient,—verily, God wastes not the hire of those who do good!'

They said, 'By God! God has chosen thee over us; and we indeed were sinners.'

He said, 'No reproach against you to-day! God will pardon you, for He is the most merciful of the merciful. Take this my shirt, and throw it over the face of my father, he will become able to see; and bring me your families all together.'

And when the caravan departed, their father said, 'Verily, I find the smell of Joseph, unless ye think I dote!'

They said, 'By God! thou art in thy old error.' And when the herald of glad tidings came he threw it on his face, and he was restored to sight.

Said he, 'Did I not tell you that I know from God that of which ye know not?'

They said, 'O our father! ask pardon for us of our sins;—verily, we were sinners!'

He said, 'I will ask pardon for you from my Lord; verily, He is the pardoning and merciful.'

And when they entered in unto Joseph, he took his father to stay with him, and said, 'Enter ye into Egypt, if it please God, safe.' And he raised his father upon the throne, and they fell down before him adoring.

And he said, 'O my sire! This is the interpretation of my vision aforetime; my Lord has made it come true, and He has been good to me, in bringing me forth out of prison, and bringing you from the desert, after Satan had made a breach between me and my brethren; —verily, my Lord is kind to whomsoever He will;—verily, He is the knowing, the wise!

'O my Lord! thou hast given me dominion, and hast taught me the interpretation of sayings; O originator of the heavens and the earth! Thou art my patron in this world and the next; take me to Thyself resigned, and let me reach the righteous!'

That is one of the stories of the unseen which we inspire thee with, though thou wert not with them when they agreed in their affair, when they were so crafty.—And yet most men, though thou shouldst be urgent, will not believe.

Thou dost not ask them for it a hire; it is naught but a reminder to the world.

How many a sign in the heavens and the earth do they pass by and turn away there from!

Nor do most of them believe in God without associating (other gods) with Him.

Are they safe, then, from overwhelming vengeance coming on them from the torment of God? or from the Hour coming upon them suddenly while they do not perceive?

Say, 'This is my way; I call now unto God on clear proof, I and those who follow me; and celebrated be God's praises, for I am not of the idolaters.'

Nor did we ever send before thee any save men whom we inspired, of the people of the cities. Have they not journeyed on in the earth, and beheld how was the end of those before them? But the abode of the future is surely better for those who believe;—what! have they then no sense?

Until when the apostles despaired and they thought that they were proved liars, our help came to them, and whosoever we pleased was saved; but our violence is not averted from the sinful people.

Their stories were a lesson to those endowed with minds. It was not a tale forged, but a verification of what was before it, and a detailing of everything, and a guide and a mercy to a people who believe.

THE CHAPTER OF THE BELIEVER

In the name of the merciful and compassionate God.

'H. M. The sending down of the Book from God, the mighty, the knowing, the forgiver of sin and accepter of repentance, keen at punishment, long-suffering! there is no good but He! to whom the journey is!

None wrangle concerning the signs of God but those who misbelieve; then let not their going to and fro in the cities deceive thee.

The people of Noah before them called the prophets liars; and the confederates after them; and every nation schemed against their Apostle to catch him. And they wrangled with falsehood that they might refute the truth thereby, but I seized them, and how was my punishment!

Thus was the sentence of thy Lord due against those who misbelieved, that they are the fellows of the Fire!

Those who bear the throne and those around it celebrate the praise of their Lord, and believe in Him, and ask pardon for those who believe: 'Our Lord! thou dost embrace all things in mercy and knowledge, then pardon those who turn repentant and follow thy way, and guard them from the torment of hell! Our Lord! make them enter into gardens of Eden which thou hast promised to them, and to those who do well of their fathers, and their wives, and their seed; verily, thou art the mighty, the wise! and guard them from evil deeds, for he whom thou shalt guard from evil deeds on that day, thou wilt have had mercy on, and that is mighty bliss!'

Verily, those who misbelieve shall be cried out to, 'Surely, God's hatred is greater than your hatred of each other when ye were called unto the faith and misbelieved!' They shall say, 'Our Lord! Thou hast killed us twice, and Thou hast quickened us twice;[1] and we do confess our sins: is there then a way for getting out?'

That is because when God alone was proclaimed ye did disbelieve; but when partners were joined to Him ye did believe; but judgment belongs to God, the high, the great! He it is who shows you His signs, and sends down to you from heaven provision; but none is

[1] Referring to the absence of life before birth and the deprivation of it at death, and to the being quickened at birth and raised again after death.

mindful except him who turns repentant; then call on God, being sincere in your religion to Him, averse although the misbelievers be! Exalted of degrees! The Lord of the throne! He throws the spirit by His bidding upon whom He will of His servants, to give warning of the day of meeting. The day when they shall be issuing forth, naught concerning them shall be hidden from God. Whose is the kingdom on that day?—God's, the one, the dominant! to-day shall every soul be recompensed for that which it has earned. There is no wrong to-day; verily, God is quick at reckoning up!

And warn them of the day that approaches, when hearts are choking in the gullets; those who do wrong shall have no warm friend, and no intercessor who shall be obeyed. He knows the deceitful of eye and what men's breasts conceal, and God decides with truth; but those they call on beside Him do not decide at all: verily, God, He both hears and looks.

Have they not journeyed on in the earth and seen how was the end of those who journeyed on before them? They were stronger than them in might, and their vestiges are in the land; but God caught them up in their sins, and they had none to guard them against God.

That is for that their apostles did come to them with manifest signs, and they misbelieved, and God caught them up; verily, He is mighty, keen to punish!

And we did send Moses with our signs, and with obvious authority, unto Pharaoh and Hâmân and Qarûn. They said, 'A lying sorcerer!' and when they came to them with truth from us, they said, 'Kill the sons of those who believe with him, and let their women live!' but the stratagem of the misbelievers is only in error!

And Pharaoh said, 'Let me kill Moses; and then let him call upon his Lord! verily, I fear that he will change your religion, or that he will cause evil doing to appear in the land.'

And Moses said, 'Verily, I take refuge in my Lord and your Lord from every one who is big with pride and believes not on the day of reckoning.'

And a believing man of Pharaoh's people, who concealed his faith, said, 'Will ye kill a man for saying, My Lord is God, when he has come to you with manifest signs from your Lord? and if he be a liar, against him is his lie; and if he be truthful, there will befall you somewhat of that which he threatens you; verily, God guides not him who is an extravagant liar. O my people! yours is the kingdom to-day, ye are eminent in the land, but who will help us against the violence of God, if it comes upon us?'

Said Pharaoh, 'I will only show you what I see, and I will only guide you into the way of right direction.'

And he who believed said, 'O my people! verily, I fear for you the like of the day of the confederates, the like of the wont of the people of Noah and 'Ad and Hâmân, and of those after them; for God desires not injustice for His servants. O my people! verily, I fear for you the day of crying out,—the day when ye shall turn your backs, fleeing, with no defender for you against God; for he whom God leads astray, for him there is no guide!

'And Joseph came to you before with manifest signs, but ye ceased not to doubt concerning what he brought you, until, when he perished, ye said, "God will not send after him an apostle;" thus does God lead astray him who is extravagant, a doubter.

'Those who wrangle concerning the signs of God without authority having come to them are greatly hated by God and by those who believe; thus does God set a stamp upon the heart of every tyrant too big with pride!'

And Pharaoh said, 'O Hâmân! build for me a tower, haply I may reach the tracts,—the tracts of heaven, and may mount up to the God of Moses, for, verily, I think him a liar.'

And thus was his evil deed made seemly to Pharaoh, and he was turned from the way; but Pharaoh's stratagem ended only in ruin, and he who believed said, 'O my people! follow me, I will guide you to the way of the right direction. O my people! verily, the life of this world is but a provision, but, verily, the hereafter, that is the abode of stability! Whoso does evil, he shall only be recompensed with the like thereof; and whoso does right, be it male or female and a believer, these shall enter into Paradise; they shall be provided therein without count. O my people! why should I call you to salvation, and you call me to the fire? Ye call on me to disbelieve in God, and to join with Him what I have no knowledge of; but I call you to the mighty forgiving One! no doubt that what ye call me to, ought not to be called on in this world or in the hereafter, and that we shall be sent back to God, and that the extravagant, they are the fellows of the Fire!

'But ye shall remember what I say to you; and I entrust my affair to God, verily, God looks upon His servants!'

And God guarded him from the evils of what they plotted, and there closed in upon Pharaoh evil woe.

The fire—they shall be exposed to it morning and evening; and 'on the day the Hour shall arise,' enter, O people of Pharaoh! into the keenest torment.

And when they argue together in the fire, and the weak say to those who were big with pride, 'Verily, we were followers of yours, can ye then avail us against a portion of the fire?'

Those who were big with pride shall say, 'Verily, we are all in it; verily, God has judged between His servants.'

And those who are in the fire shall say unto the keepers of hell, 'Call upon your Lord to lighten from us one day of the torment.' They shall say, 'Did not your apostles come to you with manifest signs?' They shall say, 'Yea!' They shall say, 'Then, call!'—but the call of the misbelievers is only in error.

Verily, we will help our apostles, and those who believe, in the life of this world and on the day when the witnesses shall stand up: the day when their excuse shall not avail the unjust; but for them is the curse, and for them is an evil abode.

And we did give Moses the guidance; and we made the children of Israel to inherit the Book, as a guidance and a reminder to those endowed with minds.

Be thou patient, then; verily, God's promise is true: and ask thou forgiveness for thy sins, and celebrate the praise of thy Lord in the evening and in the morn.

Verily, those who wrangle concerning the signs of God without authority having come to them, there is naught in their breasts but pride; but they shall not attain it: do thou then seek refuge in God: verily, He both hears and looks!

Surely the creation of the heavens and the earth is greater than the creation of man: but most men know it not.

The blind and the seeing shall not be deemed alike, nor those who believe and do right and the evildoer; little is it that they remember.

Verily, the Hour will surely come; there is no doubt therein; but most men do not believe!

And your Lord said, 'Call upon me, I will answer you; verily, those who are too big with pride to worship shall enter into hell, shrinking up.'

God it is who has made for you the night to repose therein, and the day to see by; verily, God is Lord of grace to men, but most men give no thanks!

There is God for you! your Lord! the creator of everything! there is no god but He, how then can ye lie?[2] Thus did those lie who gainsaid the signs of God.

God it is who has made for you the earth as a restingplace, and a heaven as building, and has formed you and made excellent your forms; and has provided you with good things! there is God for you! —your Lord! then blessed be God, the Lord of the worlds!

He is the living One, there is no god but He! then call on Him, being sincere in your religion to Him; praise be to God, the Lord of the worlds!

Say, 'Verily, I am forbidden to serve those whom ye call on beside God, since there have come to me manifest signs from my Lord, and I am bidden to be resigned unto the Lord of the worlds.'

He it is who created you from the earth, then from a clot, then from congealed blood, then He brings you forth a child;—then ye reach to puberty; then do ye become old men,—though of you there are some who are taken away before,—that ye may reach an appointed time, and haply ye may have some sense.

He it is who quickens and kills, and when He decrees a matter, then He only says to it, 'BE,' and it is.

Hast thou not seen those who wrangle concerning the signs of God how they are turned away? Those who call the Book, and what we have sent our apostles with, a lie, soon shall they know— when the fetters are on their necks and the chains, as they are dragged into hell!—then in the fire shall they be baked.

Then it shall be said to them, 'Where is what ye did associate beside God?' They shall say, 'They have strayed away from us; nay,

[2] Or 'turn away.'

we did not call before upon anything!'—thus does God lead the misbelievers astray.

There! for that ye did rejoice in the land without right; and for that ye did exult; enter ye the gates of hell, to dwell therein for aye; for evil is the resort of those who are too big with pride!

But be thou patient; verily, the promise of God is true; and whether we show thee a part of what we promised them, or whether we surely take thee to ourself, unto us shall they be returned.

And we did send apostles before thee: of them are some whose stories we have related to thee, and of them are some whose stories we have not related to thee; and no apostle might ever bring a sign except by the permission of God; but when God's bidding came it was decided with truth, and there were those lost who deemed it vain!

God it is who has made for you cattle, that ye may ride on some of them;—and of them ye eat, and ye have in them advantages;—and that ye may attain thereon a want which is in your breasts; upon them and upon ships are ye borne.

He shows you His signs; which sign then of your Lord do ye deny?

Have they not journeyed on in the land and seen how was the end of those before them, who were more numerous than they and stronger in might, and in their vestiges which are still in the land? but of no avail to them was that which they had earned.

And when there came to them their apostles with manifest signs they rejoiced in what knowledge they had; but there closed in upon them that whereat they had mocked.

And when they saw our violence they said, 'We believe in God alone, and we disbelieve in what we once associated with Him.'

But their faith was of no avail to them when they saw our violence —the course of God with His servants in time past, and there the misbelievers lose!

THE CHAPTER OF THUNDER

In the name of the merciful and compassionate God.

A. L. M. R. Those are the signs of the Book, and that which is sent down to thee from thy Lord is the truth; but most people will not believe. God it is who has raised the heavens without columns that ye can see; then He made for the throne, and subjected the sun and the moon; each one runs on to a stated and appointed time; He governs the affair, details the signs;—haply of the meeting with your Lord ye will be sure.

And He it is who has stretched out the earth and placed therein firm mountains and rivers, and of every fruit has He placed therein two kinds. He makes the night cover the day;—verily, in that are signs unto a people who reflect.

And on the earth are neighbouring portions, and gardens of grapes and corn and palms growing together (from one root) and not growing together; they are watered with one water, yet we distinguish one over the other as food;—verily, in that are signs unto a people who have sense.

And if thou shouldst wonder, wondrous is their speech: 'What! when we have become dust, shall we really then be created anew?'

These are they who disbelieve in their Lord, and these are they with fetters round their necks, and these are the fellows of the Fire; they shall dwell therein for aye!

They will wish thee to hasten on the evil rather than the good; examples have passed away before them: but thy Lord is possessor of forgiveness unto men, notwithstanding their injustice; but, verily, thy Lord is keen to punish.

Those who misbelieve say, 'Unless a sign be sent down upon him from his Lord . . .'—Thou art only a warner, and every people has its guide.

God knows what each female bears, and what the wombs fall short of or add; for dimensions of everything are with Him.

He who knows the unseen and the visible,—the great, the lofty one.

Alike among you is he who keeps secret his speech and he who displays it; and he who hides by night and he who stalks abroad by day. Each of them has pursuers[1] before him and behind him, to keep guard over him at the command of God; verily, God changes not what a people has until they change it for themselves. And when

[1] Guardian angels.

God wishes evil to a people there is no averting it, nor have they a protector beside Him.

He it is who shows you the lightning for fear and hope;[2] and He brings up the heavy clouds.

And the thunder celebrates His praise, and the angels too for fear of Him; and He sends the thunder-clap and overtakes therewith whom He will;—yet they wrangle about God! But He is strong in might.

On Him is the call of truth, and those who call on others than Him shall not be answered at all, save as one who stretches out his hand to the water that it may reach his mouth, but it reaches it not! The call of the misbelievers is only in error.

And God do those who are in the heavens and the earth adore, whether they will or no! as do their shadows also morn and eve.

Say, 'Who is Lord of the heavens and the earth?' say, 'God'; say, 'Do ye take beside God patrons who cannot control profit or harm for themselves?' say, 'Shall the blind and the seeing be held equal? or shall the darkness and the light be held equal? or have they made associates with God who can create as He creates, so that the creation seem familiar to them?' say, 'God is the creator of everything, and He is the one, the dominant.'

He sends down from the sky water, and the watercourses flow according to their bulk, and the torrent bears along the floating scum: and from what they set fire to, craving ornaments or utensils, comes a scum like that;—thus does God hit the truth and the falsehood;—and as for the scum it is thrown off, and as for what profits man it stays on the earth. Thus does God strike out parables!

For those who respond to their Lord is good; but those who respond not to Him, had they all that is in the earth and the like thereof as well, they would give it for a ransom; these shall have an evil reckoning up! and their resort is hell,—an evil couch shall it be!

Is he who knows that naught but the truth is sent down upon thee from thy Lord like him who is blind? Only those possessed of minds will remember!

Those who fulfil God's covenant and break not the compact, and

---

[2] I. e. hope of rain; lightning is always hailed with joy by the Arabs as a precursor of rain.

those who attain what God has bidden to be attained, and dread their Lord and fear the evil reckoning up; and those who are patient, craving their Lord's face, and are steadfast in prayer, and expend in alms of what we have bestowed upon them secretly and openly, and ward off evil with good,—these shall have the recompense of the abode, gardens of Eden, into which they shall enter with the righteous amongst their fathers and their wives and their seed; and the angels shall enter in unto them from every gate:—'Peace be upon you! for that ye were patient; and goodly is the recompense of the abode.'

And those who break God's covenant after compacting for it, and who cut asunder what God hath bidden to be joined, and who do evil in the earth, these—upon them is the curse of God, and for them is an evil abode.

God extends his bounty freely to whomsoever He will, or He metes it out; and they rejoice in the life of this world, but the life of this world is naught but a (temporary) provision compared with the next.

Those who misbelieve say, 'Unless a sign is sent down upon him from his Lord . . . .' Say, 'God leads whom He will astray, but guides unto Him those who turn again,

'Those who believe and whose hearts are comforted by the mention of God,—aye! by the mention of God shall their hearts be comforted, who believe and do what is right. Good cheer for them and an excellent resort.'

Thus have we sent thee to a nation before which other nations have passed away, to recite to them that which we have inspired thee with; yet they misbelieve in the merciful! Say, 'He is my Lord; there is no god but He; upon Him do I rely, and unto Him is my repentance.'

And though it were a Qur'ân by which the mountains were moved, or by which the earth were cut up, or the dead made to speak[3]—nay, God's is the command altogether! Did not those who believed know[4] that if God had pleased He would have guided men altogether?

[3] They would not believe. [4] The word used in the original, yâi'as, means 'despair,' but in the patois of the Na'ha'h tribe signifies 'know,' and is so interpreted by the native commentators on this passage.

And a striking calamity shall not cease to overtake those who misbelieve for what they have wrought, or to alight close by their dwelling; until God's promise comes—verily, God fails not in His promise.

Before thee have apostles been mocked at; and those who misbelieved have I allowed to range at large; and then it caught them up! How then was my punishment?

Shall He who is standing over every soul (to note) what it has earned——? And they join partners with God! Say, 'Name them; can ye inform Him of what He does not know in the earth? or is it for name's sake only (that ye call upon them)?

'Nay, then, stratagem is made seemly to those who misbelieve, and they turn folks from the path of God! But whomsoever God doth lead astray no guide has he.'

For them is torment in this world's life; but surely the torment of the next is more wretched still—nor have they against God a keeper.

The likeness of the Paradise which those who fear God are promised, beneath it rivers flow, its food is enduring, and likewise its shade! That is the recompense of those who fear; but the recompense of misbelievers is the Fire!

And those to whom we brought the Book rejoice in that which we have sent down to thee; but of the confederates are some who deny a part thereof.

Say, 'I am only bidden to serve God and not to associate any with Him; on Him I call and to Him is my recourse.'

Thus have we sent it down, an Arabic judgment, but hadst thou followed their lusts, after the knowledge that has come to thee, thou hadst not had against God a patron or a keeper.

And we sent apostles before thee, and we made for them wives and seed; and no apostle could bring a sign save by God's permission;—for every period there is a book.

God blots out what He will, or He confirms; and with Him is the Mother of the Book.

Either we will let thee see a part of what we threaten them with, or we will take thee to Ourself; but thy duty is only to deliver thy message, and ours to reckon up.

Did they not see that we come to the land and diminish the borders thereof[5]? God judges, and there is none to reverse His judgment, and He is swift at reckoning up!

And those who were before them were crafty too; but God's is the craft altogether! He knows what every soul earns; and the misbelievers shall know whose is the recompense of the abode.

And those who misbelieve say, 'Thou art not sent!' Say, 'God is witness enough between me and you; and so is he who has the knowledge of the Book!'

[5] Alluding to the conquests of Islâm.

CHAPTERS FROM THE KORAN

MEDINA SURAS

THE CHAPTER OF THE CONGREGATION

IN the name of the merciful and compassionate God.

What is in the heavens and what is in the earth celebrates the praises of God the King, the holy, the mighty, the wise!

He it is who sent unto the Gentiles a prophet amongst themselves to recite to them His signs and to purify them, and to teach them the Book and the wisdom, although they were before in obvious error.

And others of them have not yet overtaken them[1]; but He is the mighty, the wise!

That is God's grace, He gives it to whomsoever He will; for God is Lord of mighty grace.

The likeness of those who were charged with the law and then bore it not is as the likeness of an ass bearing books: sorry is the likeness of the people who say God's signs are lies! but God guides not an unjust people.

Say, 'O ye who are Jews! if ye pretend that ye are the clients of God, beyond other people; then wish for death if ye do speak the truth!'

But they never wish for it, through what their hands have sent before! but God knows the unjust.

Say, 'Verily, the death from which ye flee will surely meet you; then shall ye be sent back to Him who knows the unseen and the visible, and He will inform you of that which ye have done!'

O ye who believe! when the call to prayer is made upon the Congregation Day,[2] then hasten to the remembrance of God, and leave off traffic; that is better for you, if ye did but know!

---

[1] I. e. by embracing Islâm.

[2] Friday, called before this 'Harûbah. It was the day on which Mohammed entered Medînah for the first time.

And when prayer is performed, then disperse abroad in the land, and crave of God's grace; and remember God much; haply ye may prosper!

But when they see merchandise or sport they flock to it and leave thee standing[3]! Say, 'What is with God is better than sport and than merchandise, for God is the best of providers!'

THE CHAPTER OF THE SPOILS

In the name of the merciful and compassionate God.

They will ask thee about the spoils. Say, 'The spoils are God's and the Apostle's; fear God and settle it amongst yourselves; obey God and the Apostle if ye do believe.'

Verily, the believers are those who, when God's name is mentioned, their hearts sink with fear; and when His signs are rehearsed to them they increase them in faith; and on their Lord do they rely; who are steadfast in prayer, and of what we have bestowed upon them give in alms; these are in truth believers; to them are degrees with their Lord, and forgiveness, and a generous provision.

As thy Lord caused thee to go forth from thy house[1] with the truth, although a sect of the believers were averse therefrom. They wrangled with thee about the truth after it was made plain, as though they were being driven on to death and looked thereon; and when God promised you that one of the two troops should be yours, and ye would fain have had those who had no arms. God wished to prove the truth true by His words, and to cut off the hindermost parts of those who misbelieve—to prove the truth true, and to make vain the vain, although the sinners are averse.[2]

When ye asked for succour from your Lord, and He answered you, 'I will assist you with a thousand angels, with others in reserve.'

[3] It is said that one Friday a caravan entered the town while Mohammed was conducting the public prayers, and the congregation hearing the drums beat rushed out to see the sight, with the exception of about twelve of them.

[1] At Medînah.

[2] The occasion alluded to was one when Mohammed had made preparations for attacking an unarmed caravan on its way from Syria to Mecca, when Abu Sufiân, who was in charge of it, sent to Mecca and obtained an escort of nearly a thousand men; many of Mohammed's followers wished to attack the caravan only, but the prophet and his immediate followers were for throwing themselves on the escort.

God made it only glad tidings to quiet your hearts therewith; for victory is only from God! verily, God is mighty and wise.

When drowsiness covered you as a security from Him, and He sent down upon you from the heavens water to purify you withal, and to take away from you the plague of Satan, and to tie up your hearts and to make firm your footsteps.[3]

When your Lord inspired the angels—'Verily, I am with you; make ye firm then those who believe; I will cast dread into the hearts of those who misbelieve,—strike off their necks then, and strike off from them every finger tip.'

That is, because they went into opposition against God and His Apostle; for he who goes into opposition against God and His Apostle—verily, God is keen to punish.

There, taste it! since for the misbelievers is the torment of the Fire.

O ye who believe! when ye meet those who misbelieve in swarms, turn not to them your hinder parts; for he who turns to them that day his hinder parts, save turning to fight or rallying to a troop, brings down upon himself wrath from God, and his resort is hell, and an ill journey shall it be!

Ye did not slay them, but it was God who slew them; nor didst thou shoot when thou didst shoot, but God did shoot,[4] to try the believers from Himself with a goodly trial; verily, God both hears and knows. There! verily, God weakens the stratagem of the misbelievers.

If ye wish[5] the matter to be decided, a decision has now come to you; but if ye desist, it is better for you; and if ye turn back we will turn too, and your troop shall avail nothing, great in number though it be, since God is with the believers!

O ye who believe! obey God and His Apostle, and turn not from

[3] The Muslims were fewer in number than the enemy, and the latter had command of the water, at both of which circumstances their hearts sank. In the night, however, rain fell, refreshed them and supplied their wants.

[4] Alluding to the alleged miracle of the gravel thrown into the eyes of the Qurâis at the battle of Bedr, to which the Muslim victory was due.

[5] An address to the Meccans who, when threatened with an attack from Mohammed, took sanctuary in the Kaabah, and prayed to God that if they were right He would help them, but that if Mohammed was in the right he would help him.

Him while ye hear, and be not like those who say, 'We hear,' and yet they hear not.

Verily, the worst of beasts in God's sight are the deaf, the dumb who do not understand. Had God known any good in them, He would have made them hear; but had He made them hear, they would have turned back and have swerved aside.

O ye who believe! answer God and His Apostle when He calls you to that which quickens you; and know that God steps in between man and his heart; and that to Him ye shall be gathered. And fear temptation, which will not light especially on those of you who have done wrong; but know that God is keen to punish.

Remember when ye were few in number and weak in the land, fearing lest people should snatch you away; then He sheltered you and aided you with victory, and provided you with good things; haply ye may give thanks.

O ye who believe! be not treacherous to God and His Apostle; nor be treacherous to your engagement while ye know!

Know that your wealth and your children are but a temptation, and that God—with Him is mighty hire!

O ye who believe! if ye fear God He will make for you a discrimination,[6] and will cover for you your offences, and will forgive you; for God is Lord of mighty grace.

And when those who misbelieve were crafty with thee to detain thee a prisoner, or kill thee, or drive thee forth; they were crafty, but God was crafty too, for God is best of crafty ones!

But when our verses were rehearsed to them they said, 'We have already heard.—If we pleased we could speak like this; verily, this is nothing but tales of those of yore.'

When they said, 'O God! if this be truth, and from Thee, then rain upon us stones from heaven or bring us grievous woe!'

But God would not torment them while thou art amongst them; nor was God going to torment them while they asked Him to forgive. But what ails them that God should not torment them while they turn folk away from the Holy Mosque, though they are not the guardians thereof—its guardians are only the pious?—but most of them know not.

[6] Here used in the sense of victory.

Their prayer at the House was naught but whistling and clapping hands!—taste then the torment for that ye misbelieved!

Verily, those who misbelieve expend their wealth to turn folk from the path of God; but they shall spend it, and then it shall be for them sighing, and then they shall be overcome Those who misbelieve, into hell shall they be gathered!—that God may distinguish the vile from the good, and may put the vile, some on the top of the other, and heap all up together, and put it into hell!— These are those who lose!

Say to those who misbelieve, if they desist they will be forgiven what is past; but if they return,—the course of those of former days has passed away.[7]

Fight them then that there should be no sedition, and that the religion may be wholly God's; but if they desist then God on what they do doth look. But if they turn their backs, then know that God is your Lord; a good Lord is He, and a good help; and know that whenever ye seize anything as a spoil, to God belongs a fifth thereof, and to His Apostle, and to kindred and orphans, and the poor and the wayfarer; if ye believe in God and what we have revealed unto our servants on the day of the discrimination,—the day when the two parties met; and God is mighty over all. When ye were on the near side of the valley, and they were on the far side, and the camels were below you; had ye made an appointment then[8] ye would have failed to keep your appointment—but it was that God might accomplish a thing that was as good as done! that he who was to perish might perish with a manifest sign; and that he who was to live might live with a manifest sign; for, verily, God hears and knows!

When God showed thee them in thy dream as though they were but few; but had He shown thee them as though they were many, ye would have been timid, and ye would have quarrelled about the matter;—but God preserved you; verily, He knows the nature of men's breasts!

And when he showed them to you, as ye encountered them, as few in your eyes; and made you seem few in their eyes; that God

---

[7] That is, they have the doom of former people as a warning and an example.
[8] That is, had ye agreed to attack them.

might accomplish a thing that was as good as done; for unto God do things return!

O ye who believe! when ye encounter a troop, then stand firm and remember God; and haply ye may prosper! and fear God and His Apostle, and do not quarrel or be timid, so that your turn of luck go from you; but be ye patient, verily, God is with the patient. And be not like those who went forth from their homes with insolence, and for appearance sake before men, and to turn folks off God's way; for all they do God comprehends.

And when Satan made their works appear seemly to them, and said, 'There is none amongst mankind to conquer you to-day, for, verily, I am your neighbour!' and when the two troops came in sight of each other, he turned upon his heels and said, 'Verily, I am clear of you! verily, I see what you see not[9]! verily, I fear God, for God is keen to punish!'

And when the hypocrites and those in whose hearts was sickness said, 'Their religion hath beguiled these men,[10] but he who relies upon God, verily, God is mighty and wise.'

Couldst thou see when the angels take away the souls of those who misbelieve; they smite them on their faces and hinder parts.— 'Taste ye the torment of burning! that is for what your hands have sent on before; and for that God is no unjust one towards his servants.'

As was the wont of Pharaoh's people and those before them! they disbelieved in the signs of God, and God overtook them in their sins; verily, God is strong and keen to punish.

That is because God is not one to change a favour He has favoured a people with, until they change what they have in themselves, and for that God both hears and knows.

As was the wont of Pharaoh's people and those before them! they said our signs were lies, and we destroyed them in their sins, and drowned Pharaoh's people; and all of them were evil-doers.

Verily, the worst of beasts in God's eyes are those who misbelieve and will not believe; with whom if thou dost make a league, they break their league each time, for they fear not God; but

[9] The angels who were fighting on the Muslim side.
[10] I. e. beguiled them into attacking a force superior in numbers.

shouldst thou ever catch them in war, then make those who come after them run by their example,[11] haply they may remember then.

And shouldst thou ever fear from any people treachery, then throw it back to them in like manner; verily, God loves not the treacherous. Deem not that those who misbelieve can win; verily, they cannot make (God) powerless!

Prepare ye against them what force and companies of horse ye can, to make the enemies of God, and your enemies, and others beside them, in dread thereof. Ye do not know them, but God knows them! and whatever ye expend in God's way He will repay you; and ye shall not be wronged. But if they incline to peace, incline thou to it too, and rely upon God; verily, He both hears and knows.

But if they wish to betray thee, then God is enough for thee! He it is who supports thee with His help and with the believers; and reconciles their hearts! Didst thou expend all that is in the earth thou couldst not reconcile their hearts, but God reconciled them, verily, He is mighty and wise!

O thou prophet! God is sufficient for thee, with those of the believers who follow thee! O thou prophet! urge on the believers to fight. If there be of you twenty patient men, they shall conquer two hundred; if there be of you a hundred, they shall conquer a thousand of those who misbelieve, because they are a people who did not discern.—Now has God made it light for you; He knows that there is a weakness amongst you: but if there be amongst you but a patient hundred, they will conquer two hundred; and if there be of you a thousand, they will conquer two thousand, by the permission of God,—for God is with the patient!

It has not been for any prophet to take captives until he hath slaughtered in the land! Ye wish to have the goods of this world, but God wishes for the next, for God is mighty, wise! Were it not for a book from God that had gone before, there would have touched you, for that which ye took, a mighty punishment.[12]

---

[11] That is, make them an example to all future opponents by the severity of thy dealing with them.

[12] Mohammed here blames them for having accepted ransom from the captives which they took at the Battle of Bedr; but acknowledges that previously revealed passages of the Qur'ân did in the strict letter allow of such ransom being taken.

Eat of what spoils ye have taken, what is lawful and good; and fear God, verily, God is forgiving and merciful.

O thou prophet! say to such of the captives as are in your hands, 'If God knows of any good in your hearts, he will give you better than that which is taken from you, and will forgive you; for God is forgiving and merciful.'

But if they desire to betray thee,—they have betrayed God before! but He hath given you power over them; for God is knowing, wise!

Verily, those who believe and have fled and fought strenuously with their wealth and persons in God's way, and those who have given refuge[13] and help, these shall be next of kin to each other.[14] But those who believe, but have not fled, ye have naught to do with their claims of kindred, until they flee as well. But if they ask you for aid for religion's sake, then help is due from you, except against a people between whom and you there is an alliance; for God on what ye do doth look.

And those who misbelieve, some of them are next of kin to others —unless ye act the same there will be sedition in the land, and great corruption.

Those who believe and have fled and fought strenuously in God's cause, and those who have given a refuge and a help, those it is who believe; to them is forgiveness and generous provision due. And those who have believed afterwards and have fled and fought strenuously with you; these too are of you, but blood relations are nearer in kin by the Book of God. Verily, God all things doth know.

THE CHAPTER OF IMRAN'S FAMILY

In the name of the merciful and compassionate God.

A. L. M. God, there is no god but He, the living, the self-subsistent. He has sent down to thee the Book in truth, confirming what was before it, and has revealed the law, and the gospel before for the guidance of men, and has revealed the Discrimination.

Verily, those who disbelieve in the signs of God, for them is severe torment, for God is mighty and avenging.

Verily, God, there is nothing hidden from Him in the earth, nor

---

[13] To the prophet.   [14] The Ansârs and Muhâgerîn, that is, those who lent aid to, and those who fled with Mohammed were at first regarded as next of kin and heirs to each other's property to the exclusion of blood relationship, until the above passage was abrogated by the last words of this chapter.

in the heaven; He it is who fashions you in the womb as He pleases. There is no God but He, the mighty, the wise.

He it is who has revealed to thee the Book, of which there are some verses that are decisive, they are the mother[1] of the Book; and others ambiguous; but as for those in whose hearts is perversity, they follow what is ambiguous, and do crave for sedition, craving for (their own) interpretation of it; but none know the interpretation of it except God. But those who are well grounded in knowledge say, 'We believe in it; it is all from our Lord; but none will remember save those who possess minds.

'O Lord! pervert not our hearts again when Thou hast guided them, and grant us mercy from Thee, for Thou art He who grants. O Lord! Thou shalt gather together men unto the day wherein is no doubt. Verily, God will not depart from His promise.'

Verily, those who misbelieve, their wealth shall not help them, nor their children, against God at all; and they it is who are the fuel of the fire.

As was the wont of Pharaoh's people, and those before them, they said our signs were lies, and God caught them up in their sins, for God is severe to punish.

Say to those who misbelieve, 'Ye shall be overcome and driven together to hell, an ill couch will it be.

'Ye have had a sign in the two parties who met; one party fighting in the way of God, the other misbelieving; these saw twice the same number as themselves to the eye-sight,[2] for God aids with His help those whom He pleases.' Verily, in that is a lesson for those who have perception. Seemly unto men is a life of lusts, of women, and children, and hoarded talents of gold and silver, and of horses well-bred, and cattle, and tilth;—that is the provision for the life of this world; but God, with Him is the best resort.

Say, 'But shall we tell you of a better thing than this?' For those who fear are gardens with their Lord, beneath which rivers flow; they shall dwell therein for aye, and pure wives and grace from God; the Lord looks on His servants, who say, 'Lord, we believe, pardon Thou our sins and keep us from the torment of the fire,'—upon the

---

[1] I. e. the fundamental part of it.
[2] On the occasion of the battle of Bedr.

patient, the truthful, the devout, and those who ask for pardon at the dawn.

God bears witness that there is no god but He, and the angels, and those possessed of knowledge standing up for justice. There is no God but He, the mighty, the wise.

Verily, (the true) religion in God's sight is Islâm, and those to whom the Book was given disagreed not until after that there was given to them knowledge, through mutual envy. But whoso disbelieves in God's signs, truly God is quick at reckoning up.

And if they would dispute with thee, then say, 'I turn my face with resignation unto God, and whoso follows me.'

And say to those who have been given the Book, unto the Gentiles,[3] 'Are ye, too, resigned?' and if they are resigned, then are they guided. But if they turn their backs, then thou hast only to preach, and God looks on his servants.

Verily, those who disbelieve in God's signs, and kill the prophets without right, and kill those from among men, who bid what is just,—to them give the glad tidings of grievous woe! These are they whose works are void in this world and the next, and helpers have they none.

Did ye not see those who have been given a portion of the Book? they were called unto the Book of God to decide between them; and then a sect of them turned their backs and turned away;—that is because they say the fire shall not touch us save for a certain number of days. But that deceived them in their religion which they had invented. How will it be when we have gathered them together for a day whereof there is no doubt, when each soul shall be paid what it has earned, and they shall not be wronged?

Say, 'O God, Lord of the kingdom! Thou givest the kingdom to whomsoever Thou pleasest, and strippest the kingdom from whomsoever Thou pleasest; Thou honourest whom Thou pleasest, and abasest whom Thou pleasest; in Thy hand is good. Verily, Thou art mighty over all. Thou dost turn night to day, and dost turn day to night, and dost bring forth the living from the dead, and dost provide for whom Thou pleasest without taking count.'

[3] The word also means 'illiterate,' and refers here to the Pagan Arabs in Mohammed's time. He seems to have borrowed the expression from the Jews.

Those who believe shall not take misbelievers for their patrons, rather than believers, and he who does this has no part with God at all, unless, indeed, ye fear some danger from them. But God bids you beware of Himself, for unto Him your journey is.

Say, 'If ye hide that which is in your breasts, or if ye show it, God knows it: He knows what is in the heavens and what is in the earth, for God is mighty over all.'

The day that every soul shall find what it has done of good present before it; and what it has done of evil, it would fain that there were between itself and that a wide interval. 'God bids you beware of Himself, but God is gentle with His servants.'

Say, 'If ye would love God then follow me, and God will love you and forgive you your sins, for God is forgiving and merciful.'

Say, 'Obey God and the Apostle; but if ye turn your backs God loves not misbelievers.'

Verily, God has chosen Adam, and Noah, and Abraham's people, and Imrân's[4] people above the world,—a seed, of which one succeeds the other, but God both hears and knows.

When Imrân's wife said, 'Lord! I have vowed to Thee what is within my womb, to be dedicated unto Thee, receive it then from me. Verily, Thou dost hear and know.' And when she brought it forth she said, 'Verily, I have brought it forth a female'—but God knew best what she brought forth; and a male is not like a female— 'I have called her Mary, and I seek a refuge in Thee for her and for her seed from Satan the pelted.'[5]

And her Lord received her with a good reception, and made her grow up with a good growth, and Zachariah took care of her. Whenever Zachariah entered the chamber to her he found beside her a provision, and said, 'O Mary, how hast thou this?' She said, 'It is from God, for God provides for whom He pleases without count.' Therefore prayed Zachariah to his Lord, and said, 'Lord, grant me

[4] Amram, who, according to the Mohammedans, was the father of the Virgin Mary (Miriam). A confusion seems to have existed in the mind of Mohammed between Miriam 'the Virgin Mary,' and Miriam the sister of Moses.

[5] The Mohammedan superstition is that the devils listen at the gate of heaven for scraps of the knowledge of futurity, and when detected by the angels are pelted with shooting stars. The expression may also refer to the ceremony of 'pelting the devil,' as performed by 'Hagg pilgrims at Minâ, in memory, it is said, of Abraham's having driven Iblîs away with stones when tempted by him to disobey God and refuse to sacrifice Isaac.

from Thee a good seed. Verily, Thou hearest prayer.' And an angel cried out to him as he was standing praying in the chamber (and said) that 'God gives thee the glad tidings of John, to confirm the Word from God,—of a chief and a chaste one, and a prophet from amongst the righteous.'

He said, 'My Lord, how can there be to me a boy when old age has reached me, and my wife is barren?' Said he, 'Thus God does what He pleaseth.' He said, 'My Lord, make for me a sign.' He said, 'Thy sign is that thou shalt not speak to men for three days, save by gesture; but remember thy Lord much, and celebrate His praises in the evening and the morning.'

And when the angels said, 'O Mary! verily, God has chosen thee, and has purified thee, and has chosen thee above the women of the world. O Mary! be devout unto thy Lord, and adore and bow down with those who bow. That is (one) of the declarations of the unseen world which we reveal to thee, though thou wert not by them when they threw their lots[6] which of them should take care of Mary, nor were ye by them when they did dispute.'

When the angel said, 'O Mary, verily, God gives thee the glad tidings of a Word from Him; his name shall be the Messiah Jesus the son of Mary, regarded in this world and the next and of these whose place is nigh to God. And he shall speak to people in his cradle, and when grown up, and shall be among the righteous.' She said, 'Lord! how can I have a son, when man has not yet touched me?' He said, 'Thus God creates what He pleaseth. When He decrees a matter He only says BE and it is; and He will teach him the Book, and wisdom, and the law, and the gospel, and he shall be a prophet to the people of Israel (saying), that I have come to you, with a sign from God, namely, that I will create for you out of clay as though it were the form of a bird, and I will blow thereon and it shall become a bird by God's permission; and I will heal the blind from birth, and lepers; and I will bring the dead to life by God's permission; and I will tell you what you eat and what ye store up in your houses. Verily, in that is a sign for you if ye be believers. And I will confirm what is before you of the law, and will surely make lawful for you some of that which was prohibited from you.

6 The legend is, that the priests threw lots by casting arrows into the river Jordan.

I have come to you with a sign from your Lord, so fear God and follow me, for God is my Lord, and your Lord, so worship Him:—this is the right path.'

And when Jesus perceived their unbelief, He said, 'Who are my helpers for God?' Said the apostles, 'We are God's helpers. We believe in God, so bear witness that we are resigned. Lord, we have believed in what Thou hast revealed, and we have followed the Apostle, so write us down with those which bear witness.' But they (the Jews) were crafty, and God was crafty, for God is the best of crafty ones!

When God said, 'O Jesus! I will make Thee die and take Thee up again to me[7] and will clear thee of those who misbelieve, and will make those who follow thee above those who misbelieve, at the day of judgment, then to me is your return. I will decide between you concerning that wherein ye disagree. And as for those who misbelieve, I will punish them with grievous punishment in this world and the next, and they shall have none to help them.'

But as for those who believe and do what is right, He will pay them their reward, for God loves not the unjust.

That is what we recite to thee of the signs and of the wise reminder. Verily, the likeness of Jesus with God is as the likeness of Adam. He created him from earth, then He said to him BE, and he was;—the truth from thy Lord, so be thou not of those who are in doubt. And whoso disputeth with thee after what has come to thee of knowledge, say, 'Come, let us call our sons and your sons, and our women and your women, and ourselves and yourselves: then we will imprecate and put God's curse on those who lie.'

Verily, those are the true stories, and there is no god but God, and, verily, God He is the mighty, the wise; but if they turn back, God knows the evildoers.

Say, 'O ye people of the Book, come to a word laid down plainly between us and you, that we will not serve other than God, nor associate aught with him, nor take each other for lords rather than God.' But if they turn back then say, 'Bear witness that we are resigned.'

[7] The Mohammedans believe that it was an eidolon and not Jesus himself who was crucified.

O people of the Book, why do ye dispute about Abraham, when the law and the gospel were not revealed until after him? What! do ye not understand? Here ye are, disputing about what ye have some knowledge of; why then do ye dispute about what ye have no knowledge of? God knows and ye know not.

Abraham was not a Jew, nor yet a Christian, but he was a 'Hanîf[8] resigned, and not of the idolaters. Verily, the people most worthy of Abraham are those who follow him and his prophets, and those who believe;—God is the patron of the believers.

A sect of the people of the Book would fain they could lead you astray, but they only lead themselves astray, and they do not perceive.

O people of the Book! why do ye disbelieve in the signs of God, the while ye witness them? O people of the Book! why do ye clothe the truth with falsehood and hide the truth the while ye know? A sect of the people of the Book say, 'Believe in what was revealed to those who believed at the first appearance of the day, and disbelieve it at the end thereof,'—that (others) may perchance go back (from their faith)[9]—'do not believe save one who followeth your religion.'

Say, 'Verily, the (true) guidance is the guidance of God, that one should be given like what ye are given.' Or would they dispute with you before your Lord, say, 'Grace is in the hand of God, He gives it to whom he pleases, for God both comprehends and knows. He specially favours with his mercy whom he pleases, for God is Lord of mighty grace.'

And of the people of the Book, there are some of them who, if thou entrust them with a talent[10] give it back to you; and some of them, if thou entrust them with a dinâr,[10] he will not give it back to thee except so long as thou dost stand over him. That is because they say, 'We owe no duty to the Gentiles;' but they tell a lie against God, the while they know.

[8] The word means in Arabic 'inclining to what is right'; it is often used technically for one who professes El Islâm.

[9] This is said to allude to some Jews who professed Islâm in the morning and recanted at night, saying that they had in the meantime consulted their books and found nothing to confirm it, hoping by this stratagem to raise doubts in the believers' minds.

[10] A 'talent,' qintâr, is used for any very large sum, a dinâr ('denarius') was a gold coin worth about 10 shillings.

Yea, whoso fulfils his covenant and fears,—verily, God loves those who fear. Those who sell God's covenant and their oaths for a little price, these have no portion in the future life. God will not speak to them, and will not look upon them on the resurrection day, and will not purify them; but for them is grievous woe.

And, verily, amongst them is a sect who twist their tongues[11] concerning the Book, that ye may reckon it to be from the Book, but it is not from the Book. They say, 'It is from God,' but it is not from God, and they tell a lie against God, the while they know.

It is not right for a man that God should give him a Book, and judgment, and prophecy, and that then he should say to men, 'Be ye servants of mine rather than of God;' but be ye rather masters[12] of teaching the Book and of what ye learn.

He does not bid you take the angels and the prophets for your lords; shall He bid you misbelieve again when you are once resigned?

And when God took the compact from the prophets '(this is) surely what we have given you of the Book and wisdom. Then shall come to you the Apostle confirming what is with you. Ye must believe in him and help him.' He said, moreover, 'Are ye resolved and have ye taken my compact on that (condition)?' They say, 'We are resolved.' He said, 'Then bear witness, for I am witness with you; but he who turns back after that, these are sinners.'[13]

What is it other than God's religion that they crave? when to Him is resigned whosoever is in the heavens and the earth, will he or nill he, and to him shall they return!

Say, 'We believe in God, and what has been revealed to thee, and what was revealed to Abraham, and Ishmael, and Isaac, and Jacob, and the tribes, and what was given to Moses, and Jesus, and the prophets from their Lord,—we will make no distinction between any of them,—and we are unto Him resigned. Whosoever craves other than Islam for a religion, it shall surely not be accepted from him, and he shall, in the next world, be of those who lose.'

---

[11] I. e. pervert it.

[12] In the original Rabbânîyin, an expression identical with Rabboni, cf. John xx. 16.

[13] The legend, borrowed from Talmudic sources, is that God assembled all past, present, and future prophets on Mount Sinai and entered into the compact mentioned in the text.

How shall God guide people who have disbelieved after believing and bearing witness that the Apostle is true, and after there come to them manifest signs? God guides the unjust folk.

These, their reward is, that on them is the curse of God, and of the angels, and of men together; they shall dwell therein for aye— the torment shall not be alleviated from them, nor shall they be respited; save those who repent after that, and act aright, for verily, God is forgiving and merciful.

Verily, those who misbelieve after believing, and then increase in misbelief, their repentance shall not be accepted; these are those who err.

Verily, those who misbelieve and die in misbelief, there shall not be accepted from any one of them the earth-full of gold, though he should give it as a ransom. For them is grievous woe, and helpers have they none.

Ye cannot attain to righteousness until ye expend in alms of what ye love. But what ye expend in alms, that God knows.

All food was lawful to the children of Israel save what Israel made unlawful to himself before that the law was revealed. Say, 'Bring the law and recite it, if ye speak the truth.' But whoso forges against God a lie, after that, they are the unjust. Say, 'God speaks the truth, then follow the faith of Abraham, a 'hanîf, who was not of the idolaters.'

Verily, the first House founded for men was surely that at Bekkah,[14] for a blessing and a guidance to the worlds. Therein are manifest signs,—Abraham's station, and whosoever enters in is safe. There is due to God from man a pilgrimage unto the House, for whosoever can find his way there. But whoso misbelieves—God is independent of the worlds.

Say, 'O people of the Book! why do ye misbelieve in God's signs, while God is witness of what ye do?'

Say, 'O people of the Book! why do ye turn from the way of God him who believes, craving to make it crooked, while ye are witnesses? But God is not careless of what ye do.'

O ye who believe! if ye obey the sect of those to whom the Book was brought, they will turn you, after your faith, to unbelievers

[14] Another name of Mecca.

again. How can ye misbelieve while unto you are recited the signs of God, and among you is His Apostle? But whoso takes tight hold on God, he is guided into the right way.

O ye who believe! fear God with the fear that He deserves, and die not save ye be resigned.

Take tight hold of God's rope altogether, and do not part in sects; but remember the favours of God towards you, when ye were enemies and He made friendship between your hearts, and on the morrow ye were, by His favour, brothers. Ye were on the edge of a pit of fire, but he rescued you therefrom.[15] Thus does God show to you His signs, perchance ye may be guided; and that there may be of you a nation who shall invite to good, and bid what is reasonable, and forbid what is wrong; these are the prosperous.

Be not like those who parted in sects and disagreed after there came to them manifest signs; for them is mighty woe, on the day when faces shall be whitened and faces shall be blackened. As for those whose faces are blackened,—'Did ye misbelieve after your faith, then taste the torment for your misbelief!' But as for those whose faces are whitened, they are in God's mercy, and they shall dwell therein for aye.

These are the signs of God. We recite them to you in truth, for God desires not wrong unto the worlds.

God's is what is in the heavens and what is in the earth, and unto God affairs return.

Ye were the best of nations brought forth unto man. Ye bid what is reasonable, and forbid what is wrong, believing in God. Had the people of the Book believed, it would have been better for them. There are believers among them, though most of them are sinners.

They shall surely not harm you save a hurt[16]; and if they fight you, they shall show you their backs, then they shall not be helped.

They are smitten with abasement wherever they be found, save for the rope of God and the rope of man[17]; and they draw on themselves wrath from God. They are smitten, too, with poverty; that is

[15] Alluding to an occasion in which the ancient rivalry between the two tribes of El Aus and El 'Hazrag, which had been reconciled by Islâm, was on the point of breaking out again.

[16] I. e. only a slight hurt.

[17] That is, unless they enter into either the spiritual or temporal dominion of Islam, by professing the Mohammedan creed, or by paying a tribute.

because they did disbelieve in God's signs, and kill the prophets undeservedly. That is because they did rebel and did transgress.

They are not all alike. Of the people of the Book there is a nation upright, reciting God's signs throughout the night, as they adore the while. They believe in God, and in the last day, and bid what is reasonable, and forbid what is wrong, and vie in charity; these are among the righteous.

What ye do of good surely God will not deny, for God knows those who fear.

Verily, those who misbelieve, their wealth is of no service to them, nor their children either, against God; they are the fellows of the Fire, and they shall dwell therein for aye.

The likeness of what they expend in this life of the world, is as the likeness of wind wherein is a cold blast that falls upon a people's tilth who have wronged themselves and destroys it. It is not God who wrongs them, but it is themselves they wrong.

O ye who believe! take not to intimacy with others than yourselves; they will not fail to spoil you; they would fain ye came to trouble,—hatred is shown by their mouths; but what their breasts conceal is greater still. We have made manifest to you our signs, did ye but understand.

Ye it is who love them, but they love not you; and ye believe in the Book, all of it. But when they meet you they say, 'We believe;' and when they go aside they bite their finger tips at you through rage. Say, 'Die in your rage, for God doth know the nature of men's breasts.'

If good luck touch you it is bad for them, but if bad luck befal you they rejoice therein; yet if ye are patient and fear, their tricks shall not harm you, for what they do God comprehends.

When thou didst set forth early[18] from thy people to settle for the believers a camp to fight;—but God both hears and knows;— when two companies of you were on the point of showing cowardice; but God was their guardian, for on God surely the believers do rely. Why! God gave you victory at Bedr when ye were in a poor way; fear God, then, haply ye may give thanks. When thou didst say unto

[18] This refers to the battle of Ohod, when Mohammed experienced a severe check, and lost two teeth by a shot from an arrow.

the believers, 'Is it not enough for you that your Lord assists you with three thousand of the angels sent down from on high? Yea, if ye are patient and fear God, and they come upon you on a sudden, now, your Lord will assist you with five thousand of His angels, (angels) of mark. God only made this as glad tidings for you to comfort your hearts withal,—for victory is but from God, the mighty, the wise;—to cut off the flank of those who misbelieve, or make them downcast, that they may retire disappointed.'

Thou hast nothing to do with the affair at all, whether He turn towards them again or punish them; for, verily, they are unjust.

God's is what is in the heavens and in the earth. He forgives whom He pleases, and punishes whom He pleases; for God is forgiving and merciful.

O ye who believe! devour not usury doubly doubled, but fear God, perchance ye may be prosperous; fear the fire which is prepared for the unbelievers, and obey God and His Apostle, perchance ye may get mercy. And vie with one another for pardon from your Lord, and for Paradise, the breadth of which is as the heaven and the earth, prepared for those who fear;—for those who expend in alms, in prosperity and adversity, for those who repress their rage, and those who pardon men; God loves the kind. Those who when they do a crime, or wrong themselves, remember God, and ask forgiveness for their sins,—and who forgives sins save God?—and do not persevere in what they did, the while they know;—these have their reward:—pardon from their Lord, and gardens beneath which rivers flow, dwelling therein for aye; for pleasant is the hire of those who act like this.

Incidents have passed before your time, go on then in the earth, and see what was the end of those who called (the prophets) liars.

This is an explanation unto men, and a guidance and a warning unto those who fear. Do not give way nor grieve, for ye shall have the upper hand if ye but be believers.

If a sore touch you, a sore like it has touched people: these are days[19] which we make to alternate amongst mankind that God may know who it is that believe, and may take from you witnesses,[20] for

[19] Or 'battles.'   [20] Or 'martyrs.'

God loves not the unjust; and that God may assay those who believe, and blot out the misbelievers. Do ye think that ye can enter Paradise and God not know those of you who have fought well, or know the patient? Why, ye longed for death before ye met it! Now ye have looked upon it and ye halt!

Mohammed is but an apostle; apostles have passed away before his time; what if he die or is killed, will ye retreat upon your heels? He who retreats upon his heels does no harm to God at all; but God will recompense the thankful. It is not for any soul to die, save by God's permission written down for an appointed time; but he who wishes for the reward of this world we will give him of it, and he who wishes for the reward of the future we will give him of it, and we will recompense the grateful.

How many prophets have myriads fought against! yet they did not give way at what befel them in God's way! Nor were they weak, nor did they demean themselves:—God loves the patient. And their word was only to say, 'Lord, forgive us our sins and our extravagance in our affairs; and make firm our footing, and help us against the misbelieving folk!' and God gave them the reward of this world, and good reward for the future too, for God doth love the kind.

O ye who believe! if ye obey those who misbelieve, they will turn you back upon your heels, and ye will retreat the losers. Nay, God is your Lord, He is the best of helpers. We will throw dread into the hearts of those who misbelieve, for that they associate that with God which He has sent down no power for; but their resort is fire, and evil is the resort of the unjust.

God has truly kept His promise, when ye knocked them senseless by His permission, until ye showed cowardice, and wrangled, and rebelled, after he had shown you what ye loved. Amongst you are those who love this world, and amongst you are those who love the next. Then He turned you away from them to try you; but He has pardoned you, for God is Lord of grace unto believers,—when ye went up and looked not round upon any one, although the Apostle was calling you from your rear. Therefore did God reward you with trouble on trouble that ye should not grieve after what ye had missed,[21] nor for what befell you, for God is well aware of what ye

[21] Plunder.

do. Then He sent down upon you after trouble safety,—drowsiness creeping over one company of you, and one company of you getting anxious about themselves, suspecting about God other than the truth, with the suspicion of the ignorant,[22] and saying, 'Have we any chance in the affair?' Say, 'Verily, the affair is God's.' They conceal in themselves what they will not show to thee, and say, 'If we had any chance in the affair we should not be killed here.' Say, 'If ye were in your houses, surely those against whom slaughter was written down, would have gone forth to fight even to where they are lying now; that God may try what is in your breasts and assay what is in your hearts, for God doth know the nature of men's breasts.'

Verily, those of you who turned your backs on that day when the two armies met, it was but Satan who made them slip for something they had earned. But God has now pardoned them; verily, God is forgiving and clement.

O ye who believe! be not like those who misbelieve, and say unto their brethren when they knock about in the earth, or are upon a raid, 'Had they but been at home, they had not died and had not been killed.' It was that God might make a sighing in their hearts, for God gives life and death; and God on what ye do doth look.

And if, indeed, ye be killed in God's way or die, surely forgiveness from God and mercy is better than what ye gather; and if ye die or be killed it is to God ye shall be assembled. It was by a sort of mercy from God thou didst deal gently with them, for hadst thou been rough and rude of heart they had dispersed from around thee. But pardon them, and ask forgiveness for them, and take counsel with them in the affair. As for what thou hast resolved, rely upon God; verily, God loves those who do rely. If God help you, there is none can overcome you; but if He leave you in the lurch, who is there can help you after Him? Upon God then let believers rely.

It is not for the prophet to cheat; and he who cheats shall bring what he has cheated on the resurrection day. Then shall each soul be paid what it has earned, and they shall not be wronged. Is he who follows the pleasure of God, like him who has drawn on himself

[22] This word is always used for the pagan Arabs.

anger from God, whose resort is hell? An evil journey shall it be! These are degrees with God, and God sees what ye do.

God was surely very gracious to the believers, when He sent amongst them an apostle from themselves, to recite to them His signs, and purify them, and teach them the Book and wisdom, although they surely were before his time in manifest error. Or when an accident befalls you, and ye have fallen on twice as much, ye say, 'How is this[23]?' Say, 'It is from themselves. Verily, God is mighty over all.'

And what befell you the day when the two armies met, it was by God's permission; that He might know the believers, and might know those who behaved hypocritically; for it was said to them, 'Come, fight in God's way,' or 'repel (the foe);' they said, 'If we knew how to fight we would surely follow you.' They were that day far nigher unto misbelief than they were to faith. They say with their mouths what is not in their hearts, but God doth know best what they hid. Those who said of their brethren, whilst they themselves stayed at home, 'Had they obeyed us they would not have been killed.' Say, 'Ward off from yourselves death, if ye do speak the truth.'

Count not those who are killed in the way of God as dead but living with their Lord;—provided for, rejoicing in what God has brought them of His grace, and being glad for those who have not reached them yet,—those left behind them; there is no fear for them, and they shall not be grieved; glad at favour from God and grace, and that God wasteth not the hire of the believers. Whoso answered to the call of God and of His prophet after sorrow had befallen them, for those, if they do good and fear God, is a mighty hire. To whom when men said, 'Verily, men have gathered round you, fear then them,' it only increased their faith, and they said, 'God is enough for us, a good guardian is He.' Then they retired in favour from God and grace; no evil touched them; they followed the pleasure of God, and God is Lord of mighty grace.

It is only that Satan who frightens his friends. Do not ye fear them, but fear me, if ye be believers.

---

[23] He means that the loss at Ohod was more than counterbalanced by their previous success at Bedr.

Let them not grieve thee who vie with each other in misbelief. Verily, they cannot hurt God at all. God wills not to make for them a portion in the future life; but for them is mighty woe.

Verily, those who purchase misbelief for faith, they do not hurt God at all, and for them is grievous woe.

Let not those who misbelieve reckon that our letting them range is good for themselves. We only let them have their range that they may increase in sin. And for them is shameful woe. God would not leave believers in the state which ye are in, until He discerns the vile from the good. And God would not inform you of the unseen, but God chooses of His apostles whom He pleases. Wherefore believe ye in God and His Apostle; and if ye believe and fear, for you is mighty hire.

And let not those who are niggard of what God has given them of His grace, count that it is best for them;—nay, it is worse for them. What they have been niggard of shall be a collar round their necks upon the resurrection day. And God's is the heritage of the heavens and the earth, and God of what ye do is well aware.

God heard the speech of those who said, 'Verily, God is poor[24] and we are rich.' We will write down what they said, and how they killed the prophets undeservedly, and say, 'Taste ye the torment of burning;' this shall they suffer for what their hands have sent on before;—for, verily, God is no unjust one to His servants,—who say, 'Verily, God has covenanted with us that we should not believe in an apostle until he gives us a sacrifice which fire devours.'[25]

Say, 'There have come to you apostles before me with manifest signs, and with what ye talk about; why then did ye kill them, if ye speak the truth?'

And if they did call thee a liar, apostles before thee have been called liars too, who came with manifest signs, and with scriptures, and with the illuminating Book.

[24] Mohammed, in his message to the Jewish tribe of Kainûka, used the words of the Qur'ân, and bade them 'lend to God at good interest,' when Phineas Ibn Azûra mockingly said, 'Surely, God is poor since they try to borrow for him!' Whereupon Abu Bekr, who had brought the letter, smote him on the face and said, that, but for the truce between them, he would have smitten off his head. On complaint being made of this conduct to Mohammed the above verse was revealed.

[25] The commentators say that the Jewish Rabbis demanded of Mohammed this proof of his prophetic mission, having regard, probably, to the contest between Elijah and the priests of Baal on Mount Carmel.

Every soul must taste of death; and ye shall only be paid your hire upon the resurrection day. But he who is forced away from the fire and brought into Paradise is indeed happy; but the life of this world is but a possession of deceit. Ye shall surely be tried in your wealth, and in your persons, and ye shall surely hear from those who have had the Book brought them before you, and from those who associate others with God, much harm. But if ye be patient and fear,—verily, that is one of the determined affairs.

When God took the compact from those who have had the Book brought them that 'Ye shall of a surety manifest it unto men, and not hide it,' they cast it behind their backs, and bought therewith a little price,—but evil is what they buy.

Count not that those who rejoice in what they have produced, and love to be praised for what they have not done,—think not that they are in safety from woe,—for them is grievous woe!

God's is the kingdom of the heavens and the earth, and God is mighty over all!

Verily, in the creation of the heavens and the earth, and in the succession of night and day, are signs to those possessed of minds; who remember God standing and sitting or lying on their sides, and reflect on the creation of the heavens and the earth. 'O Lord! thou hast not created this in vain. We celebrate Thy praise; then keep us from the torment of the fire! Lord! verily, whomsoever Thou hast made to enter the fire, Thou hast disgraced him; and the unjust shall have none to help them.

'Lord! verily, we heard a crier calling to the faith, "Believe in your Lord," and we did believe. Lord! forgive us our sins and cover our offences, and let us die with the righteous. Lord! and bring us what Thou hast promised us by Thy apostles, and disgrace us not upon the resurrection day; for, verily, Thou dost not break Thy promises!' And the Lord shall answer them, 'I waste not the works of a worker amongst you, be it male or female,—one of you is from the other.[26]

'Those who fled, and were turned out of their houses, and were harmed in my way, and who fought and were killed, I will cover

[26] This passage was revealed in answer to the objection of Umm Salmâ, one of Mohammed's wives, when the women who fled with him were not mentioned as well as the men in the promised reward of the future life.

their offences, and I will make them enter into gardens beneath which rivers flow.' A reward from God; for God, with Him are the best of rewards.

Let it not deceive you that those who misbelieve go to and fro in the earth. It is a slight possession, and then their resort is Hell; an evil couch shall it be. But those who fear their Lord, for them are gardens beneath which rivers flow, and they shall dwell therein for aye,—an entertainment from God; and that which is with God is best for the righteous.

Verily, of the people of the Book are some who do believe in God, and in what has been revealed to you, and what was revealed to them, humbling themselves before God, and selling not the signs of God for a little price. These shall have their reward with their Lord; verily, God is quick at reckoning up.

O ye who believe! be patient and vie in being patient,[27] and be on the alert, and fear God, that haply ye may prosper.

THE CHAPTER OF THE RANKS

In the name of the merciful and compassionate God.

What is in the heavens and what is in the earth celebrates the praises of God, for He is the mighty, the wise!

O ye who believe! say not what ye do not. It is most hateful to God that ye say what ye do not.

Verily, God loves those who fight in His cause in ranks as though they were a compact building.[1]

When Moses said to his people, 'O my people! why do ye hurt me, when ye know that I am the apostle of God to you?' and when they swerved, God made their hearts to swerve; for God guides not the people who work abomination!

And when Jesus the son of Mary said, 'O children of Israel! verily, I am the apostle of God to you, verifying the law that was before me and giving you glad tidings of an apostle who shall come after me, whose name shall be A'hmed[2]!'—but when he did come to them with manifest signs, they said, 'This is manifest sorcery!'

---

[27] That is, with their enemies.   [1] Who fight in close and unbroken lines.

[2] A'hmed is equivalent in meaning to Mohammed, and means 'Praised,' 'Laudable.' The allusion is to the promise of the Paraclete in John xvi. 7, the Muslims declaring that the word παράκλητος has been substituted in the Greek for περικλυτός, which would mean the same as A'hmed.

And who is more unjust than he who forges against God a lie when called unto Islâm? but God guides not the unjust people.

They desire to put out the light of God with their mouths; but God will perfect His light, averse although the misbeliever be!

He it is who sent His Apostle with guidance and the religion of truth to set it above all religion; averse although the idolaters may be.

O ye who believe! shall I lead you to a merchandise which will save you from grievous woe?

To believe in God and His Apostle, and to fight strenuously in God's cause with your property and your persons; that is better for you if ye did but know!

He will pardon you your sins, and bring you into gardens beneath which rivers flow, and goodly dwellings in gardens of Eden;—that is the mighty bliss!

And other things which ye love,—help from God and victory nigh! so do thou give the glad tidings unto the believers!

O ye who believe! be ye the helpers[3] of God! as Jesus son of Mary said to the apostles, 'Who are my helpers for God?' Said the apostles, 'We are God's helpers!'

And a party of the children of Israel believed, and a party mis believed. And we aided those who believed against their enemies, and they were on the morrow superior!

THE CHAPTER OF WOMEN

IN the name of the merciful and compassionate God.

O ye folk! fear your Lord, who created you from one soul, and created therefrom its mate, and diffused from them twain many men and women. And fear God, in whose name ye beg of one another, and the wombs; verily, God over you doth watch.[1]

And give unto the orphans their property, and give them not the vile in exchange for the good, and devour not their property to your own property; verily, that were a great sin. But if ye fear that ye cannot do justice between orphans, then marry what seems good to you of women, by twos, or threes, or fours; and if ye fear that ye

---

[3] Ansár.
[1] That is, fear God, and pay respect to your mothers and wives.

cannot be equitable, then only one, or what your right hands possess.[2] That keeps you nearer to not being partial.

And give women their dowries freely; and if they are good enough to remit any of it of themselves, then devour it with good digestion and appetite.[3]

But do not give up to fools[4] their property which God has made you to stand by; but maintain them from it, and clothe them, and speak to them with a reasonable speech. Prove orphans until they reach a marriageable age, and if ye perceive in them right management, then hand over to them their property, and do not devour it extravagantly in anticipation of their growing up. And he who is rich, let him abstain; but he who is poor, let him devour in reason, and when ye hand over to them their property, then take witnesses against them; but God sufficeth for taking account.

Men should have a portion of what their parents and kindred leave, and women should have a portion of what their parents and kindred leave, whether it be little or much, a determined portion. And when the next of kin and the orphans and the poor are present at the division, then maintain them out of it, and speak to them a reasonable speech. And let these fear lest they leave behind them a weak seed, for whom they would be afraid; and let them fear God, and speak a straightforward speech. Verily, those who devour the property of orphans unjustly, only devour into their bellies fire, and they shall broil in flames.

God instructs you concerning your children; for a male the like of the portion of two females, and if there be women above two, then let them have two-thirds of what (the deceased) leaves; and if there be but one, then let her have a half; and as to the parents, to each of them a sixth of what he leaves, if he has a son; but if he have no son, and his parents inherit, then let his mother have a third, and if he have brethren, let his mother have a sixth after payment of the bequest he bequeaths and of his debt.

[2] That is, female slaves.
[3] The Arabic idiom for the enjoyment of property being to eat it up, Mohammed here gives the men permission to enjoy such portion of their wives' dowries as the latter might be pleased to remit, and adds, with a sort of humour, the colloquial expression used by the Arabs when any one is eating. The sentence might be paraphrased 'and if they are kind enough to remit any portion of it of their own accord, then enjoy it, and much good may it do you!'   [4] To idiots or persons of weak intellect.

Your parents or your children, ye know not which of them is nearest to you in usefulness:—an ordinance this from God; verily, God is knowing and wise! And ye shall have half of what your wives leave, if they have no son; but if they have a son, then ye shall have a fourth of what they leave, after payment of the bequests they bequeath or of their debts. And they shall have a fourth of what ye leave, if ye have no son; but if ye have a son, then let them have an eighth of what ye leave, after payment of the bequest ye bequeath and of your debts.

And if the man's or the woman's (property) be inherited by a kinsman who is neither parent nor child, and he have a brother or sister, then let each of these two have a sixth; but if they are more than that, let them share in a third after payment of the bequest he bequeaths and of his debts, without prejudice,[5]—an ordinance this from God, and God is knowing and clement!

These be God's bounds, and whoso obeys God and the Apostle He will make him enter into gardens beneath which rivers flow, and they shall dwell therein for aye;—that is the mighty happiness.

But whoso rebels against God and His Apostle, and transgresses His bounds, He will make him enter into fire, and dwell therein for aye; and for him is shameful woe.

Against those of your women who commit adultery, call witnesses four in number from among yourselves; and if these bear witness, then keep the women in houses[6] until death release them, or God shall make for them a way.

And if two of you commit it, then hurt them both[7]; but if they turn again and amend, leave them alone, verily, God is easily turned, compassionate.

God is only bound to turn again towards those who do evil through ignorance and then turn again. Surely, these will God turn again to, for God is knowing, wise. His turning again is not for those who do evil, until, when death comes before one of them, he

---

[5] I. e. to the heirs.

[6] Women taken in adultery or fornication were at the beginning of Islâm literally immured.

[7] The commentators are not agreed as to the nature of the offence here referred to. The text, however, speaks of two of the masculine gender. The punishment to be inflicted is also the subject of dispute, the original merely saying, as I have translated it, 'hurt them.'

says, 'Now I turn again;' nor yet for those who die in misbelief. For such as these have we prepared a grievous woe.

O ye who believe! it is not lawful for you to inherit women's estates against their will; nor to hinder them,[8] that ye may go off with part of what ye brought them, unless they commit fornication manifestly; but associate with them in reason, for if ye are averse from them, it may be that ye are averse from something wherein God has put much good for you.

But if ye wish to exchange one wife for another, and have given one of them a talent,[9] then take not from it anything. What! would you take it for a calumny and a manifest crime[10]?

How can ye take it when one of you has gone in unto the other, and they have taken from you a rigid compact?

And do not marry women your fathers married,—except bygones, —for it is abominable and hateful, and an evil way; unlawful for you are your mothers, and your daughters, and your sisters, and your paternal aunts and maternal aunts, and your brother's daughters, and your sister's daughters, and your foster mothers, and your foster sisters, and your wives' mothers, and your step daughters who are your wards, born of your wives to whom ye have gone in; but if ye have not gone in unto them, then it is no crime in you; and the lawful spouses of your sons from your own loins, and that ye form a connexion between two sisters,—except bygones,—verily, God is forgiving, merciful; and married women, save such as your right hands possess,—God's Book against you!—but lawful for you is all besides this, for you to seek them with your wealth, marrying them and not fornicating; but such of them as ye have enjoyed, give them their hire as a lawful due; for there is no crime in you about what ye agree between you after such lawful due, verily, God is knowing and wise.

But whosoever of you cannot go the length of marrying marriageable women who believe, then take of what your right hands possess, of your maidens who believe;—though God knows best about your faith. Ye come one from the other; then marry them with the

---

[8] That is, from marrying again.   [9] That is, a large dowry.

[10] This question is ironical, and intended as a warning against bringing a false accusation of infidelity against a wife for the sake of keeping her dowry when divorced.

permission of their people, and give them their hire in reason, they being chaste and not fornicating, and not receivers of paramours.

But when they are married, if they commit fornication, then inflict upon them half the penalty for married women; that is for whomsoever of you fears wrong; but that ye should have patience is better for you, and God is forgiving and merciful.

God wishes to explain to you and to guide you into the ordinances of those who were before you, and to turn towards you, for God is knowing, wise. God wishes to turn towards you, but those who follow their lusts wish that ye should swerve with a mighty swerving! God wishes to make it light for you, for man was created weak.

O ye who believe! devour not your property amongst yourselves vainly, unless it be a merchandise by mutual consent. And do not kill yourselves; verily, God is compassionate unto you.

But whoso does that maliciously and unjustly, we will broil him with fire; for that is easy with God.

If ye avoid great sins from which ye are forbidden, we will cover your offences and make you enter with a noble entrance.

And do not covet that by which God has preferred one of you over another. The men shall have a portion of what they earn, and the women a portion of what they earn; ask God for His grace, verily, God knows all.

To every one have we appointed kinsfolk as heirs of what parents and relatives and those with whom ye have joined right hands leave; so give them their portion, for, verily, God is over all a witness.

Men stand superior to women in that God hath preferred some of them over others, and in that they expend of their wealth: and the virtuous women, devoted, careful (in their husbands') absence, as God has cared for them. But those whose perverseness ye fear, admonish them and remove them into bed-chambers and beat them; but if they submit to you, then do not seek a way against them; verily, God is high and great.

And if ye fear a breach between the two,[11] then send a judge from his people and a judge from her people. If they wish for reconciliation, God will arrange between them; verily, God is knowing and aware.

[11] Man and wife.

And serve God, and do not associate aught with Him; and to your parents show kindness, and to kindred, and orphans, and the poor, and the neighbour who is akin, and the neighbour who is a stranger, and the companion who is strange, and the son of the road, and what your right hands possess,[12] verily, God loves not him who is proud and boastful; who are miserly and bid men be miserly too, and who hide what God has given them of His grace;—but we have prepared for the misbelievers' shameful woe.

And those who expend their wealth in alms for appearance sake before men, and who believe not in God nor in the last day;—but whosoever has Satan for his mate, an evil mate has he.

What harm would it do them if they believed in God and in the last day, and expended in alms of what God has provided them with? but God knows about them.

Verily, God would not wrong by the weight of an atom; and if it's a good work, He will double it and bring from Himself a mighty hire.

How then when we bring from every nation a witness, and bring thee as a witness against these on the day when those who misbelieve and rebel against the Apostle would fain that the earth were levelled with them? but they cannot hide the news from God.

O ye who believe! approach not prayer while ye are drunk, until ye well know what ye say; nor yet while polluted,—unless ye be passing by the way,—until ye have washed yourselves. But if ye are sick, or on a journey, or one of you come from the privy, or if ye have touched a woman, and ye cannot find water, then use good surface sand and wipe your faces and your hands therewith; verily, God pardons and forgives.

Do ye not see those who have been given a portion of the Book? they buy error, and they wish that ye may err from the way! But God knows best who your enemies are, and God suffices as a patron, and sufficient is God as a help.

And those who are Jews, and those who pervert the words from their places, and say, 'We hear but we rebel, and do thou listen without hearing,' and (who say) 'râ'hinâ,'[13] distorting it with their tongues and taunting about religion. But had they said, 'We hear

---

[12] I. e. slaves. [13] The Jewish Arabs used this word derisively.

and we obey, so listen and look upon us,' it would have been better for them and more upright;—but may God curse them in their misbelief, for they will not believe except a few.

O ye who have been given the Book! believe in what we have revealed, confirming what ye had before; ere we deface your faces and turn them into hinder parts, or curse you as we cursed the fellows of the Sabbath[14] when God's command was done.

Verily, God pardons not associating aught with Him, but He pardons anything short of that to whomsoever He pleases; but he who associates aught with God, he hath devised a mighty sin.

Do ye not see those who purify themselves? nay, God purifies whom He will, and they shall not be wronged a straw.[15]

Behold, how they devise against God a lie, and that is manifest sin enough.

Do ye not see those to whom a portion of the Book has been given? They believe in Gibt[16] and Tâghût,[16] and they say of those who misbelieve, 'These are better guided in the way than those who believe.' These are those whom God has cursed, and whom God has cursed no helper shall he find.

Shall they have a portion of the kingdom? Why even then they would not give to men a jot.[17]

Do they envy man for what God has given of His grace? We have given to Abraham's people the Book and wisdom, and we have given them a mighty kingdom. And of them are some who believe therein, and of them are some who turn from it, but Hell is flaming enough for them.

Verily, those who disbelieve in our signs, we will broil them with fire; whenever their skins are well done, then we will change them for other skins, that they may taste the torment. Verily, God is glorious and wise.

But those who believe and do aright, we will make them enter gardens beneath which rivers flow, and they shall dwell therein for ever and aye, for them therein are pure wives, and we will make them enter into a shady shade. Verily, God bids you pay your trusts

[14] Turning them into apes.

[15] The word in the original means a fibre in the cleft of a date stone, or the rush wick of a candle.

[16] Idols of the ancient Arabs.   [17] Literally, a dent or cleft in a date stone.

to their owners, and when ye judge between men to judge with justice. Verily, God, excellent is what He admonishes you with; verily, God both hears and sees.

O ye who believe! obey God, and obey the Apostle and those in authority amongst you; and if ye quarrel about anything, refer to God and the Apostle, if ye believe in God and the last day; that is better and fairer as a settlement.

Do ye not see those who pretend that they believe in what has been revealed to them, and what was revealed before thee; they wish to refer their judgment to Tâghût, but they are bidden to disbelieve therein, and Satan wishes to lead them into a remote error. And when it is said to them, 'Come round to what God has sent down and unto the Apostle,' thou seest the hypocrites turning from thee, turning away.

How then when there befalls them a mischance through what their hands have sent on before? then will they come to you, and swear by God, 'We meant naught but good and concord.' These, God knows what is in their hearts. Turn thou away from them and admonish them, and speak to them into their souls with a searching word.

We have never sent an apostle save that he should be obeyed by the permission of God; and if they, when they have wronged themselves, come to thee and ask pardon of God, and the Apostle asks pardon for them, then they will find God easy to be turned, compassionate.

But no! by thy Lord! they will not believe, until they have made thee judge of what they differ on; then they will not find in themselves aught to hinder what thou hast decreed, and they will submit with submission. But had we prescribed for them, 'Kill yourselves, or go ye forth out of your houses,' they would not have done it, save only a few of them; but had they done what they are admonished, then it would have been better for them, and a more firm assurance.

And then we would surely have brought them from ourselves a mighty hire, and would have guided them into a right path.

Whoso obeys God and the Apostle, these are with those God has been pleased with, of prophets and confessors and martyrs and the righteous;—a fair company are they.

That is grace from God, and God knows well enough.

O ye who believe! take your precautions and sally in detachments or altogether. Verily, there is of you who tarries behind, and, if a mischance befalls you, says, 'God has been gracious to me, since I am not with them a martyr.'

But if there befalls you grace from God, he would say—as though there were no friendship between you and him—'O would that I had been with thee to attain this mighty happiness!' Let those then fight in God's way who sell this life of the world for the next; and whoso fights in God's way, then, be he killed or be he victorious, we will give him a mighty hire.

What ails you that ye do not fight in God's way, and for the weak men and women and children, who say, 'Lord, bring us out of this town[18] of oppressive folk, and make for us from Thee a patron, and make for us from Thee a help?'

Those who believe fight in the way of God; and those who disbelieve fight in the way of Tâghût; fight ye then against the friends of Satan, verily, Satan's tricks are weak.

Do ye not see those to whom it is said, 'Restrain your hands, and be steadfast in prayer and give alms;' and when it is prescribed for them to fight then a band of them fear men, as though it were the fear of God or a still stronger fear, and they say, 'O our Lord! why hast thou prescribed for us to fight, couldst thou not let us abide till our near appointed time?' Say, 'The enjoyment of this world is but slight, and the next is better for him who fears;'—but they shall not be wronged a straw.

Wheresoe'er ye be death will overtake you, though ye were in lofty towers. And if a good thing befall them, they say, 'This is from God,' but if a bad thing, they say, 'This is from thee.' Say, 'It is all from God.' What ails these people? they can hardly understand a tale.

What befalls thee of good it is from God; and what befalls thee of bad it is from thyself. We have sent thee to mankind as an apostle, and God sufficeth for a witness.

Whoso obeys the prophet he has obeyed God; and he who turns back—we have not sent thee to watch over them.

[18] Mecca.

They say, 'Obedience!' but when they sally forth from you, a company of them brood by night over something else than that which thou hast said; but God writes down that over which they brood. Turn then from them and rely on God, for God sufficeth for a guardian. Do they not meditate on the Qur'ân? if it were from other than God they would find in it many a discrepancy.

And when there comes to them a matter of security or fear they publish it; but if they were to report it to the Apostle and to those in authority amongst them, then those of them who would elicit it from them would know it; but were it not for God's grace upon you and His mercy ye had followed Satan, save a few.

Fight, then, in the way of God; impose not aught on any but thyself, and urge on the believers; it may be that God will restrain the violence of those who misbelieve, for God is more violent and more severe to punish.

Whoso intercedes with a good intercession shall have a portion therefrom; but he who intercedes with a bad intercession shall have the like thereof, for God keeps watch over all things.

And when ye are saluted with a salutation, salute with a better than it, or return it;—verily, God of all things takes account.

God, there is no God but He! He will surely assemble you on the resurrection day, there is no doubt therein; who is truer than God in his discourse?

Why are ye two parties about the hypocrites, when God hath overturned them for what they earned? Do ye wish to guide those whom God hath led astray? Whoso God hath led astray ye shall not surely find for him a path. They would fain that ye misbelieve as they misbelieve, that ye might be alike; take ye not patrons from among them until they too flee in God's way; but if they turn their backs, then seize them and kill them wheresoever ye find them, and take from them neither patron nor help,—save those who reach a people betwixt whom and you is an alliance—or who come to you while their bosoms prevent them from fighting you or fighting their own people. But had God pleased He would have given you dominion over them, and they would surely have fought you. But if they retire from you and do not fight you, and offer you peace,—then God hath given you no way against them.

Ye will find others who seek for quarter from you, and quarter from their own people; whenever they return to sedition they shall be overturned therein: but if they retire not from you, nor offer you peace, nor restrain their hands, then seize them and kill them wheresoever ye find them;—over these we have made for you manifest power.

It is not for a believer to kill a believer save by mistake; and whosoever kills a believer by mistake then let him free a believing neck[19]; and the blood-money must be paid to his people save what they shall remit as alms. But if he be from a tribe hostile to you and yet a believer, then let him free a believing neck. And if it be a tribe betwixt whom and you there is an alliance, then let the blood-money be paid to his friends, and let him free a believing neck; but he who cannot find the means, then let him fast for two consecutive months —a penance this from God, for God is knowing, wise.

And whoso kills a believer purposely, his reward is hell, to dwell therein for aye; and God will be wrath with him, and curse him, and prepare for him a mighty woe.

O ye who believe! when ye are knocking about in the way of God be discerning, and do not say to him who offers you a salutation, 'Thou art no believer,' craving after the chances of this world's life,[20] for with God are many spoils! So were ye aforetime, but God was gracious to you, be ye then discerning; verily, God of what ye do is well aware.

Not alike are those of the believers who sit at home without harm, and those who are strenuous in God's way with their wealth and their persons. God hath preferred those who are strenuous with their wealth and their persons to those who sit still, by many degrees, and to each hath God promised good, but God hath preferred the strenuous for a mighty hire over those who sit still,—degrees from him, and pardon and mercy, for God is forgiving and merciful.

Verily, the angels when they took the souls of those who had wronged themselves,[21] said, 'What state were ye in?' they say, 'We were but weak in the earth;' they said, 'Was not God's earth

[19] Captive.
[20] Because a believer might not be attacked and plundered as an infidel might be.
[21] Alluding to some half-hearted Muslims, slain at Bedr.

wide enough for you to flee away therein?' These are those whose resort is hell, and a bad journey shall it be!

Save for the weak men, and women, and children, who could not compass any stratagem, and were not guided to a way; these it may be God will pardon, for God both pardons and forgives.

Whosoever flees in the way of God shall find in the earth many a spacious refuge; and he who goes forth from his house, fleeing unto God and His prophet, and then death catches him up,—his hire devolves on God, and God is forgiving and merciful.

And when ye knock about in the earth, it is no crime to you that ye come short in prayer, if ye fear that those who disbelieve will set upon you; verily, the misbelievers are your obvious foes.

When thou art amongst them, and standest up to pray with them, then let a party of them stand up with thee, and let them take their arms; and when they adore, let them go behind you, and let another party who have not yet prayed come forward and pray with thee; and let them take their precautions and their arms.

Fain would those who misbelieve that ye were careless of your arms and your baggage, that they might turn upon you with a single turning. And it is no crime to you if ye be annoyed with rain or be sick, that ye lay down your arms; but take your precautions,—verily, God has prepared for those who misbelieve a shameful woe.

But when ye have fulfilled your prayer, remember God standing and sitting and lying on your sides; and when ye are in safety then be steadfast in prayer; verily, prayer is for the believers prescribed and timed!

And do not give way in pursuit of the people; if ye suffer they shall surely suffer too, even as ye suffer; and ye hope from God, but they hope not! and God is knowing, wise.

Verily, we have revealed to thee the Book in truth that thou mayest judge between men of what God has shown thee; so be not with the treacherous a disputant; but ask God's pardon: verily, God is forgiving, merciful.

And wrangle not for those who defraud themselves; for God loves not him who is a fraudulent sinner. They hide themselves from men; but they cannot hide themselves from God, for He is with them while they brood at night over speeches that please Him not;—but God doth compass what they do!

Here are ye, wrangling for them about this world's life;—but who shall wrangle with God for them on the day of judgment, or who shall be a guardian over them?

Yet whoso does evil and wrongs himself, and then asks pardon of God, shall find God forgiving and merciful; and whoso commits a crime, he only commits it against himself, for God is knowing, wise.

And whoso commits a fault or a sin and throws it on the innocent, he hath to bear a calumny and a manifest sin.

Were it not for God's grace upon thee, and His mercy, a party of them would have tried to lead thee astray; but they only lead themselves astray; they shall not hurt you in aught: for God hath sent down upon thee the Book and the wisdom, and taught thee what thou didst not know, for God's grace was mighty on thee.

There is no good in most of what they talk in private; save in his who bids almsgiving, or kindness, or reconciliation between men; and whoso does this, craving the good pleasure of God, we will give to him a mighty hire.

But he who severs himself from the prophet after that we have made manifest to him the guidance, and follows other than the way of the believers, we will turn our backs on him as he hath turned his back; and we will make him reach hell, and a bad journey shall it be.

Verily, God forgives not associating aught with Him, but He pardons anything short of that, to whomsoever He will; but whoso associates aught with God, he hath erred a wide error.

Verily, they call not beside Him on aught save females; and they do not call on aught save a rebellious devil.

God curse him! for he said, 'I will take from thy servants a portion due to me; and I will lead them astray; and I will stir up vain desires within them; and I will order them and they shall surely crop the ears of cattle; and I will order them and they shall surely alter God's creation[22];' but he who takes the devil for his patron

[22] The pagan Arabs used to cut off the ears of cattle, and mutilate their slaves by branding, and filing their teeth, partly that they might recognise them and partly as a superstitious ceremony.

instead of God, he loses with a manifest loss. He promises them, and stirs up vain desires within them; but the devil promises only to deceive.

These, their resort is hell; they shall not find an escape therefrom! But those who believe, and do what is right, we will make them enter into gardens beneath which rivers flow, to dwell therein for aye,— God's promise in truth; and who is truer than God in speech? Not for your vain desires, nor the vain desires of the people of the Book. He who doeth evil shall be recompensed therewith, and shall not find for him beside God a patron, or a help. But he who doeth good works,—be it male or female,—and believes, they shall enter into Paradise, and they shall not be wronged a jot.

Who has a better religion than he who resigns his face to God, and does good, and follows the faith of Abraham, as a 'Hanîf?—for God took Abraham as a friend.

And God's is what is in the heavens and in the earth, and God encompasses all things!

They will ask thee a decision about women; say, 'God decides for you about them, and that which is rehearsed to you in the Book; about orphan women to whom ye do not give what is prescribed for them, and whom ye are averse from marrying; and about weak children; and that ye stand fairly by orphans;—and what ye do of good, verily, that God knows.'

And if a woman fears from her husband perverseness or aversion, it is no crime in them both that they should be reconciled to each other, for reconciliation is best. For souls are prone to avarice; but if ye act kindly and fear God, of what ye do He is aware.

Ye are not able, it may be, to act equitably to your wives, even though ye covet it; do not however be quite partial, and leave one as it were in suspense; but if ye be reconciled and fear, then God is forgiving and merciful; but if they separate, God can make both independent out of His abundance; for God is abundant, wise.

God's is what is in the heavens and what is in the earth! We have ordained to those who have been given the Book before you, and to you too that ye fear God;—but if ye misbelieve, verily, God's is what is in the heavens and what is in the earth, and God is rich and to be praised!

God's is what is in the heavens and what is in the earth! and God sufficeth for a guardian!

If He will He can make ye pass away, O men! and can bring others;—God is able to do all that.

He who wishes for a reward in this world,—with God is the reward of this world and of the next, and God both hears and sees.

O ye who believe! be ye steadfast in justice, witnessing before God though it be against yourselves, or your parents, or your kindred, be it rich or poor, for God is nearer akin than either.

Follow not, then, lusts, so as to act partially; but if ye swerve or turn aside, God of what ye do is well aware.

O ye who believe! believe in God and His apostles, and the Book which He hath revealed to His Apostles, and the Book which He sent down before; for whoso disbelieves in God, and His angels, and His Apostle, and the last day, has erred a wide error.

Verily, those who believe and then misbelieve, and then believe and then misbelieve, and then increase in misbelief, God will never pardon them, nor will He guide them in the path.

Give to the hypocrites the glad tidings that for them is grievous woe!

Those who take the misbelievers for their patrons rather than believers,—do they crave honour from them? Verily, honour is altogether God's!

He hath revealed this to you in the Book, that when ye hear the signs of God disbelieved in and mocked at, then sit ye not down with them until they plunge into another discourse, for verily, then ye would be like them. Verily, God will gather the hypocrites and misbelievers into hell together.

Those who lie in wait for you, and if the victory be yours from God, say, 'Were we not with you?' and if the misbelievers have a chance, they say, 'Did we not get the mastery over you, and defend you from the believers?' But God shall judge between you on the resurrection day; for God will not give the misbelievers a way against believers.

Verily, the hypocrites seek to deceive God, but He deceives them; and when they rise up to pray, they rise up lazily to be seen of men, and do not remember God, except a few; wavering between the two, neither to these nor yet to those! but whomsoever God doth lead astray thou shall not find for him a way.

O ye who believe! take not misbelievers for patrons rather than believers; do ye wish to make for God a power against you?

Verily, the hypocrites are in the lowest depths of hell-fire, and thou shalt not find for them a help.

Save those who turn again, and do right, and take tight hold on God, and are sincere in religion to God; these are with the believers, and God will give to the believers mighty hire.

Why should God punish you, if ye are grateful and believer for God is grateful and knowing.

God loves not publicity of evil speech, unless one has been wronged; for God both hears and knows.

If ye display good or hide it, or pardon evil, verily, God is pardoning and powerful!

Verily, those who disbelieve in God and His apostles desire to make a distinction between God and His apostles, and say, 'We believe in part and disbelieve in part, and desire to take a midway course between the two': these are the misbelievers, and we have prepared for misbelievers shameful woe! But those who believe in God and His apostles, and who do not make a distinction between any one of them,—to these we will give their hire, for God is forgiving and merciful!

The people of the Book will ask thee to bring down for them a book from heaven; but they asked Moses a greater thing than that, for they said, 'Show us God openly'; but the thunderbolt caught them in their injustice. Then they took the calf, after what had come to them of manifest signs; but we pardoned that, and gave Moses obvious authority. And we held over them the mountain[23] at their compact, and said to them, 'Enter ye the door adoring'; and we said to them, 'Transgress not on the Sabbath day,' and we took from them a rigid compact.

But for that they broke their compact, and for their misbelief in God's signs, and for their killing the prophets undeservedly, and for their saying, 'Our hearts are uncircumcised,'—nay, God hath

[23] The Mohammedan legend is that this was done by the angel Gabriel to terrify the people into obedience.

stamped on them their misbelief, so that they cannot believe except a few,—and for their misbelief, and for their saying about Mary a mighty calumny, and for their saying, 'Verily, we have killed the Messiah, Jesus the son of Mary, the apostle of God,' . . . but they did not kill him, and they did not crucify him, but a similitude was made for them. And verily, those who differ about him are in doubt concerning him; they have no knowledge concerning him, but only follow an opinion. They did not kill him, for sure! nay, God raised him up unto Himself; for God is mighty and wise[24]!

And there shall not be one of the people of the Book but shall believe in him before his death[25]; and on the day of judgment he shall be a witness against them.

And for the injustice of those who are Jews have we forbidden them good things which we had made lawful for them, and for their obstructing so much the way of God, and for their taking usury when we had forbidden it, and for their devouring the wealth of people in vain,—but we have prepared for those of them who misbelieve a grievous woe.

But those amongst them who are firm in knowledge, and the believers who believe in what is revealed to thee, let what is revealed before thee, and the steadfast in prayer, and the givers of alms, and the believers in God and the last day,—unto these we will give a mighty hire.

Verily, we have inspired thee as we inspired Noah and the prophets after him, and as we inspired Abraham, and Ishmael, and Jacob, and the tribes, and Jesus, and Job, and Jonas, and Aaron, and Solomon; and to David did we give Psalms.

Of apostles we have already told thee of some before; and of apostles some we have not told thee of;—

But Moses did God speak to, speaking;—apostles giving glad tidings and warning, that men should have no argument against God, after the apostles, for God is mighty, wise.

But God bears witness to what He has revealed to thee: He revealed it in His knowledge, and the angels bear witness too; though God is witness enough.

[24] See note 7, Chapter of Imrân's Family. [25] This may allude to the time of his death after his second advent, when he shall slay the antichrist.

Verily, those who misbelieve and obstruct the way of God, have erred a wide error.

Verily, those who misbelieve and are unjust, God will not pardon them, nor will He guide them on the road—save the road to hell, to dwell therein for aye;—that is easy enough to God!

O ye folk! the Apostle has come to you with truth from your Lord: believe then, for it is better for you. But if ye misbelieve, then God's is what is in the heavens and the earth, and God is knowing, wise.

O ye people of the Book! do not exceed in your religion, nor say against God aught save the truth. The Messiah, Jeṣus the son of Mary, is but the apostle of God and His Word, which He cast into Mary and a spirit from Him; believe then in God and His apostles, and say not 'Three.' Have done! it were better for you. God is only one God, celebrated be His praise that He should beget a Son! His is what is in the heavens and what is in the earth; and God sufficeth for a guardian.

The Messiah doth surely not disdain to be a servant of God, nor do the angels who are nigh to Him; and whosoever disdains His service and is too proud, He will gather them altogether to Himself.

But as for those who believe and do what is right, He will pay their hire and will give increase to them of His grace. But as for those who disdain and are too proud, He will punish them with a grievous woe, and they shall not find for them other than God a patron or a help.

O ye folk! proof has come to you from your Lord, and we have sent down to you manifest light. As for those who believe in God, and take tight hold of Him, He will make them enter into mercy from Him and grace; and He will guide them to Himself by a right way.

They will ask thee for a decision; say, 'God will give you a decision concerning remote kinship.'

If a man perish and have no child, but have a sister, let her have half of what he leaves; and he shall be her heir, if she have no son. But if there be two sisters, let them both have two thirds of what he leaves; and if there be brethren, both men and women, let the male have like the portion of two females. God makes this manifest to you lest ye err; for God all things doth know.

THE CHAPTER OF THE CONFEDERATES[1]

IN the name of the merciful and compassionate God.

O thou prophet! fear God and obey not the misbelievers and hypocrites; verily, God is ever knowing, wise!

But follow what thou art inspired with from thy Lord; verily, God of what you do is ever well aware. And rely upon God, for God is guardian enough.

God has not made for any man two hearts in his inside; nor has He made your wives,—whom you back away from,—your real mother[2]; nor has He made your adopted sons your real sons. That is what ye speak with your mouths; but God speaks the truth and He guides to the path!

Call them by their fathers' names; that is more just in God's sight; but if ye know not their fathers, then they are your brothers in religion and your clients. There is no crime against you for what mistakes ye make therein; but what your hearts do purposely—but God is ever forgiving and merciful.

The prophet is nearer of kin to the believers than themselves, and his wives are their mothers. And blood relations are nearer in kin to each other by the Book of God than the believers and those who fled[3]; only your doing kindness to your kindred, that is traced in the Book.

And when we took of the prophets their compact,[4] from thee and from Noah, and Abraham, and Moses, and Jesus the son of Mary, and took of them a rigid compact, that He might ask the truth-tellers of their truth. But He has prepared for those who misbelieve a grievous woe.

O ye who believe! remember God's favours towards you when

---

[1] When this sûrah was written Medînah was besieged by a confederation of the Jewish tribes with the Arabs of Mecca, Negd and Tehâmah, at the instigation of the Jewish tribe of Na*dh*îr, whom Mohammed had expelled from Mecca the year before. The event took place in the fifth year of the Higrah.

[2] The Arabs were in the habit of divorcing their wives on certain occasions with the words, 'Thy back is to me as my mother's back,' after which they considered it as unnatural to approach them as though they were their real mothers. This practice Mohammed here forbids. They used also to consider their adopted children in the same light as real children of their body; in forbidding this practice also, Mohammed legalised his marriage with Zâinab, the divorced wife of his freedman Zâid, who was also his adopted son.

[3] The Muhâgerîn.

[4] See note 13, Chapter of Imrân's Family.

hosts came to you and we sent against them a wind and hosts[5] that ye could not see;—and God knew what ye were doing.

When they came upon you from above you and from below[6] you, and when your eyesights were distracted and your hearts came up into your throats, and ye suspected God with certain suspicions.

There were the believers tried and were made to quake with a severe quaking.

And when the hypocrites and those in whose hearts was sickness said, 'God and His Apostle have only promised us deceitfully.' And when a party of them said, 'O people of Yathreb[7]; there is no place for you (here),[8] return then (to the city).' And a part of them asked leave of the prophet (to return), saying, 'Verily, our houses are defenceless;' but they were not defenceless, they only wished for flight.

But had they been entered upon from its environs and then been asked to show treason they would have done so; but they would only have tarried there a little while.[9]

They had covenanted with God before, that they would not turn their backs; and God's covenant shall be enquired of.

Say, 'Flight shall avail you naught; if ye fly from death or slaughter, even then ye shall be granted enjoyment only for a little!'

Say, 'Who is it that can save you from God, if He wish you evil, or wish you mercy?' but they will not find beside God a patron or a helper.

Say, 'God knows the hinderers amongst you, and those who say to their brethren, "Come along unto us," and show but little valour; —covetous towards you.'[10] When fear comes thou wilt see them looking towards thee, their eyes rolling like one fainting with death;

[5] Of angels.

[6] On the approach of the confederate army, to the number of 12,000, Mohammed, by the advice of Selmân the Persian, ordered a deep trench to be dug round Medînah, and himself went out to defend it with 3,000 men. The two forces remained for nearly a month in their respective camps, without coming to an actual conflict: until one night a piercing east wind blew so violently, and made such disorder in the camp of the besiegers, that a panic seized upon them, and they retired precipitately. Some of them had been encamped on the heights to the east of the town, the others in the lower part of the valley.

[7] The ancient name of the city; it was only called 'El Medînah, 'the city,' after it had become famous by giving shelter to Mohammed.

[8] In the trenches.

[9] I. e. if the confederates had effected an entry, these half-hearted persons would have listened to their proposals, and have deserted the prophet.

[10] I. e. chary of helping you, but greedy of the spoils.

but when the fear has passed away they will assail you with sharp tongues, covetous of the best.[11] These have never believed, and God will make vain their works, for that is easy with God.

They reckoned that the confederates would never go away; and if the confederates should come they would fain be in the desert with the Arabs, asking for news of you! and if they were amongst you they would fight but little.

Ye had in the Apostle of God a good example for him who hopes for God and the last day, and who remembers God much.

And when the believers saw the confederates they said, 'This is what God and His Apostle promised us; God and His Apostle are true!' and it only increased them in faith and resignation.

Amongst the believers are men who have been true to their covenant with God, and there are some who have fulfilled their vow,[12] and some who wait and have not changed[13] with fickleness.

That God might reward the truthful for their truth, and punish the hypocrites if He please, or turn again towards them;—verily, God is forgiving, merciful!

And God drove back the misbelievers in their rage; they gat no advantage;—God was enough for the believers in the fight, for God is strong, mighty!

And He drove down those of the people of the Book who had helped them[14] from their fortresses[15] and hurled dread into their hearts; a part ye slew and ye took captive a part: and He gave you their land, and their dwellings, and their property for an inheritance, and a land ye had not trodden, for God is ever mighty over all.

O thou prophet! say to thy wives, 'If ye be desirous of the life of this world and its adornments, come, I will give you them to enjoy and I will let you range handsomely at large! But if ye be desirous of God and His Apostle and of the abode of the hereafter, verily, God has prepared for those of you who do good a mighty hire[16]!'

---

[11] I. e. the best share of the spoils.

[12] I. e. their vow to fight till they obtained martyrdom.

[13] I. e. changed their mind.

[14] I. e. who had helped the confederates.

[15] The Quráizhah Jews, whom Mohammed attacked after the siege of Medînah had been raised, and punished for their treachery in having joined the confederates although in league with him at the time.

[16] Mohammed being annoyed by the demands made by his wives for costly dresses and the like, offered them the choice of divorce or of being content with their usual mode of living. They chose the latter.

O ye women of the prophet! whosoever of you commits manifest fornication, doubled shall be her torment twice; and that is easy unto God!

But that one of you who is devoted to God and His Apostle and does right we will give her her hire twice over, and we have prepared for her a noble provision.

O ye women of the prophet! ye are not like any other women; if ye fear God then be not too complaisant in speech, or he in whose heart is sickness will lust after you; but speak a reasonable speech.

And stay still in your houses and show not yourselves with the ostentation of the ignorance of yore; and be steadfast in prayer, and give alms, and obey God and His Apostle;—God only wishes to take away from you[17] the horror as people of His House and to purify you thoroughly.

And remember what is recited in your houses of the signs of God and of wisdom; verily, God is subtle and aware!

Verily, men resigned and women resigned,[18] and believing men and believing women, and devout men and devout women, and truthful men and truthful women, and patient men and patient women, and humble men and humble women, and almsgiving men and almsgiving women, and fasting men and fasting women, and men who guard their private parts and women who guard their private parts, and men who remember God much, and women who remember Him,—God has prepared for them forgiveness and a mighty hire.

It is not for a believing man or for a believing woman, when God and His Apostle have decided an affair, to have the choice in that affair; and whoso rebels against God and His Apostle has erred with obvious error.

And when thou didst say to him God had shown favour to and thou hadst shown favour to, 'Keep thy wife to thyself and fear God;' and thou didst conceal in thy soul what God was about to display; and didst fear men, though God is more deserving that thou shouldst

---

[17] Here the pronoun is changed from feminine to masculine, and the passage is appealed to by the Shiahs as showing the intimate relations that existed between Mohammed and 'Ali, for they say that by 'his household' are particularly meant Fatimah and 'Ali. In the next paragraph the feminine is again used.

[18] I. e. Muslims.

fear Him; and when Zâid had fulfilled his desire to her[19] we did wed thee to her that there should be no hindrance to the believers in the matter of the wives of their adopted sons when they have fulfilled their desire of them: and so God's bidding to be done.[20]

There is no hindrance to the prophet about what God has ordained for him;—(such was) the course of God with those who have passed away before,—and God's bidding is a decreed decree! Those who preach God's messages and fear Him and fear not any one except God,—but God is good enough at reckoning up.

Mohammed is not the father of any of your men, but the Apostle of God, and the Seal of the Prophets; for God all things doth know!

O ye who believe! remember God with frequent remembrance, and celebrate His praises morning and evening.

He it is who prays[21] for you and His angels too, to bring you forth out of the darkness into the light, for He is merciful to the believers.

Their salutation on the day they meet Him shall be 'Peace!' and He has prepared for them a noble hire.

O thou prophet! verily, we have sent thee as a witness and a herald of glad tidings and a warner, and to call (men) unto God by His permission, and as an illuminating lamp.

Give glad tidings then to the believers, that for them is great grace from God. And follow not the unbelievers and the hypocrites; but let alone their ill-treatment,[22] and rely upon God, for God is guardian enough.

O ye who believe! when ye wed believing women, and then divorce them before ye have touched them, ye have no term that ye

[19] I. e. divorced her.

[20] Zâid was Mohammed's freedman and adopted son. Mohammed had seen and admired Zâid's wife Zâinab, and her husband at once offered to divorce her: this Mohammed dissuaded him from until the transaction was sanctioned by the verse. The relations of the Arabs to their adopted children were, as has been remarked before, note 2, very strict; and Mohammed's marriage with Zâinab occasioned much scandal among his contemporaries. This passage and those at the commencement of the chapter abrogate all these inconvenient restrictions. Zâid and Abu Laheb are the only two persons of Mohammed's acquaintance who are mentioned in the Qur'ân by name.

[21] The same word is used as is rendered 'pray', in all the other passages in the Qur'ân, though the commentators interpret it here as meaning 'bless.' So, too, in the formula which is always used after Mohammed's name, zalla 'llâhu 'alâihi wa sallam, 'may God bless and preserve him!' is literally, 'may God pray for him and salute him!'

[22] Either, 'do not ill-treat them,' or, 'take no notice of their ill-treating thee.'

need observe; so make them some provision, and let them go handsomely at large.

O thou prophet! verily, we make lawful for thee thy wives to whom thou hast given their hire,[23] and what thy right hand possesses[24] out of the booty that God has granted thee, and the daughters of thy paternal uncle and the daughters of thy paternal aunts, and the daughters of thy maternal uncle and the daughters of thy maternal aunts, provided they have fled with thee, and any believing woman if she give herself to the prophet, if the prophet desire to marry her; —a special privilege this for thee, above the other believers.

We knew what we ordained for them concerning their wives and what their right hands possess, that there should be no hindrance to thee; and God is forgiving, merciful.

Put off[25] whomsoever thou wilt of them and take to thyself whomsoever thou wilt, or whomsoever thou cravest of those whom thou hast deposed,[26] and it shall be no crime against thee. That is nigher to cheering their eyes and that they should not grieve, and should be satisfied with what thou dost bring them all; but God knows best what is in their hearts; and God is knowing, clement.

It is not lawful to thee to take women after (this), nor to change them for (other) wives, even though their beauty please thee; except what thy right hand possesses, for God is ever watchful over all.

O ye who believe! do not enter the houses of the prophet, unless leave be given you, for a meal,—not watching till it is cooked! But when ye are invited, then enter; and when ye have fed, disperse, not engaging in familiar discourse. Verily, that would annoy the prophet and he would be ashamed for your sake,[27] but God is not ashamed of the truth.[28]

[23] I. e. dowry.   [24] Slave girls.   [25] I. e. from her turn of conjugal rights.   [26] I. e. divorced.   [27] He would be reluctantly obliged to ask you to leave.   [28] The tent of an Arab chief is looked upon as a place of general entertainment, and is always besieged by visitors. The advent of a stranger, or indeed any occasion that demands the preparation of food or any form of entertainment, is the signal for every adult male of the encampment to sit around it, and wait for an invitation to partake of the meal. This becomes a very serious tax upon the sheikh, as the laws of Arab hospitality imperatively require every person present to be invited to join in the repast. The translator has often witnessed scenes—especially among the Arabs of Edom and Moab— which gave a very living significance to these words of the Qur'ân. Mohammed's exceptionally prominent position exposed him in a peculiar manner to these irruptions of unbidden guests. Another saying bearing upon the point is traditionally ascribed to him, zur ghibban tazdâd 'hubban, 'visit seldom and you will get more love.'

And when ye ask them[29] for an article, ask them from behind a curtain[30]; that is purer for your hearts and for theirs. It is not right for you to annoy the prophet of God, nor to wed his wives after him ever; verily, that is with God a serious thing.

If ye display a thing or conceal it, verily, God all things doth know.

There is no crime against them[31] (if they speak unveiled) to their fathers, or their sons, or their brothers, or their brothers' sons, or their sisters' sons, or their women, or what their right hands possess; but let them fear God,—verily, God is witness over all.

Verily, God and His angels pray for the prophet. O ye who believe! pray for him and salute him with a salutation!

Verily, those who annoy God and His Apostle, God will curse them in this world and the next, and prepare for them shameful woe!

And those who annoy the believers for what they have not earned, such have to bear (the guilt of) calumny and obvious sin.

O thou prophet! tell thy wives and thy daughters, and the women of the believers, to let down over them their outer wrappers; that is nearer for them to be known and that they should not be annoyed; but God is forgiving, merciful.

Surely if the hypocrites and those in whose hearts is a sickness and the insurrectionists in Medînah do not desist, we will surely incite thee against them. Then they shall not dwell near thee therein save for a little while. Cursed wherever they are found,—taken and slain with slaughter!

God's course with those who have passed away before: and thou shalt never find in God's course any alteration.

The folk will ask thee about the Hour; say, 'The knowledge thereof is only with God, and what is to make thee perceive that the Hour is haply nigh?'

Verily, God has cursed the misbelievers and has prepared for them a blaze!

To dwell therein for ever and for aye; they shall not find a patron or a helper!

[29] The prophet's wives.
[30] The women to the present day always remain behind a curtain which screens off their part of the tent from the rest, but freely converse with their husband and his guests, and hand over the dishes and any other articles that may be required by the company.   [31] The prophet's wives.

On the day when their faces shall writhe in the fire they shall say, 'O, would that we had obeyed God and obeyed the Apostle!'

And they shall say, 'Our Lord! verily, we obeyed our chiefs and our great men and they led us astray from the path! Our Lord! give them double torment and curse them with a great curse!'

O ye who believe! be not like those who annoyed Moses; but God cleared him of what they said, and he was regarded in the sight of God.[32]

O ye who believe! fear God and speak a straightforward speech. He will correct for you your works, and pardon you your sins; for he who obeys God and His Apostle has attained a mighty happiness.

Verily, we offered the trust[33] to the heavens and the earth and the mountains, but they refused to bear it, and shrank from it; but man bore it: verily, he is ever unjust and ignorant. That God may torment the hypocritical men and hypocritical women, and the idolators and idolatresses; and that God may turn relenting towards the believing men and believing women; verily, God is ever forgiving, merciful.

THE CHAPTER OF PROHIBITION[1]

IN the name of the merciful and compassionate God.

O thou prophet! wherefore dost thou prohibit what God has made lawful to thee, craving to please thy wives? but God is forgiving, compassionate!

God has allowed you to expiate your oaths; for God is your sovereign, and He is the knowing, the wise!

And when the prophet told as a secret to one of his wives a recent event, and when she gave information thereof and exposed it, he

---

[32] The occasion of the revelation of this verse is said to have been that Mohammed being accused of unfairly dividing certain spoils, said, 'God, have mercy on my brother Moses; he was wronged more than this, and bore it patiently.'

[33] That is, 'the faith.'

[1] This chapter was occasioned by Mohammed's liaison with the Coptic girl Mary, with whom he lay on the day due to 'Ayeshah or 'Hafsah. The latter was greatly enraged, and Mohammed to pacify her swore never to touch the girl again, and enjoined 'Hafsah to keep the matter secret from the rest of his wives. She, however, revealed it in confidence to 'Ayeshah; when Mohammed, annoyed at finding his confidence betrayed, not only divorced her, but separated himself from his other wives for the space of a month, which time he passed in Mary's apartment. The chapter is intended to free him from his oath respecting Mary, and to reprove his wives for their conduct.

acquainted her with some of it and avoided part of it. But when he informed her of it, she said, 'Who told thee this?' he said, 'The wise one, the well-aware informed me.

'If ye both turn repentant unto God,—for your hearts have swerved!—but if ye back each other up against him,—verily, God, He is the sovereign; and Gabriel and the righteous of the believers, and the angels after that, will back him up.

'It may be that his Lord if he divorce you will give him in exchange wives better than you, Muslims, believers, devout, repentant, worshipping, given to fasting—such as have known men and virgins too.'

O ye who believe! save yourselves and your families from the fire, whose fuel is men and stones;—over it are angels stout and stern; they disobey not God in what He bids them, but they do what they are bidden!

O ye who disbelieve! excuse not yourselves to-day;—ye shall only be rewarded for that which ye have done.

O ye who believe! turn repentant to God with sincere repentance; it may be that thy Lord will cover for you your offences and will bring you into gardens beneath which rivers flow!—the day God will not disgrace the Prophet nor those who believe with him; their light shall run on before them, and at their right hands! they shall say, 'Our Lord! perfect for us our light and forgive us; verily, Thou art mighty over all!'

O thou prophet! fight strenuously against the misbelievers and hypocrites and be stern towards them; for their resort is hell and an evil journey shall it be!

God strikes out a parable to those who misbelieve: the wife of Noah and the wife of Lot; they were under two of our righteous servants, but they betrayed them: and they availed them nothing against God; and it was said, 'Enter the fire with those who enter.'

And God strikes out a parable for those who believe: the wife of Pharaoh, when she said, 'My Lord, build for me a house with Thee in Paradise, and save me from Pharaoh and his works, and save me from the unjust people!'

And Mary, daughter of Imrân, who guarded her private parts, and we breathed therein of our spirit and she verified the words of her Lord and His books, and was of the devout.

THE CHAPTER OF THE TABLE

IN the name of the merciful and compassionate God.

O ye who believe! fulfil your compacts.—Lawful for you are brute beasts, save what is here recited to you, not allowing you the chase while ye are on pilgrimage; verily, God ordaineth what He will.

O ye who believe! do not deem the monuments of God to be lawful, nor the sacred month, nor the offering, nor its neck garlands, nor those who sojourn at the sacred house, craving grace from their Lord and His pleasure.

But when ye are in lawful state again, then chase; and let not ill-will against the people who turned you from the Sacred Mosque[1] make you transgress; but help one another in righteousness and piety, and do not help one another to sin and enmity; but fear God, —verily, God is keen to punish.

Forbidden to you is that which dies of itself, and blood, and the flesh of swine, and that which is devoted to other than God, and the strangled and the knocked down, and that which falls down, and the gored, and what wild beasts have eaten—except what ye slaughter in time—and what is sacrificed to idols,[2] and dividing carcases by arrows.[3]

To-day shall those who disbelieve in your religion despair; do ye not then fear them, but fear me— To-day is perfected for you your religion, and fulfilled upon you is my favour, and I am pleased for you to have Islâm for a religion. But he who is forced by hunger, not inclined wilfully to sin, verily, God is forgiving, compassionate.

They will ask thee what is lawful for them? say, 'Lawful for you are good things and what ye have taught beasts of prey (to catch), training them like dogs;—ye teach them as God taught you;—so eat of what they catch for you, and mention the name of God over it, and fear God, for verily, God is swift in reckoning up.'

Lawful for you to-day are good things, and the food of those to whom the Book has been given is lawful for you, and your food is lawful for them; and chaste women of those who believe, and chaste

---

[1] The Qurâish, who were sent to meet Mohammed with 1400 men at 'Hudâibîyeh to prevent him from approaching Mecca, A. H. 6.

[2] Literally, 'stones set up,' Dolmens and the like, which are so common throughout Arabia.   [3] By the game of mâisar.

women of those to whom the Book has been given before you,—when you have given them their hire, living chastely and not fornicating, and not taking paramours. But whoso disbelieves in the faith, of a truth his work is vain, and he shall be in the next life of those who lose.

O ye who believe! when ye rise up to prayer wash your faces, and your hands as far as the elbows, and wipe your heads, and your feet down to the ankles. And if ye are polluted, then purify yourselves. But if ye are sick, or on a journey, or if one of you comes from the privy, or if ye have touched women and cannot find water, then take fine surface sand and wipe your faces and your hands therewith. God does not wish to make any hindrance for you; but he wishes to purify you and to fulfil his favour upon you; haply ye may give thanks.

Remember the favour of God to you and His covenant which He covenanted with you, when ye said, 'We hear and we obey[4];' and fear God, verily, God knows the nature of men's breasts.

O ye who believe! stand steadfast to God as witnesses with justice; and let not ill-will towards people make you sin by not acting with equity. Act with equity, that is nearer to piety, and fear God; for God is aware of what ye do.

God has promised to those who believe and work righteousness, that for them is pardon and a mighty hire. But those who disbelieve and call our signs lies, these are the fellows of hell.

O ye who believe! remember God's favour towards you, when a people intended to stretch their hands against you, but He withheld their hands from you[5]; and upon it God let believers rely.

God did take a compact from the children of Israel, and raised up of them twelve wardens; and God said, 'Verily, I am with you, if ye be steadfast in prayer, and give alms, and believe in my apostles, and assist them, and lend to God a goodly loan; then will I cover your offences and make you enter gardens beneath which rivers flow: and whoso disbelieves after that, he hath erred from the level way.'

[4] Referring to the oath of fidelity which Mohammed's adherents took at 'Akabah.

[5] Various stories are told in explanation of this passage, but they are all obviously apocryphal, the angel Gabriel intervening to prevent some mischief either to the Apostle or his followers.

And for that they broke their compact, we cursed them, and placed in their hearts hardness, so that they perverted the words from their places, and forgot a portion of what they were reminded of.[6]

But thou wilt not cease to light upon treachery amongst them, save a few of them; but pardon them and shun them; verily, God loves the kind.

And of those who say, 'Verily, we are Christians,' we have taken a compact; but they have forgotten a portion of what they were reminded of; wherefore have we excited amongst them enmity and hatred till the resurrection day; but God will tell them of what they have done.

O ye people of the Book! our Apostle has come to you to explain to you much of what ye had hidden of the Book, and to pardon much. There has come to you from God a light, and a perspicuous Book; God guides thereby those who follow His pleasure to the way of peace, and brings them into a right way.

They misbelieve who say, 'Verily, God is the Messiah the son of Mary;' say, 'Who has any hold on God, if he wished to destroy the Messiah the son of Mary, and his mother, and those who are on earth altogether?'

God's is the kingdom of the heavens and the earth and what is between the two; He createth what He will, for God is mighty over all!

But the Jews and the Christians say, 'We are the sons of God and His beloved.' Say, 'Why then does He punish you for your sins? nay, ye are mortals of those whom He has created! He pardons whom He pleases, and punishes whom He pleases; for God's is the kingdom of the heavens and the earth, and what is between the two, and unto Him the journey is.'

O people of the Book! our Apostle has come to you, explaining to you the interval of apostles; lest ye say, 'There came not to us a herald of glad tidings nor a warner.' But there has come to you now a herald of glad tidings and a warner, and God is mighty over all!

When Moses said to his people, 'O my people! remember the favour of God towards you when He made amongst you prophets, and made for you kings, and brought you what never was brought

6 That is, the text foretelling the coming of Mohammed.

to anybody in the worlds. O my people! enter the Holy Land which God has prescribed for you; and be ye not thrust back upon your hinder parts and retreat losers:' They said, 'O Moses! verily, therein is a people, giants; and we will surely not enter therein until they go out from thence; but if they go out then we will enter in.' Then said two men of those who fear,—God had been gracious to them both,— 'Enter ye upon them by the door, and when ye have entered it, verily, ye shall be victorious; and upon God do ye rely if ye be believers.' They said, 'O Moses! we shall never enter it so long as they are therein; so, go thou and thy Lord and fight ye twain; verily, we will sit down here.' Said he, 'My Lord, verily, I can control only myself and my brother; therefore part us from these sinful people.' He said, 'Then, verily, it is forbidden them; for forty years shall they wander about in the earth; so vex not thyself for the sinful people.'

Recite to them the story of the two sons of Adam; truly when they offered an offering and it was accepted from one of them, and was not accepted from the other, that one said, 'I will surely kill thee;' he said, 'God only accepts from those who fear. If thou dost stretch forth to me thine hand to kill me, I will not stretch forth mine hand to kill thee; verily, I fear God the Lord of the worlds; verily, I wish that thou mayest draw upon thee my sin and thy sin, and be of the fellows of the Fire, for that is the reward of the unjust.' But his soul allowed him to slay his brother, and he slew him, and in the morning he was of those who lose. And God sent a crow to scratch in the earth and show him how he might hide his brother's shame, he said, 'Alas, for me! Am I too helpless to become like this crow and hide my brother's shame?' and in the morning he was of those who did repent.

For this cause have we prescribed to the children of Israel that whoso kills a soul, unless it be for another soul or for violence in the land, it is as though he had killed men altogether; but whoso saves one, it is as though he saved men altogether.

Our apostles came to them with manifest signs; then, verily, many of them did after that commit excesses in the earth.

The reward of those who make war against God and His Apostle, and strive after violence in the earth, is only that they shall be slaughtered or crucified, or their hands cut off and their feet on alternate sides, or that they shall be banished from the land;—that is a disgrace for them in this world, and for them in the next is mighty woe; save for those who repent before ye have them in your power, for know ye that God is forgiving, merciful.

O ye who believe! fear God and crave the means to approach Him, and be strenuous in His way, haply ye will prosper then.

Verily, those who disbelieve, even though they had what is in the earth, all of it, and the like thereof with it, to offer as a ransom from the punishment of the resurrection day, it would not be accepted from them; but for them is grievous woe. They may wish to go forth from the Fire, but they shall not go forth therefrom, for them is lasting woe.

The man thief and the woman thief, cut off the hands of both as a punishment, for that they have erred;—an example from God, for God is mighty, wise.

But whoso turns again after his injustice and acts aright, verily, God will turn to him, for, verily, God is forgiving, merciful.

Do ye not know that God, His is the kingdom of the heavens and the earth: He punishes whom He pleases, and forgives whom He pleases, for God is mighty over all?

O thou Apostle! let not those grieve thee who vie in misbelief; or those who say with their mouths 'We believe,' but their hearts do not believe; or of those who are Jews, listeners to a lie,—listeners to other people, but who come not to thee. They pervert the words from their places and say, 'If this is what ye are given, take it; but if ye are not given it, then beware!' but he whom God wishes to mislead, thou canst do nothing with God for him; these are those whose hearts God wishes not to purify, for them in this world is disgrace, and for them in the next is mighty woe,—listeners to a lie, eaters of unlawful things!

But if they come to thee, then judge between them or turn aside from them; but if thou turnest aside from them they shall not harm thee at all, but if thou judgest, then judge between them with justice, verily, God loves the just. But how should they make thee their judge, when they have the law wherein is God's judgment? Yet they turn back after that, for they do not believe.

Verily, we have revealed the law in which is guidance and light;

the prophets who were resigned did judge thereby those who were Jews, as did the masters and doctors by what they remembered of the Book of God and by what they were witnesses of. Fear not men, but fear me, and sell not my signs for a little price; for whoso will not judge by what God has revealed, these be the misbelievers.

We have prescribed for thee therein 'a life for a life, and an eye for an eye, and a nose for a nose, and an ear for an ear, and a tooth for a tooth, and for wounds retaliation;' but whoso remits it, it is an expiation for him, but he whoso will not judge by what God has revealed, these be the unjust.

And we followed up the footsteps of these (prophets) with Jesus the son of Mary, confirming that which was before him and the law, and we brought him the gospel, wherein is guidance and light, verifying what was before it of the law, and a guidance and an admonition unto those who fear.

Then let the people of the gospel judge by that which is revealed therein, for whoso will not judge by what God has revealed, these be the evildoers.

We have revealed to thee the Book in truth verifying what was before it, and preserving it; judge then between them by what God has revealed, and follow not their lusts, turning away from what is given to thee of the truth.

For each one of you have we made a law and a pathway; and had God pleased He would have made you one nation, but He will surely try you concerning that which He has brought you. Be ye therefore emulous in good deeds; to God is your return altogether, and He will let you know concerning that wherein ye do dispute.

Wherefore judge thou between them by what God has revealed, and follow not their lusts; but beware lest they mislead thee from part of what God has revealed to thee; yet if they turn back, then know that God wishes to fall on them for some sins of theirs,—verily, many men are evildoers.

Is it the judgment of the Ignorance they crave[7]? but who is better than God to judge for people who are sure?

O ye who believe! take not the Jews and Christians for your patrons: they are patrons of each other; but whoso amongst you takes

[7] The time before the Mohammedan dispensation is always so called.

them for patrons, verily, he is of them and, verily, God guides not an unjust people.

Thou wilt see those in whose hearts is a sickness vieing with them; they say, 'We fear lest there befall us a reverse.' It may be God will give the victory, or an order from Himself, and they may awake repenting of what they thought in secret of themselves.

Those who believe say, 'Are these they who swore by God with their most strenuous oath that they were surely with you?'—their works are in vain and they shall wake the losers.

O ye who believe! whoso is turned away from his religion—God will bring (instead) a people[8] whom He loves and who love Him, lowly to believers, lofty to unbelievers, strenuous in the way of God, fearing not the blame of him who blames. That is God's grace! He gives it unto whom He pleases, for God both comprehends and knows.

God only is your patron, and His Apostle and those who believe, who are steadfast in prayer and give alms, bowing down. Whoso taketh as patrons God and His apostles and those who believe;—verily, God's crew, they are victorious!

O ye who believe! take not for patrons those who take your religion for a jest or a sport, from amongst those who have been given the Book before and the misbelievers; but fear God if ye be believers. Nor those who, when ye call to prayer, take it for a jest and a sport; that is because they are a people who do not understand.

Say, 'O people of the Book! do ye disavow us, for aught but that we believe in God, and what was revealed to us before, and for that most of you are evildoers?'

Say, 'Can I declare unto you something worse than retribution from God?' Whomsoever God has cursed and been wroth with—and he has made of them apes and swine—and who worship Tâghût, they are in a worse plight and are more erring from the level path. When they come to you they say, 'We believe;' but they entered in with unbelief, and they went out therewith, and God knows best what they did hide.

Thou wilt see many of them vieing in sin and enmity, and in eating unlawful things,—evil is it that they have done. The masters

---

[8] I. e. to take his place.

and their doctors prohibit them from speaking sin and eating unlawful things,—evil is what they have performed.

The Jews say, 'God's hand is fettered;' their hands are fettered
and they are cursed for what they said; nay! His hands are outspread, He expends how He pleases! and that which has been sent
down to thee from thy Lord will surely increase many of them in
their rebellion and misbelief, for we have cast amongst them enmity
and hatred till the resurrection day. Whenever they light a fire[9] for
war, God puts it out; they strive for corruption in the earth, but God
loves not the corrupt.

But did the people of the Book believe and fear, we would cover
their offences, and we would make them enter into gardens of
pleasure; and were they steadfast in the law and the gospel, and
what has been sent down to them from their Lord, they should eat
from above them and below them. Amongst them are a nation who
are moderate, but many of them—bad is what they do.

O thou Apostle! preach what has been revealed to thee from thy
Lord; if thou do it not thou hast not preached His message, and
God will not hold thee free from men; for God guides not people
who misbelieve.

Say, 'O people of the Book! ye rest on naught until ye stand fast
by the law and the gospel, and what is revealed to you from your
Lord.' But what has been revealed to thee from thy Lord will of a
surety increase many of them in rebellion and misbelief, vex not
thyself then for a people who misbelieve.

Verily, those who believe and those who are Jews, and the Sabæans,
and the Christians, whosoever believes in God and the last day,
and does what is right, there is no fear for them, nor shall they
grieve.

We took a compact of the children of Israel, and we sent to them
apostles; every time there came to them an apostle with what their
souls loved not, a part of them they did call liars and a part of them
they slew.

And they reckoned that there would be no disturbance; but they
were blind and deaf! and then God turned again towards them: and

---

[9] The ancient Arabs always lit a beacon-fire as a proclamation of war, or a notice
of the approach of an enemy.

then many amongst them were blind and deaf! but God saw what they did.

They misbelieve who say, 'Verily, God is the Messiah the son of Mary;' but the Messiah said, 'O children of Israel! worship God, my Lord and your Lord;' verily, he who associates aught with God, God hath forbidden him Paradise, and his resort is the Fire, and the unjust shall have none to help them.

They misbelieve who say, 'Verily, God is the third of three;' for there is no God but one, and if they do not desist from what they say, there shall touch those who misbelieve amongst them grievous woe.

Will they not turn again towards God and ask pardon of Him? for God is forgiving and merciful.

The Messiah the son of Mary is only a prophet: prophets before him have passed away; and his mother was a confessor; they used both to eat food.—See how we explain to them the signs, yet see how they turn aside!

Say, 'Will ye serve, other than God, what can neither hurt you nor profit you?' but God, He both hears and knows.

Say, 'O people of the Book! exceed not the truth in your religion, and follow not the lusts of a people who have erred before, and who lead many astray, and who go away from the level path.'

Those of the children of Israel who disbelieved were cursed by the tongue of David and Jesus the son of Mary; that is because they rebelled and did transgress; they would not desist from the wrong they did; evil is that which they did. Thou wilt see many of them taking those who disbelieve for their patrons; evil is that which their souls have sent before them, for God's wrath is on them, and in the torment shall they dwell for aye. But had they believed in God and the prophet, and what was revealed to him, they had not taken these for their patrons; but many of them are evildoers.

Thou wilt surely find that the strongest in enmity against those who believe are the Jews and the idolaters; and thou wilt find the nearest in love to those who believe to be those who say, 'We are Christians;' that is because they are amongst them priests and monks, and because they are not proud.

And when they hear what has been revealed to the prophet, you will see their eyes gush with tears at what they recognize as truth therein; and they will say, 'O our Lord! we believe, so write us down amongst the witnesses. Why should we not believe in God and the truth that is given to us, nor desire that our Lord should make us enter with the upright people?'

Therefore has God rewarded them, for what they said, with gardens beneath which rivers flow, to dwell therein for aye; that is the reward of those who do good; but those who disbelieve and say our signs are lies, they are the fellows of hell.

O ye who believe! forbid not the good things which God has made lawful for you, nor transgress; verily, God loves not the transgressors.

But eat of what God has provided you lawfully of good things; and fear God, in whom ye believe.

God will not catch you up for a casual word in your oaths, but He will catch you up for having what ye make deliberate oaths about; and the expiation thereof is to feed ten poor men with the middling food ye feed your families withal, or to clothe them, or to free a neck[10]; but he who has not the means, then let him fast three days. That is the expiation of your oaths, when ye have sworn to keep your oaths; thus does God explain to you His signs,—haply ye may be grateful.

O ye who believe! verily, wine, and el mâisar,[11] and statues,[12] and divining (arrows) are only an abomination of Satan's work; avoid them then that haply ye may prosper. Satan only desires to place enmity and hatred between you by wine and mâisar, and to turn you from the remembrance of God and from prayer; but will ye not desist, and obey God, and obey the apostles, and beware, for if ye turn back then know that our Apostle has only his message to preach?

There is no crime in those who believe and do right, for having tasted food, when they fear God, and believe, and do what is right, and then fear Him, and believe, and then fear, and do good, for God loves those who do good.

O ye who believe! God will try you with something of the game

[10] I. e. from the yoke of captivity.   [11] See note 3, above.
[12] This has been thought by strict Mussulmans to exclude the game of chess. Sunnis, however, play the game with plain pieces like drafts, though Persians and Indians are not so scrupulous.

that your hands and your lances take, that God may know who fears Him in secret; and whoso transgresses after that, for him is grievous woe.

O ye who believe! kill not game while ye are on pilgrimage. But he amongst you who kills it purposely, his compensation is the like of that which he has killed, in sheep—of which two equitable persons amongst you shall be judge—an offering brought to the Kaabah; or as an expiation, the food of poor persons, or an equivalent thereof in fasting, that he may taste the evil result of his deed. God pardons bygones; but whoso returns, God will take vengeance on him, for God is mighty and the avenger.

Lawful for you is the game of the sea, and to eat thereof; a provision for you and for travellers; but forbidden you is the game of the land while ye are on pilgrimage; so fear God to whom ye shall be gathered.

God has made the Kaabah, the sacred House, to be a station for men, and the sacred month, and the offering and its neck garland; this is that ye may know that God knows what is in the heavens and what is in the earth, and that God knows all things. Know that God is keen to punish, but that God is forgiving, merciful.

The Apostle has only to preach his message, but God knows what ye show and what ye hide.

Say, 'The vile shall not be deemed equal with the good, although the abundance of the vile please thee.' Fear God then, O ye who have minds! haply ye may prosper.

O ye who believe! ask not about things which if they be shown to you will pain you; but if ye ask about them when the (whole) Qur'ân is revealed, they shall be shown to you. God pardons that, for God is forgiving and clement. People before you have asked about that, yet on the morrow did they disbelieve therein.

And God has not ordained any Ba'hirah or Sâïbah, nor Wazîlah nor 'Hâmî,[13] but those who misbelieve invent a lie against God, for most of them do not understand.

[13] These were the names given to certain animals which were marked and allowed to graze at liberty. Ba'hirah was the name given to a camel which had had ten young ones; her ear was then slit and she was turned loose to feed. When she died her flesh was eaten by the men only, the women being forbidden to touch it. There were, however, cases in which any she-camel was so called and treated. Sâïbah signifies merely a camel turned loose, her being so turned out was generally in fulfilment

And when it is said to them, 'Come round to what God has revealed unto His Apostle,' they say, 'Enough for us is what we found our fathers agreed upon.' What! though their fathers knew nothing and were not guided.

O ye who believe! mind yourselves; he who errs can do you no hurt when ye are guided: unto God is your return altogether, and He will declare to you that which ye do not know.

O ye who believe! let there be a testimony between you when any one of you is on the point of death—at the time he makes his will—two equitable persons from amongst you; or two others from some other folk, if ye be knocking about in the land, and the calamity of death befall you; ye shall shut them both up after prayer, and they shall both swear by God, if ye doubt them, (saying), 'We will not sell (our testimony) for a price, though it were to a relative, nor will we hide God's testimony, verily, then, we should be among sinners.' But if it shall be lit upon that they too have deserved the imputation of sin, then let two others stand up in their place with those who think them deserving of the imputation, the nearest two in kin, and they shall both swear by God, 'Indeed, our testimony is truer than the testimony of those two, and we have not transgressed, for then we should surely be of the unjust:' thus is it easier for men to bear testimony according to the purport thereof, else must they fear lest an oath be given to rebut their own oath; but let them fear God and listen, for God guides not the people who do ill.

On the day when God shall assemble the apostles and shall say, 'How were ye answered?' they will say, 'We have no knowledge; verily, thou art He who knoweth the unseen.'

When God said, 'O Jesus, son of Mary! remember my favours towards thee and towards thy mother, when I aided thee with the Holy Ghost, till thou didst speak to men in the cradle and when grown up.

'And when I taught thee the Book and wisdom and the law and

---

of a vow. Wazîlah was a term applied to any cattle, including sheep and goats, and generally meant a beast who had brought forth a male and female at the seventh parturition. 'Hâmî was a stallion camel which, after begetting ten young ones, was turned loose. As all these customs were connected with the idolatrous superstitions of the pagan Arabs, and tended to keep alive the rites and beliefs of paganism, Mohammed forbade them, with other similar superstitions.

the gospel; when thou didst create of clay, as it were, the likeness of a bird, by my power, and didst blow thereon, it became a bird; and thou didst heal the blind from birth, and the leprous by my permission; and when thou didst bring forth the dead by my permission; and when I did ward off the children of Israel from thee, when thou didst come to them with manifest signs, and those who misbelieved amongst them said, "This is naught but obvious magic."

'And when I inspired the apostles that they should believe in him and in my Apostle, they said, "We believe; do thou bear witness that we are resigned."'

When the apostles said, 'O Jesus, son of Mary! is thy Lord able to send down to us a table from heaven?' he said, 'Fear God, if ye be believers;' and they said, 'We desire to eat therefrom that our hearts may be at rest, and that we may know that what thou hast told us is the truth, and that we may be thereby amongst the witnesses.' Said Jesus the son of Mary, 'O God, our Lord! send down to us a table from heaven to be to us as a festival,—to the first of us and to the last, and a sign from Thee,—and grant us provision, for Thou art the best of providers.'

God said, 'Verily, I am about to send it down to you; but whoso disbelieves amongst you after that, verily, I will torment him with the torment which I have not tormented any one with in all the worlds.'

And when God said, 'O Jesus, son of Mary! is it thou who didst say to men, take me and my mother for two gods, beside God?' He said, 'I celebrate Thy praise! what ails me that I should say what I have no right to? If I had said it, Thou wouldst have known it; Thou knowest what is in my soul, but I know not what is in Thy soul; verily, Thou art one who knoweth the unseen. I never told them save what Thou didst bid me,—"Worship God, my Lord and your Lord," and I was a witness against them so long as I was amongst them; but when Thou didst take me away to thyself Thou wert the watcher over them, for Thou art witness over all. If Thou shouldst punish them, verily, they are Thy servants; if Thou shouldst forgive them, verily, Thou art the mighty and the wise.' God said, 'This is the day when their confession shall profit the confessors, for them are gardens beneath which rivers flow, to dwell therein for ever and for aye.'

God is well pleased with them, and they well pleased with Him; that is the mighty happiness.

God's is the kingdom of the heavens, and the earth, and all that is therein, and He is mighty over all.